Master
SimCity®/SimEarth™

Master SimCity®/SimEarth™

City & Planet Design Strategies

Dan Derrick and Dennis Derrick

SAMS

A Division of Macmillan Computer Publishing

11711 North College, Carmel, Indiana 46032 USA

Dedicated to John Raymond Bishopp, our grandfather.

FIRST EDITION
FIRST PRINTING—1991

International Standard Book Number: 0-672-22787-8
Library of Congress Catalog Card Number: 91-64169

Publishing Manager: *Marie Butler-Knight*
Manuscript Editor: *Lisa Bucki*
Cover Art and Part Dividers: *Ned Shaw*
Production: *Brad Chinn, Joe Ramon, Lisa Wilson, Martin Coleman, Jeff Baker, Johnna Van Hoose, Tad Ringo, Sandra Grieshop*
Indexer: *Hilary Adams*
Technical Reviewer: *Testing 1, 2, 3...*

Printed in the United States of America

Contents

Acknowledgments

We looked forward to writing this acknowledgment for several reasons. The main reason is to acknowledge and thank the many people who helped us write this book.

We get to thank the professionals like Wanda Pearson, director of the Brownsburg Public Library, who cheerfully and quickly helped us get books we could have requested weeks before. Thanks go to Carolyn Kennedy at the American Planning Association for providing research directions and sources. Thanks, too, go to Steve Beckert with Maxis Software for his help from start to finish. (Is it ever really done, Steve?)

We also thank the many friends who helped. My son's friend Shawn Crane loaned us the family computer for several weeks. While all our friends provided encouragement, fellow writer Jack Nimershiem knew exactly the kind of encouragement we needed and provided liberal doses.

We want to provide a special "thank you" to Marie Butler-Knight, our development editor at SAMS. Her guidance and encouragement were greatly appreciated. And another special "thank you" is reserved for Lisa Bucki, our editor. She put up with our moaning and groaning (Will you ever forgive us?) and still managed to make the book look sooooo much better.

My (Dan's) family put up with lots of take-home suppers, weeks of a paper covered dining table, and many missed soccer games. We both (Dennis and Dan) appreciate their patience and encouragement. Thank you Cathy, T.J., and Rachael.

But there was another reason we looked forward to writing this acknowledgment. Because this the last thing we write for the book, we're done!

Dan Derrick
Dennis Derrick
January, 1991

Trademarks

All terms mentioned in this book that are known to be trademarks or service marks are listed below. In addition, terms suspected of being trademarks or service marks have been appropriately capitalized. SAMS cannot attest to the accuracy of this information. Use of a term in this book should not be regarded as affecting the validity of any trademark or service mark.

AdLib is trademark of Adlib, Inc.

Amiga is a registered trademark of Commodore-Amiga, Inc.

Apple, Macintosh, and Macintosh SE are registered trademarks of Apple Computer, Inc.

Atari is a registered trademark of Atari Corporation. Atari ST is a trademark of Atari Corporation.

Commodore and Commodore 64 are registered trademarks of Commodore Electronics Limited. Commodore 128 is a trademark of Commodore Electronics Limited.

CompuServe Incorporated is a registered trademark of H&R Block, Inc.

COVOX Sound Master and VOXKIT are trademarks of COVOX, Inc.

Creative Music System, CM/S, Game Blaster, and Sound Blaster are trademarks of Creative Labs, Inc.

EPSON is a registered trademark of Epson Corporation.

HP is a registered trademark of Hewlett-Packard Co. LaserJet is a trademark of Hewlett-Packard Co.

IBM, and IBM PC are registered trademarks of International Business Machines Corporation. IBM PS/2 is a trademark of International Business Machines Corporation.

LogiMouse is a registered trademark of Logitech, Inc.

Microsoft and MS-DOS are registered trademarks of Microsoft Corporation.

NEC Multisunc is a registered trademark of NEC Home Electronics (USA) Inc.

PC Paintbrush is a registered trademark of ZSoft Corporation.

PART

1

SimCity/SimEarth

1 Inside SimCity and SimEarth

If you have SimCity, buy this book. If you don't have SimCity, buy this book and then go buy SimCity. Oh yes, if you need a computer, buy one of those, too. The critics love SimCity. They gave it 14 awards. Over 200,000 people have it. How can you go wrong?

If you have SimCity, buy SimEarth (right after buying this book). Building a city was just the warm up. Shaping a world is the ultimate test. This book will help you master the process of building and managing a city or world. We provide tips and ideas. You'll make the final decisions as you create a SimCity or SimEarth.

"Games" with Different Goals

SimCity and SimEarth are part of the newest generation of interactive software. They offer you a constructive challenge. Rather than destroy planes or monsters, you can be creative, making cities and worlds within the computer. The simulation rules immediately show the results of each design decision you make. Through trial and error, you learn the secrets of creating cities and worlds which must thrive . . . or die.

These games/simulations are easy to use. You can accomplish most of the actions with a joystick, mouse, or keyboard. Although these software packages are as easy to use as a game, don't be mislead into thinking of them as "only a game." SimCity and SimEarth also provide a way to learn and explore real-world concepts and theories. Mastering these "games" is difficult. Finishing is impossible.

SimCity

Available for MS-DOS (IBM PC-compatible), Macintosh, Commodore, Amiga and Atari computers, SimCity is accessible to users of many different types of computers. An MS-DOS user can debate with a Macintosh player about setting funding for the Police Department at 91%. And users of different versions (except the Commodore version) can exchange computer files of their cities. Not only does SimCity work with different machines, it falls into two software categories: game and simulation.

Game or Simulation?

Most younger computer users like action-packed games. SimCity has a lot to offer a young dude or dudette—or anyone else—looking for a new challenge on the computer.

SimCity is an action-packed game with great graphics. You can learn to play in just a few minutes, but SimCity provides hours of fun. Point and click to build roads, power plants, and airports. Decide where people live, work, and play. Make highways and railroads anywhere you want. If the Sims (that is, the *Simulated Citizens* who live in SimCity) like what you have done, they begin racing up and down the highways. A train runs up and down the tracks. Build a stadium and watch the Sims play games. Put in seaports and airports. Ships will move over the water. Planes and helicopters will fly over *your* city. The helicopter even gives traffic reports over the loudspeaker.

Just when you think you have built a great city, disaster strikes. An earthquake shakes the city and leaves behind shattered buildings and uncontrolled fires. How quickly can your city recover from the damage?

Better yet, a monster lizard appears and lumbers toward the most heavily polluted section of town. She leaves fires and destruction in her wake. Can you stop her? Do the police know what do with her? And why do the Sims keep driving along the roads as though nothing is happening?

Not satisfied to wait for trouble? You can call up a disaster anytime by making a menu choice. Who knows how long that tornado will twist through the city, smashing buildings and breaking gas and power lines. If you didn't provide enough fire stations, you'll just have to get out the marshmallows for when your city turns into one huge bonfire.

If this still isn't enough action, you can bulldoze anything you want. If you don't like the housing the Sims build, flatten it with your joystick- or mouse-driven bulldozer. Of course, they can protest by moving away. But you can do anything you want to the Sims!

Simulation or Game?

Monsters? Earthquakes? Not much of this appeals to the more mature computer user. Nice graphics are for kid games, not serious computer software. "Adults" want to use the computer as a tool, to engage in interactive, real-world, rule-based simulations. OK, Mr. or Ms. Adult, here's what SimCity offers you.

Modern cities don't just happen. They are planned. The people who do the planning have degrees, belong to professional organizations, and even take certification tests. This simulation software gives you the chance to explore the process of designing and maintaining a city without taking four more years of college.

You serve as the mayor, planning commissioner, and tax assessor as you plan and build your city. But remember, you serve only as long as you satisfy your tax payers, the Sims. Make one or two mistakes, and they'll forgive you. Keep making mistakes, and the Sims will vote with their feet. They'll move out of your city and leave you with a slum, or worse.

As you zone the residential areas, you discover what the Sims like and don't like. They like waterfront views and lots of trees. They aren't happy when you forget to build roads to their subdivisions. They like commercial zones close—but not too close—to the residential zones. They don't like to live next to industrial zones. In short, the imaginary Sims like to live in the same type of city you might like.

SimEarth

"Hello, I'd like to take Planet Planning 101." No problem. The class meets near the Andromeda Cluster. Bring your own raw materials to class. We'll see you just before your local star goes nova. Oh yes, this is a seminar class. You'll have to bring samples of your previous work.

While city planning theory has been around for many years, planet planning hasn't. Only within this century have we begun to develop an appreciation for the care and feeding of planet Earth.

Scientists acknowledge that the Earth's systems are all linked. However, the ways the systems influence one another are so complex they defy clear explanations. But scientists, being scientists, still try to understand. One view, called the *Gaia theory*, is that the Earth is one large organism able to take care of itself. SimEarth uses the Gaia theory pattern to simulate planet development in four different time periods: *Geologic, Evolutionary, Civilization*, and *Technological*. Using the same types of simple commands used in SimCity, you may work in any or all of the four time periods.

Geologic Period

The planet has cooled enough for oceans and land to form. You determine the location of continents and the composition of the atmosphere. Direct material from outer space toward your new planet. Introduce single-cell organisms. You have only 10 million years to begin the evolution of multicellular organisms.

Evolutionary Period

Now that the planet has multicellular organisms, you can change the climate and biomes, and control the pace of evolution to advance the evolutionary scale. Change the temperature and moisture to control the climate. *Biomes* are the major types of ecological communities inhabited by plants and animals; "paint" rock, arctic, boreal forest, desert, grasslands, forest, jungle, or swamp biomes on the plant surface. You have 500 thousand years to develop intelligent life.

Civilization Period

Your creatures have 10 thousand years to reach a higher technology. You help by controlling the climate and biomes. You also control the use of fossil, nuclear, solar, and hydro (water) energy. Prevent wars and eliminate unwanted technologies.

Technology Period

Intelligent creatures using low-level technology settle your planet. Because the goal of all organisms is to reproduce, your planet must reproduce itself through interstellar contact. Control the climate, change biomes, and guide the technology toward space travel. You have the rest of your planet's lifetime to accomplish the task of reproducing the planet.

Somewhere Near Andromeda

"Hello, I finally made it. Here are my designs on digital magnetic media. I did have a little trouble bringing all my raw materials with me, though."

Behind the Scenes

Great projects often have many people behind them. SimCity and SimEarth are no exception. Credited with the concept and design of SimCity, Will Wright has guided the creative focus for both products. Over 200,000 copies of SimCity have been sold, and SimEarth is likely to be popular, as well.

Will Wright

Will Wright created the hearts of SimCity and SimEarth. Royalties from his 1984 success, Raid on Bungling Bay, allowed him to disappear from the mainstream. Typically working from 10 p.m. to 4 a.m., he began to develop a robotics game. After he noticed some small squares which looked like little roads on the screen, he left the robotics game behind to develop city-building software.

Wright read about cities and city design. Working on a Commodore 64, he shaped the project and called it Metropolis. In 1985, Broderbund bought the rights. The project stalled until Broderbund relinquished the rights to Wright.

Maxis

Wright assembled a small design team and renewed the project. Started by Will Wright and Jeff Braun in 1987, Maxis operated out of Braun's apartment for several years.

The team translated SimCity to run on other computers. In the spring of 1989, Maxis released SimCity, The City Simulator. Maxis moved into an office complex in the fall of 1989. They now have over 35 employees and continue to grow.

Reviews and Awards

The *New York Times*, impressed by the lack of a win or lose theme, raved about SimCity, "The object is to make the citizens of the simulated city happy by creating an optimal environment." SimCity won over 14 awards within 18 months of its release. These included the **Software Publisher's Association** "Best Entertainment Program of the Year" and "Best Educational Program of the Year." Other awards SimCity has received include the **Game Player Magazine** "Best PC Game of 1989" and the **European Computer Leisure Award** - "Best Educational - 1990." If you've worked with SimCity, you understand all this recognition. If you haven't, you will.

Stay Tuned

What will be next? Software companies are understandably reluctant to say much about their current efforts. Now that SimCity and SimEarth are out, an inside source claims Maxis is working on SimUniverse. (We suspect that the statement was made with tongue firmly planted in cheek.)

Other new Maxis products include Robo Sport and Super Collider, due to be "released soon". Also look for enhanced versions of SimEarth that use all the features of multimedia: still and moving images, sound and music, and huge databases for queries.

How We Wrote This Book

It all began at the Indianapolis Children's Museum. Watching several lab assistants work with SimCity for five minutes convinced me (Dan) that the software package was worth buying. As a computer consultant, it was my job to know about all the "significant pieces of software" in the marketplace. I spent some time on SimCity but didn't really grasp the subtleties of the program. I gave my brother Dennis the disk and manual a few weeks later.

Dennis has been in the computer field for several years but previously had not seen a "game" he liked. Other games interested him for 10 minutes, then he was done. SimCity was different. Dennis built towns. He built cities. He recovered from nuclear meltdowns. He invited friends over for SimCity parties. He cranked up the stereo and created cities for hours. In short, he did learn the subtleties of SimCity, and he loved it.

When we had the opportunity to write a book about SimCity and SimEarth, we jumped at the chance. We had been having fun before, and now we had to get serious about our fun. We talked to other Simmers, read computer bulletin board messages, talked with the nice people at Maxis, and created even more Sim cities.

For SimEarth, we worked with test versions. These "beta copies," as they are called, were just short of being ready for publication by Maxis. We were some of the first "outsiders" to see SimEarth. While we spent many exciting hours creating new worlds, we didn't have anyone else to talk with about the software. (Beta testers can't admit to having a copy of the software.)

We hope you have as much fun learning SimCity and SimEarth as we did. We hope this book helps you get even more fun and satisfaction out of learning about SimCity, SimEarth, and the world of computer simulations.

Oh, yes. To answer that nagging question from the second page of the SimCity manual—Cassidy is Will Wright's daughter.

Using This Book

Master SimCity/Sim Earth is a tutorial and reference for SimCity and SimEarth. In these games/simulations, there is no story line to follow, no end to reach. There are no characters to profile or items to pick up on a quest. We provide tips, hints, and examples. You create your own cities and worlds. You are the main character on your own quest.

We divided this book into four parts. Part 1 (you're in it now) contains general information about both SimCity and SimEarth. Part 2 contains the tutorial and reference for SimCity. Part 3 covers SimEarth. Part 4 covers hardware differences between the game versions. If you have trouble running or using the software, Appendix A provides hints. Appendix B contains a list of resources for more information and additional city and world files.

Based on Your Skill

We all like to have some standard or yardstick against which we can measure our performance. Even though you do not focus on winning or reaching an end goal in SimCity and SimEarth, we thought you might like to gauge your skills. For each "yes" answer to the questions in the following quizzes, give yourself one point. Total your points for each set of questions, see how you rank in our arbitrary rating system, and read on to find out which chapters in this book you'll find most useful.

In the SimCity simulation, do you know . . .

1. What a flashing lightning bolt means?
2. How to lay straight roads and tracks?
3. Where to place parks?
4. The correct ratios of different zoned areas?
5. How to embezzle funds?
6. How to keep from getting caught embezzling?
7. How to build stadiums and airports at the right time?
8. How to have the proper amount of fire/police protection?
9. How to keep from going broke...frequently?
10. How to keep your satisfaction rating over 80%?

Ratings:

0 to 2 points: **Beginner**
Have you taken the shrink wrap off?

3 to 5 points: **Novice**
You've spent some time with SimCity.

6 to 8 points: **Experienced**
Several cities named after you?

9 to 10 points: **Professional**
Call yourself "Mayor."

In the SimEarth simulation, do you know . . .

1. How life begins and how you help?
2. How to create land with continental drift?
3. How to bring up the Globe window?
4. How to get the most out of your Energy allocation?
5. How and why to use a Terraformer?
6. How to win the planet creation contest?
7. What ice meteors are used for?
8. What Gaia says when poked in the eye?
9. When to use nuclear power?
10. How to keep the oceans from boiling away?

Ratings:

0 to 2 points: **Beginner**
Haven't even been watching "Nova," eh?

3 to 5 points: **Novice**
Bet you've boiled a few oceans away in your day.

6 to 8 points: **Experienced**
The force is with you.

9 to 10 points: **Professional**
Reaching for the stars.

Beginners and Novice Users

If you have just begun your career as a city planner, read Chapter 3 to get hints on installing SimCity and building your first city. After you've worked with SimCity for a while, continue with other chapters in this book for additional hints and ideas about city planning.

As a novice world planner, you may be unclear about how to create a world. Go directly to Part 3 on SimEarth. (Do not pass *Go*. Do not collect $200.)

For both software packages, you might want to refer to Part 4 for notes related to your specific computer version of SimCity or SimEarth.

Experienced Users

If you have been using SimCity for some time, read Chapter 5, "Set Your Goals," then skim Chapters 6 and 7 to pick up some new tips. Dive into Chapter 10 for more information about city planning.

Not too many people have experience with world planning. Part 3 provides ideas and hints for *SimEarth*.

If you have been thinking about purchasing a higher resolution (nicer) screen, sound board, mouse, or joystick for your MS-DOS computer, you will definitely want to read sections of Part 4. You might save yourself some money. If you want to get in touch with other Simmers (that is, other SimCity and SimEarth players), note the section on CompuServe in Appendix B, "Resources." There are thousands of other Simmers out there, waiting to compare notes, ideas and cities. (Oh, yes. If they haven't heard about this book, tell them for us, will you? Thanks.)

Professional Users

If you have *Terrain Editor* or if you are interested in gaining more control over your cities, read Chapter 12, "SimCity Extras." With this separate software product, (included with the Commodore and Color Mac versions) you can create your own rivers, lakes, and trees before or after starting a city.

Chapter 12 also tells you about new graphics sets available for SimCity. With these graphics sets, you can build ancient or future cities based on the SimCity rules, but with different-looking buildings and services.

For Cooperative Learning

If you are a classroom teacher and SimCity user, read Chapters 3 through 5. Chapter 11, "Cooperative Learning," contains 10 lesson plans to use with SimCity. You can use these lesson plans as part of math, government, geography, or problem-solving classes. Give your students time on the computer to master the basics and use the hints described in this book. In the process of learning SimCity or SimEarth, they'll discover a great deal about decision-making.

On Different Computers

Because SimCity and SimEarth have been written for many different machines, there may be differences between our instructions in this book and what you see on your screen. Part 4 discusses these differences. We did most of the work for this book on an MS-DOS machine. We also tested the Macintosh SE version thoroughly. We spent time with the Amiga, Commodore, and Atari ST versions as well. To our knowledge, the rules and ideas presented here are consistent on all machines. You can read about your machine in Part 4.

What's Next?

Whatever your level of experience, this book will help you

- ❑ Build your own cities and worlds.
- ❑ Explore ways to make changes.
- ❑ Learn how each feature works and affects your creations.

- ❑ Discover hints and tips on design and disaster recovery.
- ❑ Explore the concepts of city and world planning.
- ❑ Compare the versions for each computer.
- ❑ Decide if you want to upgrade your system.

Warning: Addictive

It's only fair to warn you: SimCity and SimEarth are much more than typical computer games. They are system simulations offering endless ways to combine elements. The designers have provided a learning tool which happens to be easy (and fun) to use. You can become caught up in the challenge and forget the necessities of life (except cola and pizza, of course.) Remember that finishing this "game" is next to impossible.

That being the case, if your family (or boss) complains that you are spending too much time in front of the computer, show them how to build a city. When they grasp the significance of your project, you can all discuss and plan and build a city together. They may even become Sim addicts, too.

2 Before You Create

You may have already opened SimCity or SimEarth, loaded the software, and worked with the program. If so, we still urge you to look over the next few pages. This chapter contains important information about your use and enjoyment of these software packages.

Software Registration

As you sort through the material that comes with either SimCity or SimEarth, you'll find a software registration card. (Actually, all software packages come with one.) This card is the second most important part of the package—after the proper size diskettes, of course. There are several reasons why you should complete and return the registration card.

Establish Ownership

By returning the card, you establish ownership of the software. You paid for the software, and returning the card is your proof. Maxis Software provides a 90-day warranty on the SimCity and SimEarth diskettes. If something happens to your software, Maxis will replace it free of charge, provided you have registered your copy of the program.

Receive Update Notices

Registration also enables the software company to update you about new versions of the program. Many companies provide new and improved software versions to current owners at a significantly reduced price. Typically, updated versions are more powerful, have more features, and may fix any bugs (problems) in the previous version.

When you receive an update notice, you don't have to upgrade to the next version. If the version you're using does everything you want, and you've not discovered any bugs, you may want to stay with that version. You'll still get a notice about the next update and will have the option of adding the newer features.

In some cases, software companies automatically send new program versions. This may happen if lots of users discover a problem and call the company for help. If many users experience a software problem or if a problem could result in the loss of data, the company may send a notice or new program diskettes. We're not implying that Maxis Software has had to fix bugs in any of their software. The point is to send in the registration card so Maxis can find you if necessary.

Mailing Lists

Maxis Software states emphatically that the company *WILL NOT* release your name or address. Some other software companies may put your name on a mailing list if you send in your card. While some of us love pouring over new computer catalogs, others would rather avoid the extra mail.

If you fall within the latter category, make a note on the registration card. State that you do not want your name to be sold or rented for other mailings. Any company that values customer relations will make sure to keep your name out of the general mailing list database.

If you want to make doubly sure that your name is not passed around, make a slight change in your address. Make the change small—one that won't keep you from getting the mail but will be easy to identify if you get a label with that change. For example, you could rename yourself slightly, from Robert to Roberto. If you get junk mail addressed to "Roberto," take the software company to task and request that the company remove your name from the mailing list. If you make a habit of slightly changing your address, start a list with the slight variations for each name and the company to which you gave the name. This technique works and will be worth the effort if you really don't like "junk" mail.

Get Technical Support

Simulation software users are, by nature, an adventuresome type of computer user. Simulations require an interest in trying things out, and seeing what works and what doesn't. But what if trial and error will not resolve a significant problem? What if it is the software? Could there be a bug in the program? If you encounter a problem with SimCity or SimEarth, first try the steps in Appendix A, "Troubleshooting." If you can't resolve the problem, you may need to contact Maxis Software for assistance or answers to your questions.

Contact Maxis by phone or FAX machine. Maxis will want to know they are helping a registered customer. They'll know who you are if you sent in your registration card.

Be Included in Consumer Profiles

When software companies develop and market a program, they target their efforts toward a particular type of consumer. The registration cards provide an idea of who is buying the company's product. Your responses to questions on the card help the company focus design efforts on revisions or new products. As a result, you can get products which better meet your interests and needs.

Giving software companies the information they need to develop better products is another good reason to send in software registration cards to Maxis Software, as well as other companies. If you haven't done so, fill the card out and send it NOW!

Copy Protection

Software publishing companies, like any other businesses, want to make a fair profit as the result of labor and investment. Software makers want people to pay for the products they use. Seems fair enough, doesn't it?

But software is easy to copy. Note that you can repeat the SimCity installation process over and over. You can make as many copies of the SimCity and SimEarth software as you like. People can copy a diskette and hand it over to someone else to use. Then two people are using the product for the price of one. Because there is no limit to the number of copies you can make from a diskette, virtually any number of people could use one copy of a program. People who spend a lot of time writing programs don't care much for that loss of income.

OK, It's a Soapbox

As you might have guessed, we're up on a soapbox. Please hear out our views on software copyrights. For years, software publishers created special schemes to prevent casual program copying. The schemes were generally a pain in the whazoo and caused real problems if a user's one copy of the program was lost or damaged. Over the years, publishers responded to users and removed the software protection methods. Very few programs have protection now.

Some people are not very concerned about the legality of "sharing" programs. They see nothing wrong with making copies and giving them out.

After conducting a survey several years ago, one software company estimated there was one illegal copy of its software being used for every purchased copy. Such a ratio means that millions of illegal copies of a program can exist—representing millions of dollars in lost income for the software publisher.

Software publishers now focus on public education, letting people know that making copies of programs to give to others is theft. Handing a program diskette to someone takes money out of the producer's pocket. This is a heavy message, but users are beginning to hear it. Users make backup copies for their own safety and don't ask for, or give out, programs they didn't purchase.

Maxis' Approach

There are a lot of reasons why users should respect the rights of the software publishers. The most compelling, from the user's viewpoint, were outlined in this chapter's discussion about registering software. A legitimate software owner makes a connection with the company. This connection enables the user to access help and information on updates and new products. Besides, paying for software is the right thing to do.

Maxis Software chose a protection method—the external lookup chart—which guards the company's rights and allows the user to make as many backup copies of the diskettes as is necessary. (The Commodore version of SimCity is on a copy-protected disk.)

Installation

Various computer systems require different methods of software installation. The manual supplied with your version of SimCity or SimEarth provides more details about the installation process. Chapters 3 and 13 of this book provide details on installation for SimCity and SimEarth respectively. Usually, the computer has a standard configuration, and the installation program copies files from one floppy diskette to another or to a hard disk. Except for the Commodore version, you can and should make backup copies of the diskettes before installing the program.

Because MS-DOS systems have more variations, Part 4, "Hardware," provides an explanation of the possible combinations for running the SimCity or SimEarth software. If you want to compare systems or are considering adding equipment to enhance your enjoyment of these programs, take a look at Part 4 before you spend your money.

Controlling SimCity and SimEarth

The developers at Maxis have designed SimCity and SimEarth so you can control either program in the way you find most comfortable. Throughout this book, we explain specific keys and shortcuts. We repeat them several times, at the risk of being redundant over and over. It's easier to read about commands several times than to flip through the book looking for a particular shortcut.

For *mousers* and *stickers* (mouse and joystick users), moving the control moves the pointer in the same direction on-screen. The *boarders* (keyboard users) direct the pointer around the screen using Arrow keys. While each method is different, with experience you'll find the shortcuts.

Mouse/Joystick Movement Techniques

It's quickest to develop and run a simulated city or world with a mouse or joystick. Move the on-screen pointer to select items, make menu choices, move around the city, and change your views of the city. Except for typing information from the Lookup Chart (a red sheet that comes with the program for copy protection purposes) or typing your city name, you can do everything with a mouse or joystick.

For most purposes, the mouse and joystick affect the pointer the same way. The only difference is in the actual use of the device. You move a mouse across a flat surface, but move the joystick itself. The on-screen effect is the same. The pointer moves in the direction you moved the device. Each device also has buttons in similar locations. The following terms describe actions with the mouse or joystick. The angle brackets, < and >, indicate when you should perform the enclosed action.

<POINT>

After each **<POINT>** instruction, we include a word or description of an object upon which to place the pointer. Additional actions to perform while the pointer remains on that spot follow the **<POINT>** instruction. For example, the instruction

<POINT> to a residential zone; **<Q & HOLD><CLICK & HOLD>**

means to move the screen pointer to any residential zone, press the letter Q on the keyboard and hold it, then press the joystick button, mouse button, or space bar and hold it. This unusually complicated command sequence activates the Query function on individual tiles and zones.

<SELECT>

The **<SELECT>** operation combines several actions. Instructions which include **<SELECT>** also provide a word or object description. Move the pointer to the designated word or object, and then press the left button on the mouse or joystick. For example,

<SELECT> Residential icon

would mean to move the pointer to the picture (icon) which represents Residential and then press the left button. That action makes the Residential icon the active icon.

The keyboard method for **<SELECT>** will follow the same sequence, but will use a different method. Use the Arrow keys to position the pointer on the menu item or icon. Then press **<SPACE BAR>** to make the selection. In the example just mentioned, you would use the Arrow keys to move the pointer to the Residential zone icon and then press the **<SPACE BAR>** key.

<RIGHT-CLICK>

In some cases, the right button is a shortcut for a specific action. **<RIGHT-CLICK>** usually does not require pointing first. Because the **<RIGHT-CLICK>** takes effect immediately, the pointer must be in position before you use the right button.

<DOUBLE-CLICK>

<DOUBLE-CLICK> also is a shortcut for some actions. This technique combines several actions. For example,

<DOUBLE-CLICK> on `DULLSVIL`

selects the file name (during the Load City operation) and initiates loading the file. In this case, the **<DOUBLE-CLICK>** performs the following steps in one action:

<SELECT> `DULLSVIL`
<SELECT> `LOAD`

Rapidly pressing the button twice may take some practice. Some systems require presses so rapid they're almost a twitch on the button instead of two distinct taps. You can keep repeating the **<DOUBLE-CLICK>** action until you get two clicks close enough together to perform the action. Be careful that you don't move the pointer as you concentrate on double-clicking.

Keyboard users also can use the **<DOUBLE-CLICK>** trick. When this book instructs you to **<DOUBLE-CLICK>**, just place the pointer on the item or icon and press the **<SPACE BAR>** twice quickly. Additional keyboard tips appear later in this chapter.

<CLICK-DRAG>

This action is, again, a time saver. **<CLICK-DRAG>** means to press the left button and hold it down as you move the pointer in some direction. For example,

<CLICK-DRAG> right six tiles

means to hold the left button down as you move the pointer six tiles (places). The result could be a straight line of road, six tiles long.

Keyboard Movement Techniques

As we've hinted, there are quick ways to move the pointer around the screen with the keyboard. It may appear that the only way to move the pointer where you want is by pressing the Arrow key and waiting for the pointer to catch up. With this technique, it's easy to overshoot your destination and have to move the pointer back again. The makers of SimCity and SimEarth added some shortcuts to help you. There are some quick ways to accomplish things using the keyboard.

Pointing

You can control the on-screen pointer, a small hand in SimCity and an arrow in SimEarth, with the Arrow keys (also called the cursor keys) on the right side of the keyboard. Once the pointer is in the proper location, pressing **<SPACE BAR>** makes the selection. You'll use this technique to perform any work within a window. But when it comes to using icons or making menu selections, there are several tricks for keyboarders.

Hopping Around with +

Keyboard users can move the pointer quickly by pressing the + (plus) and –(minus) keys. While there is more than one plus key, the gray + key on the far right side of the keyboard (on the numeric keypad) is the easiest to use. Pressing that key moves the pointer to the next icon or decision box on the screen. In some cases, as in the Edit window, there are 12 different icons. Pressing the **<GRAY+>** key 12 times moves you to each of those icons. If you overshoot the intended icon with the **<GRAY+>** key, the **<GRAY–>** key allows you to back up. Imagine an analog clock (with hands). Each time you press **<GRAY+>**, you move your pointer clockwise to the next number. Press the **<GRAY–>** key, and you move back.

Once you have landed on the icon, press **<SPACE BAR>** to select that icon. (In some cases, pressing the **<ENTER>** key will also work.) You'll still have to use the Arrow keys to move the pointer to the section of the screen where you want to use the icon.

Key Combinations

Most keyboards contain at least 84 keys, and some have over 100 keys. We all know how to use the **<SHIFT>** key to get UPPERCASE letters. Computer keyboards also use special keys called *Alternate* and *Control* keys. Usually the keys just have *ALT* and *CTRL* on their tops, so we just show **<ALT->** and **<CTRL- >** to indicate the use of those keys.

Like the **<SHIFT>** key, these two keys don't do anything on their own. They are used in combination with other keys. For example, **<ALT-S>** means to press the Alternate key and also press the S key. This special key combination brings up the System menu in SimCity. Keep in mind that these key combinations are unique in almost every program. So in SimEarth, pressing **<ALT-S>** brings up the Speed menu.

Key combinations are convenient and common in most programs. SimCity and SimEarth both have keyboard charts you might prop up next to the monitor as you use the programs. After a few hours of use, you'll find the handiest combinations become second nature, and you'll use them without thinking.

PART

2

SimCity: The City Simulator

3 Getting Started with SimCity

After anxiously tearing the plastic shrink-wrap off the SimCity package and examining the contents of the box, every user is confronted with the same task—starting the program. We'll assume you have completed the registration card, and it is ready to mail.

You must *install* most programs before they will work properly with a specific computer. Installation copies the program files to another disk and tells the program exactly what kind of equipment your system has.

Installing the Program

This chapter gives the installation instructions for the MS-DOS version of SimCity. To learn about installing and running versions for other computer systems, see Part 4, "Hardware."

You can install SimCity on one of three possible disk drive combinations: a hard disk drive, dual floppy disk drives, or a single floppy disk drive. The SimCity manual combines floppy and hard disk installation instructions in the same section. In this book, separate sections cover hard disk drive and floppy disk drive installation. Floppy disk users can skip to the appropriate section on installation.

Copying Your Program Diskettes

To be exceptionally safe, you should make copies of your program diskettes using the DOS command DISKCOPY. We've never seen the SimCity INSTALL program write anything on the diskette, but it would not hurt to make the backups. At least put write-protect tape over the notch on the original diskettes.

To make a copy of the program disk in drive A: to a blank diskette in drive B:, type the following at the DOS prompt:

```
DISKCOPY A: B:
```

If you only have one floppy disk drive, you can use

```
DISKCOPY A: A:
```

to make a copy of each diskette. You will have to remove the program (source) diskette and insert the blank (backup) diskette when prompted.

If you type `DISKCOPY` and get the message `Bad Command or File Name`, you'll have to check your DOS manual for more informaiton about the DISKCOPY program.

Installing and Starting the Program on a Hard Disk

These days, there are more PC-compatible computer systems with hard disk drives than without them. So, it's likely that many of you should use the following procedure to install SimCity.

1. Start your system as you normally do. For hard disk users, this usually involves turning on all the switches and waiting for the opening screen to appear.

2. If you have a menu system, exit the menu and return to the DOS prompt, which will appear on-screen as `C:\>` or `C>`.

3. Insert the first SimCity disk in drive A:, usually the top or only floppy drive in the computer.

4. Type `A:` and press **<ENTER>**. The prompt should change to `A>`.

5. Type `INSTALL` and press **<ENTER>**.

The INSTALL program now takes over the installation process. The program will present you with a series of choices. The program displays the default answer (really, what the program guesses is correct) by placing an asterisk in brackets, as follows: `[*] A:, [ ] B:` Use the → and ← keys to move the asterisk, if necessary.

We've found that you'll rarely need to make any changes. The program is very good at guessing the proper answers. If you need to make changes, you may do so later by rerunning the INSTALL program.

Most hard disk users install the program from drive A: to drive C:. INSTALL creates a subdirectory on drive C: called SIMCITY and copies all the necessary program files to the hard disk. Then INSTALL asks what type of screen you have, whether you have a joystick, and what type of sound you want. Unless you are certain you need to make a change, accept the answers provided. Remember that if you have a mouse, it takes precedence over a joystick. Even if you tell the installation program that you have a joystick, INSTALL still chooses the mouse if it is attached. (You'd rather use the mouse anyway, trust us.)

For more information on these choices, take a look at Part 4, "Hardware." Appendix A discusses possible installation problems. Once the installation is complete, use the following steps to start SimCity:

1. Remove the diskette now in the floppy disk drive. Don't put the SimCity program diskettes too far away. You'll need them if you want to run INSTALL again to change the program set up.

2. Type `C:` then press **<ENTER>** to return to the hard drive prompt.

3. Type `CD\SIMCITY` then press **<ENTER>** to move to the subdirectory with the SimCity program. The prompt may look like `C:\SIMCITY>` or it may still look like `C>`.

4. Type SIMCITY then press **<ENTER>** to start the program.

5. In a few moments, the SimCity opening screen should appear.

Each time you want to start SimCity, repeat steps 3 and 4 to start the program. This moves you from the root directory on the hard disk into the SIMCITY subdirectory and starts the SIMCITY program.

Installing and Starting the Program on Floppy Diskettes

Running SimCity from a floppy diskette does not affect the actual performance of the program. It only increases the time necessary to load the program and city files. Saving the city files you create on a floppy diskette also increases the time it takes to start the game.

The INSTALL program creates a floppy *program diskette* that you'll use to run SimCity. If you have a dual drive system, the INSTALL program copies the necessary files from the SimCity diskette in drive A: to your program diskette in drive B:. If you are just using one disk drive, the program installs from drive A: to drive A:. The INSTALL program does a good job of telling you when to insert which diskette into drive A: during the process.

The INSTALL program *cannot* use a disk which doesn't have enough space. Make sure you have a newly formatted blank diskette for the new SimCity program diskette when you start. While you are making or cleaning off a diskette for the program files, go ahead and make a new blank diskette to hold your city files as well. We'll call this the data diskette from now on. Following are the steps for starting the INSTALL program on a floppy disk system.

1. Start your system as you normally do. For floppy disk users, this usually involves inserting a system diskette in drive A:, turning on all the switches, and waiting for the opening screen to appear.

2. If you have a menu system, exit the menu and return to the DOS prompt, which will appear on-screen as A:\> or A>. Remove the system diskette from drive A:.

3. Insert the first SimCity disk in drive A:, usually the top or only floppy drive in the computer.
4. Type `INSTALL` and press **<ENTER>**.

The INSTALL program now takes over the installation process. The program will present you with a series of choices. When INSTALL is finished, you'll have a program diskette for SimCity. Use the following steps to start SimCity.

1. Make sure the program diskette is in drive A:.
2. Type `SIMCITY` at the `A>` to start the program. If the opening screen does not show up in a minute or so and the disk light goes off, you (or the INSTALL program) may not have selected the proper screen. Go through the INSTALL program again and write down the choices you make. You'll need this information if you contact Maxis Software for help. (See Appendix A, "Troubleshooting," and Appendix B, "Resources.")

The manual for the MS-DOS version of SimCity notes that not all of the files necessary to run SimCity will fit on one 360K (5.25-inch, double-sided, double-density) diskette. However, we installed several variations, and all the files which *run* the program fit onto one 360K diskette. The only files INSTALL didn't copy were the SCENARIO files. If you are using just one disk drive, you'll have to insert the diskette with the SCENARIO file to load it. The SIMCITY program prompts you when it needs the diskette with the SCENARIO file.

Once all the files are "installed" on the floppy diskette, there is not much room left on that diskette. Once you have loaded SimCity from this newly created program diskette, you'll have to insert a data diskette into a floppy drive to later save your new cities. If you use a single drive, you'll have to insert a data diskette into drive A:. Dual drive users will insert the data diskette in the second drive.

Extra Cities

Both floppy and hard disk users may want to look at additional cities available on other diskettes in the SimCity software package. (*Terrain*

Editor, described in Chapter 12, has additional cities.) INSTALL does not copy these city files to the hard disk. Hard disk users should use the DOS COPY command to copy the city files into a subdirectory. Floppy disk users can insert the diskette with the city files as a data diskette to load the files. Later you can save these city files to your data diskette (after you improved the city, no doubt). Both loading and saving files are covered in Chapter 6.

Test the Controls

Even before you decide which choice to make on the opening screen of SimCity, you should make sure the controls are working properly. Just grab the mouse or joystick and move it in a circle. The pointer should move around the screen in a similar pattern. Like a batter swinging the bat to get used to its weight, testing the controls helps you find the pointer or get used to the movement. Keyboard users can test the plus (+) key to move the pointer through each of the three choices on the opening screen.

We mention this "warm-up" because we've seen the opening screen appear with no pointer visible. But don't worry—your mouse isn't dead. Scoot the mouse up and down, and the pointer will come out of hiding.

Opening Screen

The opening screen presents three choices: `START NEW CITY`, `LOAD A CITY`, and `SELECT SCENARIO`. Use the pointer to select one of these choices. Mouse and joystick users can move the pointer and **<CLICK>** the left button. Keyboard users can use the cursor keys or the plus (**<GRAY+>**) key to hop from choice to choice and the **<SPACE BAR>** to make the selection. Begin now by selecting `START NEW CITY`.

Start New City

After you select START NEW CITY, the pop-up menu shown in Figure 3.1 appears and requests a new name for your city. Use this menu to enter a city name and select the Game Play Level. Use the **<BACKSPACE>** key to erase the name shown (HERESVILLE), and type in a suitable city name. (Go ahead and use your name. Everyone does.) After pressing **<ENTER>**, you can select the Game Play Level. Because the Easy level is already selected, point to OK and **<CLICK>** to move to the next screen.

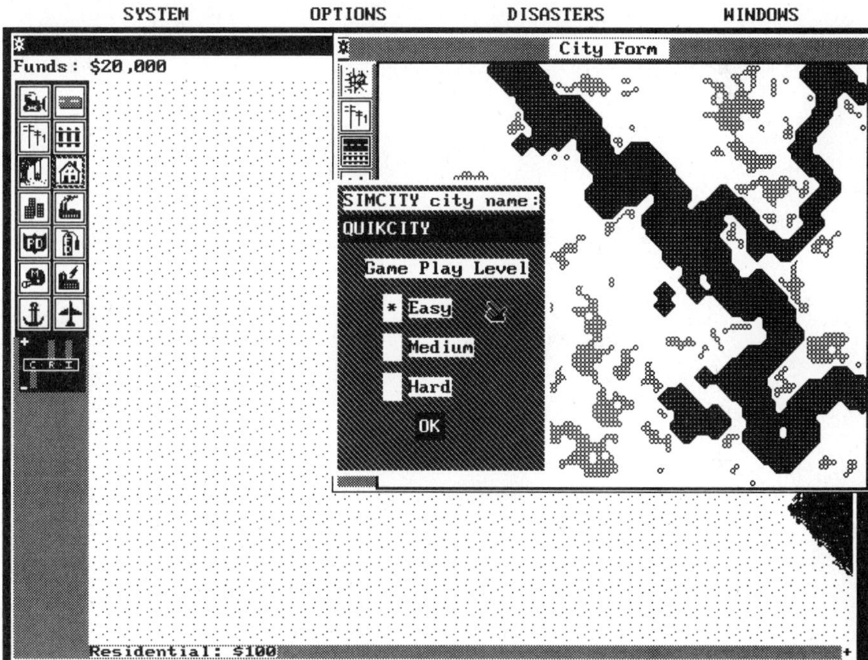

Figure 3.1 *The pop-up menu you use to name a new city and select the Game Play Level.*

From now on, this book uses a two-column "shorthand" method to show you how to complete operations like starting a new city. The left column gives the steps to execute. The right column contains details about the action and results. If you are unclear about the **<SELECT>** and **<POINT>** instructions, review the end of Chapter 2. When the book gives only one set of instructions, stickers, mousers, and boarders should follow them. Otherwise, we point out separate shortcuts for boarders.

 Special shortcuts for keyboard steps are indicated with the keyboard icon.

 In some parts of this book, shortcuts for the joystick and mouse are preceded by the mouse icon.

Instructions	**Notes**
Start the game	The opening screen, with `SIMCITY` and three menu choices, appears when the game has successfully loaded.
<SELECT> `START NEW CITY`	A pop-up menu appears so you can name the new city.
<SELECT> `HERESVILLE`	This is the default new city name. We want to put in another (yours).
Press **<BACKSPACE>** 10 times	This removes the default name.
Type your name (up to 17 letters) and press **<ENTER>**	This step enters your name as the new city name.
<SELECT> `OK` Press <0>	This closes the pop-up menu.

Lookup Chart

Maxis Software developed an external reference sheet to prevent more than one person from using each copy of the SimCity program. Included in the software package is a red lookup chart (the chart is titled *SIMCITY ALL TIME HIGH SCORES*) that cannot be duplicated on a copy machine. If you hold the lookup chart, you are the legitimate user of the program.

After SimCity terraforms your city, a copy protection box appears. (For more on copy protection, see the end of this chapter.) As shown in Figure 3.2, this pop-up box contains a question and graphic boxes which are codes for the answer. The box requests either the city name or population. Use the red lookup chart to decode the graphic squares. The first graphic box identifies one of the four lookup pages. Match the next two boxes with a row on the lookup chart, which contains the city name and population. Based on the question, type in the city name or population number appearing on the correct row of the chart. You may type the name in upper- or lowercase letters. The number does not require commas.

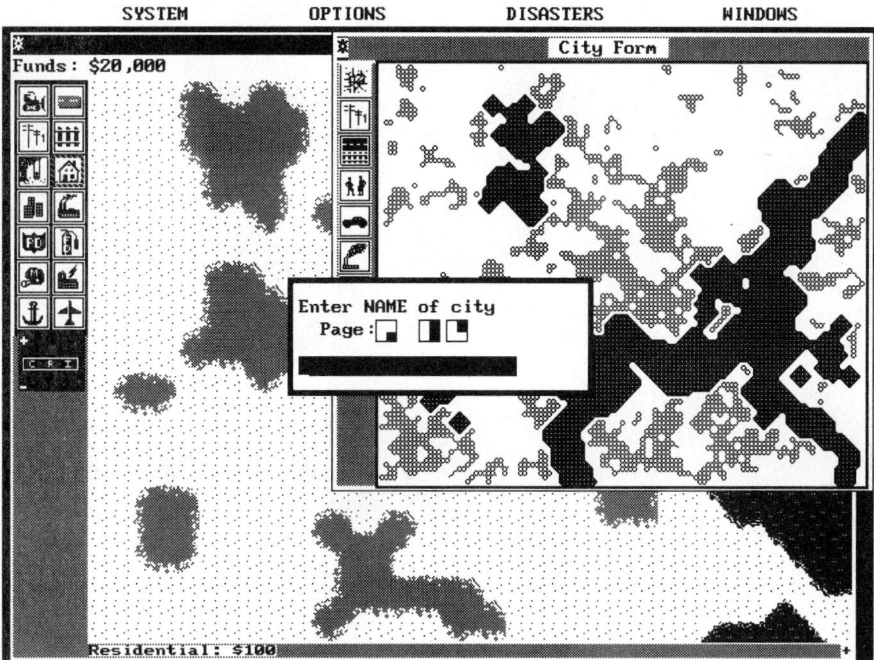

Figure 3.2 *The copy protection pop-up box. Match the graphic boxes with information on the red lookup chart to answer the question.*

Three Tries

SimCity allows you three attempts to enter the proper information. If you just press **<ENTER>** or mistype the answer, SimCity flashes a warning, shown in Figure 3.3. Once SimCity gives this warning, disaster after disaster wreaks havoc on your city. You need to start the program again. Pressing

<CTRL-X> (hold the **<CTRL>** key and press X), or **<CLICK>**ing on SYSTEM and using ↓ to select EXIT, is the only way to end the disasters—and the game.

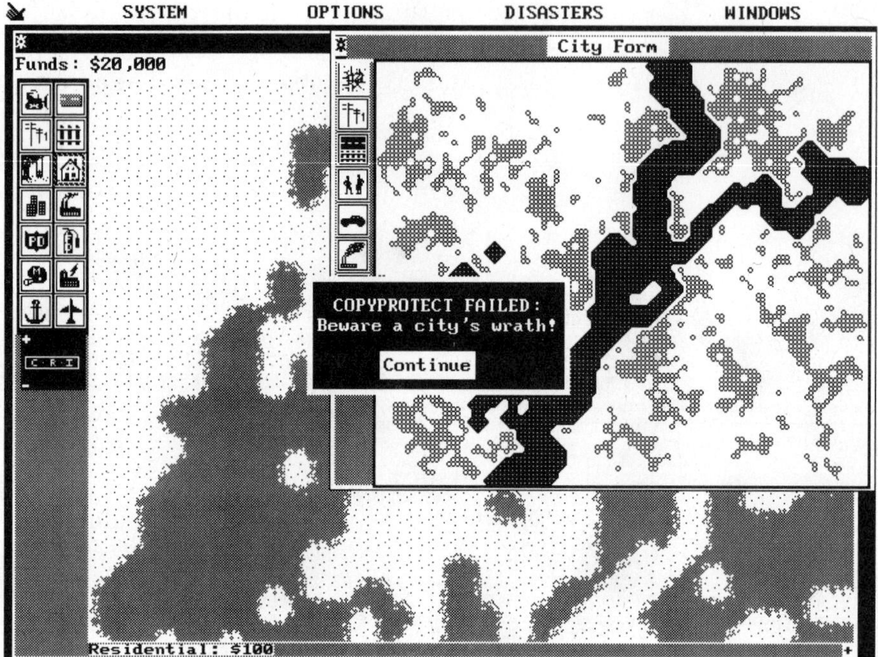

Figure 3.3 *A pop-up box foretells disaster for your city and all the Sims if you don't answer the city name/population question.*

We've tried every way we can think of to fool the copy protection feature of the game—just out of curiosity, of course. For example, we tried selecting SCENARIO, ignoring the question in the copy protection pop-up box by pressing **<ENTER>** three times, and then saving that city file. Reloading this city should have stopped the disasters, but it didn't. Just use the lookup sheet to answer the copy protection question, and you'll be in good shape.

Manuals for some of the SimCity versions say that the copy protection pop-up box will appear throughout the game. Because we'd never seen the box appear during the game, we asked Maxis Software about that note. Maxis admitted that once you respond to the initial query, the program does not request the copy protection information again.

Screen Quick Tour

After you make a choice from the opening screen (`START NEW CITY`, `LOAD A CITY`, or `SELECT SCENARIO`) and answer the copy protection question, the basic working screen, the playing field for your city, appears. Chapter 4 gives you step-by-step instructions to create a working city. For now, you can learn enough to get started using the tools to create a city. We encourage you to learn the basics of building a city first. Then go on to the next chapter to learn how the basic techniques apply in the overall context of SimCity.

Windows

In SimCity, you work in various on-screen windows as you create your simulated city. The *active* window, or the window where you can currently perform commands, appears on top of other on-screen windows. For example, Figure 3.4 shows the window holding the City Form, which appears after you answer the copy protection question. The City Form shows the entire 120 square miles of terrain. You'll find there are many ways to view the city in this, and other, windows. For now, you want to close this window and get down to the Edit window underneath it.

To close the City Form window, mousers and stickers can point to the asterisk in the upper-left corner of the City Form and **<CLICK>**. Boarders can use the **<CTRL-C>** key combination to close the window. The Edit window remains on the screen.

Moving Around

The Edit window shows a section of the entire terrain available. The view is from above, similar to looking at the ocean floor through a glass-bottomed boat. By moving the window up and down, right and left, you can see every section of your city.

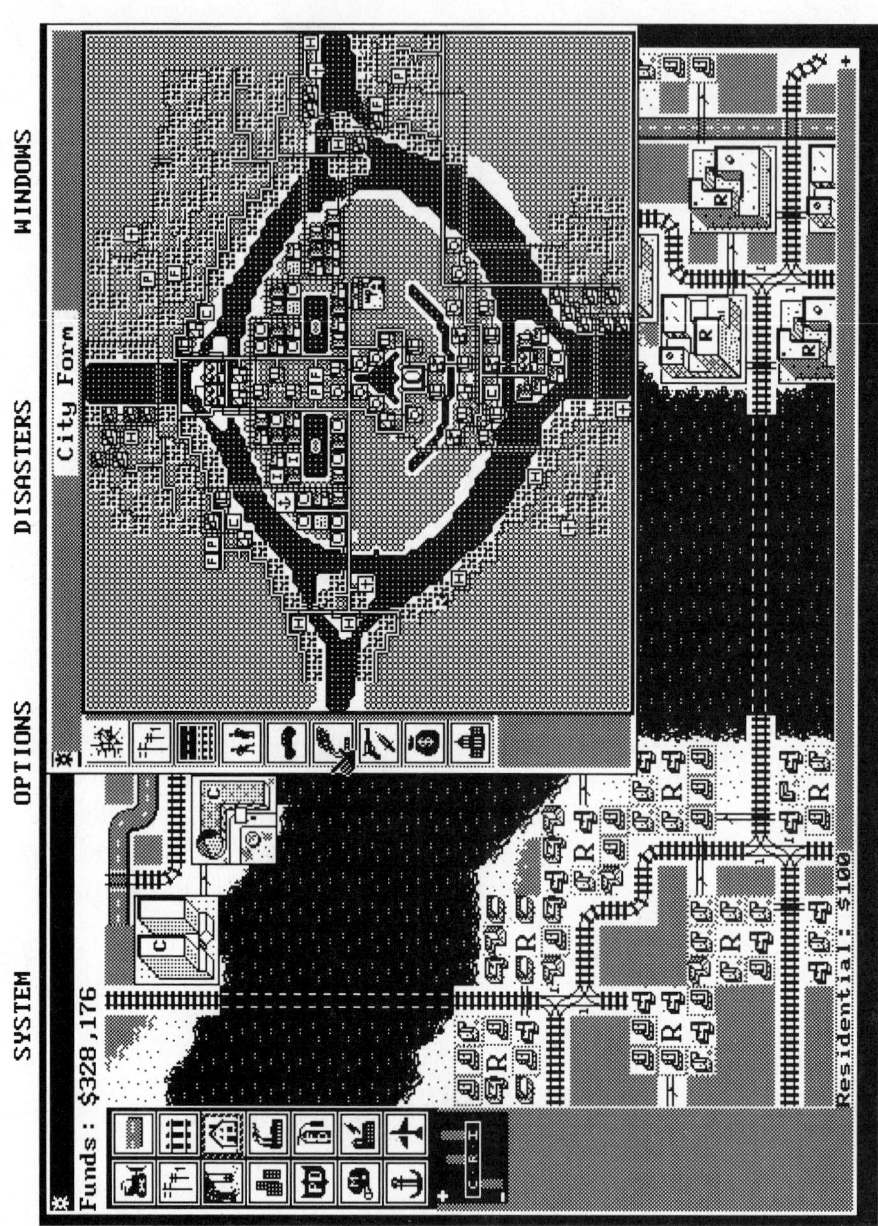

Figure 3.4 *The City Form window for FACE CITY shown over the Edit window.*

Moving the pointer to the right edge of the window moves the terrain to the left. The pointer disappears as the terrain moves rapidly across the window. This process is a bit confusing at first. Just tap the edge of the window with the pointer, then move it back to move the view a bit and stop. Keep tapping the edge of the window with the pointer to move slowly across the terrain. If you don't like this effect, you can press the **<SCROLL LOCK>** key (which turns on scroll lock). If you turn on scroll lock, you'll have to move the Edit window in other ways. Chapter 6 provides full details on using the SimCity windows.

Using Icons

The left side of the Edit window holds the icons you'll use to zone and build your city. These icons select services you (the mayor) provide for the city, including police, fire, transportation, and power. In addition, the icons designate building zones you create for the Sims.

To choose one of these icons, **<SELECT>** it with the keyboard or mouse techniques described in Chapter 2. When you return to the window, the size of the item will be represented by a box. To place the item on the terrain, move the box to the area in the window you want, and **<CLICK>** or press **<SPACE BAR>**. Move the box and **<CLICK>** or press **<SPACE BAR>** again to zone or build another of that icon.

Nothing is free. Notice that the dollar amount that appears after `Funds:` on the bar just above the Edit window decreases each time you use an icon to build something or zone an area. Don't worry about funding for now. Just practice using the icons. If you run out of funds, you can start a new city.

Making Menu Selections

The top of the screen contains menu selections. When you **<POINT>** to a menu choice and **<CLICK>** or press **<SPACE BAR>**, another series of choices drops down in a box called a *pull-down menu*. One of the most important menu choices to make when you start a new city is on the Disaster menu. Because you'd rather not have any disasters in your city, **<POINT>**

to the word DISASTERS and **<CLICK>** or press **<SPACE BAR>**. The word DISABLE appears at the bottom of the pull-down menu. **<POINT>** to DISABLE and **<CLICK>** or press **<SPACE BAR>**. The pull-down menu disappears, and the disaster feature is inactive, preventing random disasters like earthquakes or tornados from spoiling your day.

There are lots of other operations you can perform from the menus. Go ahead and explore. At this point, don't worry about creating the ideal city—just try out your tools.

Opening Screen II

Choosing LOAD A CITY or SELECT SCENARIO from the opening menu allows you to pull up existing cities or scenarios. *Existing cities* are files you've created or files provided on other diskettes. Even if you decide to load an existing city, you can change your mind and exit using the SYSTEM menu, as described in Chapter 6.

Scenarios are cities headed for trouble and are so much fun that this book has an entire chapter on them. For all scenarios except DULLSVILLE and DETROIT, a disaster occurs after you load the scenario. Your task is to handle the results of the disaster. As we point out in Chapter 8, the scenarios are not necessarily examples of good city design. Chapter 8 describes how to select a scenario.

4 Build QUIKCITY

Part of the fun of getting a new program for your computer is putting the disk in, starting the program, and figuring out some basic commands. But it's even more fun when you can really dig in and actually do things with the program.

Now that you've installed SimCity and practiced some of the basics, you're ready to—gulp—take on a whole city. This chapter presents a city project called *QUIKCITY*. After you've completed this chapter, you'll have a city which will grow and prosper!

Your First City, Step-by-Step

This QUIKCITY tour just provides the keystrokes or mouse/joystick movements to get your city started. Later chapters have much more detailed information. As explained in Chapter 3, we'll use two-column instructions to tell you what to do. The left column gives specific steps. The right column explains the results of taking the steps. (If the left column contains only one set of instructions, everyone—mousers, stickers, and boarders—should use them.) You may want to read the right column first to understand what you want to accomplish before you take a step.

Because the mouse and joystick allow you to move the screen pointer more freely than the Arrow keys, we'll give directions such as **<SELECT>** `EASY`. This instruction means you should move the screen pointer to the `EASY` on-screen and press the mouse left button or joystick left fire button.

Some of the keyboard instructions we give are similar to the mouse/joystick movements. Use the Arrow keys to move the pointer, and then press the **<SPACE BAR>** to click on that object. In other cases, you can use quick keys such as the **<GRAY+>** key. We'll show you some shortcuts later in Chapter 6.

Notice that specific keys or buttons are contained in the < and > symbols. For example, **<ENTER>** means the Enter (sometimes called Return) key on the keyboard.

We're ready to start the game and go. If you are having trouble getting the game to load, refer to Appendix A for possible solutions. We suggest that you read through each set of instructions and look at all the figures before you begin.

Starting a New City

Start building QUIKCITY by starting and naming a new city. The following steps review the procedure, which you learned in Chapter 3.

Instructions	Notes
Start the game	The opening screen, with `SIMCITY` and three menu choices, appears when the game has successfully loaded.
<SELECT> `START NEW CITY`	A pop-up menu appears so you can name the new city.

Tip:** If you get in trouble later, restart the game and return to this point; then use the following keyboard instructions:* ***<ALTS><S><ENTER><ENTER><ENTER>.

<SELECT>HERESVILLE	This step selects the default new city name so you can enter a new name.
Everyone must use the keyboard for these two steps: **<DELETE>** 10 times	This removes the default name.
QUIKCITY **<ENTER>**	Type this to name your city QUIKCITY, as shown in Figure 4.1.
<SELECT>Easy **<SELECT>**OK	This step sets the Game Play Level to Easy and accepts the new city name. The computer creates a terrain for you to use.
???????? **<ENTER>**	The copy protection pop-up box appears, with graphic boxes representing information on the red lookup chart. Type the information from the red lookup chart which corresponds to the three graphic boxes, and press **<ENTER>**. The first box stands for one page of the chart, and the other two designate the line on the page which holds the correct information. The correct answer may be a city name or city population, as shown in the example in Figure 4.2.
Now look at the screen.	The screen should contain two windows, one on top of the other. We need to move the blinking box to the center of the City Form window, as shown in Figure 4.3.

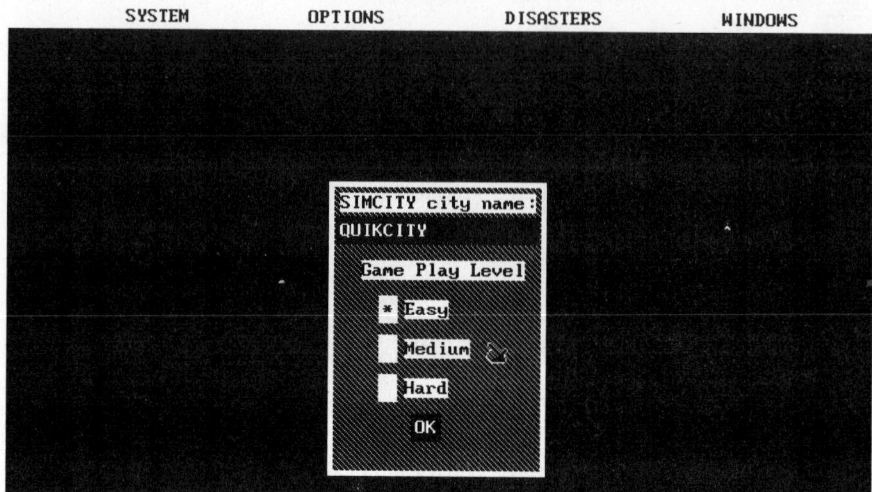

Figure 4.1 *The new city opening screen with the QUIKCITY name entered.*

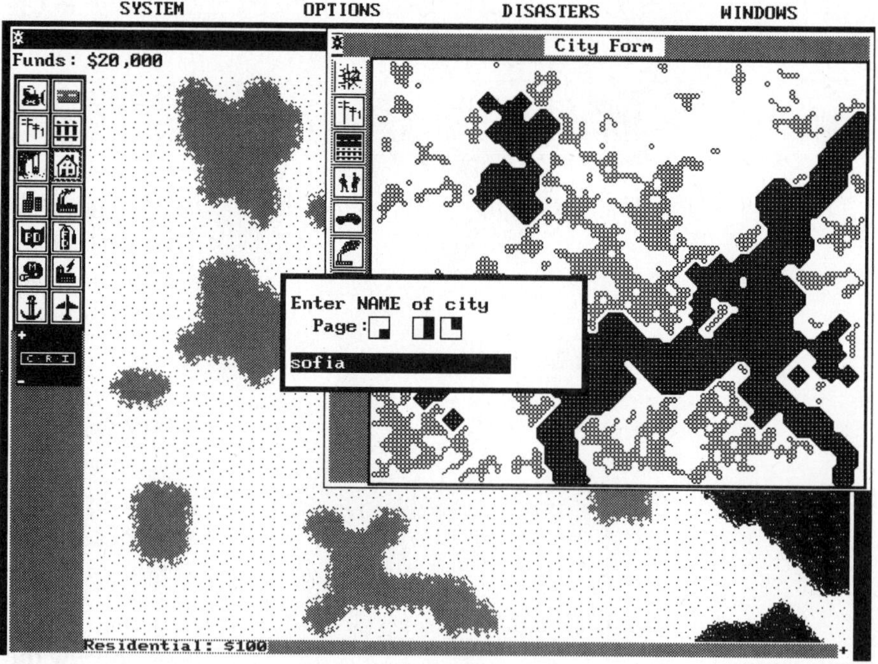

Figure 4.2 *The copy protection question in a pop-up box, with the answer from the red lookup chart entered.*

Move the pointer to the center of the City Form window and **<CLICK>** or press **<SPACE BAR>**

This step moves your map to the middle of all the land provided. **Try not to include any water (blue or dark areas) in the box for now—you can't build on water.** Choose a good space to start the city.

<SELECT> * (upper left corner of the City Form window) move the pointer

You close the top window for now. Special note about pointer movement: If you go beyond the edge of the screen, the entire window begins to move. To get back to the original position, move to the other edge of the window until you reposition the window. Boarders: There are some quicker ways for you to move around. We cover them in Chapter 6.

 **<SELECT>** `DISASTERS`

Press **ALT-D**

A pull-down menu opens under the word `DISASTER`.

<SELECT> `Disable`

This menu selection disables the disaster feature. (You don't want any disasters, just yet. You can have those later, if you like.)

 **<SELECT>** `OPTIONS`

Press **ALT-O**

Figure 4.4 shows the pull-down menu that appears. You are going to make the budget process automatic, for now. You do not need to complete the next step if the `Auto-Budget` feature already has a little triangle to the left.

<SELECT> `Auto-Budget`

Now you won't be interrupted each year to review the budget. (And how many mayors do you know who don't have to worry about budgeting?) You can change this feature later.

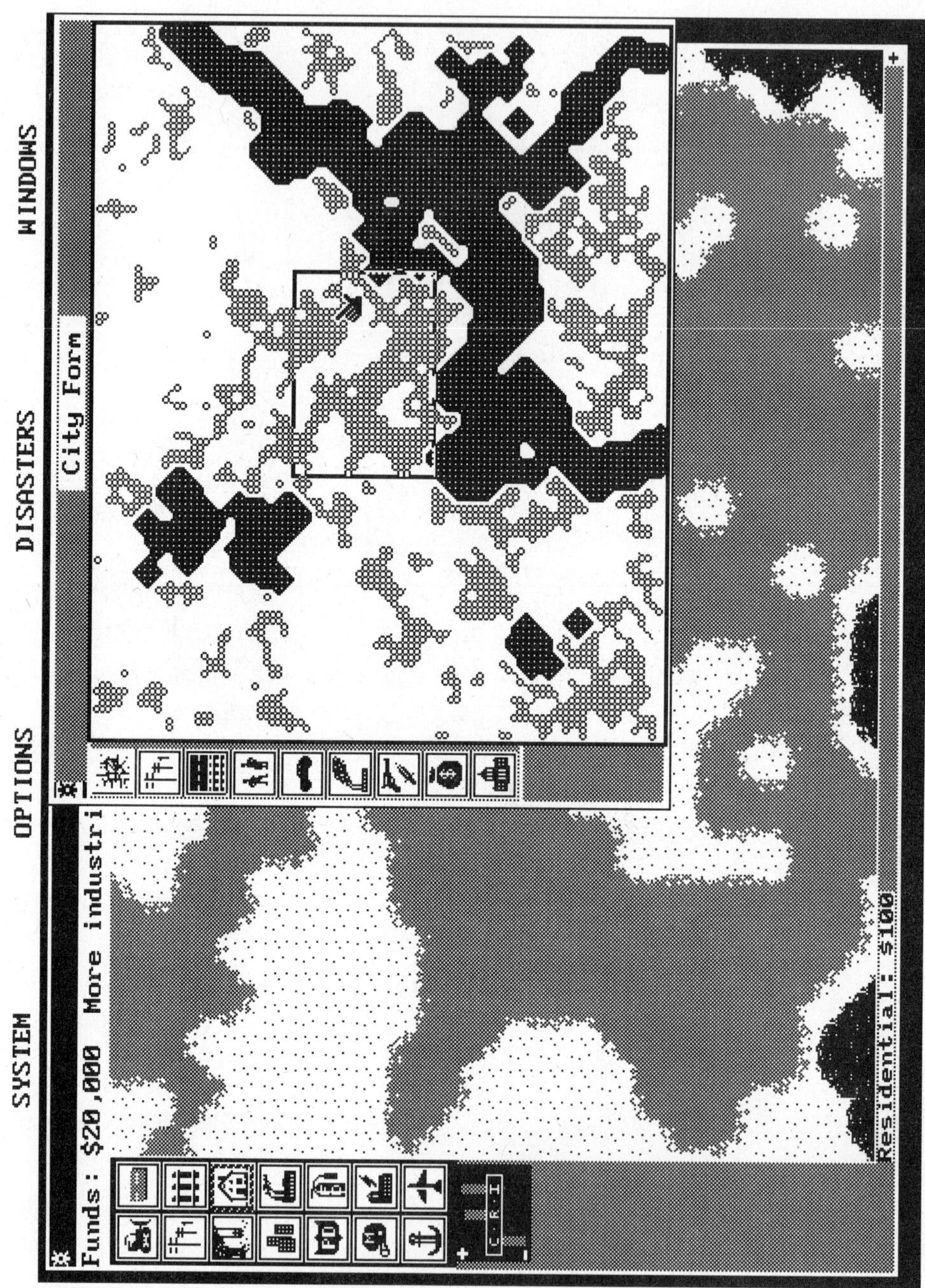

Figure 4.3 *The new city opening screen with the City Form window active.*

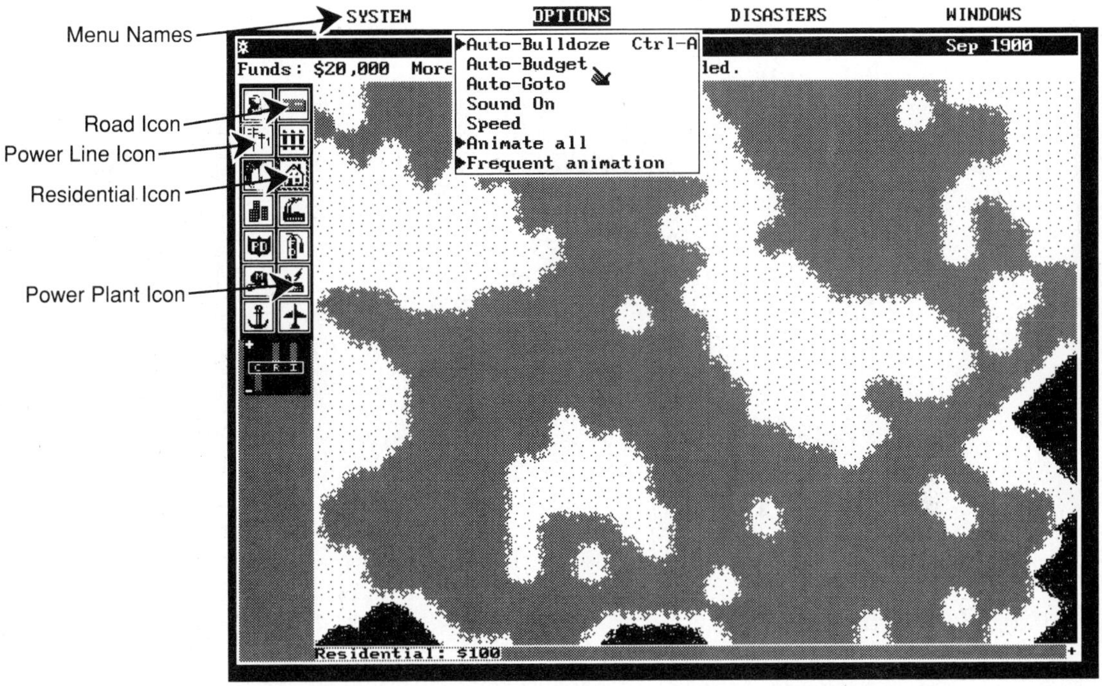

Figure 4.4 *The Options pull-down menu. The triangles along the left indicate which features are active.*

<SELECT> Power Plant icon

This icon has a lightning bolt in the upper right corner.

<SELECT> `Coal`

This step selects a coal plant, which is cheaper and produces more electricity than a nuclear plant. You'll need the money later.

Move the box that appears to the lower right corner of the screen and **<CLICK>** or press **<SPACE BAR>**

You've just zoned and built a power plant.

<SELECT> Residential icon

The Residential icon has a little house in it. A box appears on-screen after you select the icon.

Move the box to the left edge of the screen and **<CLICK>** or press **<SPACE BAR>**

You've just created a Residential zone. It should have an R in the middle. Don't worry about whether it is on ground or trees. (If you try to zone on water, SimCity won't let you.)

Now move the BOX to the right and **<CLICK>** or press **<SPACE BAR>** until you have six Residential zones side by side (See Figure 4.5)

The zones should all have a flashing lighting bolt in them. (They were flashed off when we took the picture in Figure 4.5.)

<SELECT> Power Line icon

The Power Line icon has several utility poles in it.

<CLICK-DRAG> power lines between the power plant and the Residential zones

Press the left button or **<SPACE BAR>** as you move the pointer to lay the power lines. Flashing in the Residential zones continues for a moment after the connection has been made. As long as all the Residential zones are connected, they all have power.

<SELECT> Road icon

This icon looks like a road. A small box appears after you select the icon.

Move the small box to the bottom of the left Residential zone

We want to start our road in front of this section of Residential areas.

<CLICK-DRAG> across the bottom of the Residential zones

You'll be creating a straight section of road.

Look at the screen

By now you may have noticed houses appearing in the zones. (See Figure 4.5.) You also may have noticed that anything you zone or build costs money. The dollar amount in the upper left corner keeps decreasing as you work.

Action	Result
<SELECT> Commercial icon	The Commercial icon has several high-rise buildings. A box appears on-screen after you select the icon.
Create three Commercial zones starting at the left of the main street (See Figure 4.6)	Your Commercial zones should have a `C` in the middle. No complaining about a boring city allowed. We're just getting started here. Are the Commercial zones blinking?
<SELECT> Power Line icon	The Power Line icon has several utility poles in it.
<CLICK-DRAG> to lay power lines	You may provide power to the C zones just by connecting them to an R zone across the street.
<SELECT> Industrial icon	These are the factories, little smoke stacks on the icon.
Using the same method you used for the Commercial zones, create three Industrial zones starting to the right of the Commercial zones (See Figure 4.6)	Because the Industrial zones are next to the Commercial zones, they are automatically connected with power lines.
 **<SELECT>** `SYSTEM`  Press **<ALT-S>**	The System pull-down menu appears.
 **<SELECT>** `Save City`  **<CTRL-S>**	You named the city when you started (remember?) so the program will save the city as QUIKCITY.CTY. Boarders can actually use the **<CTRL-S>** to save at any time during the game. Mousers should use **<CTRL-S>** every 15 minutes to make sure you don't accidentally lose work.

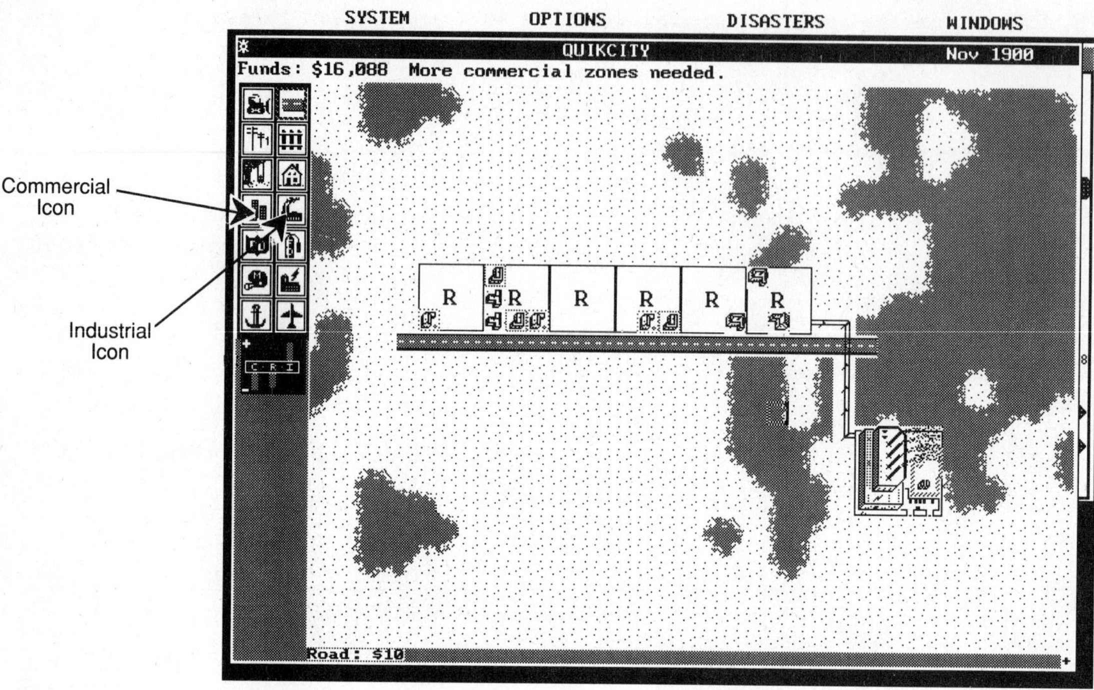

Figure 4.5 *QUIKCITY has six Residential zones connected to the power plant and a main street.*

Look at the screen	Now you've saved this city to disk. and can call it up later.

Speed Up

If you want to speed the game up, use the Options menu, choose `Speed`, and **<CLICK>** on `Fastest`. Boarders can just press the number `4` to get the Sims juiced up and the city growing at the maximum rate.

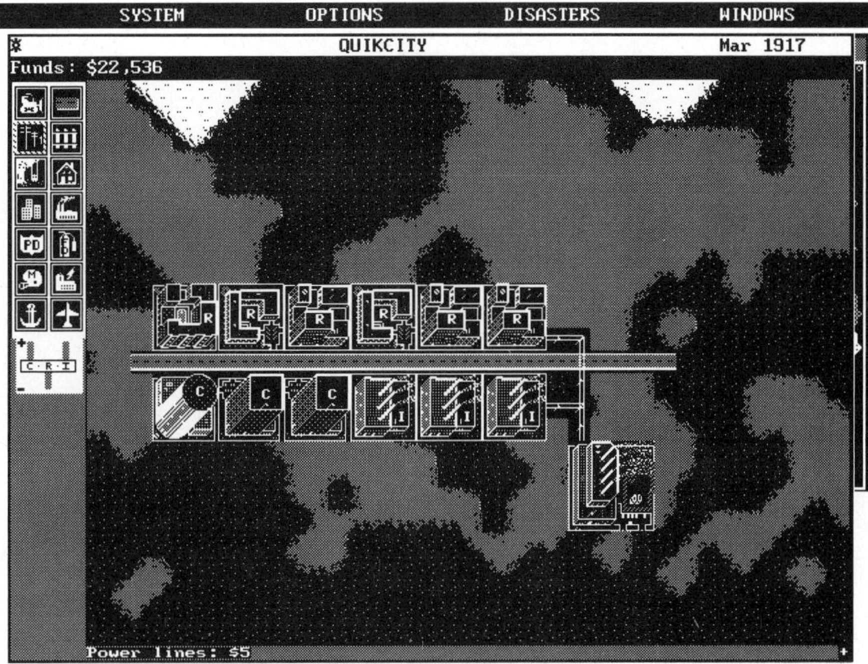

Figure 4.6 *QUIKCITY with Residential, Commercial, and Industrial zones. Your version will look different, depending on the terrain and where the Sims build their houses.*

Quitting

To quit SimCity, use the System menu, then select `Quit`. Or you can press **<CTRL-X>**. Because your city continues to change, SimCity will ask if you want to save the city. Select `YES`. Then say `YES` again to the `OVERWRITE FILE?` question. You will be able to load the city the next time you enter SimCity.

A Few Quick Guidelines

Because you want to jump in and create cities right NOW, here are a few ideas which will help. We explain these tips in more detail later, but start employing them right away.

- ❑ **Always make sure DISASTERS have been DISABLED.** It is disheartening to have a great city going and lose much of it to an unexpected earthquake. If you want to test the city's ability to withstand a disaster, save the city first, and then invoke the disaster.
- ❑ **Save your game frequently.** When we try radical ideas (like bulldozing downtown), we save the file under new names with Save As... on the System menu, and use successive numbers to create the new city names. After a long evening, we might have CITY001 through CITY023 saved on a disk.
- ❑ **Sims are taxpayers.** Discover what they want and give it to them. Choose `Evaluation` under the Window menu frequently to see what the Sims think. If the Sims aren't happy, they leave. (HINT: If you go broke, you've lost.)
- ❑ **Let cities grow for a while.** Go play Frisbee or read more of this book. More time allows the Fund balance to increase. Be sure and put the game on the fastest speed for maximum results.
- ❑ **Connect all zones with roads or rails.** Sims will build a house or two in Residential areas without a road, but that's all. Commercial and Industrial zones don't do any good without connections to the rest of the city.
- ❑ **Check funding levels for city services.** When you start building police and fire stations, you'll have to make sure they are funded, otherwise the buildings do nothing. Set funding by selecting `Budget` from the Windows menu.

5 Set Your Goals

Could you build a house if you had never seen one? Even if you knew how to use a hammer on a nail and a saw on a 2x4, you'd be lost without a blueprint.

Do you know everything about building a SimCity? Not yet, you don't. We've discussed some of the basic tools available in SimCity. But as with most new software, you need to understand some larger concepts—an overall picture—before you become really proficient with the program. So . . . the pages in this chapter provide some history about computer simulations, and a perspective on SimCity.

We assume you've been using the program and/or have progressed through Chapters 3 and 4. If you haven't read those chapters, the following discussion may not make as much sense to you.

In the Beginning...

One of the first microcomputer simulation programs was about lemonade. The game asked how much sugar and how many lemons each glass took, and the price for each glass sold. Even before providing these answers, you had to look at the weather forecast generated by the computer. After accepting your responses, the computer provided a report on the number of glasses sold that day. You knew your profit (or loss) immediately. You were running a simulated lemonade stand!

By watching the results, you learned the best (most profitable) way to run the lemonade business. In that early simulation program, the rules were simple, and you could discover them after only a few sessions of work. But the basic keys to making the business successful were obvious to even the youngest of players: find the right price; don't overproduce; and, remember that you can't control some factors (like weather), but you should consider them in decision making.

Simulations

Computer simulations provide a way to examine the world. Computer simulation software contains rules intended to represent a small segment of reality called a *system*. The system can be as small as a lemonade stand or as large as a world. There may be as few as 10 rules or thousands of rules. (SimCity has well over 100 rules!)

Many computer simulations mimic the control of exotic machines—jets, tanks, race cars, and submarines, to name a few. The government and large companies have simulations that include visual (display screen), auditory (sound), and tactile (motion) clues about the system. Such simulations include training programs for jet and helicopter pilots, gunners, and automobile drivers. Some amusement rides also employ system simulation principles.

The sophistication of these simulations requires large computers, multiple displays, and entire rooms providing the total environment. Expensive stuff here.

Microcomputers, in their own way, have been keeping up with the big boys. The *classic* simulation program was Microsoft's original Flight Simulator. The user controlled a small plane with the keyboard. Limited graphics consisted of large shapes which twitched around the screen as you "flew" the plane. If you got your plane off the ground at Chicago's O'Hare airport after 20 tries, your landmark was the Sears Tower. (Some of us promptly flew straight into the tower, hoping for a scene from Towering

Inferno. No such luck. We just got message on the screen that we had crashed.)

Battlefield simulations, which provide a way to engage in the "art of war" from the armchair, have also been popular. While these programs are destructive, they help players satisfy a basic urge to be aggressive without leaving the comfort of a neutral environment. (That's psycho-babble for "creaming the other guys without really hurting anyone.")

Good Eye-Hand Coordination?

System simulations are also different from arcade games. These programs require good eye-hand coordination, something younger players enjoy. These games don't have many rules. Just move the starship or gun or figure around the screen and press one button to launch or shoot or kick. (Actually, Flight Simulator does require some coordination to fly and, especially, land. Maybe that's why many players celebrate getting off the ground by crashing into the Sears Tower.)

With Flight Simulator the goal is to take off, fly around (across the country, if you want), and land. In the process, you do learn about the plane controls and navigation. There is no winning or winner with this type of software. Gaining experience is the goal. But there is little to show for all the time spent working with and learning the software. While there is nothing at all wrong with having a learning experience (like the ones you had in high school and college), many people like to have a little more to show for their efforts. That's where SimCity comes in.

SimCity by Maxis provides a simulation of the real world that the user can change and study. The user builds and watches the results, then makes changes. This type of software is non-violent, constructive, and rule-based, and results in a final (actually, a city is never final) product.

The Role You Play

SimCity challenges you to design and build a city. You have limited resources (money), and you must satisfy the residents of your city, the Sims.

Like a very small town, your city starts with only one town official—you. Even as the city grows, you retain control. You can't be voted out. You don't have to run for election. The worst that can happen is that the Sims all leave!

You sit high in the SimCity blimp. This is your only view of the city, but it is the best way to maintain control. With a wave of your wand (mouse, joystick, or keyboard), you lay out the zones for Residential, Commercial, or Industrial development. You build power plants, football stadiums, and airports. You lay the railroad and roll out the asphalt. You make many of the decisions about creating the city the Sims will occupy.

Sims build the houses, stores, and factories. They use the roads and trains. They rate your efforts and complain often and loudly. They pay the taxes which allow you to continue zoning and building the city. You have to make dozens of decisions in a Sim month, one minute to you. You have to make decisions quickly and carry them out. You wear the hats of mayor, city planning commissioner, city services, tax board, and many others . . . . Care to take all this on?

Mayor

You are the mayor of your city. You can even name the city whatever you like. We haven't seen anyone yet who didn't name their first city after themselves. Dennis used DENNVILLE. Dan used the more typical computer file naming convention of DAN01, planning, of course, for DAN02, DAN03, and more.

As mayor, you serve as the ceremonial representative of the city. You attend all the banquets given by the Sims in your honor. (BYO food, of course.) The much more important part of your job will be checking the Evaluation box under the Windows menu bar. A mysterious organization polls the Sims constantly about how they think the mayor is doing and what their greatest concerns are. The evaluation helps you to guide city planning.

City Planning Commissioner

You decide what the city will look like by zoning the land. As city planner, you decide how many zones to place and where each zone will go.

Residential zones give the Sims a place to live. Industrial zones offer a place to work. Commercial zones hold places to spend money.

You have to decide if the Sims can build better homes next to water and trees. (Hint: They do.) How do Sims react to nearby Industrial zones? You can decide if you should place Residential zones side by side or spread them out. Just how many Residential zones do the Sims need in a growing city?

And what about the Industrial zones? Should you group these together so the pollution accumulates in one spot? Can you spread these zones out and still be productive? How many Residential zones can each Industrial zone support?

The Honorable Mayor of SimCity hereby directs the City Planning Commissioner to do a study and report the results. The Mayor highly recommends a book which details the process of building a SimCity. You, the City Planning Commissioner, report that you have anticipated the Mayor's request and have found such a book. This book you have so cleverly located, Master SimCity/SimEarth, will provide answers to the questions we just asked and more.

So, how do you like talking to yourself? Just don't get into an argument and lose. Commercial zones are critical. Why go to work if you have no place to spend your money? Should you cluster these zones like a downtown or spread them out like shopping centers? Do the Sims want to live close to Commercial zones or just have efficient transportation to get there? Say, who's in charge of transportation, anyway? Could it be the . . .

City Services Deputy

You've guessed it! You're the city services deputy, too! Not only do you get to attend banquets and zone the city, you have to direct the city services. The services include transportation, electricity, fire, police, parks and recreation, and others. Provide efficient, timely services, and your city will grow. Neglect these areas, and the Sims will leave. No Sims, no taxes. No taxes, no city. Oops!

Transportation

As the transportation director, you build the roads and railroads through and around the city. Each section costs money to build and money to maintain. How much rail and road meets the Sims's needs without draining the yearly transportation budget? Are roads or rails more effective in your city? What do you do when the Sims complain about heavy traffic? (You'll know when they're getting uptight. A warning, shown in Figure 5.1, flashes on the screen.) When you talk to the tax board, what level of funding should you request?

Figure 5.1 *The type of complaints you'll get as the transportation director.*

Electricity

Your SimCity won't grow unless you build a power plant. Will it be a coal or nuclear plant? You can spend $3,000 or $5,000. Should you worry more about pollution or nuclear meltdown? What's the most efficient way to place the power lines? Should you supply each area with two lines? What do you do about brown-outs?

Fire

Effective fire and disaster control depends on the location of the fire stations. You decide how much to overlap the fire protection areas. What about the funding level for the fire stations? Not enough coverage or funding, and you can have fires that burn . . . for centuries.

Police

No surprise here. The Sims like police protection, too. They are quick to complain about the crime rate, as shown in Figure 5.2. Some sections of the city need more police protection, or the Sims will leave. What is the minimum funding level for adequate police protection? Can you spot potential high crime areas before the Sims leave?

Parks and Recreation

The Sims do like their recreation. Build plenty of parks, and they'll build expensive homes next to the parks. (More taxes, remember?) When the city gets big enough, the Sims will want a stadium. Do you rezone around the stadium or build it out in the suburbs? As parks and recreation supervisor, you can even watch the games for free.

Figure 5.2 The Sims complain about crime, among other things.

Port Authority

Essential for a large city, airports and seaports provide commercial traffic in and out of your city. Be ready to lay out big bucks to build an airport or seaport. Are you prepared for a plane wreck? If not, you can lose your airport. It'll cost you $10,000 to build a new one.

Remember that the Sims are very vocal about what they need. They'll tell you when they want more police protection. They demand a stadium when the time comes. When they gotta have an airport, they'll holler. (When you build an airport, a chatty traffic helicopter starts making the rounds.)

Tax Board Chair

That city services deputy sure has a lot of demands! Each zone costs $100. A section of road is $10. Power lines are $5. Airports are $10,000! How do you, the tax board chair, fund all this expensive work?

Taxes! You *ARE* the senior (and only) member of the tax board. You decide the tax rate—from 0% to 20%. Set taxes too low, and you go broke; too high, and the Sims complain. Keep up the tax squeeze, and they'll leave.

You respond to requests from the city services deputy for funding levels on transportation, police, and fire services. When the deputy asks for an appointment, you

- ❑ Listen to the reasons to raise the service funding rate.
- ❑ Take them into consideration.
- ❑ Hold a committee meeting.
- ❑ Turn the transcript over to a study group.
- ❑ Review the results.
- ❑ Leak your decision to the press.
- ❑ Reverse your decision when the Sims complain.
- ❑ And call yourself a moron and deny the requested increase.

Now you've got the bureaucratic spirit!

Hard Hat and More

Guess who operates the bulldozer, when necessary? Emergency repairs from earthquakes, fires, and monster attacks require clear land. The Sims only rebuild damaged sections after you've scraped away the rubble with your bulldozer.

You think that kind of work is hard! Huh, how about urban renewal? Lower the blade of your mouse bulldozer, and push houses and buildings into the ground. One click, and hundreds of Sims lose their homes. You don't even have to ask them. Can you just imagine their faces when a mouse the size of a building, with a gleaming, steel blade comes down the str . . . .Well, never mind. Somebody has to do it.

You have the power. You have the glory. You even get to play (Can I admit this?) *God*. When things are too calm, when the Sims complain one too many times, when you're tired of the city anyway, you can call a disaster down. You have fires, floods, earthquakes, and tornados at your fingertips.

Or, if you prefer, turn all the disasters off. It is up to you, the Honorable mayor, city planning commissioner, city services deputy, tax board chair, and 'dozer driver, to make all the decisions for your city.

The Sims' City

Spend a day in a city, and you'll get to know the buildings. Spend a week in a city, and you'll get to know the places. Spend a month, and you'll get to know the people. Spend a year, and you'll stay forever. (Well, it sounds good, and anyway it introduces the next section.)

We've spent centuries in dozens of Sim Cities. We've gotten to know the Sims pretty well, even if we've never seen one. They move too fast for a mere human to see. But we can see what they build and where they go. We always know what they think of our efforts (via the Evaluation window).

What Makes Sims Happy?

Sims are taxpayers. They come to your city because they like the number and location of the zones. They like the way you've designed the transportation. They like stadiums, airports and sea ports. They like what you might like.

Population

Sims always have a positive birth rate. Remember, little Sims become big taxpayers. You influence the Sims by having enough Residential zones. Typically, you want to have twice as many Residential zones as Commercial and Industrial zones combined. The mathematical formula for this would be: R+R+C+I=S where S equals *Success with your city*. (Pretty scientific, huh?)

The better the location of a zone, the higher the value, the more taxes generated. Therefore, put the Residential zones near water or trees or, better, both. Make sure that each Residential zone has a road or track touching it. Parks are nice, too. Sims move in, build nice houses and apartments. The tax assessor says the land is valuable, and bingo, nice return on your investment.

Making Money

Sims must have somewhere to work. In your city, you must zone some areas for industrial development. The Sims decide what to build in those areas. Make sure these zones have power and access (roads or rails), and they'll use the area. The Industrial areas producing goods to export out of the city. Location does not seem to affect the Sims' use of these zones, but just don't put Industrial zones next to Residential areas!

You have no control over the external market which buys the exports. The market operates in economic conditions outside of the city. The simulation varies these conditions. Your job is to adjust your city, if necessary, to respond to these external, uncontrollable influences.

Spending Money

Sims like to be happy. They want to spend their money. The Commercial zones form the city's marketplace. The Sims decide what goes in these zones: stores, gas stations, and banks. The Sims leave Commercial zones vacant until they really need them. Don't bother to create Commercial zones until the Sims ask.

What Makes Sims Mad?

Not having met a Sim face-to-face, we don't know exactly what upsets a Sim. We can guess that they don't like to be called names, or have anyone sit on the fender of their car or cut in front of them in line at McDonalds. And, we definitely wouldn't ask one what they think of the mayor after a nuclear meltdown.

On the other hand, as a group they are very vocal and express their opinions quickly. The Evaluation window (in Figure 5.3) provides insight into their pet peeves. Sims complain about

- ❑ Heavy traffic (replace roads with rails).
- ❑ High crime (add police stations).
- ❑ Pollution (disperse Industrial zones).
- ❑ Housing (add Residential zones).
- ❑ Housing costs (add Residential zones in low rent areas).
- ❑ Fires (add fire stations).
- ❑ Taxes (lower taxes).
- ❑ And unemployment (zone more Commercial and Industrial areas).

We've never noticed the Sims complain that only one train is on the tracks at one time. They don't seem to complain if you bulldoze some of their nicest buildings. They are amazingly unconcerned when a monster crunches her way across the city. They even continue to drive around during the attack. (Just can't resist the sight, we guess.) And we've never heard any complaints after a nuclear power plant meltdown . . . .

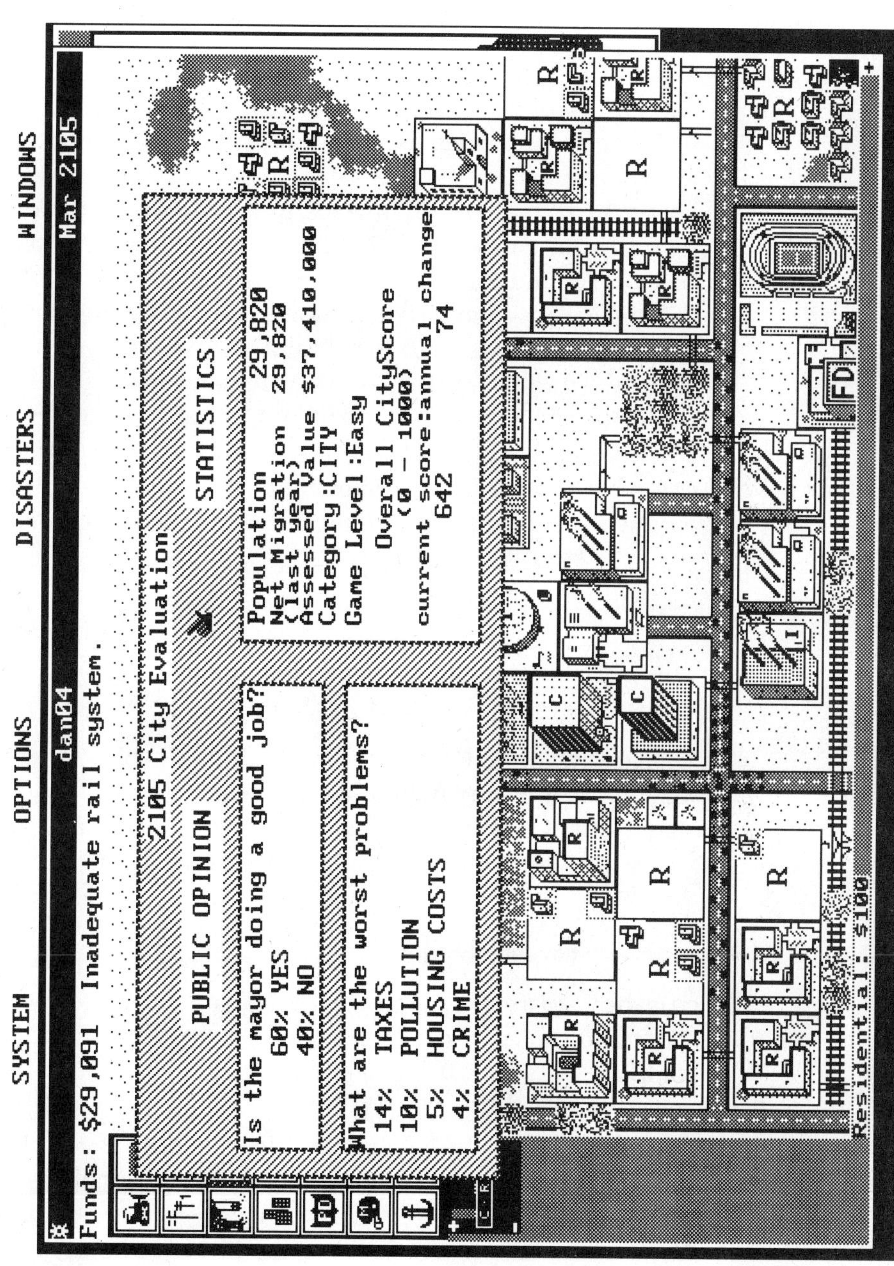

Figure 5.3 The screen showing what the Sims think of the mayor.

How to Handle Their Demands

Hey, you're a politician aren't you? Give them what they want! If they ask for a stadium, build one. If they want cheaper housing, build a suburb or two. When they complain about taxes, ignore them. If they keep complaining, just call up an earthquake. That'll get their attention. At least then they won't be complaining about the taxes anymore.

Even if you don't pay attention to the Sims' complaints, keep an eye on the statistics provided in that Evaluation window. (Chapter 6 covers the statistics.) If you have a negative Net Migration and/or a negative Overall City Score, your city is going downhill. On the other hand, if you have not collected taxes recently and are out of money, you are already at the bottom of the hill, and SimCity will shut down. Ah, don't worry. That won't happen to you more than 10 or 15 times before you reach pro status.

Predictable

Unlike anyone we know, the Sims are predictable. We suspected this and talked with the very helpful people at Maxis. They agreed that the Sims, because they are driven by a rule-based simulation system, will *always* follow the rules. This doesn't mean you have to be predictable, does it?

Measures of Success

A couple of authors named Derrick once said about SimCity and SimEarth: "Mastering these 'games' is difficult. Finishing is impossible." Although theoretically it is possible to achieve a perfect Overall City Score of 1,000 in the Evaluation window, no one that we know has scored 1,000. (We asked Maxis about this, too.) Of course, the Maxis game designer says there is a chance that you can reach 1,000, but the real limit is 900.

OK, before you start scratching your head in confusion at *that one*, what the wag was saying is that you are really playing against yourself. You set the criteria for a "winning" city. For example, when you first start building cities, you can make it a goal to build a city that survives for more than 10 years. Later, you'll rejoice when you have a town which grows to a population of 10,000 and city status, as shown in Figure 5.4. Our criteria now is that we make it to bed by 1 a.m. after firing up SimCity at 9 p.m. Here are a few ideas for rating your cities that we gathered from other Simmers.

Figure 5.4 *SimCity announces the city's population progress at every step.*

Complaints

Of the eight most common complaint areas, the Evaluation window can only show four. If complaints are under 10% in all four areas, you're doing pretty well. Even if complaints in each area are at 10%, that means only 40% of the population has a complaint. (More likely, the whining comes from just 10% of the Sims who provide four complaints each.) So, you can make it a goal to keep complaints below a certain percentage of the population.

If more than 55% of the Sims say the mayor (that's you, heh, heh!) is doing a good job, you're on the right track. If more than 75% like what you are doing, hold a fundraising dinner, fast.

Taxes

Sure, you can raise taxes to 20%. That won't last long, though. When the Sims leave town, 20% of nothing is still nothing. A tax rate of 6% to 7% seems to be the optimum. Needless to say (but we'll say it anyway), a positive cash flow is a good measure of success. The population growth rates could even be pretty level. You might decide that the challenge is trying to stabilize a city (and maintain tax revenue) instead of growing a megalopolis (500,000+ Sims).

City Services

You have a duty to protect your citizens. They don't want do deal with high crime areas. Carefully placed police stations help. If the Evaluation window shows that the Sims (even less than 10%) are complaining, there is a problem with crime. Your goal could be to control the crime rate.

There is nothing more discouraging than to have fires burning for years. Leave gaps in the fire coverage, and that's what will happen in your city. And guess who's gonna complain. Fire control is another area where you can focus your efforts.

Using the City Maps provides a quick view of the coverage of both fire and police protection. If the maps show overlapping coverage, and the complaints are not too bad, then relax. You've done your job here.

Migration

Sims vote with their feet. Sims moving in: good. Sims moving out: better take a look at how you've planned your city.

Overall City Score

You may think you have everything under control. No major complaints, no large fires, and activity in most zones—yet your Overall City Score is low. This score is based on low crime, low pollution, affordable and available housing, reasonable taxes, low unemployment, fire protection, unpowered zones, and the city growth rate. To a lesser extent, other factors influence this score. For example, if the Sims request stadiums, seaports, or airports, and you don't build them, the overall score goes down. Inappropriate funding levels for fire, police, and roads also decrease this score. Longstanding fires don't help, either.

Remember that the Overall City Score is someone else's idea of what makes a city work. For example, stability counts against you with this scoring system. But you may be working to create a stable city, not one that's always growing. If you've decided to zone areas but leave them unpowered, that's up to you. If you don't like the overall city score, don't worry. (On the other hand, if you want to build a city you'd show your mother, a score over 700 is not too bad.)

Measures of Un-Success

No one wants to admit, ah . . . OK, we'll say it . . . failure. But you'll know it when you see it in SimCity. Take heart. Nothing is really a failure if you learn from it. If a city does go down the tubes, try to discover what went wrong. We'll provide tips on avoiding failure in Chapter 10. If one of the following situations develops in your city, you may want to scrap it and build a new one.

Going Bust

The most noticeable measure of failure is running out of money. There's no state or federal government to bail you out, so it's all over. You were silly enough to keep on building even when you saw the funds dwindling. You knew you were running out of money, but still you just kept spending.

Gee, someone that silly wouldn't be willing to, say, embezzle money, would they? If they were in the Edit window, they might discover that they could hold down the **<SHIFT>** *key and type* `fund`. *Suddenly, they might have another $10,000 in their budget. What do you know? We hope they don't get greedy. Try this too many times and you get an earthquake, even if Disasters are off. The Sims will pay for the mayor's greedy ways.*

Everyone Leaves

Finding out that all the Sims have left your city is pretty traumatic. You may even have money left, but it still isn't enough to buy any friends. Your Overall City Score might be over 500, but you still have a ghost town.

The City That Won't Die

And then there are those nagging sorts of failures. The city survives—sort of. If you badly underfund your fire department and place the stations too far apart, you may have fires which burn for a long time. Or a monster just won't go away. Or those darn power brown-outs keep interrupting the Sims. You can deal with these situations or not, as you choose. Bragging about them probably isn't going to get you re-elected, though.

Ultimate Destruction

It is conceivable, but just barely, that you might become upset with the Sims. They may not have listened to your pleas, your cajoling, your begging. After hours of work, they still packed up and left your city. You've tried not one, but two stadiums. You gave them an airport, a seaport, and dozens of condos on the river. You lowered the taxes until you had no income at all. You even had to embezzle funds to give them all they wanted.

Maybe, just maybe, you didn't have the solution to all that industrial pollution (bulldozing all the Industrial zones). In a final fit of frustration, you push your computer off the table. No more SimCity. No more Sims. No more computer. No more frustration (or fun), eh?

6 Menu Choices

The SimCity menus allow you to use the city files, turn settings off and on, set off disasters, and examine your city more closely. You'll use some settings and windows more than others, based on personal preference. For example, we always turn Disasters off and rarely use the Graphs window.

As you practiced by following the steps in Chapter 4, to make a menu choice with the mouse or joystick, you move the pointer to the menu title along the top of the SimCity screen and **<CLICK>** with the button. This two-step process of pointing to the menu choice and then **<CLICK>**ing the left mouse button we designate as **<SELECT>**. Keyboarders can use special **<ALT>** key combinations for these menus. When you choose a menu with either method, a box appears below that menu name. This is a *pull-down menu*.

In some cases when keyboarders are in a menu, the menu bar must be moved up or down to point to the desired choice. Once this menu choice is highlighted, pressing the **<SPACE BAR>** makes the selection. As noted above for mouse and joystick users, this two step process of moving to the menu choice and pressing the **<SPACE BAR>** is designated with the **<SELECT>** command.

The pull-down menu shows all the available options. When you select an item with the mouse, joystick, or keyboard, something happens. Some choices show another box. Some turn and option on or off (that is, the selection *toggles* an option between active and inactive states). A mark appears next to active options on the pull-down menu. The following sections describe the choices with items on each menu.

This chapter gives both joystick or mouse and keyboard instructions for selecting each menu and menu item. Joystick/mouse instructions appear first, indicated by the mouse icon. Keyboard instructions, preceded by the key icon, follow.

***Tip:** To exit a menu without making a selection, press **<ESC>** (the escape key).*

System Menu

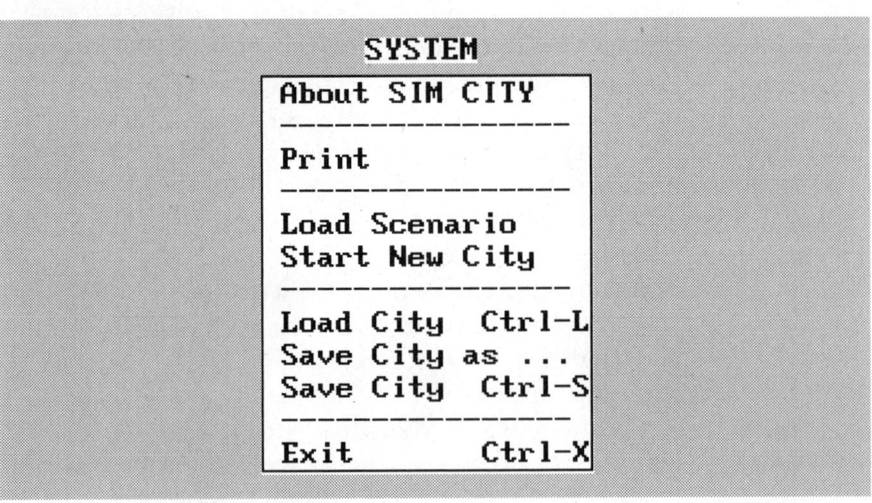

 **<SELECT>** `SYSTEM`

<ALT-S>

The System menu provides choices for the use of city files, printing the city, and quitting the game. For some menu options, you can use **<CTRL>** key shortcuts to bypass this menu and directly select the option. Information about the options on the System menu and how to select them follows.

About SimCity

<SELECT> `About SIM CITY`

Make this choice, and a box with information about your software version of the simulation pops up. The box gives the version number and names the people who worked on this version. It also tells you how to contact Maxis Software by mail, telephone, or FAX.

Print

 **<SELECT>** `SYSTEM` **<SELECT>** `Print`

 **<ALT-S> <SELECT>** `Print`

There are two ways to print your city. Assuming you have the proper printer type (Epson or Proprinter for MS-DOS), you can print out an eight-page city poster to hang on the wall, right next to your favorite moose head. Or, lacking the wall space, you can just print out a one-page city map. One page or eight pages, the choice is up to you.

Load Scenario

 **<SELECT>** SYSTEM **<SELECT>** Load Scenario

 **<ALT-S> <SELECT>** Load Scenario

Scenarios are city files provided with SimCity. Each has a unique problem. When you select Load Scenario, a screen of city names appears. You choose a scenario by moving the pointer to the icon (picture) for that city and **<CLICK>**ing or pressing **<SPACE BAR>**. For more information on scenarios, read Chapter 8.

Start New City

 **<SELECT>** SYSTEM **<SELECT>** Start New City

 **<ALT-S> <SELECT>** Start New City

Use this menu choice only when you want to start a fresh city. When you make this choice, a *pop-up box* (a box in the middle of the screen) appears, asking, Are You Sure? If you answer No, you return to your current city. If you choose Yes, and if you hadn't saved the current city, SimCity erases the current city.

Another pop-up box then prompts you to select the Game Play Level. The Game Play Level determines the funds you get to start the city and the tolerance level of the Sims. The Easy level starts you off with $20,000, while the Hard level only gives you $5,000, and the Medium level provides $10,000. At the hardest level, you can only build a coal power plant ($3,000) and zone a few areas before you run out of funds. At this level, you must plan carefully. Until you have mastered the Easy level, it is difficult to score well in the higher levels.

You then have a chance to name your city or accept the previous settings (defaults). If you had accepted the default name (HERESVILLE) for another city, you can save your new city over the old version of HERESVILLE (we think it's best to enter a new city name each time). The system asks if you want to overwrite the old version. After you enter a name or accept the default, the game automatically terraforms, and you are ready to start building.

Load City

 **<SELECT>** `SYSTEM` **<SELECT>** `Load City`

<CTRL-L>

The Load City function displays a pop-up box similar to the one shown in Figure 6.1. Notice that the Figure shows several saved cities in the current directory. If you save cities, (as we have) the box displays them as a list in a scrollable box. **<CLICK>** in the arrow along the right side of the list of cities, and the list scrolls up. **<CLICK>** on the city you want. The city then appears below `Select filename for SIMCITY load` at the top of the window. **<CLICK>** on the `LOAD` box, and the city loads. If you know the name of the city, you can point to the empty `Select filename` box and **<CLICK>**. Then just type in the city name and **<CLICK>** on `LOAD`.

Tip: *As a shortcut for loading a city, just* ***<DOUBLE-CLICK>*** *on the city name in the file list box. This saves the step of pointing to* `LOAD` *and <CLICK>ing again.*

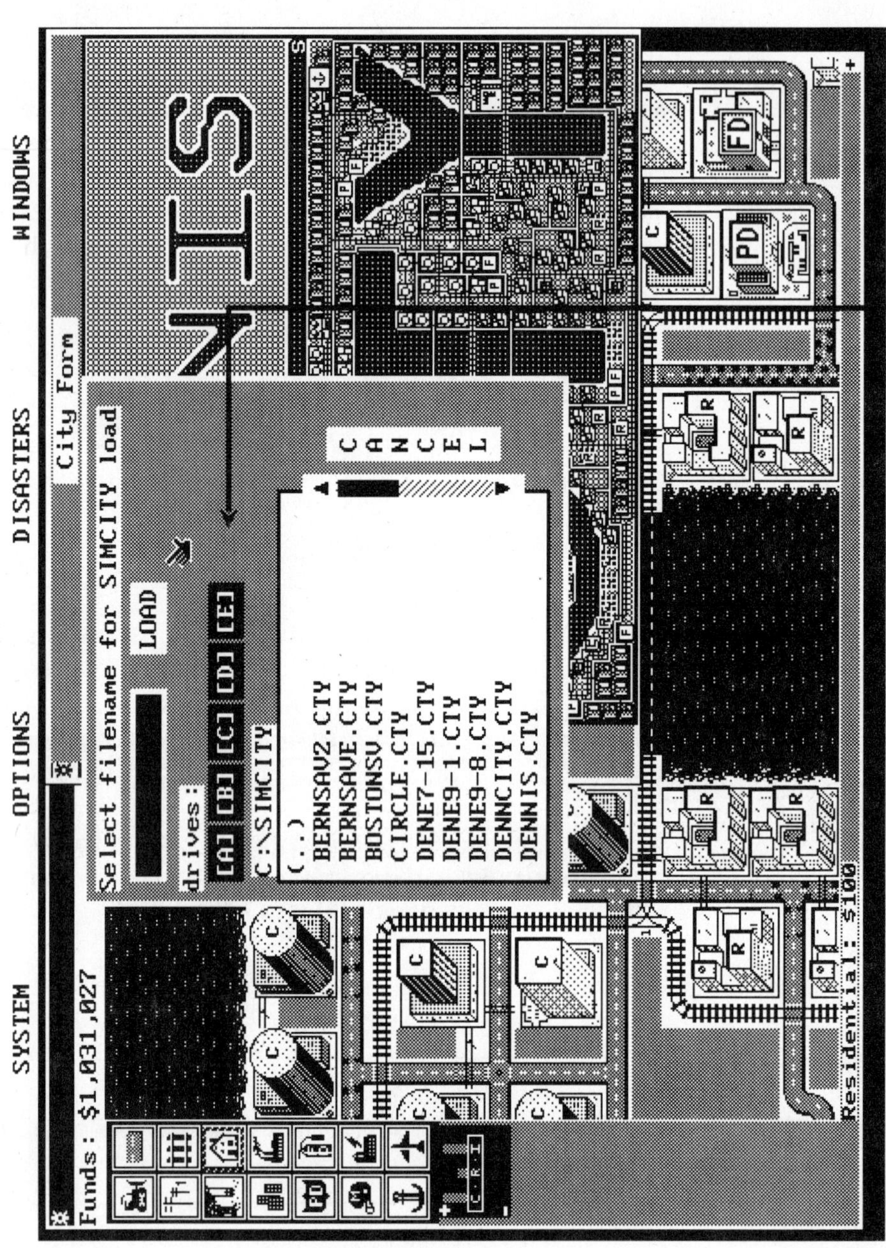

Figure 6.1 *The Load City pop-up box. Notice that our computer system has five drives, A through E.*

If the city is in another directory, **<CLICK>** on the (. .) to display the other directories. The list only shows subdirectories or SimCity files with the .CTY extension. If your cities are stored on another drive, **<CLICK>** on the corresponding drive letter box to display the directories or city files in those drives. If you have a city that you've changed but not saved, a pop-up box prompts to see if you want to save before loading the next city.

Remember, if you are using the keyboard, the **<GRAY+>** and **<GRAY->** keys on the numeric keypad move you from choice to choice on the Load City screen. You need to use the arrow keys or type in the file name, and move to `LOAD` to call up a city.

Save City As...

 **<SELECT>** `SYSTEM` **<SELECT>** `Save City as...`

 **<ALT-S>** **<SELECT>** `Save City as...`

The pop-up box that appears when you choose this menu item works similar to the pop-up box for Load City. Select this option to save your cities under different names. If you save your city using the Save City option, you lose the last version of the city because the computer writes over (destroys) the old copy. With Save City as..., you may rename the current city and save it to disk.

As you experiment with a city, save the file often to see your improvement. One way to save each level of progress is to use the Save City as... command. We save each version as a number, for example, DENNIS01, DENNIS02, and so on. If something goes wrong at version 23, Dennis can return to version 22 or 21 or even earlier to try a new approach to his city design.

Save City

<SELECT> SYSTEM **<SELECT>** Save City

<CTRL-S>

This is the fastest way to save your city frequently. The first time you choose this menu item, SimCity prompts you to name your city or to accept the current name. After this first prompt, SimCity only prompts you if you want to overwrite an existing city file. If you like the progress you are making and do not want to save successive versions of your city using Save City as..., use **<CTRL-S>** every 15 minutes or so to keep the most recent version on disk.

Exit

<SELECT> SYSTEM **<SELECT>** Exit

<CTRL-X>

Choosing Exit produces a pop-up box asking, Are you sure?, as shown in Figure 6.2. **<CLICK>** on Yes or press Y, and you return to your system prompt. If you choose Yes and have not saved your city recently, you'll lose some work.

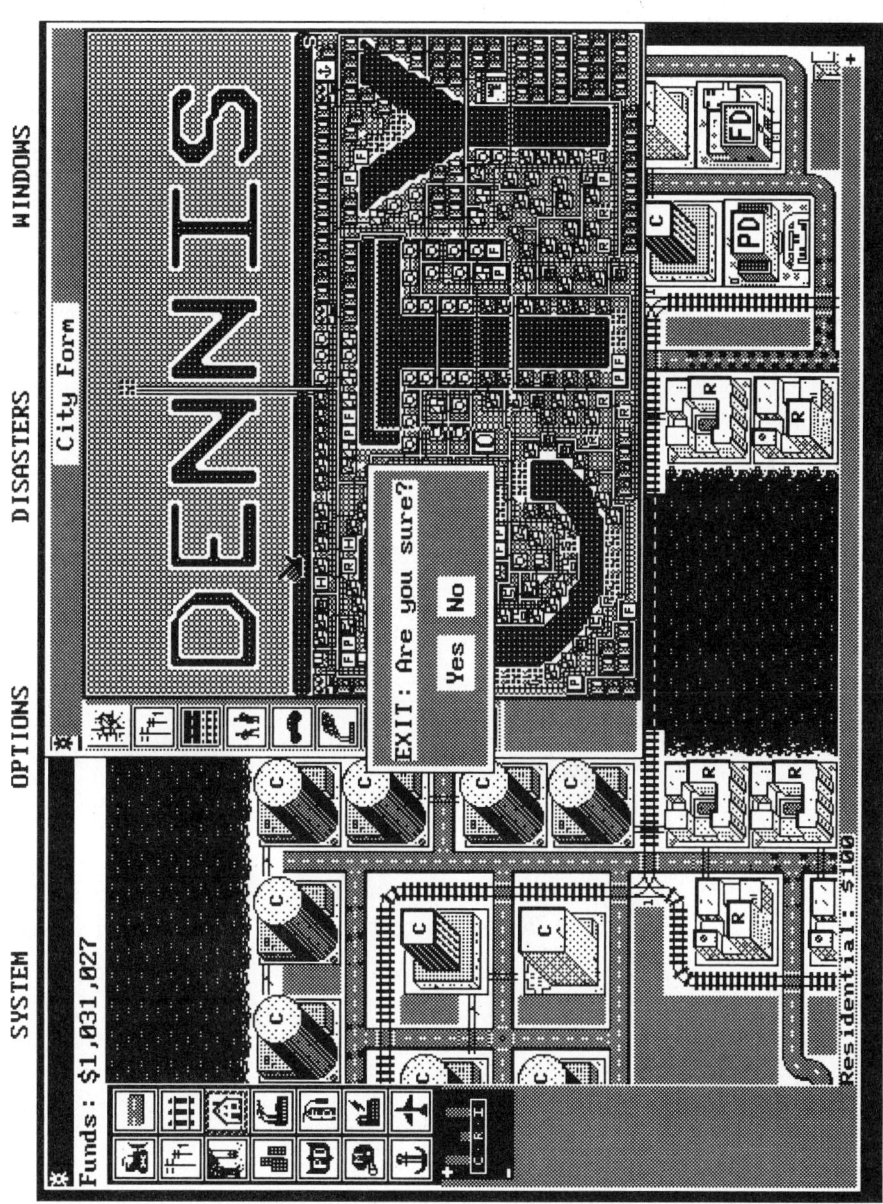

Figure 6.2 *The Exit pop-up box. Check out the funding level in the upper left corner of the SimCity screen!*

Options Menu

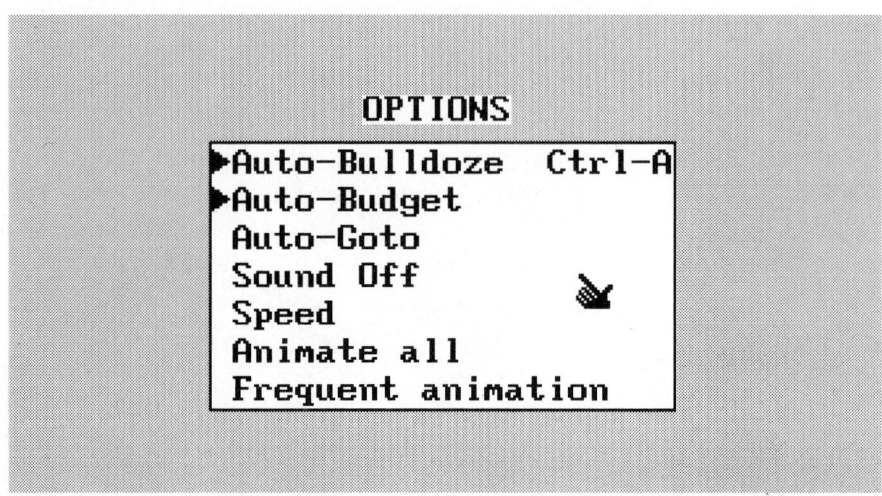

 **<SELECT>** OPTIONS

<ALT-O>

The Options menu provides several toggles (on/off choices) to enhance your using pleasure. Leaving the Auto features on saves some time, but you don't have as much control. Other choices on the Options menu affect how quickly the simulation works. The following sections describe the choices on the Options menu.

Auto-Bulldoze

 **<SELECT>** OPTIONS **<SELECT>** Auto-Bulldoze

<CTRL-A>

This option toggles the Auto-Bulldoze function. **<SELECT>**ing this menu item turns it on or off. An arrow to the left of Auto-Bulldoze indicates that the feature is on. Auto-Bulldoze allows you to zone or build over any natural objects, such as trees and shoreline, without having to manually bulldoze first. Auto-bulldozing still costs you $1 per section, but it provides a much easier way to work. (We turn it on and leave it on.)

Auto-Budget

 **<SELECT>** `OPTIONS` **<SELECT>** `Auto-Budget`

 **<ALT-O> <SELECT>** `Auto-Budget`

This menu choice is also a toggle. Normally, SimCity asks you to set your budget for taxes and city services each year. With Auto-Budget toggled on, your budget rate remains as last set, and you can concentrate on other tasks. Leaving Auto-Budget on means you have a great deal of faith in your Sim bookkeeper. While he is quite honest, he won't tell you when you have a negative cash flow. Use the Window menu to check your budget occasionally if you have this function on. We suggest you initially toggle Auto-Budget on (unless you just love to count the money every year).

Auto-Goto

 **<SELECT>** `OPTIONS` **<SELECT>** `Auto-Goto`

 **<ALT-O> <SELECT>** `Auto-Goto`

Toggling Auto-Goto on zooms you to a disaster or trouble spot as it occurs. For example, when there's a *heavy traffic report*, you're jerked away from whatever you are working on and placed in the heavy traffic area. If the

Skywatch One helicopter is reporting too many cars driving in circles, Auto-Goto places you there immediately.

We like to leave this choice off. If you are about to build something, you may click your mouse just after being "zoomed" to the trouble spot. Now you've built something in the wrong place! It is also unnerving to be whisked to another area while planning a multimillion dollar subdivision.

If you do leave Auto-Goto off, you can quickly move to a trouble spot by **<CLICK>**ing on the * Goto button as the trouble occurs. SimCity displays the Goto message on the message bar next to the Funds message. Alternately, you can hit the **<TAB>** key to be whisked to the circling cars or other trouble spots. Hit the **<TAB>** key again to return to your previous location in the city.

Tip: *Mousers need to use the* ***<TAB>*** *key to return from a trouble spot because there is no "Return from Goto" button.*

Sound

 **<SELECT>** `OPTIONS` **<SELECT>** `Sound Off`

 **<ALT-O> <SELECT>** `Sound Off`

This toggle choice displays `On` and `Off` next to the word `Sound` to indicate whether it's active. If `On` appears, choosing `Sound` turns the sound off. Enjoy(?) all the sounds of Simmin' in your city. You'll hear noise when you zone or build, ships tooting, and other city noises. In addition to the Goto button on the message bar, a warning sound lets you know when a disaster strikes.

After listening to these noises for several hours, you probably won't think they're quite as cute and you may want to turn the sound off. If you are Simmin' on your system at work (Ha! We caught you!), we strongly recommend you disable the sound. Otherwise, you have to explain the weird groans from the monster. With the sound off, your computer also runs the simulation a little faster, which brings up the next Option menu choice . . . .

Speed

 **<SELECT>** `OPTIONS` **<SELECT>** `Speed`

 Press **1**, **2**, **3**, **4** (slowest to fastest), **0** to pause

<SELECT>ing produces another submenu that lists the speeds for the simulation. You can choose Fastest, Fast, Average, Slow, and Pause. When you are letting a city run to build up funds, the Fastest setting makes the years fly by. Also, if you are using a computer with a slow clock speed, like an 8088 at 4.77 Mhz, we highly recommend the Fastest speed.

The game starts at Average, but some cities load at different speeds. You should check your speed when you load a city. Selecting `Pause` stops the simulation, but you can still zone and build. Nothing will grow or change until you select another speed.

We normally like to collect taxes as often as possible, so we run on the Fastest setting. We love to imagine those Sims drinking lots of coffee (with lots of caffeine) and zipping around day after day.

Animate All

 **<SELECT>** `OPTIONS` **<SELECT>** `Animate All`

 **<ALT-O>** **<SELECT>** `Animate All`

This menu item controls how the SimCity program updates the screen. Turning Animate All off allows only the front window to show the action, which helps computers working hard to keep the screen updated. With an 8088 system (PC or XT), toggling Animate All off allows the game to work a little faster. Even if you don't have a slow machine, making sure that Animate All is off helps increase the speed in Simtime. When you save your city, the program does not save the off setting.

Frequent Animation

 **<SELECT>** OPTIONS **<SELECT>** Frequent Animation

 **<ALT-O> <SELECT>** Frequent Animation

This menu option determines how often the computer stops running the simulation to refresh the screen. If Frequent Animation is off, the Sims on your screen will seem to move in slow motion. Actually, the system runs a little faster, but the program doesn't update the screen as often. Saving your city does not save this setting. After loading the city the next time, return to the Options menu and reset Frequent Animation.

***Tip:** If you want the Sim-ulated time to move at its fastest, disable Animate All, disable Frequent Animation, disable Sound, and set the speed at Fastest. Then sit back and collect your Simtaxes.*

Disasters Menu

DISASTERS

Fire
Flood
Air Crash
Tornado
Earthquake
Monster

▶Disable

 **<SELECT>** `DISASTERS`

<ALT-D>

The first versions of SimCity did not have disasters. But, after noticing how people enjoyed flattening their newly created cities with the bulldozer, Maxis Software added disasters. Now the Disasters menu choices can cause several problems for both you and the Sims. The Sims get maimed, killed, made homeless, or even deprived of coffee (*gasp!*). You deal with the results of the disaster you just set loose on your own city. (Kind of like shooting yourself in the foot, huh?)

We recommend using this menu when you are ready to go to bed after many hours of trying to please those little pinhead Sims. They don't appreciate all the good things you have done for them. So . . . unleash the monster on them. Or shake 'em up with a 'quake. This menu reassures you that you really are in charge. We do suggest very strongly that before starting a disaster you save your city.

Fire

 **<SELECT>** `DISASTERS` **<SELECT>** `Fire`

 **<ALT-D> <SELECT>** `Fire`

Choosing this disaster starts a fire in some lucky Sim's area. The fire starts small, but if your city has inadequate fire protection, the fire spreads rapidly. You could set a fire to test your fire protection in your best city (after you've saved a version of it, naturally).

Of course, you might find that your funding level does not please the Sims in the firefighters union and, as a result, the city burns. Until you increase funding for fire protection, the firefighters quickly rush to the fire—with hot dogs and marshmallows to roast. Maybe they will put it out, maybe not. Otherwise, you can call up the city version you saved (You did save it, didn't you?), adjust the funding level, and set another test fire.

Flood

 **<SELECT>** DISASTERS **<SELECT>** Flood

 **<ALT-D> <SELECT>** Flood

Choose this disaster, and blue (or whatever represents water on your screen) slowly spreads over an area bordering water, and over any buildings, roads, and power lines. Eventually, the water will disappear, leaving empty land. But if you want something fast and destructive, skip this disaster.

Air Crash

 **<SELECT>** DISASTERS **<SELECT>** Air Crash

 **<ALT-D> <SELECT>** Air Crash

Normally, the planes zigzag across the friendly skies. Selecting this disaster immediately puts a pilot to sleep. The plane then plows straight into the ground, usually near the airport. An explosion follows and starts a few fires. If your fire protection is good, the whole incident ends quickly. Select this disaster when you have no airport, and a plane appears out of nowhere to crash immediately. Only the Sims crash on demand.

Tornado

 **<SELECT>** DISASTERS **<SELECT>** Tornado

 **<ALT-D> <SELECT>** Tornado

Selecting Tornado creates an unpredictable funnel cloud, which skips around and acts like the real thing, sort of. Those wacky Sims don't even run away. They continue to drive around and watch as the tornado smashes buildings, destroys pavement and railroad tracks, and crashes through the woods. We saw a tornado hit a Sim stadium, and the Sims didn't even stop the game. (Must have been sudden death overtime.) After destroying planes, trains, and park fountains, the twister wander off the edge of the screen or just disappears. Rebuild and find out who won the game—you or the tornado.

Earthquake

 **<SELECT>** `DISASTERS` **<SELECT>** `Earthquake`

 **<ALT-D> <SELECT>** `Earthquake`

The most devastating SimCity disaster, these earthquakes destroy major sections of any city. Not only does this MAJOR earthquake shake apart buildings, but it also causes fires to break out everywhere. Even if your city has good fire protection, the earthquake destroys the power grid and leaves many fire stations without power. Firefighters can't respond when the power's out, and they can't use the electric door opener. When you have grown tired of a city, this is the way to commit city-cide.

Monster

 **<SELECT>** `DISASTERS` **<SELECT>** `Monster`

 **<ALT-D> <SELECT>** `Monster`

This any kid's favorite choice. Turn the monster loose and watch her knock down planes, push over buildings, and do all the things monsters are required to do.

Industry smoke and pollution *seem* to attract her. Like the tornado, she wanders aimlessly about, sometimes circling and redestroying areas she just left. If you add a special COVOX sound board to your system, you can hear her moans of terror. She seems to have indigestion and belches rather rudely. (If you don't have a system with the authentic SimCity sounds, this is not a reason to get one. See Part 4.) Now, if we could only figure out how to get King Kong to show up . . . .

Disable

 **<SELECT>** `DISASTERS` **<SELECT>** `Disable`

 **<ALT-D> <SELECT>** `Disable`

This is our favorite choice. We disable Disasters immediately after loading or starting a city. This choice is an on/off toggle. If you want the disasters to be disabled, make sure you see an arrow to the left of the word `Disable`. It's enough of a challenge to build a city with a high score. You don't need disasters ruining your work.

When you start or load a city, it *does not* come up with Disasters disabled. Remember to *disable the disasters immediately*. If you don't, the simulation can randomly start a disaster in your city at any time. After you lose a few great cities to earthquakes, you'll soon remember to turn Disasters off first thing after loading your city.

Others Disasters (Not on Menu)

Not all disasters are listed on the Disaster menu. If conditions are right and you have not turned the Disasters off, you may be lucky enough to experience a . . .

Shipwreck

When you have one or more seaports, a ship cruises your waterways and, like the planes, it zigzags all over the water. Occasionally, a bridge jumps out in front of the ship and boom, shipwreck. The ship sinks. Another takes its place. And life goes on. The ship also sinks if a monster or tornado crosses its path.

Nuclear Meltdown

Naturally, meltdowns only happen if you have nuclear power plants. Without warning, the plant can burst into flames, and the surrounding area becomes radioactive. The radioactive area is useless to normal Sims. Some Sims continue to live in the area, but in a few years they disappear. (They go underground as mutant Sims, and yes, some are green pizza-loving teenagers.) Little radioactive symbols decorate the area around the meltdown and do not go away for a long, long time.

***Tip:** Here's a sneaky trick. To solve this radioactivity problem, use the Terrain Editor to scrape all the radioactivity symbols off. The land may still be radioactive, but the Sims won't know it (until years later).*

Train Wreck

Train wrecks happen when the engineer ignores any tornado bearing down on the train and drives right into the funnel cloud. Or, sometimes a speedy monster catches the train and uses it as a back-scratcher. (Just kidding.) Like the ship, another train appears, and the commuters climb aboard without a second thought.

Beer Shortage at the Stadium

"No more beer? Is this place for real?" Running out of beer at the stadium (one of the biggest disasters we personally can imagine) results in a riot that tests your police department's skills. To avoid this, build a commercial zone next to your stadium. A hot dog stand opens to sell the Sims dogs 'n' suds. You'll find that a happy Sim is not a sober Sim.

Now we are REALLY just kidding. We made up this disaster. It would be kind of fun to see, wouldn't it?

Windows Menu

WINDOWS	
Maps	Ctrl-M
Graphs	Ctrl-G
Budget	Ctrl-B
Edit	Ctrl-E
Evaluation	Ctrl-U
Close	Ctrl-C
Hide	Ctrl-H
Position	Ctrl-P
Resize (Edit)	Ctrl-R

 **<SELECT>** WINDOWS

<ALT-W>

You do most of your city work in the Edit window. By choosing WINDOWS from the menu bar, you can open a series of other windows. Each of the windows you can select from this menu provides different information about or a different view of your city. The City Form window shows the entire city at one time. Like an x-ray machine, it also shows otherwise invisible features of the city, including areas with police and fire protection. The Budget window lets you review and change the tax rate. The Evaluation window shows you how the Sims think you are doing, as well as giving your overall City Score.

The following descriptions tell how to reach each window, including a keyboard shortcut for each. Once you are in a specific window, move the pointer and **<CLICK>** to make the selection, or use the **<GRAY+>** and **<SPACE BAR>** keys to make changes or selections.

Maps Window

<SELECT> `WINDOWS` **<SELECT>** `Maps`

<CTRL-M>

The Maps window, shown in Figure 6.3, has icons which allow you to view different features of the city. For example, you can see a layout of your city's transportation system. The bar at the top of the window displays the name of the currently selected icon. The * button in the upper left corner of the box closes the window when you **<SELECT>** it. Boarders can use **<CTRL-C>** to close this window. To choose one of the map views, **<SELECT>** the corresponding icon.

City Form Icon

<SELECT>ing this icon displays the entire city and terrain. Figure 6.3 shows Dennis' complete EVANSVIL city in the City Form window. This overview provides the perspective for the areas best suited for Residential, Industrial, and Commercial zones. For example, you can use the City Form map to locate the water and trees to decide the best location for Residential zones. You can keep Industrial zones away from the Residential zones. And, you can see where you have room to place Commercial zones between

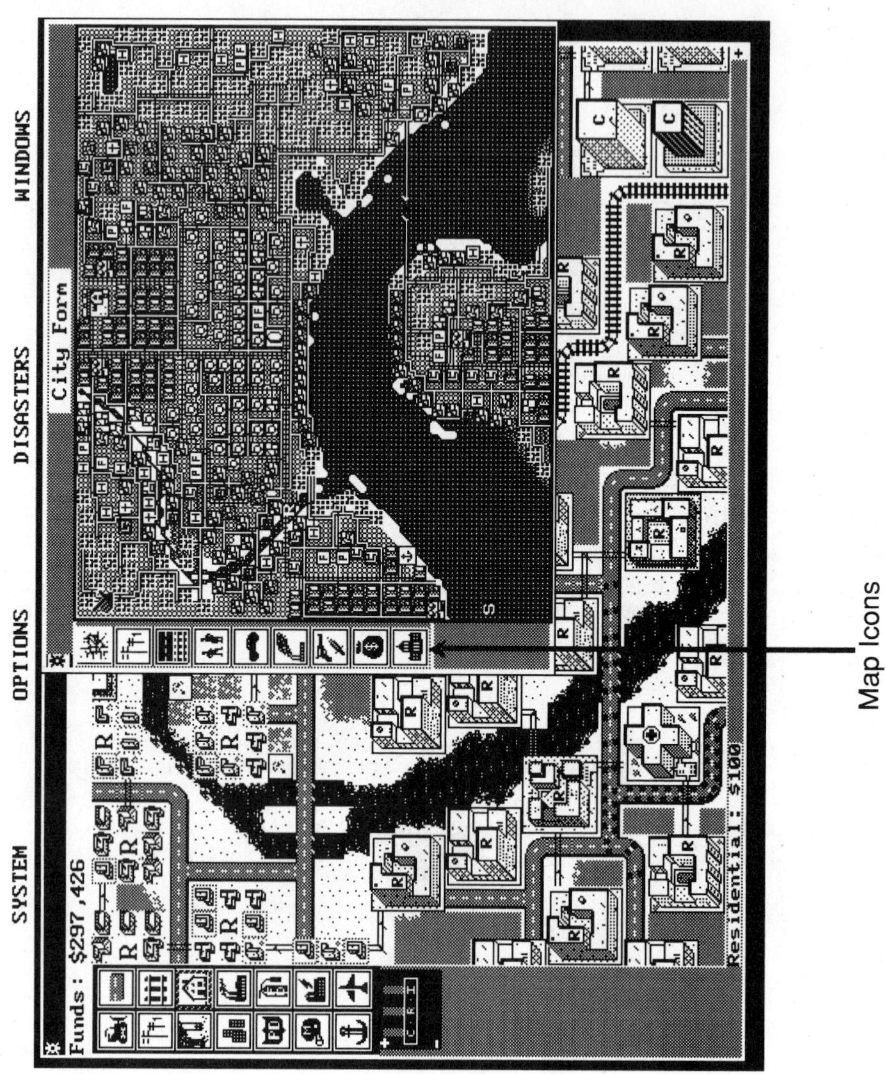

Figure 6.3 *The Maps window appears on top of the Edit window. The icons are along the left side of the window, and the name of the currently selected icon appears at the window's top.*

Residential and Industrial zones. (You did notice these hints, didn't you?) Once a city is spread out over your entire terrain, this window helps you see where you can squeeze in new zones.

When a disaster strikes and you miss the GOTO button, use the City Form map to locate the disaster quickly. For example, an M on the City Form map represents the roaming monster. The map also shows other objects, such as the train, with corresponding letters: A for airplane, R for railroad train, T for tornado, S for ship, and H for the traffic helicopter. Finding the H points you to a traffic problem.

While you are working the City Form map window, a blinking rectangle outlines the area showing in the Edit window. To select another area of the city to show in the Edit window, **<POINT>** to the rectangle, hold the left button down, and drag the box to the new location (**<CLICK-DRAG>**). You can also **<CLICK>** on the box, move the pointer to the new location, and **<CLICK>** once.

Remember keyboarders: **<SPACE BAR>** is the same as **<CLICK>**. If you leave both windows open at the same time, leave this City Form view in the Map window.

Power Grid Icon

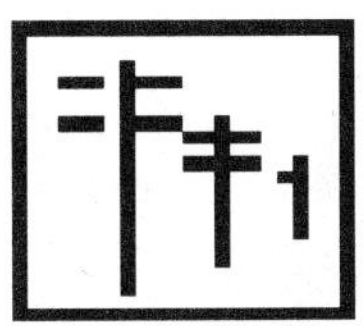

This map displays a layout of the power lines to all zones. The zones without power are dark, as in *no lights*. Use this map to locate zones that lose power due to a disaster. Repairing the power lines restores the lights.

Transportation Icon

To get an overall view of the roads and railroads, choose this icon. The Maps window displays the entire transportation network. If you have a color monitor, the railroad lines look different from the roads. If you are having traffic problems, use this map to locate the congested areas. Then start up the bulldozer. Tear down the buildings, and build a new highway, just like they do in real life.

Population Icon

Choosing this icon pops-up two more options: Population Density and Population Growth. Choose `Population Density` to show the areas full of Sims and devoid of Sims. The light areas on the screen show the minimum population density, ranging up to the darkest screen areas, which indicate the highest population density. (This difference may be difficult to see without a color monitor.) Overpopulated areas are problem areas. Bulldoze these Simslums to the ground, then build some projects on the edge of the city.

The Population Growth map shows where the city is hot, and where it's not. Where the growth is high, add more zones because the Sims like the area for some reason. They will continue to build there unless you do something wrong. In the low growth areas, clean up—build parks and maybe a police station to get the cheap-wine-loving Sims off the streets. Check again later to see if the Sim neighborhood association noticed your improvements.

Traffic Density Icon

Beep, beep. Honk, honk. This map shows where all the cars are. (Hint: They aren't home.) The screen shows the minimum (light) to maximum (dark) traffic density to help you locate the congestion. For some reason, many Sims find one street and just go in circles. The best way to solve traffic problems is to bulldoze the roads and replace them with rails. Even though the Sims are determined to drive everywhere, they don't like the bumpiness of driving on railroad tracks and start taking the train, solving the traffic problem at hand.

Pollution Index Map Icon

If you want to sell oxygen masks, first select this icon to see a map of the most unbreathable air. This map shows the polluted areas. A lot of Industrial zones grouped together appear as large, dark areas on the map. Spreading out the industry thins out the pollution but brings down surrounding property values.

We don't want to affect the tax base, and we don't have to breathe the air. Because we can't have both clean air and a low tax base, we'll go for the money, even if it gives the Sims a lung ache. If public opinion shows displeasure with pollution, (that is, if more than 10% of the Sims whine about it), use this map to eliminate some of the problem and spread it elsewhere. Sound familiar? Build some parks and plant some trees to help offset some of the lower land values caused by the polluted areas.

Crime Rate Icon

Industrial areas or areas with high population often have a lot of crime. If your police coverage on the City Services Police map (see "City Services Icon," later in this chapter) looks OK, use this icon to pinpoint the worst crime areas and build more police stations there. Low land values also add to the crime rate. Increasing the value of these areas should decrease the crime rate.

Land Values Icon

Where are the rich neighborhoods? Where are the dumps? This map shows home locations of the Sims starring in *SimStyles of the Rich and Sorta Famous*. (How famous can a Sim be in a simulation full of Sims?) The land values show the Simslums. Improve the area with parks to bring up the land values and taxes! If you notice what affects the land values, such as water, you can plan your cities to include these areas next time.

City Services Icon

Choosing the City Services icon brings up a small pop-up menu with two choices, Police and Fire. Use both these maps when building your stations to avoid overbuilding. Remember, each station costs tax dollars each year. Overdoing coverage of these services does not add to the City Score, but just drains your funds needlessly.

Select the Police choice, and the window shows a map with the effective range of each of the police stations. Use this map to keep from overlapping your coverage too much. The Sim Police are only effective if properly paid. With a low funding rate, the Sim police stay in the donut shops and Sim thugs rule. With the highest funding levels, you get the largest area of coverage for each station. Good coverage increases the land values and brings in more taxes. (But if you have too many stations, it costs you too many tax dollars. Fire up the 'dozer!) Transportation access to the city also affects the coverage for each station. Make sure the roads and railroads provide the police Sims a way out of their station.

Like the Police map, the Fire map shows the coverage of each of the fire stations. Again, the funding affects the area that each station protects. Good fire protection is important to the Sims. Coverage must be good for fire fighters to extinguish fires rapidly. This is especially important for the disasters that create fires when they strike, like earthquakes. Like the police Sims, the firefighter Sims like to be able to drive their fire trucks to the fire, so connect each station to a road or track for coverage.

Graphs Window

 **<SELECT>** `WINDOWS` **<SELECT>** `Graphs`

 `<CTRL-G>`

The Graphs window provides a graphic representation of changes in the city for the past 10 or 120 years. As shown in Figure 6.4, you can choose several items from the icons on the left side of the pop-up box containing the graph. The graph can display the last 10 or 120 years, depending on which icon you choose. Then choose the icon for the type of information you want to display. There are six items you can graph by selecting the icons that follow. The box can display all six at once with the color around the box corresponding to the color on the graph. Simmers with black and white screens have to guess a lot.

Residential icon (house)	Displays the population growth or decline in the Residential zones for the chosen time period.
Commercial icon (buildings)	Displays the Commercial zone population variances for the given time period.
Industrial icon (factories)	This shows the Industrial zone population increases, or decreases, over the years given.
Crime icon (gun/knife)	Displays the crime rate fluctuations through the given time period.
Pollution icon (smokestacks)	Displays the pollution for the entire city as it changes from year to year.
Cash icon (money bag)	Displays the amount of cash left at tax time after all services are funded—that is, your cash flow. The center of the graph represents $0, so anything below midline means there was a negative cash flow during that period.

These graphs show trends that you won't notice in the normal game timeframe. For example, you might see an upward trend in crime with the increase in industrial pollution. Paying attention to these graphs provides valuable perspectives for your next city. When you finish, **<CLICK>** on the button (*) in the upper left corner or use **<CTRL-C>** to close this window.

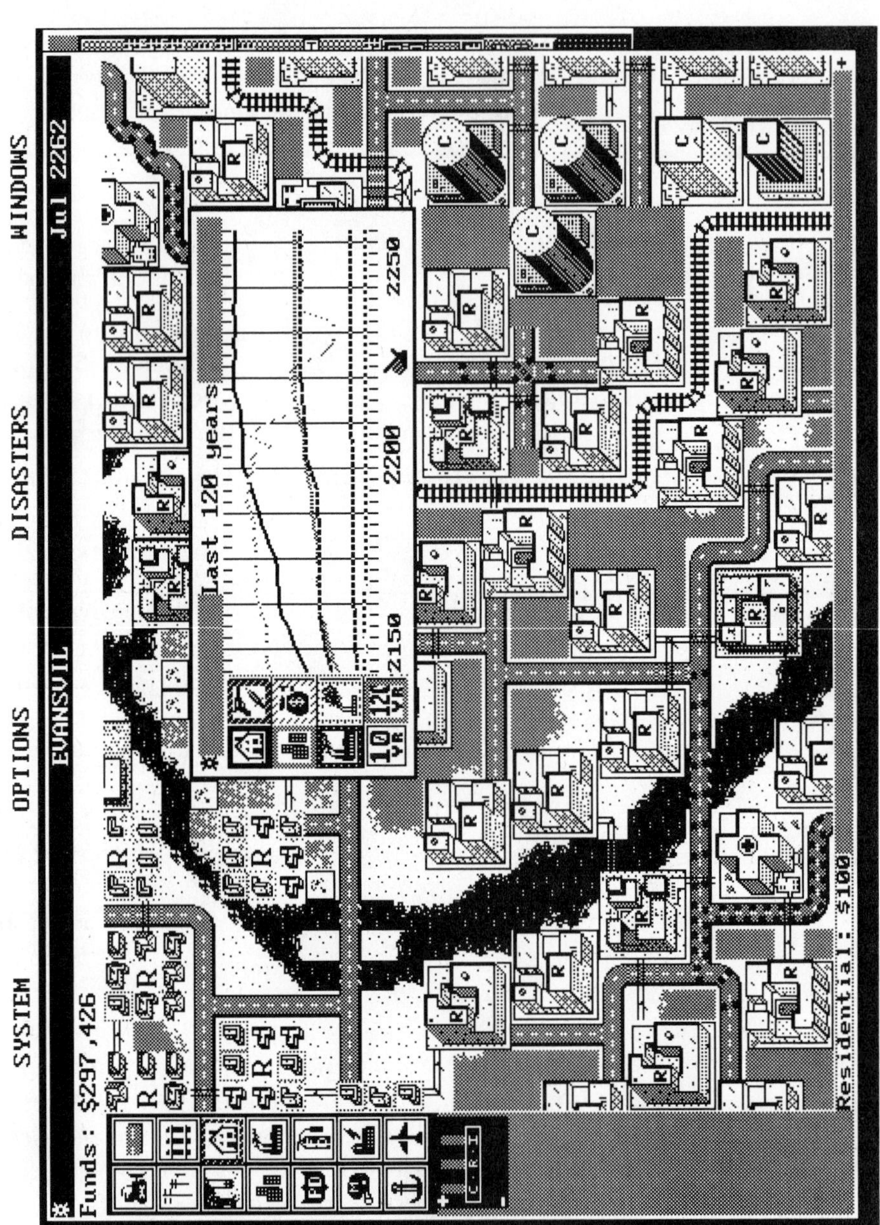

Figure 6.4 *The Graphs window showing the past 120 years of EVANSVIL.CTY. Housing is high, crime low. The Sims must be happy.*

Budget Window

 **<SELECT>** `WINDOWS` **<SELECT>** `Budget`

<CTRL-B>

It's important to watch the Budget window (shown in Figure 6.5) if you want to "win" this simulation. This window pops up once a year when taxes are collected if you don't have Autobudget on in the Options pull-down menu. You use this window to control the taxes collected from the Sims. Set the percentages of the funding and the tax rate by **<CLICK>**ing on the arrows beside them. When you are satisfied with the rates, **<CLICK>** on `Go with these figures` or press the **<ENTER>** key.

Keyboarders might not find the **<GRAY+>** key as handy to move from point to point in this window. Because each up or down control arrow (next to the percentages in Figure 6.5) is a stopping point, boarders would have to press the **<GRAY+>** key numerous times to move around the window. Just using the Arrow keys to point and the **<SPACE BAR>** to select might be easier.

The taxes collected according to the following formula: Tax = Population * Land Value * Tax Rate * Scaling Constant. SimCity sets the Scaling Constant variable based on the Game Play Level you chose at the beginning of your game. This window shows the difficulty of the Hard level, because you can see that not all the Sims pay their fair share. This keeps the SIRS (Sim Internal Revenue Service) busy and cuts into your cash flow. As we said earlier, don't try the harder levels until you understand what the Sims want for their tax dollars.

The simulation collects taxes for the current Sim year (which ends December 31 each year.) When you change the tax rate, you don't see the difference until the next tax collection. You may tax the Sims from 0% to 20%. The best rate for growth is 5% to 7%, while 8% to 9% slows growth but assists in building funds. Set taxes any higher, and you'll end up with a Sim tea party.

You should fund city services as close to 100% as possible. Per year, roads cost $1 for each section and bridge sections, $4. The railroads cost $4 per section and $10 per tunnel section. You must fund your transportation system at 90% or better for it to remain stable. Any value below 75% causes

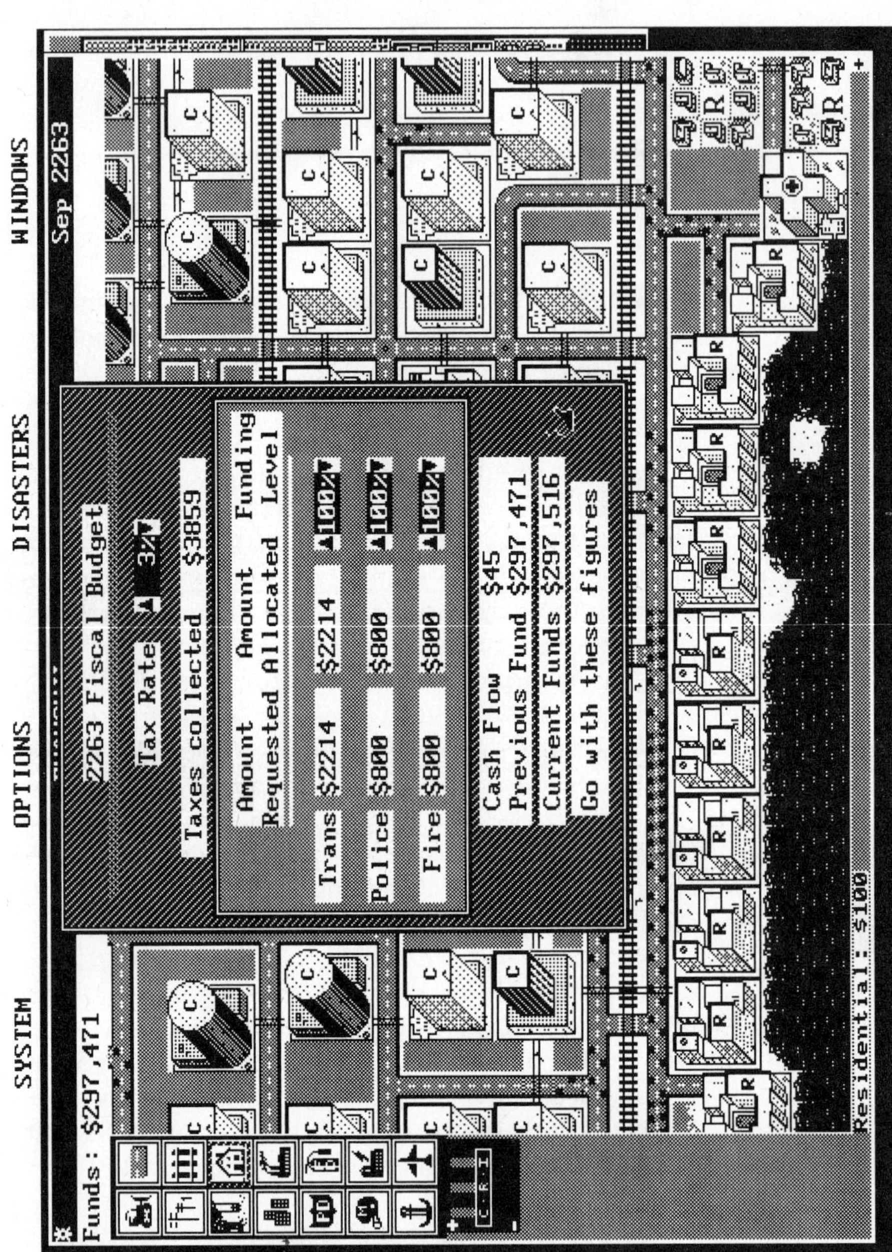

Figure 6.5 *The Budget window displays low taxes (3%), but an equally low cash flow.*

rapid deterioration. It will cost a bundle and lots of time keep up with the repairs in this case. If you fund transportation below 75%, the rails and roads deteriorate with potholes and rotten ties. The potholes are the size of an entire section of road and seriously hamper the Sims' ability to drive where they want. The damage to the tracks limits the train to a short section of useable track. Neither of these conditions helps your Overall City Score.

You are charged $100 per station per year for your police and fire services at the 100% funding level. Low funding for police and fire affects the coverage of the stations. If you spend more money to build more stations to make up for the smaller coverage areas, the additional stations take more funding, so fund the city services at a high level. When you develop negative cash flow, the police service loses its money first, followed by fire protection and transportation.

Pay attention to the costs of maintaining your funded services. You don't want to spend more than you take in. A positive cash flow is essential. If you have a negative cash flow, the city goes downhill. The Sims leave in droves (or anything else they can find to ride in).

The ideal way to build up funding is to create a city with a large tax base (lots of happy Sims) and set up the budget with a positive cash flow. Allow your simulation to run overnight with Disasters disabled. If you have a stable city, you'll be a rich mayor in the morning. If the city is not stable, you'll have a ghost town.

As we mentioned before, a sneaky way to get more money is to embezzle. Type `fund` while in the Edit window, and yours funds increase by $10,000. (Oh my!) If you embezzle too often, your city has an earthquake, even if Disasters are disabled. Like cheating at Solitaire, creating a healthy city by embezzling funds doesn't provide much of a thrill. You can only increase your funding level for a while by embezzling. After the fourth grab (or was it the third?), the earthquake hits.

Edit Window

 **<SELECT>** `WINDOWS` **<SELECT>** `Edit`

 **`<CTRL-E>`**

The Edit window allows zoning and building. It shows you a close-up of an area. The open land appears as brown on color displays. Monochrome screens display a very light tone with specks. You can build on this open land without bulldozing first.

Trees appear in green or a medium shade (so to speak). You must first bulldoze trees to zone or build, unless Auto-Bulldoze is on. Don't destroy too many trees or else the Sim environmentalist, Yule Simmons, will lead a campaign that could damage you politically. Trees help increase land values. Build Residential areas in and near plenty of trees to attract more affluent Sims.

Look for blue or a dark shade to find water. You may only build roads, tracks, and power lines over water, and you may not zone water areas. You can bulldoze the edge a little to zone an area on the shore, but you are limited to one tile into the water. Look for areas with both trees and shoreline to zone as Residential areas. This brings the Sims with megabucks, and, if the city center is nearby, condos sprout like trees. When building roads over or railroad tunnels under water, you cannot make any turns. Plan to span the water carefully, and shortly, because maintenance is much higher for these sections of road and track.

Title Bar

The *Title bar* is at the top of the Edit window, as shown in Figure 6.6. It contains the name of your city and the city's current date. The Edit window Close button (*) is in the upper left corner of the Title bar, as it is in most windows. **<CLICK>**ing on this button closes the window. Keyboarders can use **<CTRL-C>** to close the top (active) window.

<CLICK-DRAG> on the Title bar enables you to reposition the window within the screen. **<CTRL-P>** enables the Arrow keys on the keyboard to move the active window. Press **<Enter>** to set the window at that location.

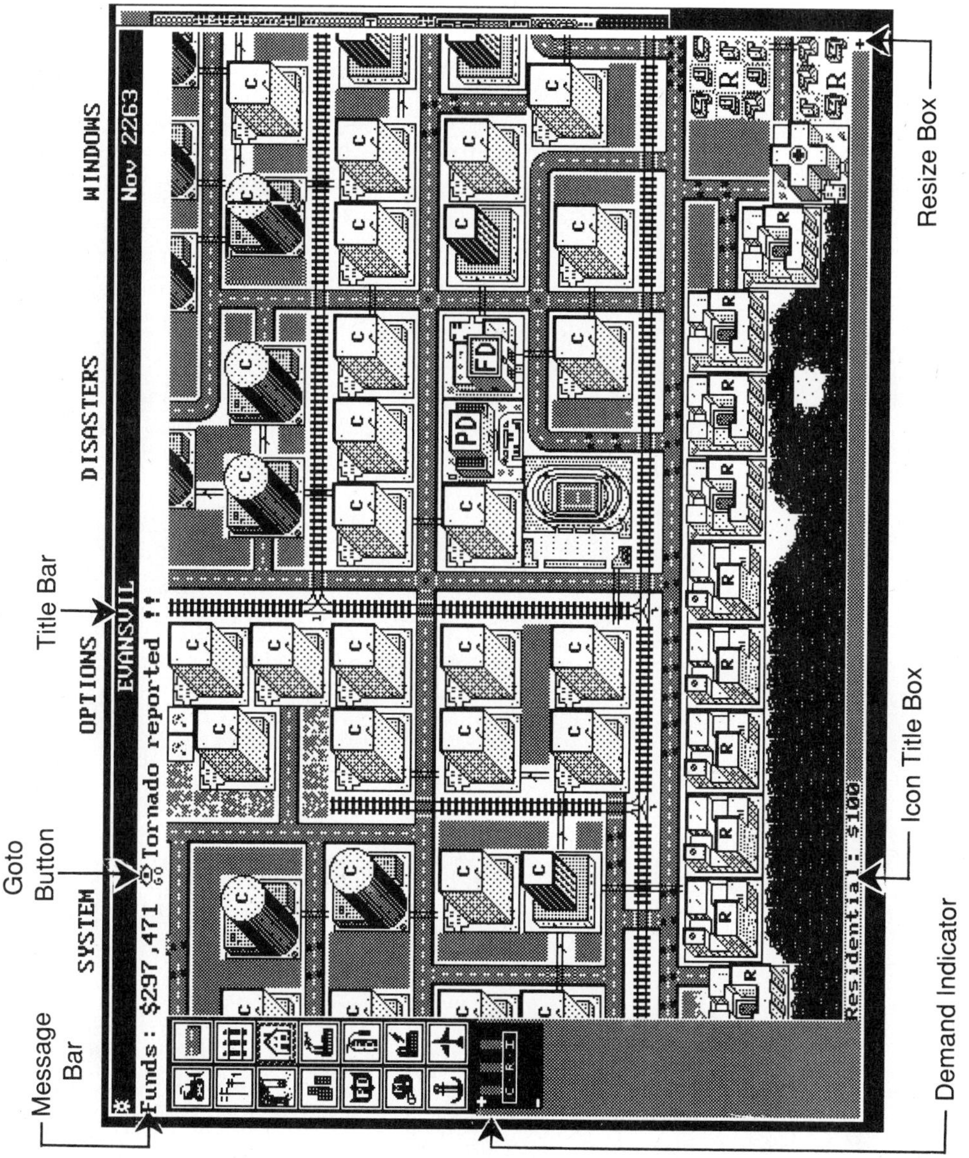

Figure 6.6 The Edit window and all its features.

Message Bar

The *Message bar* is below the Title bar. The left end shows the current `Funds` available. Next to the funding message, the bar will display other messages, including the Sims' demands and status messages from the simulator. For example, the simulation might tell you `More residential zones needed`, or `Brownouts, build another power plant`. Complaints from the Sims might be `Citizens demand a stadium`, or `Citizens demand a Police station`.

Goto Button

When a disaster or event occurs, the *Goto button* (that looks like an eye) and a description of the problem appear on the message bar, as shown in Figure 6.10. **<CLICK>**ing on the Goto button takes you to the scene of the event. You can also hit the **<TAB>** key to go to the event. Pressing **<TAB>** again takes you back to Kansas, er, where you were before the event occurred.

Icons

The left side of the Edit window contains icons. These little pictures represent the tools with which you zone, build, and bulldoze. Use the **<GRAY+>** key to cycle through the icons or just move the pointer to that icon. When you **<SELECT>** an icon, a rectangle (which is a different size depending on the chosen item) appears in the Edit window. Drag the rectangle or use the arrow keys to place it wherever you wish to zone or build. If, for some reason, the simulation will not allow you to use an icon, a message appears in the message bar. If any icons appear ghosted (that is, they appear faded on the screen), then you do not have enough funds remaining to use those icons. See Chapter 7 for more information about the icons.

Demand Indicator

The *Demand Indicator*, below the icons, shows the demand for each of the three zone types. If the bars are pointing up (positive), then the Sims are demanding more of these types of zone. If the indicators are pointing down, there are too many of a type of zone.

The Demand Indicator doesn't always make sense. For example, it sometimes shows a demand for Commercial zones when several of these zones are empty. We didn't place much value on the Demand Indicator, but rather looked for the zone type Sims built up quickly. These were the zones in demand. Don't ever zone a lot of one zone just because the Demand Indicator shows a high demand. These zones may remain empty while the indicator still shows a high demand for them.

Icon Title Box

At the lower left of the Edit window is the Icon Title box. This simply displays the currently selected icon and the cost of using that icon.

Resize Button

This button (+) appears in the lower right corner of the Edit window and enables you to change the size of the window. Use **<CLICK-DRAG>** on this button to resize the window. Keyboarders can use **<CTRL-R>** to activate the window resize. The Arrow keys will then change the window shape. Resizing windows can be useful if you want your Edit and Maps windows open concurrently. Resizing only changes the amount of the city area you see, not zones and buildings.

Evaluation Window

 **<SELECT>** `WINDOWS` **<SELECT>** `Evaluation`

<CTRL–U>

Closely watch the Evaluation window, shown in Figure 6.7. This window shows what the Sims think about you and your government. **<CLICK>** the window again or hit **<ESC>** to return to the Edit window. This window provides the Sims' and the simulation's opinion of you under two categories: `PUBLIC OPINION` and `STATISTICS`. The simulation updates the figures in this window once a Sim year.

Public Opinion

Your public wants you to know how you are doing. In fact, you can't keep them from saying what they want. Once a year, they respond to two poll questions: `Is the mayor doing a good job?` and `What are the worst problems?`

If you have been ignoring the demands displayed on the message bar, the percentage of Sims who say you're doing a good job (the `YES` percentage) will be low. If any of the `What are the worst problems?` percentages are above 10%, you also will experience a low approval rate. If you have cut funding of the city services to increase the fund reserve, suffer the Sims' wrath. When more than 60% of the Sims say you're doing a good job, you should be able to win the elections. If the rating is above 75%, you might consider running for a higher office.

Sims, like real people, will always find something to gripe about. Fortunately, the `What are the worst problems?` question limits them to eight gripes and the Evaluation window only displays the top four problems. If more than 20% of the Sims mention a problem, you'd better work to improve the situation, or the Sims vote with their feet and leave. In general, if fewer than 10% of the Sims are complaining about one of the following

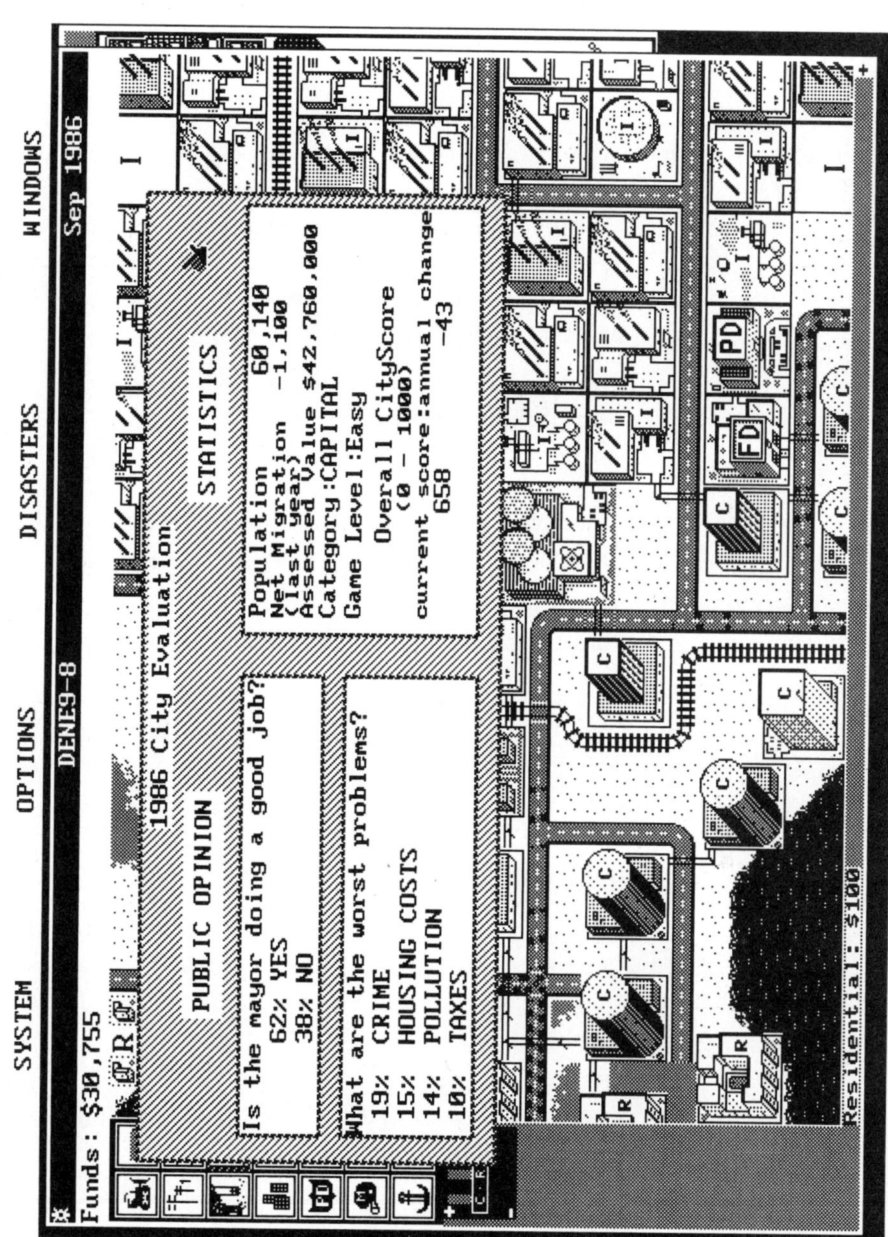

Figure 6.7 *An Evaluation window showing an evaluation of an 86-year-old city worth over $42,000,000.*

issues, it's probably just the Sims who have nothing better to do but complain.

- **Traffic**—When the Sims complain about traffic, you are probably aware of the problem from other sources. The traffic helicopter reports where more than a dozen cars are circling. The simulation warns you in the message window and displays a pop-up box telling you to watch out for stray bullets from frustrated motorists. The best thing to do is replace the most traveled routes with railroad tracks.
- **Crime**—This is a common complaint from the Sims. You can fund your police department at 100% and still get complaints about crime. If this complaint is over 10%, review your police coverage and build at least one station. If you can increase the property values in a high crime area, this helps to reduce the overall complaints.
- **Pollution**—When there is nothing good to complain about, the Sims notice that the air smells funny (see the `POLLUTION ALERT` in Figure 6.8). Even if it is because of an acute shortage of soap, they will blame you, the mayor. Sims have said "That mayor was responsible for zoning the industrial areas which give us these high paying jobs and make us drink lots of beer and produce foul smelling air." You will notice that the Sim did not indicate who produced the foul air. If you disperse the industrial zones and eliminate the congested traffic, you can bring down the pollution to a breathable condition.
- **Housing**—The Sims complain when there is a high demand for housing. This is a good sign, because it means the migration rate is positive. The complaints subside after you zone more Residential areas.
- **Housing costs**—If you zone too many areas with high Residential land values, the Sims complain. You could either zone some Residential areas in low value areas, or say "tough bananas!" so the poor Sims have to move elsewhere and live off somebody else. Isn't it fun to have such power?

- **Fires**—This is another problem which will be obvious before you see the Sims' complaints. Sims only complain about fires if they have been burning several years. Put out the fires, and the Sims will shut up—about fires at least.
- **Taxes**—The Sims will always complain about taxes. Sounds familiar, doesn't it? If you don't change your tax rate, the percentage of Sims who complain will still change from year to year. If you have a high tax rate, (above 9%), expect to hear about it. Otherwise just ignore the little *@#%s and squeeze them for every last penny.
- **Unemployment**—If only one Sim does not have a job, he will be the "Sim on the street" who is asked the about the worst problems. Complaints about unemployment will show up from time to time but are easy to fix. Zone more Industrial and Commercial areas. Then the Sims will go back to complaining about foul air.

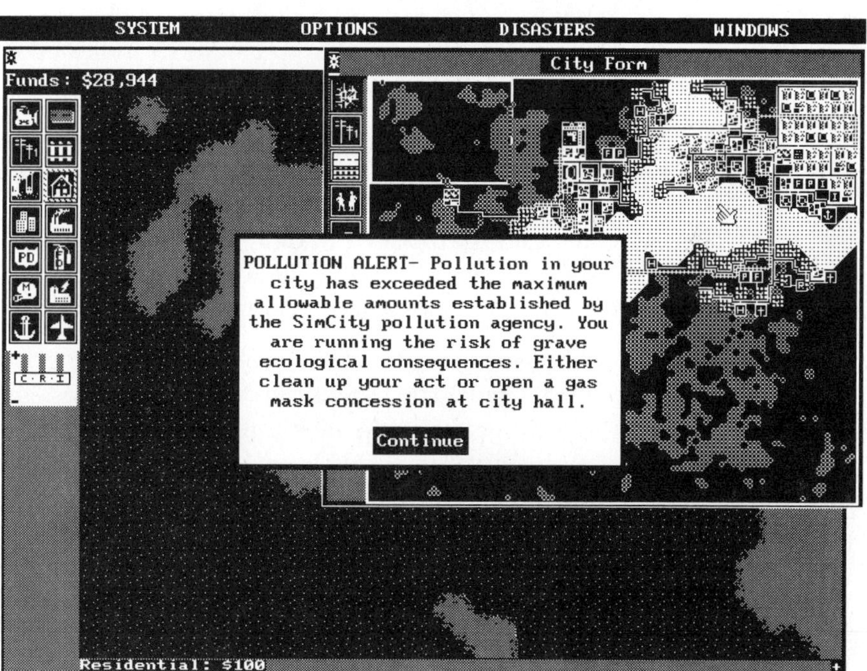

***Figure 6.8** A pollution alert just ruins the Sims' day.*

Statistics

As you work with the SimCity simulation, you learn its rules. As it checks your actions against the list of rules, it also keeps track of the results. These figures provide a numerical evaluation of how you're doing. As shown in the Evaluation window, SimCity checks the following statistics:

- **Population**—This is the Population of your city as of the last yearly census. The Sim census includes all the Sims in the city area.
- **Net Migration**—Net Migration tells you how well the Sims like your city. As we've said before, the Sims vote with their feet. If you are doing a lousy job, Net Migration will be a large *negative* number. If you are pleasing the current Sims, and they phone their relatives in other cities, more Sims will continue to move into your city. And you will collect more taxes. Net Migration is the difference between incoming Sims and outgoing Sims during the previous year. A constant low *positive* number indicates a stable population.
- **Assessed Value**—Assessed Value is the total value of all the city-owned properties. These include police and fire stations, airports, seaports, and railroads. Don't forget the roads, the power plants, or the parks. When you place parks in the right areas, they increase the value of the surrounding zones and the assessed value of your city. The assessed value does not include the privately owned Sim property in the zoned areas.
- **Category**—SimCity fits your city into a category based on the total population. The Evaluation window displays a message when your city moves up to the next category. Every city starts as a village, then moves up as the population increases. Table 6.1 shows a complete list of the categories. The category does not affect the Overall City Score. Unless your city has become a Ghost town, the category is for your information only. As your city grows from level to level, a pop-up box like the one in Figure 6.9 announces the change of status.
- **Overall City Score**—This is the ultimate measure of the Simcity "game." The Overall City Score is a rating of your city based upon several factors. Major determinants include traffic, crime, unemployment, pollution, housing costs, fire protection, taxes, problems

with power to zones, and the overall city growth rate. Other minor factors include ignoring the messages to build stadiums, seaports, and airports; funding levels on roads and city services; and fires which burn for years. If you have developed a good city and stabilized the population to keep your city from outgrowing your design, your overall city score will drop. City growth is a positive (necessary) factor in the City Score. Our average scores ranged from 550 to 750. One city that became a Ghost town had a score of 500. As far as we know, no one has achieved a perfect City Score of 1,000.

Table 6.1 Population categories.

Classification	*Population*
Village	0 to 1,999
Town	2,000 to 9,999
City	10,000 to 49,999
Capital	50,000 to 99,999
Metropolis	100,000 to 499,999
Megalopolis	500,000 and above
Ghost town	When everybody leaves

Close Window

 **<SELECT>** `WINDOWS` **<SELECT>** `Close`

<CTRL-C>

When you choose `Close` from the Windows menu or use **<CTRL-C>**, the front (active, top) window will close. To reopen that window, use the same menu or keyboard commands.

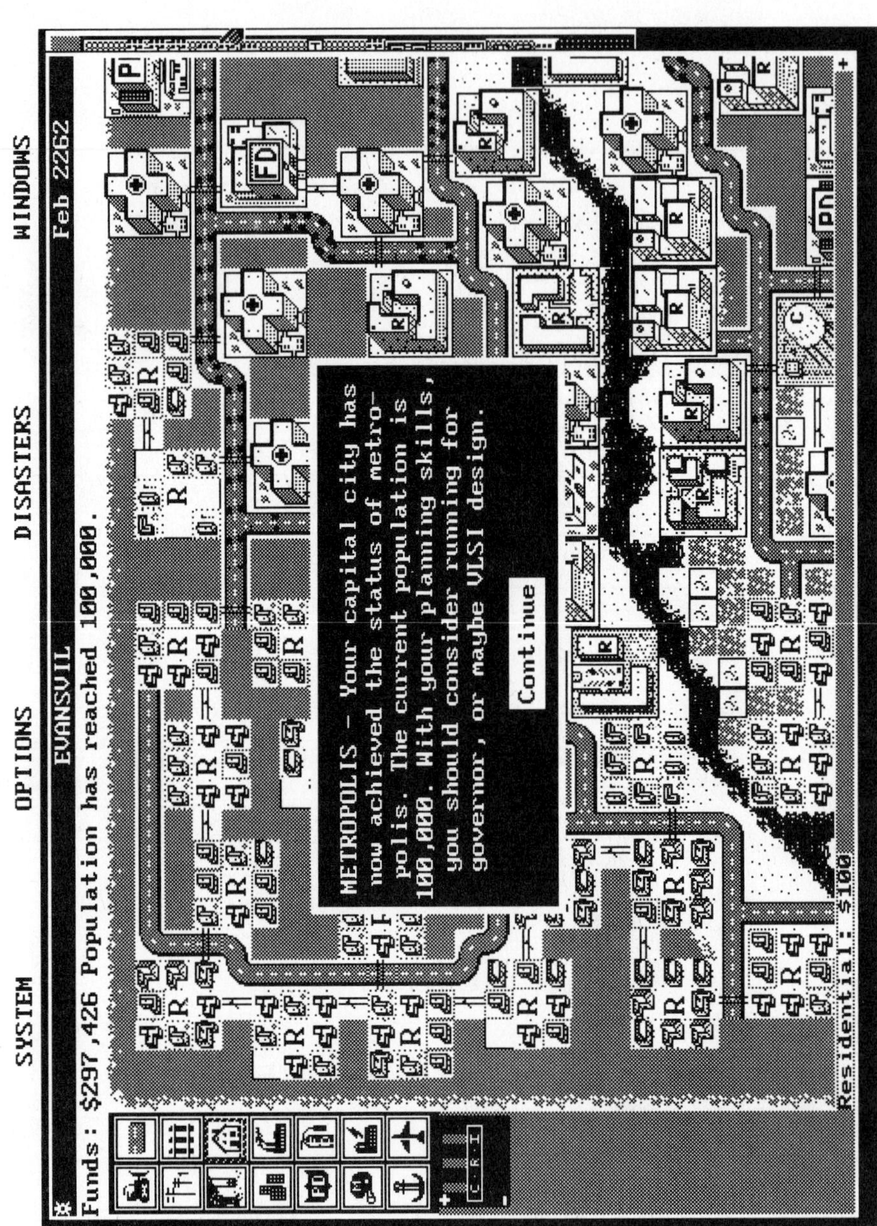
SYSTEM
OPTIONS
DISASTERS
WINDOWS
EVANSVIL
Feb 2262
Funds: $297,426 Population has reached 100,000.
METROPOLIS - Your capital city has now achieved the status of metro- polis. The current population is 100,000. With your planning skills, you should consider running for governor, or maybe VLSI design.
Continue
Residential: $100

Figure 6.9 *Every time your city's population advances to the next level, you get a message like this.*

Hide Window

 **<SELECT>** `WINDOWS` **<SELECT>** `Hide`

<CTRL-H>

When you select `Hide`, the front window moves behind any other open windows. Remember that you can also **<CLICK>** on a window to bring it to the top. The other window drops to the background but remains open. Having more than one window open at one time with Animate All on does slow down the simulation somewhat.

7 Using Edit Window Icons

The icons along the left side of the Edit window are the tools you use to design and build your city. This chapter describes each of the icons and what they do, as well as giving tips on how to use the icons. We also talk about the Query key at the end of this chapter.

Using a mouse or joystick, **<CLICK>** to select the icon you want. With the keyboard, press the plus and minus keys (**<GRAY+>** and **<GRAY->**) on the numeric keypad at the right side of the keyboard to move from icon to icon, and then use **<SPACE BAR>** to select. You can also use the keyboard to choose some icons temporarily. As long as you hold down the icon's shortcut key, that icon is active. This chapter's icon descriptions list the shortcut key for those icons that have one.

When you select an icon, its name appears in the lower left corner of the Edit window, along with the cost of using the icon. Move the pointer (a rectangle in the Edit window) to the desired location, and **<CLICK>** or press **<SPACE BAR>** to build or zone on that location. The bulldozer icon destroys whatever was in that location. The rectangle that moves around as the pointer is the size of whatever you are building or zoning. Remember, you can't "undo" building, zoning, or any other action in SimCity.

Tip: *To build power lines, roads, railroads, or anything else in a straight line, hold the* ***<SHIFT>*** *key down and move the pointer in the desired direction.*

Bulldozer Icon

Cost: $1
Shortcut Key: B

Have you ever watched someone driving a bulldozer and wished that you could drive one for a day? Now you can feel that power as you bulldoze in your city by selecting the Bulldozer icon at the top of the on-screen icons. Once you've selected the Bulldozer icon, positioning the small square box that appears and **<CLICK>**ing or pressing **<SPACE BAR>** clears the land of everything. Because you must clear everything from an area before you can build or zone, you can turn on the Auto-Bulldoze feature on the Options menu to eliminate manual bulldozing.

Because Auto-Bulldoze only clears natural objects, roads, tracks, or power lines, you still have to destroy zones with the bulldozer. If you place the pointer in the middle of a zone, you can destroy the entire zone with one **<CLICK>**. Use the bulldozer to clean up areas after a disaster, reshape the shoreline, or destroy a zone that has problems.

If you are using a mouse or joystick, the *right button* is the full-time bulldoze button. For each section you bulldoze, SimCity charges $1. When you bulldoze a zone, the charge equals the number of sections (tiles) in that zone.

Roads Icon

Cost: $10, or $50 for bridges
Shortcut Key: R

The instant paving machine is at your disposal. Next to the bulldoze icon, this icon contains a section of road. As you build with the road icon, SimCity automatically creates the intersections and curves. Areas where you place roads must be clear of trees unless Auto-Bulldoze is activated. You can't build roads within a zone. Roads can cross power lines, railroad tracks, and water, but only at right angles. Building roads over water costs more, because SimCity automatically creates a bridge. Bridges can't have turns or intersections.

Don't build unnecessary roads. Every tax year, each road section costs $1 to maintain. Bridge sections cost $4 per year. At least one road (or rail section) should touch each zone to enable it to develop fully.

Soon after you build your first road, traffic appears. As the area develops, the traffic increases. The traffic has no real destination and continues in a circular motion. This lets you know how much traffic is on a particular section of road. If the traffic is heavy, you will receive messages from the simulation and warnings from the Sims. You have to plan your city well to avoid traffic problems. We found managing traffic flow was quite a challenge in itself.

Remember that to build straight roads, you can hold down the **<SHIFT>** key as you move the cursor in the direction you want the road. Otherwise you may find that the road "twitches" as you move the pointer. You'll end up with curves where you don't want curves, and that costs money to repair.

Power Lines Icon

Cost: $5, or $25 under water
Shortcut Key: P

This icon contains a utility pole. You must connect all zones to a power plant with power lines. As you lay out your zones, connected zones power each other. Because you cannot place all the zones together, use power lines to connect the separate zones.

The area for a power line must be clear of trees. (Auto-Bulldoze clears trees automatically.) Power lines can cross roads and tracks only at right angles. Zones without power display a flashing symbol (lightning bolt) until connected to zones with power. Zones will not develop without power.

As your city grows, the time between when you connect a zone with power to when the flashing symbol disappears increases. The computer works harder to keep up all the data for the simulation. It costs $5 for each section of power line you string on land, $25 underwater. Lines running underwater can go only in a straight line. Plan your city well, and you will need to run very few power lines.

Transit (Railroad) Lines Icon

Cost: $20, $100 underwater
Shortcut Key: R

Look for the icon with a section of railroad track. This icon builds a mass transit rail. Lay out the tracks like roads. The tracks cost $20 per section. Tracks that go underwater in a tunnel set you back $100 per section to build. The tunnels are always in a straight line.

Soon after you lay track, a single train moves around. This is not the only train, so don't worry about the Sims having to wait for the one train. (The other trains move so fast you can't see them.) If you have traffic problems on the roads, replace these with tracks, and the Sims will be happy. We actually built entire cities with nothing but tracks.

Parks Icon

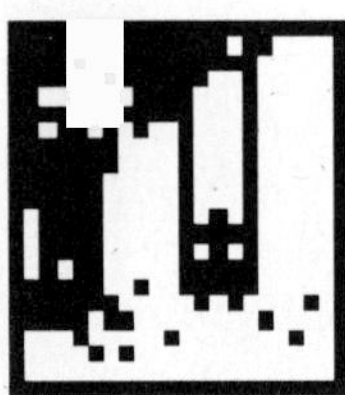

Cost: $10

The parks icon has a tree with a Sim child on a swing. (Look closely. It's the only known picture of a Sim in SimCity.) Parks increase land values. If you have a low value/high crime area, build parks there. If necessary, destroy some other zones and replace them with parks. While this technique seems drastic, it's just urban renewal. It will help increase the land values and thus, your score.

On-screen, the parks have sidewalks and sometimes fountains. The appearance of fountains seems to be random, but we've seen some cities with fountains arranged very carefully in the parks. The only way we know to get a fountain in a specific location is to build a section of park and destroy it until you get a fountain. This is expensive but, as we all know, the government is good at wasting money. And, after all, you are the government. Each section of park costs $10 to build.

Residential Zones Icon

Cost: $100

This icon contains a house. The Sims live in the Residential zones you place. If you don't place your Residential zones carefully, the Sims will not move in. If the Sims don't move in, your city won't grow. Carefully placed Residential zones create higher land value. Well-to-do Sims pay more taxes.

Two factors influence land value the most: water and trees. With Residential zones at the edge of water, the Sims will develop better homes or condos. When there is no water in part of your city, zone Residential areas in and around groups of trees. Try not to destroy too many of the trees in the process.

Residential zones develop into four classes: slums, lower-middle class, upper-middle class, and upper class. The main factors that influence the development of your zones include pollution, population and traffic density, roadway and utility access, and the surrounding terrain.

Residential areas zoned in a line, with no space between them, will not have many houses. Any houses built will have very low land values. The zones will become a Simslum. If there are no trees in an area, separate your zones with parks. When you first start your city, look at the City Form map and select areas with water and trees for Residential zones. Plan to make half of all the zones Residential, leaving the rest of the space for Commercial and Industrial zones.

Commercial Zones Icon

Cost: $100

The Commercial icon has the tall buildings. Selecting this icon zones terrain for retail stores, office buildings, parking garages, and gas stations. You do not have to place these zones in high land–value areas. If you do, they develop into high dollar buildings more quickly. But we've discovered they will anyway if you develop the area correctly. It's best to place Commercial zones between Residential and Industrial zones. This way, the Sims can stop by the store on the way home from work to pick up bread, milk, and a six-pack of pop.

Commercial zones develop most slowly, so never build too many at a time. Otherwise, they sit undeveloped for long periods. Commercial zones develop into the same four classes as the Residential zones: slums, lower-middle class, upper-middle class, and upper class. The factors that influence Commercial zone growth are residential and transit access, internal markets, labor supply, airports, crime rate, pollution, traffic density, and utilities. It costs $100 to create a Commercial zone.

Industrial Zones Icon

Cost: $100

The Industrial zone icon shows a factory with smokestacks. When they develop, Industrial zones offer heavy industrial and manufacturing services. When you place these zones, don't worry about land values. They will plummet no matter what you do. Place Industrial zones in connecting rows and with good transportation to each; then watch them grow. This arrangement produces a highly polluted area, but frees the rest of your city from bad effects. Place this Industrial complex at the edge of your city, and the overall effect on the rest of the city will be low.

Factors which influence Industrial zone growth include external markets, labor supply, seaports, transit and residential access, and connection to utilities. The land value is either high or low, with four levels of density. As long as you continue to develop your Residential areas well, factories will appear in the Industrial zones to employ the Sims. Like the Commercial and Residential zones, Industrial zones cost $100 each.

Police Department Icon

Cost: $500

The Police icon has a badge with `PD` on it. Our experience suggests that the police are the least important of the city services, but don't neglect them. Without police protection, the Sims will eventually move out of your city. Police stations lower the crime rate in the surrounding area and, as a result, raise your land values.

If you watch the message bar, it tells you when to build a police station. The message tells you to build a station or you might get a warning of rampaging Sims. Don't build too many stations. Extra stations increase the cost of running the city but won't improve the city. Usually one well-placed station quiets the Sims for a while.

Use the Police Protection map (select `Maps` from the Windows pull-down menu) to show you the area with the highest crime rate. Place the stations so the edges of the covered areas touch. This technique gives you effective coverage for your city. In some areas of high crime, (Industrial and city center), you might have to place a couple of stations with overlapping coverage. Add overlapping stations slowly during the life of the city.

Budget the police stations at 75% or more. If you don't want any complaints like `Police Department needs more funding`, fund it at 100%. At the lower rates, the Sim police get lazy and will not cover as much area. Funding at a higher rate insures the largest coverage per station, and you'll need fewer stations. For the best coverage, make sure that the station has power and a road or railroad connecting it to the rest of city.

Your Evaluation window may show that crime is the biggest complaint. First, check all your stations to make sure they are not damaged by a disaster and have power and access. Then check the funding level. If you have a negative cash flow, police services will be cut first from the budget. The Sim thugs take advantage of the lack of coverage, and the crime rate increases. If this happens, the Sims begin moving out. Then the taxes collected will go down even further.

Watch your budget. If the funding is OK, use your Police Protection map to identify an area with a high crime rate, and place another station there. This should reduce the crime rate until your city grows more. At 100% funding, it costs $100 per year to maintain each station.

Fire Department Icon

Cost: $500

The fire department icon contains a fire extinguisher. Each fire station makes the surrounding area less susceptible to fires. Having good fire protection is critical if you leave the Disasters enabled. Without the proper protection, your city will burn for years.

When disaster strikes, the fire department's response will determine how long it takes the city to recover. Don't build too many stations. Like the police stations, each fire station costs $100 each year at the 100% funding level. Use the fire protection map to place your stations so coverage doesn't overlap. When placing your stations, make sure the stations cover developed areas. Dirt, water, and trees don't pay taxes.

You get the largest area of coverage with the higher funding levels. Complete (100%) funding covers a large area and results in fewer complaints from the Sims. If you have a lower funding rate and a disaster strikes, increase your funding immediately or the Sim firefighters will take their own sweet Sim time extinguishing any blazes.

Watch your message bar. It tells you to build fire stations every now and then. Usually one well-placed station satisfies the Sims for awhile. As usual, place them on a road that connects them to the rest of the city. A railroad connection works as well because the Sims have fire trains. Firefighters really don't like being left in the dark. Make sure they have power or they will not answer the phone. No ringy-dingy, and the city will burn.

Stadium Icon

Cost: $3,000

The stadium icon has the football helmet. You don't need to build a stadium until your city is fairly large. The Sims will send a message, `Residents demand a stadium`. Notice they don't ask for it, they demand it. The stadium encourages growth in the residential population. Development of the Commercial zones increases due to indirect revenues from Sims attending the games. The stadium also increases traffic.

Place the stadium near roads and mass transit (railroads). On a routine basis, the Sims will play games at this stadium. If you have a disaster nearby, they will still play. If you have a small city, but want games anyway, you can build a stadium without any negative effect. There are no yearly costs for maintaining a stadium.

Power Plant Icon

Cost: $3,000 (Coal)
$5,000 (Nuclear)

Selecting the building/electric bolt icon produces a pop-up menu. You must choose `Coal` or `Nuclear` from this menu. After you zone some terrain, you should build a power plant because all zones and buildings must have power to function. As your city grows, the simulation provides messages about ***brownouts*** (low power). You must then build another power plant to satisfy the demand. If you don't, the zones furthest from the power plant(s) lose power sometimes, and the Sims will abandon those areas. When you build a plant, just connect it anywhere to the power grid. We usually build power plants side by side in one area, adding more as needed. The plants are self-sufficient and need no yearly funding.

Each coal power plant costs $3,000 but increases the amount of pollution in the area around it. Because coal plants supply less power, you end up building more coal plants. A coal plant will supply about 50 zones with power. That works out to $60 per zone.

A nuclear power plant costs $5,000 to build. It also carries the risk of a nuclear meltdown. Meltdowns are rare, but when they happen, the surrounding area is worthless for many, many years. Nuclear plants supply about 150 zones with power. That's $33 per zone, so you get more for your dollar. We build nuclear plants, but we don't place any Residential zones too close. We don't want any mutant Sims.

Seaport Icon

Cost: $5,000

This icon has an anchor. Wait until your city becomes fairly large before building a seaport. (Hint: Place it on the shoreline, but close to the Industrial area of the city.) A seaport increases the industrial growth in your city. When you build one, a ship appears and occasionally toots its horn. There are no maintenance costs for a seaport.

Airport Icon

Cost: $10,000

The Airport icon contains a large airplane full of Sims eating airline food. If you look closely, you can see them looking out the windows, waiting for a chance to eat real food at McDonald's.

You must build an airport to increase your growth in Commercial zones in a large city. Wait until your city growth has leveled off. The infusion of trade from the airport makes the expense worthwhile. You want to keep it away from the city center, preferably with the flight paths over water. This decreases the chance of a disastrous plane crash into a Residential zone.

When you build an airport, you will see the radar begin to turn and a plane flying around. Then the infamous traffic helicopter begins to cruise around and report the heavy traffic. After about the third or fourth traffic report, you'll probably turn the Sound `Off` at the options menu. Once you have built the airport, there are no more costs involved except when a plane crashes.

Tip: *Place a fire station next to the airport. This helps reduce the plane crash disaster recovery time.*

Query Box

For every part of the city you see, at a deeper level the simulation tracks, and sometimes controls, what's going on. And what the simulation tracks, it can tell about.

Move the pointer to any part of the city, press and hold the **<Q>**, then press and hold the left mouse button to activate a pop-up box. The box contains all sorts of information about that location, as shown in the example in Figure 7.1. Because the Query box becomes the size of an individual tile, it provides information only about that part of the zone or area. Leaving your finger on the **<Q>** allows you to view this information as you move the Query box around, sort of like a stethoscope. Each tile within a zone has different readings from one side to the other. Use this sweeping technique to pinpoint what has the negative or positive influences on each zone. The box provides information on the following:

- ❑ **Zone/Structure Type**—The top line of the Query box shows what type of zone or structure the report covers. This includes services like roads and stations as well as all zones. In some cases the box provides the score of the games being played in the stadium or tells if the area is radioactive.

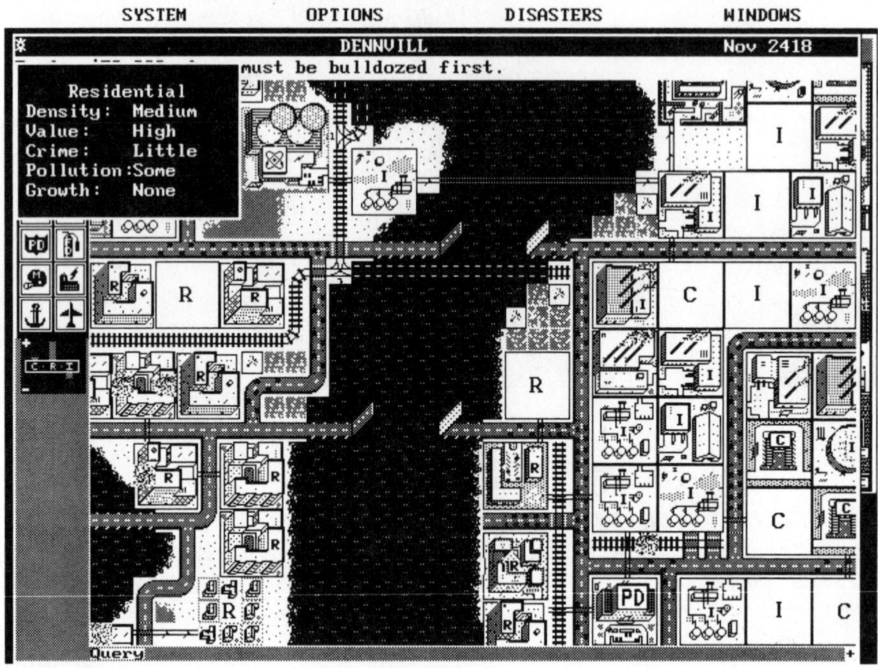

Figure 7.1 The Query box.

- **Population Density**—Population density varies even within a zone. It ranges from `Sparse` through `Low` and `Medium` to `High`. The box lists empty areas as `Sparse`, while large buildings have `Medium` to `High` populations.
- **Value**—The value of the property or land is `Low`, `Medium`, `High`, and `High!` The higher the value, the more taxes collected. Waterfront property typically has a `High!` value.
- **Crime Level**—The Query box reports the crime level in an area as `Little`, `Some`, `Much`, or `Severe`. High population density and low land values cause a severe crime level reading.
- **Pollution Level**—The Query box also shows the pollution level as `Little`, `Some`, `Much`, or `Severe`. Areas around the Industrial zones always have severe pollution levels.
- **Growth**—`None`, `Some`, or `Rapid` describes the current growth rate. If most of the other readings are positive, this reading will be `Rapid`.

8 Scenarios and Cities

If you are not content to create your own messes, calling up a scenario supplied with SimCity will keep you busy. This chapter reviews each of the eight scenarios and provides hints about solving the problems in the scenario cities.

City files are available with other programs, so the chapter also gives brief summaries of several cities from various sources. The comments about these cities may help you because you may notice the same types of problems in your cities.

Scenarios

Each scenario file provided with the SimCity software contains a complete city—with a problem. Usually, the city is about to be hit by a major disaster: earthquake, monster, nuclear meltdown, or boredom. Beginning players may try scenarios to learn the whims of the Sims and to see the destructive impact disasters have on a complete city.

Scenarios are more like a "game" than building a SimCity. You have a specific goal you must achieve. Each scenario has a time limit. You must beat the conditions before the game is over. With scenarios, there is an end, and you can win or lose the game. The simulation watches as you attempt to solve the problems. If you do accomplish the goals stated at the beginning of the session, a window will pop up and announce that you won.

To play a scenario, choose `SELECT SCENARIO` from the opening SimCity screen by **<POINT>**ing to the choice and then **<CLICK>**ing or pressing **<SPACE BAR>**. You also can choose `Load Scenario` from the System menu. SimCity diplays a screen of scenario choices similar to the one in Figure 8.1. Choose your poison by **<POINT>**ing to the choice and then **<CLICK>**ing or pressing **<SPACE BAR>**.

Figure 8.1 *The screen with scenario selections.*

The Sims in these cities are edgy. They may suspect that they've been set up. You're at a disadvantage. Because you were not there to plan the city, you can blame the previous administration. (Won't help win any points, though.) You must discover what these Sims demand from you, the mayor. If you succeed at the challenge, SimCity steps in and announces your success. Otherwise, the Sims simmer for a few years until they finally become angry enough to impeach you, returning you to the screen of scenario choices. You lost.

***Tip:** You can avoid disasters in any scenario by saving the scenario as a city immediately after loading it. When you reload the city, the simulation has "forgotten" the disaster. Of course, if you don't disable Disasters on the Disasters menu, another disaster will soon occur.*

If you really want to "win," though, work on the scenario as you brought it up. The Sims suffer through the disaster, and then you must rescue the city from the mess. For example, in the Dullsville and Detroit scenarios, you must accomplish the objectives (increase crime and decrease excitement, or something like that) for the simulation to decide you won the engagement. If you save a scenario as a city file and reload it, it just becomes a city with a problem for you to handle. There are no longer win/lose objectives.

The poor design of these cities may more closely represent real cities than the urban paradises you plan and build. Even if you choose to avoid the disaster, day-to-day operations are still difficult. You'll need both skill and luck to keep these cities running.

Dullsville USA

Difficulty:	Easy
Time Limit:	30 years
Starting Year:	1900
Problem:	Boredom
Win Condition:	Metropolis

Beginners may want to start with Dullsville. There are no disasters around the corner, just boredom (with a capital B). The Dullsville Sims have been sitting on their hands with nothing to show but pants creases on their palms. The big event of the summer is when they paint the park bench and all gather around to watch the paint dry. Unless this is what you did last summer, you should have a good idea of what to do for Dullsville. This scenario has the most potential because it's set in good terrain and wasn't too screwed up by the previous administration.

Real estate developers would salivate at all the prime, available waterfront land near Dullsville's downtown. Zone all this land as

Residential, and watch the houses grow like crazy. (Sims do love the water.) Place some Industrial zones to the east of the city (right side of your screen), and sprinkle some Commercial zones where you can squeeze them in close to the downtown area. This gives the Sims someplace to work (and shop—let's not forget the great Simerican pastime). Build a football stadium in the downtown vicinity so they can have something to do after the paint dries. As long as you have the funds, build more Residential zones to increase the tax base.

Make sure you create enough Industrial and Commercial zones so residents can earn enough money to pay taxes. As mayor, your salary comes from those tax dollars. Once the city has grown into a Metropolis, the citizens award you your own paint brush so you can be the official bench painter the following summer.

Just when you've relieved the Dullsville boredom, we suggest you turn a monster loose to create one last dash of excitement. How can any Sims be bored when they have to spend all their time cleaning up after a monster? After you've cured the Dullsville blues, you're ready to move on to the next challenge.

San Francisco, California

Difficulty:	Hard
Time Limit:	5 years
Starting Year:	1906
Problem:	Earthquake, 8.0 Richter
Win Condition:	Metropolis

Poor planning set up the city in this scenario for major problems. The previous administration built the city with total disregard for the danger of living in an area where the ground can buck like a teeter-totter at any moment. When the earthquake hits this city, it's an awesome sight. Everything jumps wildly back and forth on the screen, and the buildings look like they're moving a few hundred yards in each direction. Do you think that this would leave the Sims squashed on the walls inside the buildings or splattered on the outside? Nah, they bounce!

Right after the earthquake, the Sims bug you to build an airport. (In 1906? But, you'd probably do anything to get off the ground, too!) Immediately after the 'quake, locate the major fires, and build a fire station nearby, placing it where it won't catch on fire, too. Make sure everything in the area has power, and quickly move to the next spot. In the more extreme places, bulldoze a firebreak around the fires. Don't hesitate to demolish still-standing buildings. Concentrate on stopping the fires at this point.

Remember, if a disaster damages a fire station or any other city service building, just bulldoze the damaged part, and the Sims repair the damage themselves. As you inspect the city, make sure to connect the power to all the zones because the fires keep destroying the power grid. Firefighter Sims will not work without power to the station (something about the TV always being on—must be in their contract).

Once the fires are out and power to all zones restored, you must rebuild. Don't limit yourself to rebuilding the city the way it was before. Improve the terrible design. If you do your job well, enough Sims will stick around to maintain the Metropolis status at the 5-year mark.

And sure, why not? Go ahead and build an airport so the smart Sims can get out. They'll only have to wait about 18 years for the first commercial airplane to be built.

Hamburg, Germany

Difficulty: Hard
Time Limit: 5 years
Starting Year: 1944
Problem: Fire
Win Condition: Metropolis

When you start this scenario, you might just notice that these German Sims are a little jittery. They have been hearing that the Allied forces are a tough bunch. But even if they knew what was going to happen, they couldn't prepare for the coming destruction. Their city has the basic design flaws common to many European cities. Figure 8.2 shows the opening screen for this scenario.

For a city about to be bombed, Hamburg doesn't have many fire stations. As soon as you start this scenario, pull down the maps and look at your fire coverage. Begin placing stations to cover the city thoroughly, because the bombing starts quickly. To your dismay, you'll realize that the firefighters have already left town. Finish building fire stations, and connect power to everything. Build firebreaks around the worst of the fires with the bulldozer.

Clean up that annoying after-fire mess, and rebuild the Residential zones to increase the population. After the bombing ends, the Sims try to go to work like nothing happened, silly Sims. Watch the Sims go about their business of building Mercedes Simze and Simwagons. If they think you have done a good job, they might let you live in a bunker. If you can keep the city the size of a Metropolis, you'll convince the Sims that all is well. You really would make a good politician.

Figure 8.2 Hamburg—just before the trouble begins.

Bern, Switzerland

Difficulty:	Easy
Time Limit:	10 years
Starting Year:	1965
Problem:	Traffic
Win Condition:	Low Average Traffic Density

Though this scenario lacks thrills and action, it's challenging because many real mayors today face the same problems. The city has outgrown the roads, and the citizens face constant traffic jams.

Apparently, Swiss Sims are not fond of walking. You'll notice that the cars go in circles. If you guessed that this is a problem, you're right. Now, clever Simmer, you have to come up with a solution. Twist our arms; we'll give you the answer. Replace roads with railroads. It works, but it ain't cheap.

If you have few funds, you aren't likely to win this scenario. Of course, you can always embezzle funds and continue to build. But that's like peeking at your buried cards in Solitaire. (If you really want to cheat, the embezzle hint is elsewhere in this book. Sheesh! We can't make it *too* easy.)

If you achieve a low average traffic density by the 10-year mark, you win this scenario, as shown in Figure 8.3. We did it (and we didn't embezzle a dime).

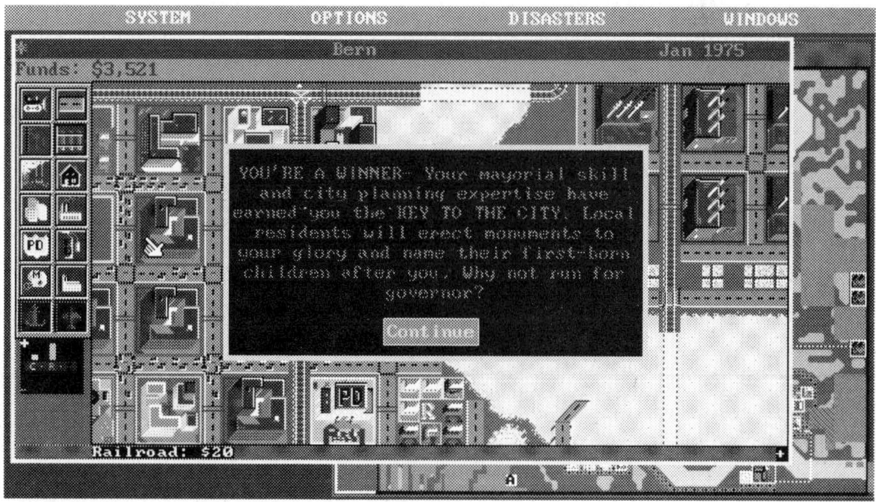

Figure 8.3 *You can even win some of the scenarios, like Bern.*

Tokyo, Japan

Difficulty: Moderate
Time Limit: 5 years
Starting Year: 1957
Problem: Monster attack
Win Condition: Overall City Score above 500

The Sims haven't seen any Godzilla movies yet, but in this scenario they're about to learn what a monster like Godzilla can do. This is a simple disaster to handle. When the monster shows up for the party, simply follow her around as she aimlessly boogies through the city. She really puts on a show. She knocks down planes, smashes ships, and all the other things that movie monster does. Meanwhile, the Tokyo Sims continue as if nothing were happening.

Traffic reports (in English) still come in from the helicopter, and Sims still make demands. But pay attention to your friend, so you can clean up her mess. She may wander into the city and then right back out. She may stick around for years. Just when you think she is gone, she'll pop back up, and you'll find yourself as busy as Santa on the 24th.

Even if you keep everything repaired, you'll find it tough to earn the winning Overall City Score of over 500 points. Other disasters keep you busy for the entire 5-year period. Make sure that the Sims are happy, and you might get free tickets to the opening of their latest movie "Simzilla."

Detroit, Michigan

Difficulty: Moderate
Time Limit: 10 years
Starting Year: 1972
Problem: Crime
Win Condition: Low Average Crime Density

The Motor City has "bitten the big one" because of an oil embargo by the Arab Sims. The city has lots of problems, and crime is the worst. What do Sims with no job, no money, and nothing to do all day do? They steal Sim money. You must play ace enforcer and bring down the crime rate, or else you may be mugged.

First increase the number of police stations. Use the Police option for the City Form map (shown in Figure 8.4) that you access by pressing **<CTRL-M>** and selecting the top icon. The dark areas on the map indicate high crime density. This is where you need to build more stations. Place a station or two at a time, and then check the crime map again.

With the Police map in view, use the query function to pinpoint the most crime-ridden areas. If you press and hold **<Q>**, move the pointer to an area, and **<CLICK>** or press **<SPACE BAR>**, you get more detailed statistics. Identify the worst areas, and then place a station right there.

Tip: *You also can do as we did and bulldoze high-crime zones, (with Sim criminals inside). Make sure to place more Residential zones in the 'burbs so displaced Sims will have someplace to go.*

If you do achieve a low crime rate, keeping it that way for 10 years is not easy. You may even have to deal with other disasters, as well. If you are indeed a successful crime stopper, the Sims may give you a new Ford Simto, fresh off the assembly line.

Boston, Massachusetts

Difficulty: Hard
Time Limit: 5 years
Starting Year: 2010
Problem: Nuclear meltdown
Win Condition: City Score above 500

This situation could stop life as we know it. But, as in most scenarios, the Sims continue about their business in the midst of disaster. Look closely, and you may see some glow-in-the-dark Sims.

There's not much you can do to prepare for this one. Like the San Francisco quake of 1906, the meltdown in action is awesome (see Figure 8.5). Little radioactive symbols spread out over the city. (And they always tell us that you can't see radioactivity.)

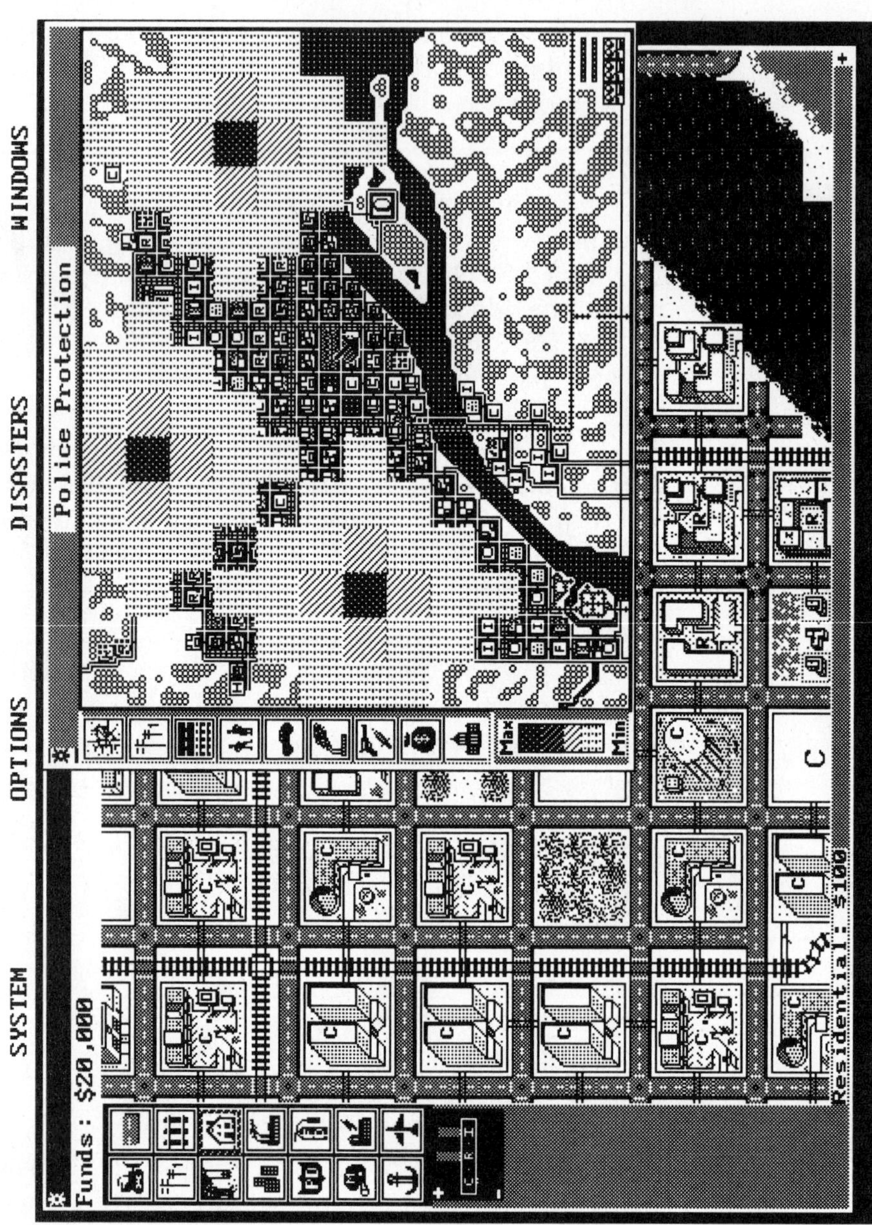

Figure 8.4 *The Police map for this scenario shows Detroit lacks coverage in a few areas.*

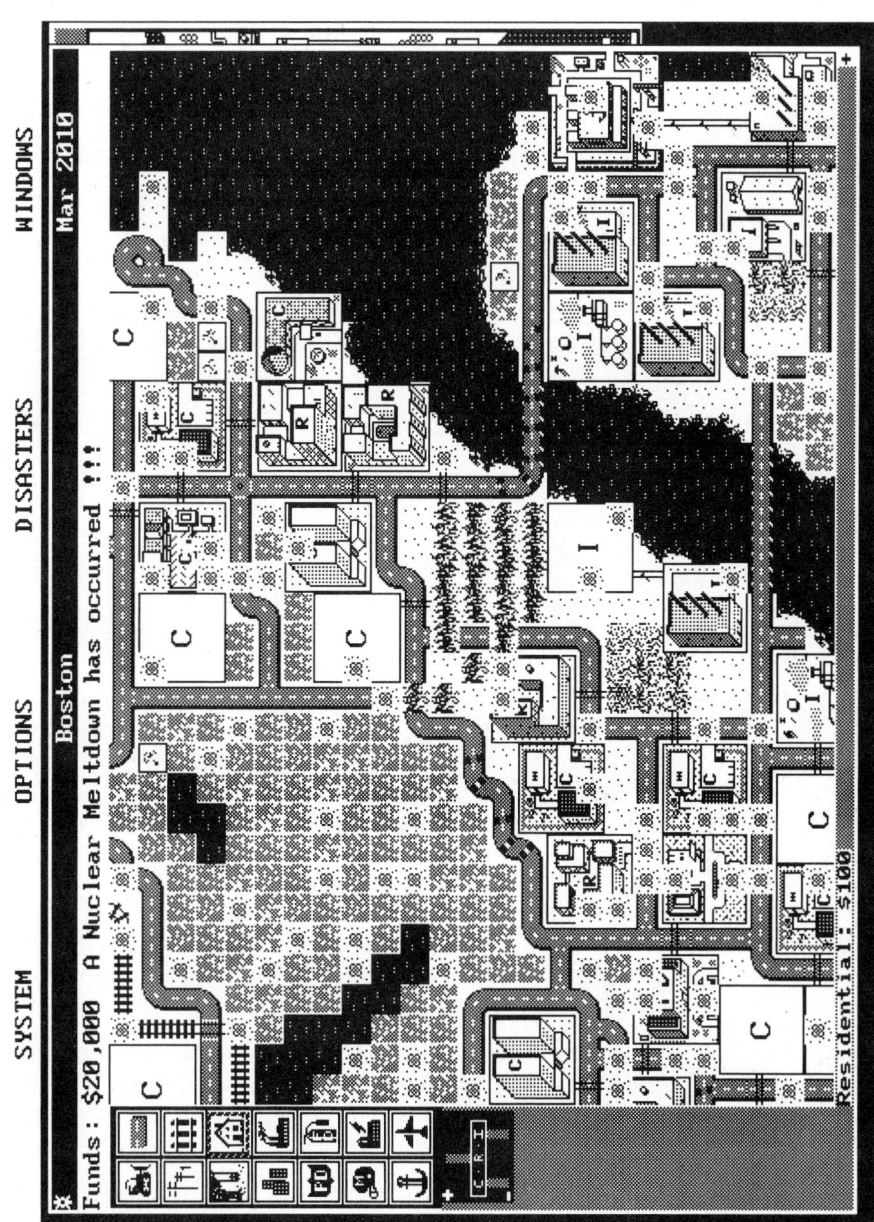

Figure 8.5 *A nuclear meltdown ensures that Boston will glow in the dark for years to come.*

Zone some areas away from the radiation to replace the ones which, at this point, are useless to any Sims except those who want a quick tan. The Sims will carry on normally and demand those simple things that everyone wants, better traffic conditions, lower taxes, and a park that doesn't glow in the dark.

If you can hold the overall score above 500 at the 5-year mark, the Sims might name a park in your honor. That park with your name on it will be around for a long time.

Here's a sneaky trick. If you have Terrain Editor (see Chapter 12), use it to bury the radiated area with dirt, trees, or water. You can then build on it normally. Because it'll take more than five years for the effects of the radiation to show up, you'll win. Besides, this is what a real administration would do. In this scenario, it works.

Rio de Janeiro, Brazil

Difficulty: Moderate
Time Limit: 10 years
Starting Year: 2047
Problem: Flood
Win Condition: City Score above 500

As the polar caps melt, the sea around the city in this scenario rises. Despite extensive flooding, the Brazilian Sims are not ready to live like fish. Other problems occur regularly. Planes crash. Fires start. (We found that the flooding helped put out the fires.) And, if you are lucky, you'll get an earthquake.

Once again, the poor city design works against you. With the city the scenario provides, the winning score is hard to achieve. Build a power plant to start. Every time you rebuild something, try to improve the area to upgrade the land values and help your Overall City Score. Building parks in damaged areas is a cheap way to improve land value. If you don't make much headway in this scenario, you might consider opening a boat dealership for the Sims before they're all in the swim . . .glug!

Cities

The Terrain Editor diskettes include a few sample cities. The documentation doesn't mention the cities, so if you didn't look at the disk directory, you wouldn't know they exist. These city files show different styles of development. This section reviews some of these cities and a couple of cities Maxis sent us. One city from Maxis contains a message for all Simmers.

Big City

This inefficient city from Terrain Editor diskette #2 resembles many large cities in the real world. Look at Figure 8.6 to see how the planners wasted taxpayer money by placing the police stations next to each other. Same story with the fire stations! Placing stations so close does not increase the coverage area but does cost much more money. This city also has a lot of empty zones. The unhappy Sims are leaving (at least the smart ones are).

Fredsvil

The guy who designed this one must own a paving company. Roads take up lots of space. Too many roads cost too much to maintain. With each section at $1 per year, and $4 per section of bridge, the expenses add up. This city has a large transportation bill every year. The city's rail system could carry much of the traffic from the roads. As the message in Figure 8.7 shows, the police department needs funding. They probably need to hire more traffic cops. Fredsvil also is on Terrain Editor diskette #2.

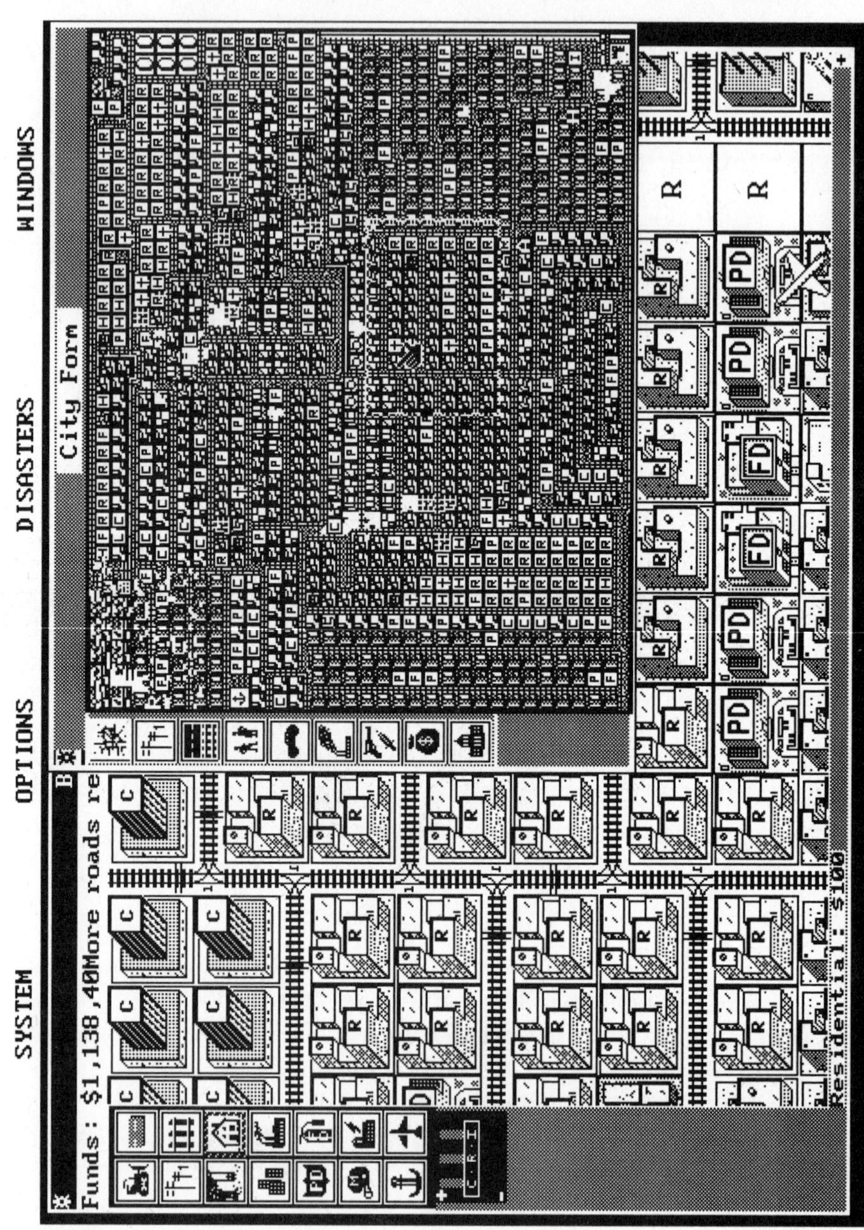

Figure 8.6 *Typical (bad) government planning—too many fire and police stations in small areas waste taxpayer money.*

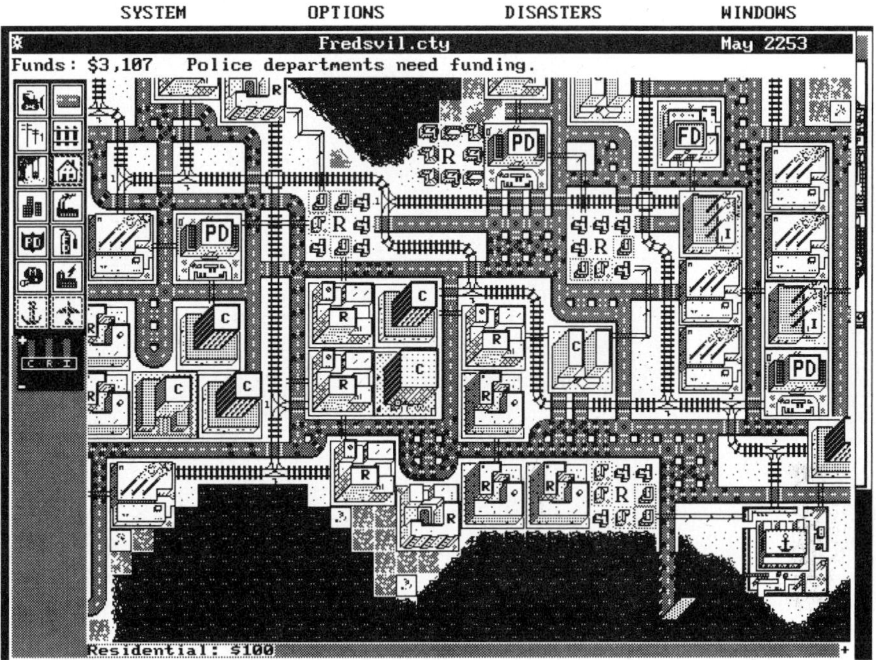

Figure 8.7 *The mayor paved paradise and put up a parking lot—or at least someone in Fredsvil tried to.*

Meddeve

Ah, the island resort of Meddeve (from Terrain Editor diskette #2)! We've never heard of it, but this Simmer thought he (or she) would design a city without traffic problems. There are no roads, only rail transit. When you load this city, you'll discover that only a small portion of the island is developed. The `More roads required` demand in the message bar (see Figure 8.8) does not go away until you build roads. Because you can build a rail-based city, just ignore the request. But in this city, even the rails are not efficient. They loop around each block. A zone only needs to have a road or rail touching it to have rail access.

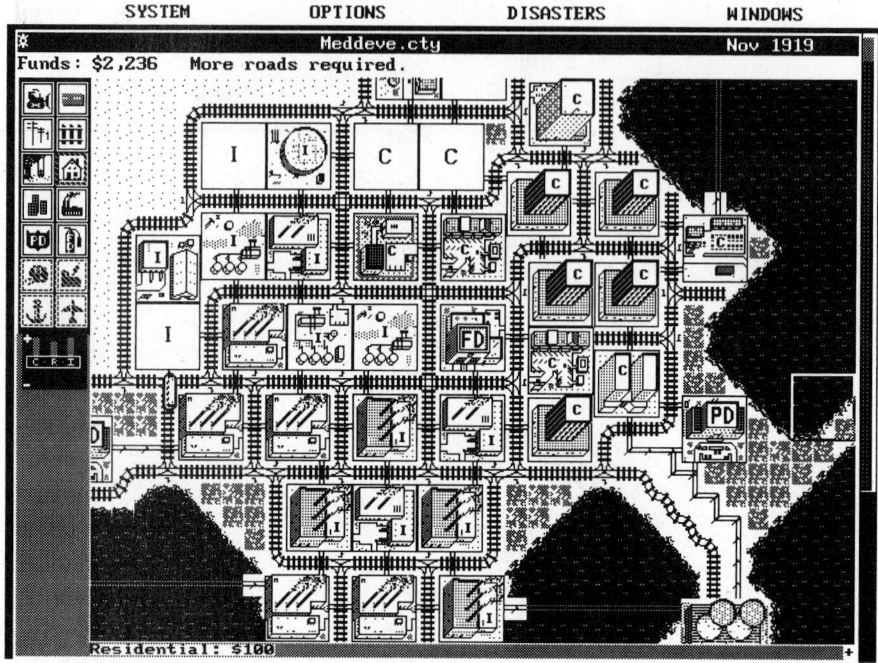

Figure 8.8 *A small corner of an island, heading for transportation problems.*

Deadwood

Building an entire city with the game on Pause might let you build a city similar to Deadwood, which Figure 8.9 shows. When you Pause the game by pressing **<0>**, you can zone and build, but the Sims can't move in. When you load this city, it's still in the Pause mode. Reset the speed, and watch the Sims flock in. Well . . . they don't exactly love the design, so they move in slowly. The Simmer who designed this city didn't put many Residential zones next to the river. What a waste! This would have brought in the Sims to work at the factories and buy from the stores. This city will have serious problems (even after you unPause it), because the maintenance will cost more than the income from the few Sims that do move in. Don't try to build your city this way. Deadwood is also from Terrain Editor diskette #2.

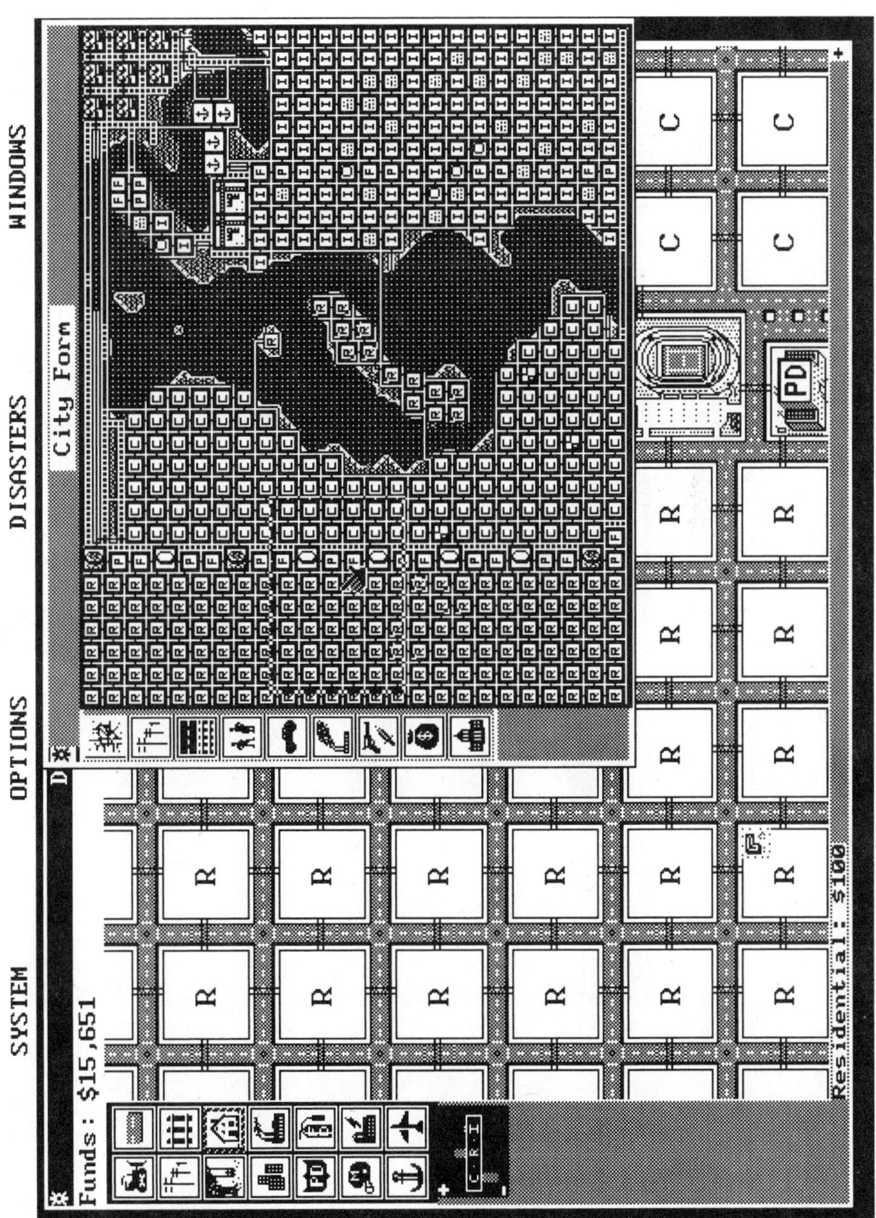

Figure 8.9 *A ghost town even before you load it, someone built Deadwood with the game paused.*

Linear

You've seen those small towns along a lonely stretch of highway. Linear in Figure 8.10 is one of 'em. If you were driving along, dropped your sunglasses, and fumbled around until you found them, you would miss the town. This might be an interesting way to start your Megalopolis. And then again, it might not. (From Terrain Editor diskette #2.)

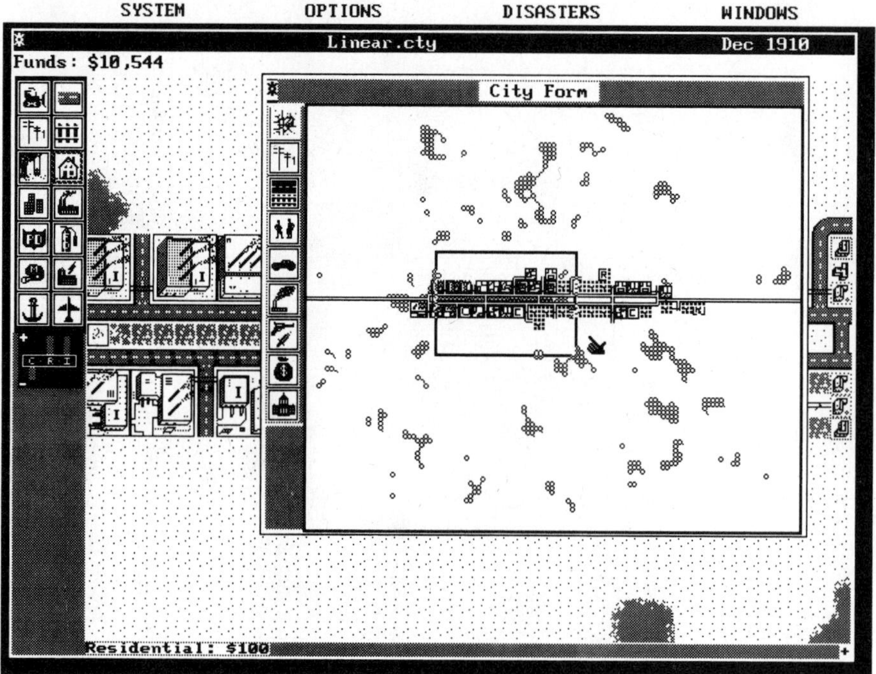

Figure 8.10 *Built along the straight and narrow, Linear is easy to miss, but you won't regret missing it.*

Hamburg

Would you live in a city with a half-million residents within 100 square miles? That's 5,000 Sims per square mile! Figure 8.11 shows how some Simmer placed the Residential zones in a tight formation. But golly, the city had over 15,000 years to develop. That's enough time to figure out how to pack a lot of Sims in one space. The mass transit system does help limit the traffic problems. This may be why this area has become Sim-ply full. This is one way to build a Megalopolis, but we don't have to live there, thank goodness. Maxis Software provided the Hamburg city file.

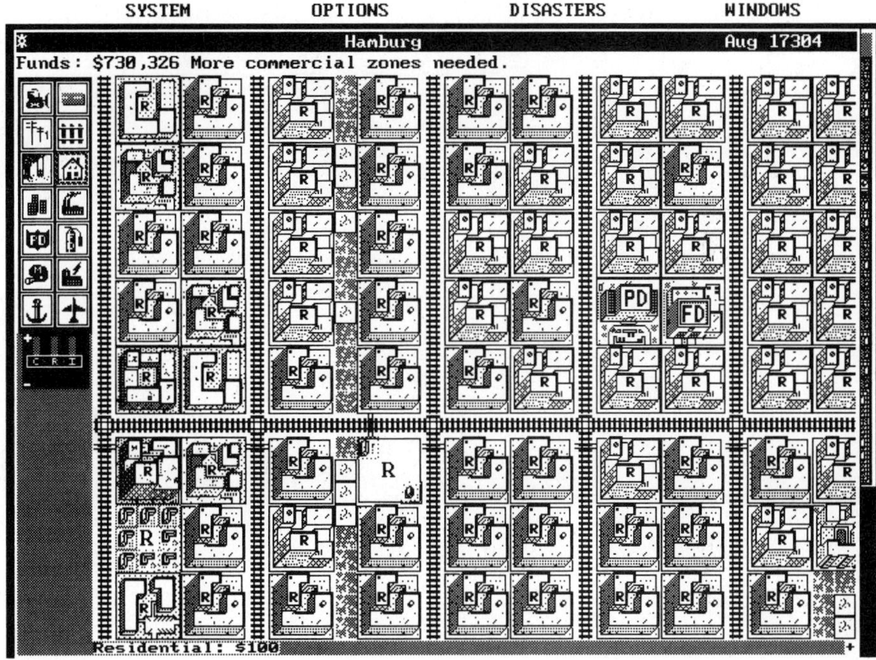

Figure 8.11 *Fortunately, Sims are very small. This city has 5,000 of them in each square mile.*

Chicago

Chicago, from Maxis Software, is a Megalopolis with 500,000 Sims in the city. It takes a real mayor to run a city this size. Looks like Maxis would like to talk to you if you build another city this big, as the message in Figure 8.12 shows. The presidential elections are coming up soon, and . . . maybe the Sim

Newsletter will mention you or you'll end up on the Top 10 Simmers list. First, you have to build your own Megalopolis. Good luck!

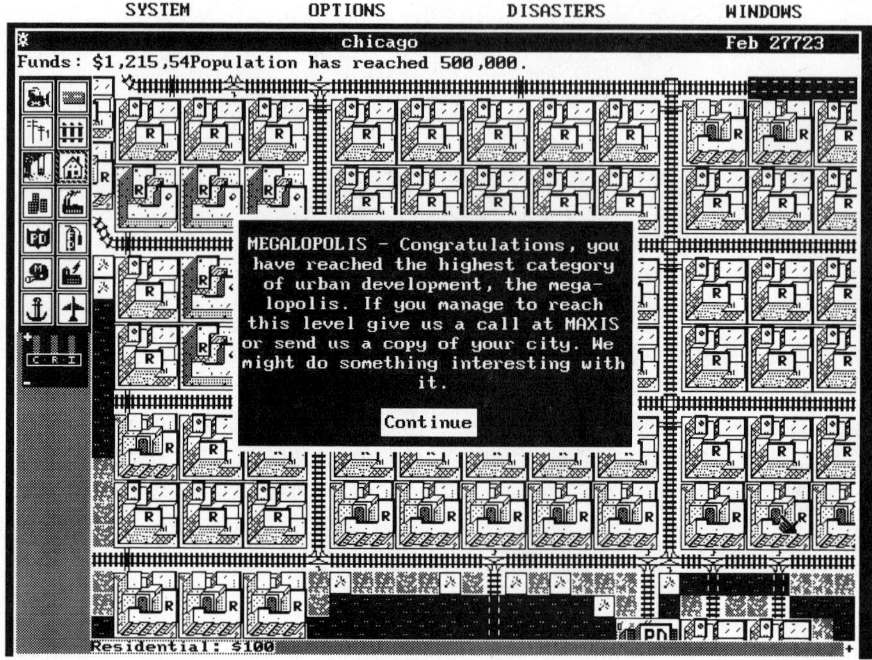

Figure 8.12 *Is creating a Megalopolis an achievement or disaster? Ask the Sims packing into this city.*

9 SimCity Planning

The last few chapters examined SimCity one feature or icon at a time. You use those tools to interact with the rules written into the SimCity program. In the process of using these tools, you'll discover the simulation rules and how those rules affect the city you create. This process of discovery and learning provides the fun and challenge of using a program like SimCity.

Now that we've covered these individual tools, we need to look at the larger process of building a city. What steps must you take to build a successful city? While we can't promise that you'll build great cities every time (we all have our off days), the guidelines in this chapter certainly can make you a better city planner. So, there are no "rules" for building a city. The best we can provide are a few ideas.

This chapter covers city planning theory, the real-world application of city building. Then the chapter puts city planning theory in perspective with the special SimCity world, contrasting the things you can control with things you can't control. Just before we tell you about interviews with fellow Simmers at the end of the chapter, we toss out a few activities, challenges and experiments to keep you Simming into the night.

City Planning

Like most complicated disciplines, city planning requires many skills for use in many contexts. There are at least four theories behind city planning. In this section, we'll look at city planners, urban design theories, levels of city planning, and zoning. These topics provide a contrast between SimCity and the real world. You can find additional information about city planning resources in Appendix B.

One person can plan a city. By using SimCity, you provide the basis for a city plan. You lay out the streets and zones. You plan for the city services of fire and police protection. You estimate the power requirements and the location of the utility poles to connect the zones. You may or may not have planned all these carefully. Getting other people to accept the city design and really carry it out is a bit more difficult.

Unlike designing a house or factory, planning all essential city elements is difficult. For example, the Sims do not protest when you bring in the bulldozer to make changes to a city block. In real life, that one action could take months to plan and even longer to be approved. And after all that time, residents and politicians may not accept the proposal for change. Does your city plan take public resistance into account?

Planning Background

People who work in city planning must have a variety of skills. Not only do they need to know about the physical design process, including land use management and transportation, they must know a great deal about people, economics, legal systems, politics, and more.

To gain this knowledge, most city planners spend at least four years in college, usually specializing in one or more areas. They may serve as interns as part of that training. They may also join a professional organization, such as the American Planning Association, and take certification exams.

Planning Environments

City planners work in many different environments and locations. In some cases, they may work within a government planning agency, reviewing proposed real estate developers' plans and potential zoning changes. Urban renewal requires a great deal of planning. The city planner would be involved with physical design, as well as coordinating property purchase and renovation.

Other city planning jobs might be in either the public or private sectors. Environmental impact studies may draw upon the wide range of city planning skills. Private organizations may develop a comprehensive plan, created by a city planner, to preserve historical buildings. Real estate developers are likely to have planning specialists help design any large project such as a subdivision.

Urban Design

While city planning includes social, economic, and political considerations, SimCity more closely reflects the process of zoning and providing services. *Urban design* is the most obvious aspect of planning, because it creates physical evidence. Build the fire station, and it stays there. Lay the road, and it carries traffic.

Because we have no way to talk with the Sims, SimCity does not emphasize the economic, social, or political aspects of city planning. But the Sims do respond to the yearly poll. They build their churches and hospitals in the residential areas as needed. They complain or make demands when their needs are not being met. Because we can't hold planning meetings or hold elections or present information via TV and print media, there is no two-way communication in SimCity. Nevertheless, economic, social, and political factors play a part in SimCity. They affect how well your city functions and grows.

For our purposes, consider urban design the physical aspect of planning the city. Because there is no *one* theory of urban design (Is there one theory for anything?), we'll look at the major approaches to urban design.

Monumental Design

When planned according to *monumental design* theory, a city has large boulevards and grand buildings laid out in a very orderly fashion. Parts of Paris, France and Washington, D.C. show the influence of this type of design. Streets laid out in grids and axially (like rays from the sun) provide a focus on the city center as well as a standard block size for design. This approach evolved from a "city beautiful" movement that developed in the early 1900s.

During that period, some designers thought that tall buildings and automobiles should be kept out of the city entirely. They preferred that people walk in the city to appreciate its design. If a city has a monumental design, the statues in the city parks may be the city designer's knickknacks.

Garden Suburbs and Garden Cities

As cities grew outward, the focus of urban design changed. Private transportation (cars) allowed the city to spread out. People measured travel in minutes instead of blocks to walk. *Garden suburbs* featured space for parks and curving streets. The parks and curving streets provided different viewpoints, similar to and influenced by English gardens. Most suburbs built today use these ideas.

Garden cities also displayed these ideas. Designed as self-sufficient communities, they were linked in clusters to other garden cities. Each city also had a "greenbelt" around the city center. This greenbelt included parks and open spaces, planned to provide a relief from the buildings in the city. Cul-de-sacs, streets closed at one end to reduce traffic, provided further variety in these cities.

Modernistic Design

The most recent urban design theory, *modernistic design*, uses ideas from both the monumental and garden approaches. Focus on the city center returns, with management and commerce located in the middle of the city while the residential and industrial zones ring the city separated by the green zone.

This design accommodates automobiles and includes tall buildings to concentrate the city government and business activity in the center of the city. Limited access highways provide easy entry to the downtown from the garden suburbs. The garden city influence keeps the tall buildings apart for maximum sunlight and great executive office views. City plazas and careful orientation to the compass are evidence of the modernistic planning method.

Megastructure Design

How big is big? Connect the buildings to form one large structure, part of the totally connected city that exemplifies *megastructure* design theory. Based on royal palaces and exhibition buildings of the 1900s, as well as modern shopping malls, these designs require a great deal of cooperation to complete. Tunnels and walkways between structures may reflect a renewed interest in the pedestrian perspective.

Levels of Planning

When you use SimCity, you work on the broadest of levels to design and build a city. Because the Sims are so quick to respond, the actual time you spend planning your city may be minimal. You learn by trial and error. But just imagine that Sim days are like real days. Then, you might actually plan ahead.

Comprehensive Planning

The highest level of planning is the overall view of what is to go where and when, *comprehensive planning*. In some cases, the details come later.

For example, the town of Brownsburg, Indiana recognized in the early 1980s that it was having difficulty providing water and sewer services for the current population. The town council contracted with a planning agency to develop a comprehensive plan for growth. The agency's first recommendation was to halt all residential zoning for five years while the city adjusted to, and planned for, the services needed.

The city developed a comprehensive plan which required approval from all sorts of agencies and the residents. Once the plan was accepted, the city redesigned the water and sewer system to handle an eventual increase in residential dwellings. When the system construction progressed to a specific, planned point, the city lifted the moratorium on residential zoning.

Real estate developers then took the lead role in designing the city by purchasing land and planning the subdivisions in the town. And now, as the result of all this careful planning, we (Dan's family) live in a nice new subdivision in a nice new house, and pay $60 a month for water and sewer services.

In this comprehensive plan, the town council set the land use policies, as well as the general course for the development of the town. They contracted with a planning agency for the next level of planning, *system planning*.

System Planning

At the system planning level, planners figured out what the city needed to support the structure approved in comprehensive planning. They designed a system to meet the approved specifications (no more building until the water and sewer systems are in place). To do so, planners considered the current situation, then looked at the potential growth zones, including the type and size of buildings in each zone. Then they designed the water and sewer system to handle the projected growth.

Area Planning

Because Brownsburg is small enough to consider in one plan, the planning agency didn't need to work at the next level of planning, the *area plan*. In much larger cities, much planning is based on a specific area, such as a neighborhood or industrial park. Considerations for the area would include transportation in and out of the area, the city service resources available for that area, and the effects changes in the area would have on the areas around it. Like pieces of a jigsaw puzzle, all the improvements considered for one area must fit with the terrain and services in all other areas.

Subsystem Planning

When you consider the fire or police coverage in SimCity, that's *subsystem planning*. Like all the city map views, each subsystem represents a layer over the area or city. Lay the transportation map on top of the police map. Without roads, the police can't function as effectively. Consider all the subsystems in relation to each other, as you considered bordering areas when area planning.

Site Planning

The smallest level of planning, *site planning*, includes activites such as determining how to build a library, fire station, or park. Again, planners must consider the location and services available to and for the site.

SimCity Planning

Use both system and subsystem planning in SimCity. Because you can consider the entire 100-square-mile area at one time, you can lay out systems in advance. Sims don't demand changes to the zones (discussed below), so you can create a master plan for a Sim city. But, like a plan for a large city must change to meet resident needs, your city plan is likely to change.

The SimCity city form map views makes subsystem planning much easier. You can easily examine the different layers of subsystems, including police, fire, transportation, and growth. As in the real world, careful design of these subsystems can provide the best coverage for the least cost. Both Sims and taxpayers appreciate that approach.

Zoning

If the theories of city planning and planning levels represent the ideas and steps necessary to develop a city, zoning represents the tools to realize the design. By zoning specific sections of land, city planners control how that land will be used. Because the planners developed the comprehensive plan, zoning assures conformance with the plan. (Notice we didn't say "success of this plan.")

Land Control

So the city can keep *land control*, zoning defines areas for residential, commercial, industrial, and agricultural uses. SimCity uses the first three of these zone types in their simplest form, similar to the way smaller towns use this zoning method. Larger cities have dozens of levels within each zone.

Planners control the use of each zone by limiting the size of the buildings in the zone. The *floor area ratio* specifies the number of square feet of building allowed within the size of the land. Zoning rules also specify building height, lot coverage, and building setback (from the road).

The need to control use of the land came, in part, from health and safety concerns. Before zoning, houses and apartments were often so crowded together there was no sunlight or ventilation for the residents. Closely packed wooden dwellings also allowed fires to spread quickly.

Setting the floor area ratio spread out the buildings to allow sunlight and air, and limited the spread of fires.

Economic concerns also influence city planning. Anyone who owns land wants the value to increase. Any combination of disparate buildings decreases the value of the land. Store owners want to be clustered together to promote sales. No one wants to live next to factories. Factories must be near major transportation routes to operate effectively. City planners must consider such economic concerns and facilitate the city's economic health by zoning the land effectively.

Zoning History

One of the major events which influenced the use of zoning was the Supreme Court's decision in a 1926 case, *Village of Euclide v. Ambler Realty Co.* While New York had adopted the first comprehensive zoning code in 1916, the code's legality was not firmly established until the Euclide decision. In this case, a landowner challenged the zoning, upset because his land was worth $10,000 per acre as industrial ground but only $2,500 as residential ground. The Court's decision upheld zoning the land as residential. Like most early zoning, this land was zoned to protect the neighborhoods with single-family homes. This decision set the philosophical basis for zoning. The case presumed that the value of the single-family home is more important than other considerations.

Many zoning laws were adapted from a model law drafted by the U.S. Department of Commerce in 1922. All 50 states ultimately incorporated that law, basically in its original form. This was a remarkable record for a model law that remains in effect in all but six states.

But, because the first zoning laws were based on the conditions of the 1920s, they do not address contemporary zoning issues. Early planners could not anticipate the problems of large-scale developments, shopping centers, industrial parks, and even billboards. How could they have envisioned the controversial issues related to "sex businesses," including massage parlors and adult bookstores and theaters?

Zoning Decisions

The process of zoning and rezoning has a number of steps. Because many people are involved, rules define the steps and the responsibilities at each step.

The city's governing body, typically composed of elected officials, is responsible for making the final decision for each zoning change. Before they decide, though, the planning commission makes recommendations based on a study of the request by the planning commission staff. The steps to request a zoning change, or *variance*, might be as follows:

1. Someone submits a request for a change, all on the proper forms, of course. This might be from a neighbor who wants to run a car repair shop in his garage (not likely). It might be a request to increase the floor area ratio in an apartment complex (maybe). Or, the request might be for a light industrial park employing more than 100 taxpaying voters (very likely).

2. The planning commission staff reviews the application as submitted and notifies the planning commission of the need for a hearing.

3. The planning commission sends a notice about the hearing to all parties who would be affected by the rezoning. This might include other business owners or residents in the area. A public notice is also run in the newspapers.

4. The planning commission staff prepares a preliminary report of the requested change, reviewing the applicant's plan for use of the land.

5. The planning commission conducts a hearing. Any interested or concerned individual may speak up at the hearing.

6. The planning commission decides what recommendation to make to the governing body.

7. The governing body then issues a notice of a second hearing.

8. The governing body listens to all interested parties at the hearing.

9. Based on statements by interested parties and the recommendation of the planning commission, the governing body decides about the requested zone change.

In real life, this process involves dozens or hundreds of people, including professional planners, politicians, and the people affected by the proposed changes. In SimCity, you **<POINT>** to an icon and **<CLICK>**, then you **<POINT>** to the area you want zoned and **<CLICK>**.

Making Choices

With a delicate **<CLICK>** here and a gentle bulldoze there, you control the lives of thousands of imaginary citizens. You make decisions based on careful thought, intuition, or caprice. But some decisions you cannot make in SimCity. Set rules prevent you from making some changes. Next, this chapter reviews what you can, and can't, control in SimCity.

What You Can Control

You can select icons and make menu choices. You can move around to view any location on the map. You can choose to load, save, or abandon any city you want. You can even turn off the computer in the middle of a session. But all these elements of control are really just the "user interface" (to use computerese). This part of the simulation must be easy to control to allow you to concentrate on the more difficult choices.

Zoning

It's a toss-up. Are the zones more important, or the transportation system? Have too many of one without the other, and the city does not grow. Both are equal, then.

In your 100 square miles of city, you could theoretically place over 1,300 zones—even more if you want to overlap edges of the zones. You have total control of which zone goes where. (Well, all right, you can't place a zone in water.) You can lay the zones out in a checkerboard pattern if it suits you.

Checkerboards are not likely to amuse the Sims, though. You can't control what the Sims build in each zone. The rules the Sims follow consider proximity to trees, water, transportation, power, and other zones. You can't force the Sims to build anything specific within the zone.

Transportation

The other critical factor in the simulation, the method and routing of transportation, is totally under your control. If you start using the standard American bias towards roads, your city will grow reasonably well. If you try the European standard and use more rails, your city will grow much more quickly. A rail system can move more Sims more quickly for less expense.

This is as good a point as any to mention the bias built into a simulation. When creating SimCity, or any other program, the designers started with a list of features. For even a small program, this list can be quite large. For a simulation, it can be huge. The list might include rules like the following:

- ❑ A road tile can handle six "trip generations" in one pass.
- ❑ A rail tile can handle 18 "trip generations" in one pass.
- ❑ Each road tile costs a Sim six units of energy to use.
- ❑ Each rail tile costs a Sim two units of energy.

These rules, when incorporated into a program, determine the amount of traffic and distance a Sim could travel in one trip generation. (*Trip generation* is a method in which SimCity simulates the traffic flow.) As is apparent from the rules, the rail transportation system has the advantage in the program. But what if the designer of the program didn't like trains, seeing them as only necessary for freight? Just by changing the basic rules, there would be no benefit to using rails, and the simulation would react differently to each city design.

As much as a simulation allows the user freedom to design, it still controls the outcome. If the simulation designer thinks that trains are more effective than cars, the simulation's rules reflect that bias. There is nothing wrong with this in SimCity or any other computer simulation, but you must understand the built-in bias of the rules.

City Services

Place your zones. Connect them with roads. They still must be powered and protected. You control whether or not a zone has power, and even what kind of plant produces the power. You can lay out the power lines in any fashion you like. Remember that they do "bleed" power like real power lines. The greater the distance, the less juice at the other end.

You also control the police and fire coverage in your city. While transportation and power must be present for a city to grow, police and fire coverage can wait until the Sims ask for the services. You also control the coverage area for the services by setting the funding level.

Tax Rate/Budget

You, too, can learn the fine art of extracting money from your taxpaying Sims without making them mad enough to move away. You can control several aspects of your city's monetary health. The first and most important is the tax rate.

Setting the tax rate from 6% to 9% provides the city with money and won't make the Sims too mad. Anything over 9%, and they complain and move away. The higher the rate, the quicker they move out. A lower rate decreases the cash flow but encourages growth. Because the simulation collects taxes at the first of each year, the changes made won't do any good until the next January.

Not only can you collect the taxes, you control how much the city spends in three areas: transportation, police, and fire services. Set funding for these services at anything less than 90%, and the roads and railroads begin to fall apart, the Sims complain about crime, and fires can burn for years.

Disasters

Yes, you can turn Disasters off. But, if you perpetrate some very questionable actions, (embezzling funds, bulldozing churches), Disasters will ruin your day and part of your city. Some disasters are quick and damaging, like earthquakes and airplane crashes. You can't stop such disasters once they've started. The Sims just have to ride them out. Saving your version of the city just before you call for a disaster is the best defense here.

On the other hand, once a monster or tornado appear, the quickest way to control the problem is to save the city immediately and then load the city. When you reload, the monster or tornado is gone. Otherwise, both can stick around for years.

Fires just burn and burn. The save/load trick won't put them out. You can bulldoze areas around the fires to provide a zone of rubble as a firebreak. Immediately building a Fire station near the fire can also help.

Speed of the Game

You don't need quick reflexes to use SimCity successfully. You succeed with careful planning and consideration. Still, the Sims may move faster than you like. You can set the game's speed from Slow to Fastest. Try using Slow when you're building and Fastest when you want to accumulate funds.

Level (Difficulty)

Only when you start a new city (or have Terrain Editor) can you set the difficulty level. The Easy level provides $20,000 in starting funds. The Medium level provides $10,000, while Hard just gives you $5,000. The *factoring constant*, the method SimCity uses to calculate taxes collected, also changes with each level. If you base your pleasure on a high Overall City Score, you'll have to reach to the hardest level for enjoyment.

What You Can't Control

Some parts of the simulation are beyond your control. There would be no challenge if this were not the case. Even with this lack of control, you can take comfort that the rules don't change in the middle of the game.

Sims

The Sims become very real to a dedicated player of SimCity. We don't want to make anyone cry, but there is really no such thing as a Sim. (We won't go into Mr. Claus or that big springtime Rabbit.) You can view Sims only as a response to your actions, the elements you do control. The simulation displays approval of the rules by showing bigger and better buildings built in the zone you create. Whether you imagine Sims or rules, you still can't make any changes to either.

External Market

The simulation controls the import and export of goods and services to and from SimCity. While you can't control these factors, you can observe the effects and adjust planning strategy as necessary. Watch the Industrial zones for growth or decay as an indication for the impact of the external market.

Point Spread of the Game

As much as you, the mayor, would like to dictate the point spread of the stadium games, you can't. In fact, you can't even acknowledge the point spread, because gambling is not allowing in SimCity!

City Challenges and Ideas

SimCity is dynamic, changing within the rules set for the Sims' behavior. The master city builder creates cities to suit his or her specifications, and watches the results. Except for random terrain, (which you can control with Terrain Editor) all design considerations come from the builder. This total control does not represent reality. Budget considerations, current land use, and even (gasp!) the peoples' interests restrain real city planners.

The rest of this chapter offers about two dozen city activities, design challenges, and experiments. Some of these illustrate more about the real world of city planning. Others are whimsical and happen only in a Sim city. In all the cases presented, there are points to discover about the Sims, and maybe the real world.

You'll create the city as you work out the challenge or explore the experiment. If you create a city you are particularly proud of, feel free to send us a copy on disk to: SimCity SAMS, 11711 North College Ave., #141, Carmel, IN 46032. Sorry, we can't return the disks. If we use your ideas or city, we'll be sure to give you credit.

Each idea includes parameters and a description of the steps to implement the idea. The parameters include the *file name*, the idea *type*, the *time frame*, and the *tools* needed. Following are descriptions of the parameters.

Name—The idea name and possible file name(s).

Type—Project types include *activity*, *challenge*, or *experiment*.

Activity—This type gives another way to look at a city or cities for comparison or perspective. Activities may need tools other than SimCity.

Challenge—This type includes city structures or design ideas which have been attempted or are very likely to be possible. Some are very difficult and others easy.

Experiment—Experiments have unknown possibilities. We can't predict the results of these ideas. Grip your mouse tightly when you enter this realm.

Time Frame—This is the number of years to reach a goal or, in some cases, the number of real hours to complete the task.

Tools—Tools include Terrain Editor, other software, or other items. We'll explain where you can get anything unusual in such a situation.

Win—Some ideas *could* include a win condition, but we didn't put them in. Accepting the challenge and making the attempt is all you need to know that you've won.

New Rail City

File Name: NRC.CTY
Type: Activity
Time Frame: No limit
Tools: SimCity

Using rails over asphalt gives significant advantages, especially in SimCity. Because trains can transport more for less, using rail exclusively ends traffic problems and pollution from cars.

Create your typical city, but use only rails for transportation. The Sims will fuss occasionally that they need more roads, but this does not seem to affect the city score. You can consider those requests a small price to pay for the vast improvement in city traffic flow in your **New Rail City**.

Rail City Conversion

File Name: RCC01.CTY & RCC02.CTY
Type: Activity
Time Frame: No limit
Tools: SimCity, an existing city

Make sure you have a stable or growing city with a "normal" number of roads. Save this city as RCC01. Save it again as RCC02. You'll come back to RCC02 in a few years.

Let RCC01 (the original city) grow for at least 10 years. Don't make any changes to the city while the city grows. At the end of that period, make a note of the funding level, how long it grew, and all the other information in the Evaluation window.

Now load RCC02 and replace all the roads with rails. Let this city grow as long as you grew RCC01 (the original city). At the end of that growth period, make a note of the same factors noted in RCC01. What differences are there between the two cities?

75% Water

File Name: SWAMP.CTY
Type: Challenge
Time Frame: No Limit
Tools: SimCity, Terrain Editor

You can set the random terrain generator in Terrain Editor to provide specific percentages of water. Set the water to 75% to create a very wet city. You may also want to set river curviness to 0%. The result is nothing but little and not so little lakes. You'll have lots of waterfront property for high value Residential zones. Will you have enough land to create an industrial and commercial base to grow a city?

No Water, No Trees

File Name: DESERT.CTY
Type: Challenge
Time Frame: No limit
Tools: SimCity, Terrain Editor

The Terrain Editor starts with a barren tract of land, just dirt. Use Terrain Editor to save this most basic city terraform as DESERT.CTY. This city won't require much land-use planning. It might lend itself to a nice grid layout. Don't count on creating a seaport, either. Can the Sims be enticed to move into such an unappealing landscape? Will the city thrive?

Easy, Hard Comparison

File Name: EASY.CTY, HARD.CTY
Type: Activity
Time Frame: No limit
Tools: SimCity, Terrain Editor

Set the Game Play Level when beginning a new city, or change it with Terrain Editor. Not only do harder levels start you with less money, the Sims are much more critical about your city design. According to some reports, some don't pay their full share of taxes.

Create or use a city with the Easy setting. Save a version as EASY.CTY after a few years of growth. (The larger the city, the less time you'll need to allow it to grow.) Save it again as HARD.CTY. We'll get back to it in a moment.

Allow EASY to grow for several years without making changes. Note the ending statistics in the Evaluation window. Use Terrain Editor to load HARD.CTY. Change the Game Play Level to Hard. Save the city again. Allow HARD to grow for the same number of years you allowed EASY to grow. Record the ending statistics and compare EASY and HARD.

Note to MS-DOS users: From our observation, Terrain Editor does not reliably change the level on a city. Until this apparent bug is fixed, you can't complete this activity.

Sim Party

File Name: None
Type: Activity
Time Frame: 3+ hours
Tools: SimCity, snacks

Because SimCity is both easy and complicated, it provides a good example of what computers can do. It only takes five minutes to demonstrate the basic moves to someone. Enticing a computer novice to use the mouse does not take much effort then. Observers rarely stay silent. Building a city becomes a group project. Discussions about the Sims's behavior, how to zone the city, and how to deal with each crisis can go on for hours.

Depending on the interest shown by the novice Simmers, you can introduce several basic computer concepts. And then they will see the LIGHT and know the power and the . . . er, never mind.

The two biggest problems when you throw a Sim Party will be keeping food away from the computer and getting everyone to go home. This observation comes from personal experience.

Compare Growth

File Name: COMPARE.CTY
Type: Experiment
Time Frame: No limit
Tools: SimCity, modem

Except for the Commodore version of SimCity, the city format files are interchangeable. The difficulty is that the diskettes are not. Even though you can't create a city data diskette on an Amiga and use it in an MS-DOS system, you can still use the universal exchange afforded with telecommunications. All systems use the same standard way to "talk" to one another. For example, you can transmit an Amiga file to a Macintosh system. The Mac saves the file in its own format and can then load the city in the Mac version of SimCity.

The user of one type of system can create a complete city, then transmit it to the user of another system type. The sender would then let the city continue to grow. The recipient would also then grow the "transplanted" city. The sender and recipient should establish the number of years of growth to allow before measuring the changes. They could then compare notes or even transmit the new versions of the cities back to one another.

Note: Actually connecting two personal computers to each other takes quite a bit of experience and special software to accomplish. The more practical solution is to use a common BBS to upload and download the files. More information about telecommunications is available in Appendix B, "Resources."

CIS Challenge

File Name: None
Type: Challenge
Time Frame: 3 hours
Tools: SimCity, modem, membership to CIS

Subscribers to CompuServe Information Service (known also as CIS) can send and receive city files. At an appointed hour, one user could upload a basic terrain on the service. Other participants would then download the file to their computers. They would have an allotted time to create and grow a city. When the time was up, they would have to upload their efforts. Once all the cities were available, everyone could download the cities by other participants. After a suitable time for study, two or three days, the group could hold a forum conference to discuss the results.

Disaster Recovery

File Name: Any small city
Type: Challenge
Time Frame: No limit
Tools: SimCity

Anticipating disaster is part of any city planner's job. How well can a city recover from a tornado or earthquake? SimCity gives you the advantage of calling specific disasters at any time. Because most disasters result in fire and structural damage, recovery depends on the fire department's response time as well as your ability to lead the damage clean up.

Save a city in a pre-disaster file, for example PREEARTH.CTY. Invoke the disaster, and see what it takes for the city to recover. How long does it take to put out all the fires? This is up to the Sim fire departments. If the power grid is broken, you'll have to fix it. You'll have to bulldoze any burnt ground before the zone can recover. How long does it take you to return the city to normal?

Now, after having watched the damage, return to the original PREEARTH file and make design changes. Do you add another power plant to the other side of the grid? Should you add more fire stations? Do what you think is necessary, and save this version as RECOVER1.CTY. Now invoke the same disaster. How long did it take you to recover this time?

Return to RECOVER1 and make additional changes. Can you create a city which recovers fairly quickly from disasters? What did it take? Does it add an extra maintenance burden to the city because you have more roads, stations, and power lines? How much protection is enough?

Money Machine

File Name: MONEY.CTY
Type: Challenge
Time Frame: No limit
Tools: SimCity

This is a no-holds-barred challenge. Create a city which makes money, the more the better. Don't worry about pretty parks. Don't worry about pollution. Don't worry about whining Sims. Just do what it takes to make money. Let the city run as long as you like. While the grand total accumulated is nice, you'll have to divide that amount by the number of years the city has grown to determine the real winner here. (Our highest was over $40,000,000 with a final annual growth rate of $5,000 a year.)

Chart Growth

File Name: Any city
Type: Activity
Time Frame: No limit
Tools: SimCity, chart paper

While the Windows menu provides charts for population, crime, taxes, employment, pollution, and cashflow, it does not chart many of the factors in the Evaluation window. Select a stable city, put the city on the Fastest speed, and watch the growth. Every January, jump into the Evaluation window (press **<CTRL-E>**), and write down the statistics you want to chart.

After checking the window for 10 years, create a chart of the figures. Do the selected factors change together? For example, does the mayor's rating fluctuate with the crime rate? Does the tax rate affect the net migration? What changes could you make to influence these figures? How do you know the changes will work?

Residential Sprawl

File Name: SPRAWL.CTY
Type: Experiment
Time Frame: No limit
Tools: SimCity

Residential zones with high-rises provide the best tax return, because more people live in less space. More people pay more taxes. But, some people (Sims?) don't like living in the city. Is it possible to create a city of Residential zones which remain at the lowest tax level, just houses? Can these zones generate enough income to pay for the roads and power lines out to them? Will there be enough people to work in the Industrial zones to keep the city growing?

The trick to keeping a zone to only houses is to place a park in one of the nine tiles. This prevents the zone from developing any further.

Local City

File Name: (Your city name)
Type: Experiment
Time Frame: No limit
Tools: SimCity, Terrain Editor, local map

The idea of creating a SimCity based on your city is too much to resist if you have Terrain Editor. Before beginning, though, get a city map and mark out a 10" x 10" square at the center of the map. This represents all the area you can include. Use this map to sketch the approximate zones in your city. If you are familiar with the city, this may not be too difficult. If you want a more authentic effort, contact your local city planning commission for an overview map of the city.

Don't be too disappointed when the Sim version does not respond much like your real city. Your city planners can zone in much more detail than you can with SimCity. On the other hand, you can create your version of your city and then fix it as you think it should be fixed. You won't even have to talk to the planning commission.

Multi-City

File Name:	Several
Type:	Challenge
Time Frame:	Lots of time
Tools:	SimCity, Terrain Editor, printer

For those of you who really like to think big, this project is it. Create at least four cities of any design, but make sure you create connections off the edge of the map. Place the connections so you can align all the cities when you print them out. You can't use SimCity to work with more than one city at a time, but printing out a multi-city will place you well within the ranks of Serious City Simmer. If you like this exercise, you'll love the SimEarth simulation.

Wave Growth

File Name:	WAVE.CTY
Type:	Experiment
Time Frame:	No limit
Tools:	SimCity

As a city grows, most of the zones might be rezoned at least once. The rezoning reflects the changing needs of the city. Rather than assume that once you zone an area in SimCity it should remain that zone type forever, plan on rezoning land as the city expands outward.

Think of the zones in rings. Commercial is the center. Industrial surrounds Commercial, with Residential on the outside. What happens when the Industrial area outgrows the current zoning? In this experiment, bulldoze the ring of Residential zones to make room for more Commercial and Industrial zones. You might want to zone the residential areas further out, so the Sims have somewhere to go when you begin tearing up their condos for office buildings.

Planning Theory

File Name: GARDEN.CTY and MODERN.CTY
Type: Experiment
Time Frame: No limit
Tools: SimCity

Try creating cities based on the garden city and modernistic urban planning theories outlined earlier in this chapter. Using the garden city model, can you create different self-sufficient areas? (You'll always have to rely on outside commerce, though.) What principles of the modernistic design can you use in you city? How will the Sims take to it?

Yearly Expenses

File Name: Any small city
Type: Activity
Time Frame: No limit
Tools: SimCity, calculator/spreadsheet, printer

Print the city in the large format. Tally the items on each which require yearly maintenance, including roads, railroads, power lines, and police and fire stations. (See why a small city is a good idea?) On a sheet of paper or using a spreadsheet, calculate the yearly cost to the city. Check this against the Budget window. If the figures are significantly different, determine why.

Don't make any changes to the city as you allow it to grow. Observe and record the cost of running the city each year. Using the cost against the tax income, project the city's fund balance in 10 and 20 years. Continue to let the city grow, and check your projections against the actual results. Why did or didn't this work as expected? (If you really enjoyed this activity, consider a career in accounting.)

Ghost Town

File Name: Any large city, population 10,000+
Type: Challenge
Time Frame: 5 years
Tools: SimCity

Oh, you've already created a few ghost towns? In that case, you've already discovered that building faster than you can afford to upsets the Sims, so they leave. But what about creating a ghost town deliberately? A few disasters would do the job, but we didn't say to level the city. Just make the Sims mad so they move out. Try the subtle approach first. Take away (bulldoze) the city services one a time: police, fire, air- and seaports. Then check the Net Migration score in the Evaluation window. By withdrawing different services, you can see which creates the fastest migration. This information will help you when you want a city to grow quickly.

No Industrial

File Name: NOSMOKE.CTY
Type: Experiment
Time Frame: No limit
Tools: SimCity

We know that the most effective ratio for city zoning is two Residential zones for one each of the Industrial and Commercial zones. Is it possible to create a city without any Industrial zones? Because the simulation relies on an external import and export factor for city income, can a city grow without any industry? At least pollution will be less severe without Industrial zones, assuming the city survives at all!

Gift City

File Name: HAPYBDY.CTY
Type: Activity
Time Frame: Soon
Tools: Cash or credit

Next time your favorite computer enthusiast has a birthday looming, search their bookshelves for SimCity or this book. If they are missing one or the other, correct the omission with a gift of the missing item. If they are missing both, present them with a copy of this book. (That's cheaper than buying the SimCity software for them.)

Interviews with Simmers

Knowing how to use the tools and knowing about each icon is not enough to guarantee success when building a city. Putting all the parts together is what counts. Each Simmer who builds more than one city develops his or her own style. Because we can compare cities but not the process of building them, we talked with a few SimCity enthusiasts about their building styles.

Getting Details

One interview was extensive, hours in the telling. We extracted every possible bit of information from this Simmer. An edited portion of the highlights of the summary follows.

Master SimCity/SimEarth: Where do you start a typical city?

Simmer: I always use Terrain Editor. I like having control of the terrain. I don't even use the random feature, I start from scratch, bare dirt.

MSC/SE: What then?

Simmer: I've tried lots of different ways to create my terrain, but in the end, I always find myself focusing on the water, lots and lots of water. Then when I've created all the water I need, I forest all the remaining land. I like lots of trees. More importantly, I've found that the Sims like water and trees, too.

MSC/SE: Doesn't that cost more when you do zone or build? You have to pay $9 a zone to bulldoze the trees.

Simmer: Yes, it does cost that extra $9, but it is worth it to have the trees wherever the buildings are and roads aren't. Once I have created my terrain, I go to SimCity to build.

MSC/SE: What level do you choose?

Simmer: I use the Easy level. I know that seems like a cop-out, but the Medium and Hard levels just offer more aggravation than they're worth. I wouldn't mind the lower amounts of money *(Medium starts with $10,000, and Hard starts with $5,000)*, but the Sims are just too picky to be useful when building a city at those levels.

MSC/SE: Do you print out the terrain for study?

Simmer: Having used the Terrain Editor, I know exactly what the terrain looks like and have already chosen my city center. When I let the simulator create random terrain, I would study the entire map for quite awhile, looking for the best location for the center of the city.

MSC/SE: What is so important about the city center?

Simmer: Do you know many cities that don't have a downtown area? This is where I'll put my commercial zones, and . . .

MSC/SE: What settings do you use when you start?

Simmer: As soon as I start the game, I make sure Disasters are off, Auto-budget is on, and Speed is Fastest. That's just my personal working style. I work fast and don't want to be bothered with budget issues for the first 10 or 15 years of building the city.

MSC/SE: Do you build a power plant first?

Simmer: Sure do. I want my zones to be working from the moment I lay them down. I build a power plant slightly to one side of my downtown. I always start with Coal. It's cheaper and more appropriate for a small town. Then, I'll place about four Industrial zones behind the power plant, making sure they have power lines and rail access.

MSC/SE: Rails? Why not roads?

Simmer: I'll tell you about rails in a minute. On the opposite side of the city center, I'll place about eight Residential zones. These are carefully placed to take advantage of any water and trees available. In the middle of these two areas, I'll put about four Commercial zones. I make sure this is all connected with rails and power lines.

MSC/SE: So now we have Industrial on one side, Residential on the other and the Commercial in the center. Now what?

Simmer: Well . . . . I'd just say "develop as needed." That's my recipe for a successful city.

MSC/SE: Let's get back to the "rails instead of roads" issue. Why rails?

Simmer: Once you get over the cute cars zooming up and down the highways, you begin to realize the significant savings of money and pollution that trains provide. While the Sims may complain that they "Need more roads", I've never seen them move out just because they had to commute by train. It is kind of funny watching the traffic helicopter try to decide where to circle when there are no roads.

MSC/SE: Do you use any particular city planning theory in your development?

Simmer: The closest I can imagine would be the concentric circles, the way most cities develop. As my city grows, I'll bulldoze and rezone Residential areas to allow for Commercial growth. Take a look at almost any city. You'll see where the old houses are close to the center of the city. They were overcome by the Commercial zones as they expanded to accommodate the needs of the downtown.

MSC/SE: How about city services, such as police and fire stations?

Simmer: I always wait until the Sims demand those types of services. I just don't have staff to monitor all the needs of the city. The Sims are active and will tell me when they want something. When they do, I use the City Form map to decide the best placement for the services, whether transportation, police, or fire.

MSC/SE: How about the airport and stadium?

Simmer: The Sims seem happy when they have either of those anywhere in their city. Location does not seem to be that critical. Extras are a waste of money and space.

MSC/SE: Any other parting tips for Simmers?

Simmer: Sure. Look at as many cities as you can. Watch the city grow and work for a while. Use all the maps to find the weak spots in fire and police coverage. Just because a city has some growth does not mean it is a properly developed city. Create and grow cities to suit yourself.

MSC/SE: Thanks for the interview, Dennis.

Simmer: You're welcome, Dan.

Around the Country

It was hard to find a SimCity player who *didn't* want to talk about their city building. A message posted on CompuServe brought six responses in as many hours. "Willing to be interviewed? Well sure, here's my phone number. Give me a call," was the typical response. We talked with those six people, and more. They ranged in age from 15 to over 40 and were in New

York, San Francisco, and points in between. They all enjoy playing SimCity and passing along their favorite tips.

Tom Talbott

When we talked with Tom, he had been playing SimCity for over four months. He found out about SimCity from friends, and plays on an MS-DOS 80386 system with a VGA screen. His average sessions last two to three hours. During one such session, Tom built four major cities. One city was over 200 years old. He leaves the Disasters on, adding "that's part of the challenge." He tends to leave his speed on Fast as he works. He must work quickly because, he suggests that "density is the key" to a successful city. He contrasted that theory with his home city of Seattle, which he says is spread out "all over the place." His tips: Build slowly and replace busy roads with rail.

Roy Mengot

Roy first played SimCity at a friend's house in Dallas. When the friend began hinting that he should begin paying part of the rent, Roy bought an Amiga. "Well sure, there were lots of things I knew I could use the computer for, so I went ahead and bought one. I haven't done much else (except SimCity), but someday I will." We discovered Roy from a lengthy message he left on CompuServe. Roy spends anywhere from three to six hours per session, and has built more than 20 cities. He described a six-city series he created, which, when printed out, became a 4-by-6-foot master city. He spent over $50 in color ink for his friend's computer to print all six cities to connect them together. He's thinking real hard about the $200 it would cost to get his master city mounted and framed.

Several of Roy's tips are scattered throughout this book. (Thanks again, Roy.) He was delighted to have discovered another tip just days before we talked with him: Residential areas away from the city center must be "squished together" to develop. If left spread out, they just stabilize at the house level. To suggest that Roy is enthusiastic about SimCity would be an understatement. As Roy said, SimCity was the first program to really "capture his imagination." (And your wallet, Roy?)

Neil Rubenking

As an editor for a computer magazine, Neil has access to dozens of software packages. He read several names from the bookshelf across the room. For Sim months, SimCity has had his attention. As a programmer, Neil has his own way of "playing" with games. After exploring the internal structure of SimCity, he still enjoys two-hour sessions of city building. He says he has about eight cities he's worked with, and leaves cities running overnight and part of the next day to build up funds. He varies his playing speed, depending on what he is doing: Slow for building, and Fastest for funding. Neil's tip: Don't build roads. But he adds quickly, "everybody already knows that." Maybe they didn't Neil, but they do now.

Janet Rubenking

Fellow Simmer and wife of Neil, Janet has her own ideas about SimCity. She's been playing almost a year and has built about 10 cities. She used to leave Disasters on, but now keeps them off. She tried some of the scenarios, but discovered that she'd rather create cities than try to solve someone else's problems. Her oldest creation is more than 4,000 years old and still stable.

Janet passed along several tips: Keep crime low with careful location of the Police stations; keep industry away from the Residential zones and; don't even bother with roads, build rails, rails and more rails. Do Janet and Neil ever compare cities? I knew better than to ask. They are still married, aren't they?

Adam "Longshot" Tullis

We knew where Adam lived even before we asked: New Yawk. He discovered SimCity on CompuServe about three months ago. He likes to put together his cities and then wander off to let the funds "build up." He "always" disables the Disasters while he builds. He likes to keep his simulation running on Fastest. He found most of his tips on CompuServe ("What, read the manual?") and suggests that you start small with cities.

When we mentioned that we would send a copy of this book to him for talking with us, he responded enthusiastically "All right! Thanks." You're welcome, Longshot.

Scott Calamar

Another member of the computer publishing industry, Scott creates cities on a Macintosh. He first saw a demonstration of SimCity at a computer show and, being the cool, calculating software user we all are, bought it on the spot. In over eight months he has built six cities he calls his own. Scott admits that there are few 15-minute sessions with SimCity. A more typical session lasts three or more hours.

Scott likes to design his own cities and uses Terrain Editor in the process. Disasters distract him from the creative process, so he always leaves them off. (Most of the Bay Area people didn't seem to care too much for disasters, actually.) He switches speeds depending on his current growth or building phase. He lets his cities run but finds that they deteriorate when left alone on the Mac too long. Scott's tip: Don't build bridges near the airport. The planes seem determined to hit them when they crash.

Scott also mentioned a trick to fake out the budget, something about changing the rate and then changing it back. It seemed very complicated, but he claimed it worked. Say Scott, do you handle the accounting at the office? Is your boss going to read this book?

Mayor Charles E. Hofmann, M.D.

The residents of Baker City, Oregon have an advantage over most other cities. Their mayor loves to build cities. In fact, His Honor has built and saved more than 25 cities in his year of using SimCity. He even confessed to having a city called **Baker City**, designed as he "would have built it." With SimCity he can try out all kinds of arrangements and watch the results. He likes quick results, too. Dr. Hofmann sets his speed on Fastest and works with Disasters off.

He likes nuclear power, leaves Auto-Goto on, and rarely has sessions lasting less than an hour. SimCity is a family activity, too. Mr. Mayor likes working with his family at home. He points out that the simulation lets the kids "use their imaginations." This, he adds, is "much better than watching T.V."

He was also one of the few people we talked with who liked working with the scenarios. He's played them "several times," and really enjoys Tokyo and Hamburg, having won each several times. He may be pleased with the suggestion at the end of some of the winning scenarios that `You may consider running for Mayor.`

How is SimCity different from the real duties of a mayor? Chuck went into great detail explaining Oregon's Open Meeting Law. Basically, every decision made by government officials must be made in front of an audience. He says the process to hold any kind of meeting is "overwhelming." With his Sim cities, he can do whatever he wants without filling out one form or consulting one official.

How is SimCity the same as real city planning? The problems with traffic are very consistent with real life. It is, he adds, a constant struggle. His Honor says he has "all (his) staff using SimCity." He did make it a point to mention that he does not use some of the tricks available to Simmers. He chuckled as he added, "for example, I'd never consider absconding with the funds." Ever the politician, aren't we, Mr. Mayor?

10 Cooperative Learning

Teachers recognize the term "cooperative learning." It occurs most often in the school classroom. Students work together toward a common learning goal. In the classroom setting, the teacher provides the structure and materials. The students organize themselves to complete the task. As a group, they make the decisions and evaluate the results. The comparable situation in a less academic or structured setting is a group of kids playing together.

Tip for Teachers

This book is "perfect bound," the publishing industry's term for the way these pages are put together. When you just read the book, this type of binding is functional. For teachers, it can be a pain. You want the book to open flat and stay open. You can break the spine (back) of the book, but the pages may begin to fall out.

As a solution, get a three-ring binder. Mark where to punch (drill) the holes on the book cover. Then take the book to a printer for drilling and spine trimming. Printers use a paper drill for the holes and a paper shear to cut off the spine. It takes them two minutes at the most. Offer $2 but pay what it's worth to you. Returning the loose pages to the ring binder gives you a very functional book for the classroom. (It also allows you to make copies of the pages more easily. It's OK. We said so.)

Learning Tool

The computer is a great learning tool. It provides the chance to explore possibilities and observe the results. While it is not a substitute for life in the real world, it allows the learner to form impressions and develop theories about how things work. It makes you think!

Because of the quick response, assortment of colors, and variety of sounds, computers easily draw young learners. Whatever the computer is doing looks like fun. Figuring out how to use it is a challenge. Kids enjoy all the possibilities represented by so many buttons (keys). In the process of discovery, they'll learn. And they won't mind learning.

We just can't resist contrasting a young person's response to computers with the typical response we've observed in adults. Adults think that

- ❑ Colors are pretty. Pretty things are not useful, just pretty. The computer screen is too colorful therefore the program is not useful.
- ❑ Music is for entertainment. Entertainment is not productive. The computer music is entertaining, and therefore the program is not productive.
- ❑ As if both color and sound were not distracting enough, there are too many keys to press. It is all too complicated, and must be a waste of time.

When trying cooperative learning on computers, maybe the best thing adults can do is to step aside and let the kids go crazy. Well, OK. We agree that kids still need structure. Teachers know that. Parents know that. The kids will even admit it (when they know that's what teachers and parents want to hear). The trick is to let kids explore the computer while providing enough structure for them to learn as well.

Kids at Work

This chapter contains lesson plans for teachers and parents to structure childrens' exploration of SimCity. Left on their own, they can master the basics of zoning, building roads, and making power connections. Because the program is so easy to use, five minutes of demonstration can get the kids started. For the first 30 minutes, let the kids take off on their own.

They'll build a haphazard city. It'll have some houses, factories and stores. They'll have some roads and railroads. If they have connected zones, they'll even see traffic. If they are enthusiastic, they'll build until they run out of money. Once that happens, they can't do much but watch and wait for the taxes to restore their building fund. When this does not occur within two minutes, there is only one thing left to do.

They will start a disaster to destroy what they have created. With a simple menu choice, they can call out the monster or create an earthquake or start any other equally destructive event. After watching the monster or tornado or earthquake, they tend to lose interest. Now they have a city with whole blocks destroyed, fires burning, and complaining citizens. And they don't have any money to repair their city.

They've done the obvious: make it and tear it down. This is what kids do with building blocks and clay. Now they've done it on the computer, too. Building an entire city and destroying it completely only took 30 minutes. This chapter provides ideas for the 31st minute and beyond.

Subjects

SimCity illustrates many school subjects. You can "tie it in" to specific classes. Teachers call this the *interdisciplinary approach*. Here's how SimCity pertains to several school subjects.

Math SimCity tracks expenses against available funds. Students must add and subtract to plan for growth. They can view graphs created by the program or make their own. Funding levels for transportation, police, and fire services illustrate how percentages work.

History	Creating a city is creating history. The simulation condenses years to minutes. Students can compare what happened to a real city with what happens as a SimCity grows.
Economics	What must every city have for growth? Students see what accounts for commercial and industrial activity. How do changes in the tax rate affect growth?
Geography	Map reading skills are essential. SimCity provides the same view of a city as a map. It includes streets, railroads, trees, and water.
Government	Government class is the most obvious application for SimCity. Who is responsible for what areas of a city? What do leaders change based on what the residents request? What happens if they ignore the citizens?

Audience

Bright six year olds can use SimCity. Professional city planners benefit from working with the program. Cooperative learning works within any group of any age. Participants can all succeed with SimCity. We provide the lesson plans in order of increasing complexity. Second grade to high school teachers can use these ideas in the classroom. The lesson plans also provide a great way for the family to work together building a city.

Computer Access

Some schools have at least one computer in each classroom. Others have all their systems in a computer lab. In some cases, one computer travels among several rooms. Access to a computer is not equal within a school or classroom. We've designed these lesson plans for use by a small group working independently at one computer. If computer access is limited, the entire class could serve as one team, with subgroups taking the roles described in the lesson plan.

Lesson Plans

This chapter's lesson plans help you use SimCity in the classroom. If you normally use lesson plans as a base to work from and adapt them to suit the class, use these plans the same way.

Teacher's Experience

While we'd love to make this a complete computer training manual, we can't. The SimCity program has varying versions for many different types of computers, so we have to be vague in some places. For example, when we suggest you make a copy of a diskette, we can't provide a method for doing it. With some systems, you run a program. With others, you just issue a command.

Out of necessity then, we have to assume that you have some basic computer skills before working with SimCity. While this program would be a good place to start for a student's introduction to computers, we hope you've had some time to become familiar with the computer and SimCity before class.

We assume you know about, or how to accomplish, the following:

- ❑ Turn on (boot) the computer system.
- ❑ Start different programs.
- ❑ Use the mouse or joystick, if available.

- ❑ Load the printer with paper and ribbons.
- ❑ Copy disks (make backups).
- ❑ Save files to disk (specific to each program).
- ❑ Turn off the computer properly.
- ❑ Take care of floppy disks.

As always, should any member of your Mission Impossible team be caught or captured . . . Oh, wrong book. As always, if you get stuck, remember to look in the computer manual for possible solutions to computer problems. Problems specific to SimCity might be covered in Appendix A.

Structure

Each lesson plan follows a typical outline for educational settings: objectives, materials, preparation, activities, teamwork, and discussion questions. Each lesson plan has been reviewed by a certified representative of the field of education.

Complete the 10 lesson plans in order. They provide sequential steps to learn more about SimCity. Depending on the average age of the team, each lesson may take from 15 minutes to hours. If your students complete the lessons, you may suggest they take on the challenges in the scenarios, described in Chapter 8. Students may also want to read Chapter 10, "SimCity Planning." That chapter contains planning tips, design challenges, and information about city planning theory.

Each lesson begins on a new page. Handouts referenced in a lesson plan appear at the end of the lesson. References to other parts of the book identify background information. Table 10.1 provides an overview of the lesson plans.

Table 10.1 This chapter's lesson plans.

This Lesson Plan	*Teaches How to*
1. Computer Orientation	Operate the computer.
2. SimCity Tour	Control the SimCity software.
3. Save the City	Save city files.
4. QUIKCITY	Build a city step-by-step.
5. Team Members	Form the city building team.
6. Planning Meeting	Plan ahead.
7. Build a City	Implement the team design.
8. Disaster Strikes	Test for the unexpected.
9. Running a City	Ensure maintenance and growth.
10. Take a Trip	Look at other teams' efforts.

1

Computer Orientation

For your students who have not used the computer independently, this lesson provides the basics of computer operation. It does not cover how a computer works, but how to work the computer. The lesson includes rules about working on the computer and working with other students on the computer. If the students have used the computer before, you may just want to review the rules with the class.

Objectives

- ❑ To identify the main parts of the computer.
- ❑ To know how to turn the computer system on and off.
- ❑ To use the computer properly.
- ❑ To know how to work with others on the computer.

Materials

For the class demonstration

Computer system with monitor (screen), keyboard, disk drive, and printer.

Boot diskette (if necessary).

SimCity software.

For each team

Copy of the Computer Rules handout.

Preparation

Make sure the computer works as expected. Review the process of turning the computer on. If it requires a boot diskette, make sure you have one. Check everything by turning on the computer and loading the software.

Activities

- ❑ Identify the parts of the computer, paying special attention to the on/off switches on the computer and monitor.
- ❑ Explain how to be careful with diskettes. (Avoid bending, heat, magnets, and touching the surface.)
- ❑ Demonstrate how to turn on the computer, inserting the diskette before or after as appropriate.
- ❑ Load the software, pointing out any special commands as necessary.
- ❑ Show only the opening screen of SimCity.
- ❑ Explain a little bit about SimCity and the class/team project.
- ❑ Review the material in the Computer Rules handout.
- ❑ Remove the diskette (if necessary), and then turn off the computer.
- ❑ Have a team member turn on the computer, load the program, and then turn it off properly in front of the class. (Always wait 10 seconds before turning a computer off and then back on.)

Teamwork

- ❑ Have each team practice turning the computer off and then back on, making sure they wait 10 seconds between turning it off and back on.
- ❑ Have one member of the team draw the computer on the Computer Rules handout and identify the parts.
- ❑ Team members should also write any special notes about starting the program on the back of the handout.
- ❑ Each team may make up a team name and write it on the Computer Rules handout, as well.

Discussion Questions

1. What will happen if you abuse the computer?
2. How can you make sure that each team member gets a turn?
3. What do you do if you have a problem?

Notes

While the process of turning on the computer may not seem particularly exciting, the first teamwork session builds confidence and provides a chance to work with the computer. If students start using the SimCity program without the teamwork session, they are likely to forget the basic rules and safe practices for computer use that you demonstrated in the activities portion of the lesson.

Computer Rules

Team name: ______________________________

1. Make sure only clean hands touch any part of the computer.
2. No food or drink near the computer.
3. Never pound the keys.
4. Don't remove a diskette when the drive light is on.
5. Replace the diskette dust cover when finished.
6. Return diskettes to their proper place.

Helping each other

1. Offer advice only when asked.
2. The user at the keyboard makes all final decisions.
3. Never reach over someone to type when it is their turn.
4. If needed, you may call out the keys for them to type.
5. Be patient—others may not type as quickly as you do.
6. Don't tell what's coming next, even if you know.
7. Take equal turns at the keyboard.

2

SimCity Tour

Once your students know how to use the computer, they are ready to learn how to use SimCity. On your computer system, they'll learn to use the keyboard, mouse or joystick to make menu choices, select icons, and build a city. After a demonstration by you or a computer helper, give each team a chance to try everything out.

Objectives

- ❑ To review loading the program.
- ❑ To understand windows, menu choices, and icons.
- ❑ To know how to make selections.
- ❑ To recognize and place Residential, Industrial, and Commercial zones.
- ❑ To create roads and make power connections.
- ❑ To move around and view parts of the city/terrain.

Materials

Computer system and software.

SimCity Help Sheet handout

Preparation

You or the computer helper should be familiar with the SimCity program. Make sure the pointing device (keyboard, joystick, or mouse) works prior to the demonstration. A review of Chapters 6 and 7 might help.

Activities

- ❑ Review the process of starting the computer and software.
- ❑ Load the Dullsville scenario.
- ❑ Demonstrate how to use the red copy protection sheet.
- ❑ Show the menu system and how to make choices.
- ❑ Demonstrate the windows available and how to move from one to another.
- ❑ Show how to choose an icon and place an object on the map.
- ❑ Briefly explain the symbols on the map.
- ❑ Explain the areas to fill in on the SimCity Help Sheet.
- ❑ Show how to exit the program properly.

Teamwork

- ❑ Have each team select the "driver" for the first round.
- ❑ Once they have started the program, each member should practice making menu choices, moving between windows, and selecting icons.
- ❑ Each team should complete the SimCity Help Sheet.

Discussion Questions

1. What happens when you make a mistake on the computer?
2. How does the computer help you learn?

Notes

It's important that you practice for this lesson. You need not have a complete understanding of how to build a city, but know how to use the software for the demonstration. If you don't have time to become familiar with the program, consider letting a student with computer experience spend some time with the program. Let the student demonstrate while you explain. Completing the help sheet provides notes the students can refer to later and reinforces the material.

SimCity Help Sheet

By exploring the menu system, you can learn how to use the SimCity program. You can answer each of these questions by looking around SimCity.

1. What are the main menu choices?
2. What are the Disasters?
3. How do you Pause the program?
4. Draw the Residential, Industrial, and Commercial icons.
5. Can roads curve?
6. What does a flashing lightning bolt mean?
7. Can you see the Sims? Why or why not?
8. How long does a Sim year last?

3

Save the Cities

Each team will soon build a city, but it helps to be comfortable with the basics first. In this lesson plan, teams practice placing zones, laying roads, making power connections, and saving cities to disk. The resulting city may not function very well, but at least they'll have created and saved it.

Objectives

- ❑ To create a basic city with zones and roads.
- ❑ To save and reload a city on the data diskette.
- ❑ To find the Evaluation window.
- ❑ To move to all edges of the terrain.
- ❑ To use all three types of zones.
- ❑ To connect zones with power.
- ❑ To create roads.

Materials

Several soft tipped pens.

Computer and software.

A blank formatted diskette for each team.

A label for each diskette.

A Save the Cities Sheet handout for each team.

Preparation

Make sure the diskettes have been formatted. Gather the labels but don't apply them to the diskettes. (Mailing labels work well if diskette labels are not available.) If the diskettes are already labeled, provide several soft tipped pens to use on the labels.

Activities

- ❑ Have each team put the team name on the diskette label. Emphasize the need to write on the label before it is on the disk or use a soft tipped pen after it is on the disk.
- ❑ Review the need to keep all disks in their disk sleeve when not in the computer. See also the note below.
- ❑ Review the questions on the Save the Cities Sheet handout.

Teamwork

Each team should work through the Save the Cities Sheet handout.

Discussion Questions

1. Why do we save the files to a diskette?
2. What happens to your work if the disk is damaged?
3. Can you recreate your city if you lose or damage the disk?
4. How are the zones different from each other?
5. Why doesn't a zone without power get buildings?
6. Must roads connect each zone?

Notes

If your computer system uses 3.5-inch hard plastic diskettes, they don't need to be kept in a sleeve. Their sliding metal shutter serves as a protection system.

Remember to provide instructions for saving the city to the drive which contains the team's floppy diskette. With a single-drive system, the students will remove the SimCity diskette and replace it with their own. On a two-drive system, students need to include the drive letter, typically **B:**, before the city name. When saving to a floppy using a hard drive system, students should also include the drive letter, more typically **A:**, in front of the name.

Save the Cities Sheet

1. Create four Residential zones.
2. Create two Commercial zones.
3. Create two Industrial zones.
4. Create one power station.
5. Connect everything with power lines.
6. Create some roads.
7. Use the menu to save a city to the diskette and name it FIRST.
8. Exit the program.
9. Start the program.
10. Load the city called FIRST.
11. Is it just like you left it?

If you have time:

12. Find the Evaluation window.
13. Move to all edges of the terrain.

4

QUIKCITY

Chapter 4, "Build QUIKCITY," contains more detailed instructions on the steps here. You'll use these step-by-step instructions to build and save a city. Students can compare cities and building styles. The lesson also provides more practice with the program.

Objectives

- ❑ To create order out of chaos (a city which grows).
- ❑ To begin to understand city growth patterns.
- ❑ To follow written instructions.

Materials

For each team:

Computer and software.

Data diskette.

QUIKCITY handout.

Preparation

Using the handout, build a QUIKCITY prior to class.

Activities

- ❏ Begin by discussing the differences between a random city versus a planned city. Point out that growth becomes more likely when students place neighborhoods together and connect zones with roads and power.
- ❏ Ask for their observations about their FIRST city. Did it grow? How did they know if it was growing?
- ❏ Where was the Evaluation window? What did it say? How is this different from a real city?
- ❏ How long would it take to build a real city the size they created?
- ❏ What are zones? Who decides what zones go where?
- ❏ What happens to a zone without power? Roads?

Teamwork

- ❏ Have the students follow the QUIKCITY handout and answer the questions as they go.
- ❏ Remind them to save the city as they work on it.

Discussion Questions

1. Does a mayor really run a city?
2. What if he or she ignores the citizens' complaints?

Notes

The QUIKCITY handout steps closely resemble the steps in Chapter 4. We left off the explanation to save space. You may want to have Chapter 4 handy as a guide. This lesson plan begins to introduce city planning. Neighborhoods, stores, and factories don't just happen, someone plans them. Students may begin noticing the Sims asking (demanding) certain things, like more Residential zones or roads.

Remember that **<SELECT>** means to move the pointer to the specified icon or word and press the left mouse button or **<SPACE BAR>**. In some cases, there are shortcut keys for the keyboard. Shortcuts are noted in the keyboard column.

QUIKCITY

Start the program and start a new city. The following steps will help you create a city which will grow. You can add to it later and watch it grow even more.

Mouse Instructions	Keyboard Instructions
<SELECT> DISASTERS	**<ALT-D>**
<SELECT> Disable	**<SELECT>** Disable
<SELECT> Options	**<ALT-O>**
<SELECT> Auto-Budget	**<SELECT>** Auto-Budget
<SELECT> Power Plant (icon)	**<SELECT>** Power Plant (icon)
<SELECT> Coal	**<SELECT>** Coal
Move the box to the lower right corner of the screen and **<CLICK>**	Move the box to the lower right corner of the screen and press **<SPACE BAR>**
<SELECT> Residential (icon)	**<SELECT>** Residential (icon)
Move the box that appears to the left edge of the screen and **<CLICK>**	Move the box that appears to the left edge of the screen and press **<SPACE BAR>**
Move the box to the left and **<CLICK>** five times, until you have six Residential zones side-by-side	Press →, then **<SPACE BAR>** five more times, until you have six Residential zones side by side
<SELECT> Power Line (icon)	**<SELECT>** Power Line (icon)
<POINT> and **<CLICK>** to connect the Power Plant with the Residential zones	**<POINT>** and press **<SPACE BAR>** to connect the Power Plant with the Residential zone
<SELECT> Road (icon)	**<SELECT>** Road (icon)

Move the small box to the bottom of the far left Residential zone	Move the small box to the bottom of the far left Residential zone
<CLICK-DRAG> across the bottom of the Residential zones. Hold the button down as you move the box across the screen. Repeat to create the city shown in Figure 10.1	Move the pointer across the bottom with the →, then press **<SPACE BAR>** to lay the road. Repeat to create the city shown in Figure 10.1
<SELECT> Commercial (icon)	**<SELECT>** Commercial (icon)
Using the same method you used to make Residential zones, create three Commercial zones starting at the left end of the main street.	Using the same method you used to make Residential zones, create three Commercial zones starting at the left end of the main street.
<SELECT> Power Line (icon)	**<SELECT>** Power Line (icon)
Provide power to the Commercial zones by connecting them to a Residential zone	Provide power to the Commercial zones by connecting them to a Residential zone
<SELECT> Industrial (icon)	**<SELECT>** Industrial (icon)
Using the same method you used with the Commercial zones, create three Industrial zones starting to the right of the Commercial zones. Your city should look like Figure 10.2	Using the same method you used with the Commercial zones, create three Industrial zones starting to the right of the Commercial zones. Your city should look like Figure 10.2
<SELECT> `SYSTEM` (menu) **<SELECT>** `Save City`	**<ALT-S>**

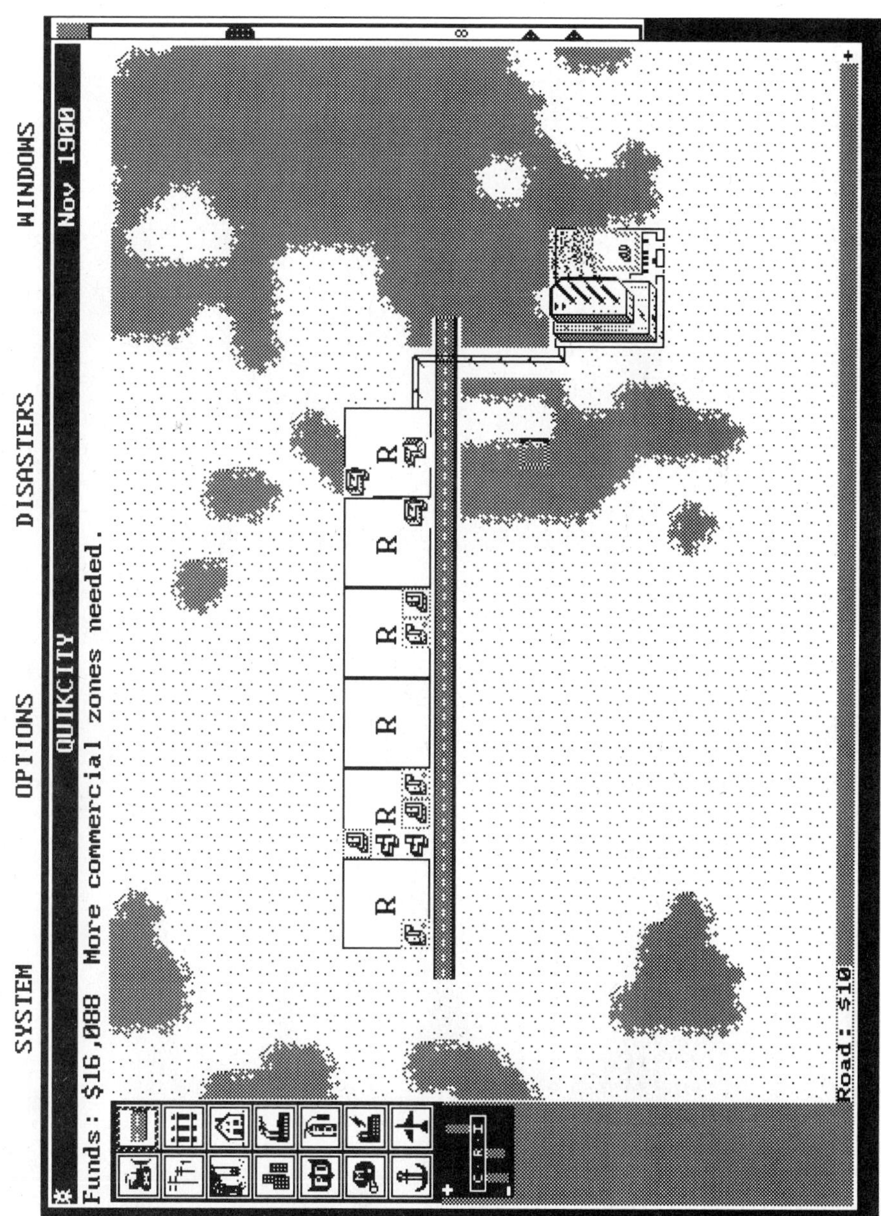

Figure 10.1 *QUIKCITY has six Residential zones connected to the power plant and a main street.*

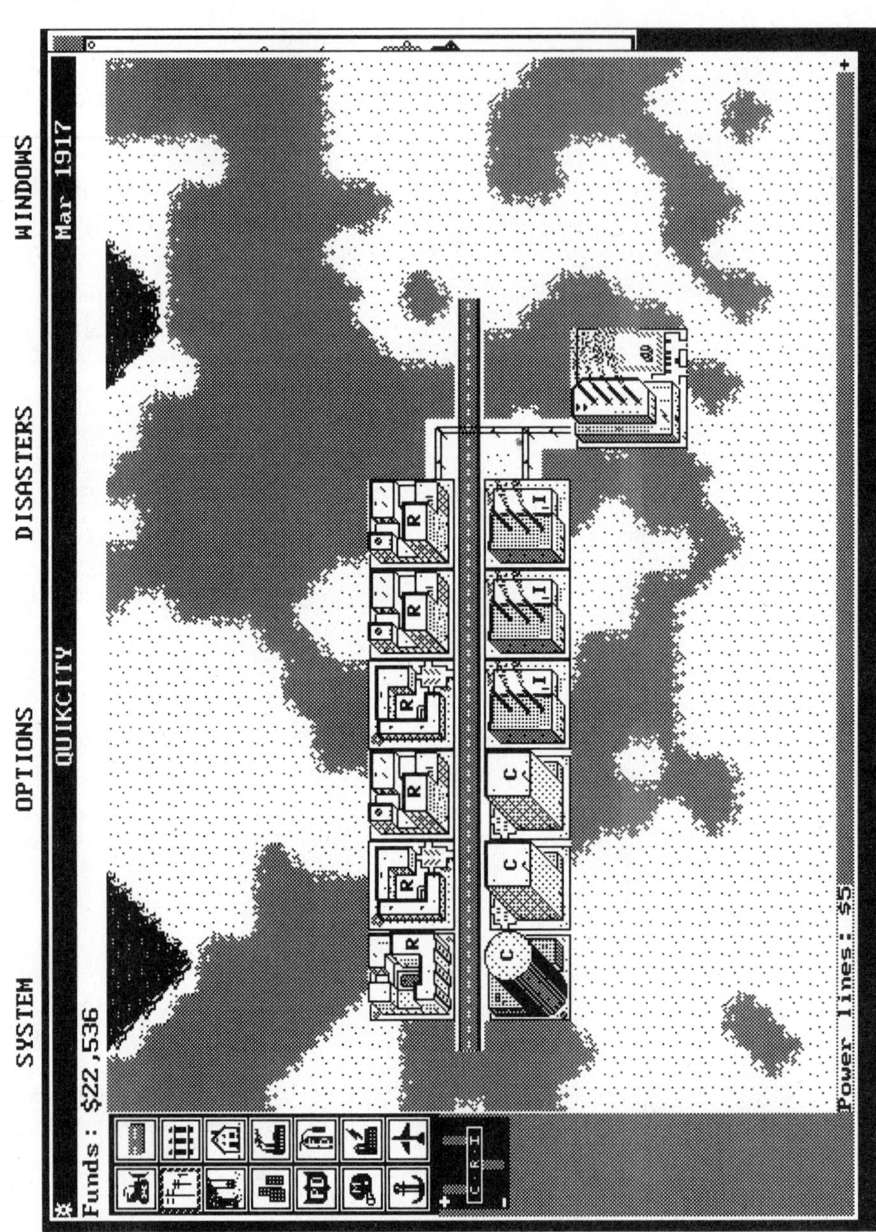

Figure 10.2 *The finished QUIKCITY.*

5

Team Members

At this point, the students have been working together, learning how to use the computer and SimCity. Now it is time to divide the responsibilities among the team members. Each member will be responsible for building and running a different part of the city. This lesson plan outlines several jobs: mayor, tax commissioner, city planner, fire marshall, police chief, transportation manager, financial officer, and power director. Hold this session in a classroom because computers would be distracting.

Objectives

❏ To define team members and their roles.

Materials

Each team needs the City Leaders handout.

Activities

❏ Read and discuss the team members roles in class.

Teamwork

❏ The teams then meet to decide who will serve the various roles. You might suggest they "elect" the mayor from within their group, or you may want to appoint a mayor to manage each team.

Discussion Questions

1. Do projects just happen without planning?
2. Why does a team need a leader?
3. What is the election process?
4. Why do we use elections to choose leaders?

Notes

This activity may or may not appeal to the students. It is a great chance to learn to make decisions as a group. It may help them understand the jobs of local officials. Gathering additional, local job descriptions can reinforce students' understanding of local government.

City Leaders

Job Descriptions

Mayor: Elected by the citizens. Makes all the final decisions about how the city will be built and run. Gets to name the city.
Planning Commissioner: Decides where to place the Residential, Commercial, and Industrial zones. Also decides the placement of airports, seaport, and stadiums.
City Services Deputy: Decides where to locate the power plant. Makes sure the power lines run to each zone. Decides where to locate the police and fire stations.
Transportation Director: Designs the transportation system, including roads and railroads.
Tax Board Chair: Sets the tax rate and funding for roads, police, and fire services. Must work closely with everyone to make sure there is enough money for planned expansion.
City Auditor: Keeps track of all expenses, including the cost of each zone, and how much each section of road costs to build and maintain. Advises the tax board chair about the tax funding needed to accomplish the planned city. Makes yearly reports on the taxes collected and migration rate.

Team name: ______________________

City name: ______________________

Mayor: ______________________

Planning Commissioner: ______________________

City Services Deputy: ______________________

Transportation Director: ______________________

Tax Board Chair: ______________________

City Auditor: ______________________

6

Planning Meeting

Now that each member of the team has specific responsibilities, they have to decide what their cooperative effort will look like. They'll have to hold a town board meeting and design their city. Each member of the team will make proposals covering their area.

Objectives

- ❏ To design a city before building it.
- ❏ To discover costs associated with running a city.

Materials

Each team needs

Copy of the City Planning Sheet handout.

Terrain map of starting city (you make).

Templates (you make).

Mayor's Speech handout.

Preparation

Create and save a city terrain. Print it and make a copy for each team (you'll need an Epson or Epson-compatible printer to do this). This is the terrain map, the basis upon which each city will be built. To aid in the design, you may want to create small templates, cut out of heavy construction paper, for the zones, fire, and police stations and other buildings.

Activities

- ❏ The mayor of each team will make a speech to the team or class about the city. We've provided a short speech for the mayor. The speech should raise more questions than it answers. You may want to explain the job of a speechwriter. You may point out that promises made are not always kept. Review the mayor's promises and why they may, or may not, be kept.

Teamwork

- ❏ The team will sketch out their city using the terrain map you provided. Tell them to count the zones, power lines, and road sections they draw. This will help them estimate the city budget.
- ❏ Teams should trace the templates to decide placement for zones, fire and police stations, and other city features.
- ❏ The teams then complete the City Planning Sheet. In the process, they have to make decisions using little experience or information. If they have read other parts of this book, they may have more information on which to base their decisions.

Discussion Questions

1. What happens when team members can't agree what to do?
2. Why do we want to start with the same terrain?
3. What are the advantages to planning the city first?

Notes

The program lends itself to experimentation. This lesson plan becomes more like work. If the students resist these planning efforts, you may point out that they can call up a disaster later.

Mayor's Speech

We are here today on a very important mission. We must design a city. Not just any city, but a city which grows because the citizens are happy with what we build.

I have been elected to serve the people of our great city. It will be named

____________________.

I promise we will have low taxes.

Our pollution will be somewhere else.

We will have a low crime rate and complete fire protection.

We will build a stadium and have a great team.

Our roads will be well-maintained and allow you to go anywhere you want.

Thank you.

City Planning Sheet

	Number	x	Cost	=	Total
Power plant	____	x	____	=	____
Residential zones	____	x	____	=	____
Commercial zones	____	x	____	=	____
Industrial zone	____	x	____	=	____
Road sections	____	x	____	=	____
Power lines	____	x	____	=	____
Railroad sections	____	x	____	=	____
Police/fire stations	____	x	____	=	____
Total initial building phase:					_____

7

Build a City

The sessions all come together now. Now that they have the plan, the team members can use SimCity to try out their ideas. This stage may last for weeks as the city grows (or doesn't).

Objectives

- ❑ To put plans into action.
- ❑ To observe cause and effect.
- ❑ To develop an understanding of the Sims' behavior.

Materials

Computer and software for each team.

City Notes handout.

Preparation

Review the last page of Chapter 4 on QUIKCITY. The suggestions there will be helpful. Chapter 9 provides more in-depth information. Provide only as much information as the students need or ask for.

Activities

❑ Point out that although they budgeted for a certain number of zones, they don't have to place them all at once. The most effective ratio is two Residential zones for one Commercial and one Industrial zone.

❑ Remind the students to save their cities frequently. You may suggest they use the Save As... option to keep naming their cities sequentially, as in CITY01 and CITY02. Depending on the system and disk size, students will be able to keep quite a few versions that way. If they run out of space, they can delete some of the cities.

Teamwork

❑ The teams will use the City Planning Sheet to layout the city.

❑ The students may also want to keep notes on the City Notes handout as they build the city. As they save city versions, they can note the year, funds, complaints, mayor's rating, city score, and other factors. This handout could provide great data for charting later. It may also record the beginning of the end for some cities.

Discussion Questions

1. How are the Sims like us?
2. How are they different?
3. How do the Sims "know" what to do?
4. Are the Sims real?
5. Do they seem real?

Notes

This and the final three lessons are trial-and-error city building sessions. Focus more on the cause and effect of the students' actions. Careful observation is the key to discovering all they can about the Sims.

City Notes

Name	Date	Funds	Pop.	Rating	City Score	Notes

Name = Name of the city file
Date = Date file saved
Funds = Funds remaining
Pop. = Population
Rating = Mayor's rating in evaluation window
Score = Overall City Score in evaluation window

8

Disaster Strikes

Because the city should be saved to disk as often as possible, the team may test their disaster preparation. They may predict how their city will react and how long it will take to recover. Otherwise, the students can load an old, intact version of their city and continue the city growth.

Objectives

- ❑ To give in to the urge to make a mess of things.
- ❑ To test the design of the city.

Materials

Computer and software for each team

Activities

- ❑ If they haven't already set loose a disaster, encourage the teams to try one. They may want to save the current version of the city just before calling up the disaster.

Teamwork

- ❑ Available disasters include tornados, earthquakes, floods, fires, and monsters. Once a disaster starts, not much can be done about it. If the city lacks fire protection, the after-disaster fires may burn for years.
- ❑ The teams can use the Load command to recall the city they saved just before the disaster.

Discussion Questions

1. Why keep track of each city file?
2. Can you remember each city and how you created it? Why or why not?
3. Are the best learning experiences based on mistakes?
4. How can a computer simulation help or hinder learning?
5. Do disasters help you learn about your city? How?

Notes

It's likely that the teams tried the Disaster menu before now. Kids like to see things torn down. Remind them that they can turn Disasters off. We start new cities by making sure unexpected disasters won't bother us.

9

Running a City

Well planned, mature cities will not require as much management (in SimCity). They function unattended if you let them run, especially overnight. On the other hand, if the city is out of balance, the Sims will leave. A complete analysis of the problems will help prevent the same situation in the next city built.

Objectives

- ❑ To contrast city growth and maintenance.
- ❑ To observe patterns of the simulation.
- ❑ To determine imbalances leading to city decay.
- ❑ To compare a Sim city with a real city.

Materials

Computer and software for each team.

Preparation

Arrange to leave the computer(s) on overnight. Change the class lab times to just before the end of the school day and at the beginning of the next day. To see even more variation, let the simulation run over a weekend.

Activities

- ❑ Talk about running a city versus building it. One measure of success is a stable city which will run for years.
- ❑ If you only have access to one computer, a team could start the cities in the morning, and the class could observe the results throughout the school day.

Teamwork

- ❑ Instruct the teams to pick an existing city or create a new one to run overnight.
- ❑ Instruct the teams to set the fastest speed and just watch the city, checking the Evaluation window every new year. They may want to chart the changes year by year. Using the Graphs window also shows the city history.

Discussion Questions

1. What is a balanced city?
2. What would happen to make the Sims move away?
3. What happens to make real people move away?
4. How do we learn from watching patterns of growth and decay?
5. What would a stable city look like?

Notes

Running the computers does not hurt them any more than leaving a light bulb on hurts it. You may turn the screens off without affecting the program or computer.

10

Take a Trip

Mayors and other city officials travel to other cities to make comparisons. Students can view other teams' cities just by making copies of the cities to a diskette. After reviewing the cities, team members may talk to their counterparts on the other teams.

Objectives

- ❑ To view other teams' cities.
- ❑ To enable each team to contrast other cities with theirs.

Materials

Computer and software for each team.

An extra formatted diskette for each team.

Preparation

Before class, make a copy of each team's data diskette. Mark the diskette with the team name and place a write-protect tab on the diskette.

Activities

- ❑ Explain that each team will tour other cities by using each team's extra disk. They'll load the cities normally. If they want to save that city to their diskette, they can insert their data diskette and save the city. They may want to keep notes to keep track of where each city came from.

- ❑ Depending on how organized the teams are, they could include a sheet with the disk explaining the cities on the disk and various features of each city.

Teamwork

- ❑ This lesson is likely to cause more chaos than any other. Teams are likely to want other teams to explain their cities or provide tours. This activity may take a few class sessions to satisfy the students.

Discussion Questions

1. What differences did you see in the cities?
2. Is one type of city better than another?
3. How do the individual team members influence the city?
4. Do individual teams develop a style?

Notes

Write-protect disks by either placing an opaque piece of tape over the notch on a 5.25-inch floppy or by moving the write-protect tab on 3.5-inch pocket diskettes to the open position. This will keep a team from accidentally erasing cities on a diskette. But because this is a copy of the team's original disk, even accidental erasure would not be a disaster.

Advanced Projects

Just covering these lesson plans will take many class periods. If some teams are interested in additional challenges, they may want to look at Chapter 8 for information on using scenarios. Students may also want to read Chapter 9, "SimCity Planning."

11 SimCity Extras

It doesn't take long before you want even more control of your cities. Not only do you want to zone the land, build the roads, and set the tax rate, but you also want to create lakes, expand shorelines, and grow forests. Terrain Editor allows you to do all that.

If you get tired of the way your terrain looks, you can call up additional graphics sets to replace the original images and icons. Graphics Set #1 includes *Ancient Asia*, *Wild West*, and *Medieval Times*. Graphics Set #2 has *Future USA*, *Future Europe*, and *Moon Colony*. While the city simulation rules remain the same behind the scenes, the graphics sets create a whole new series of images to work with.

Terrain Editor

Terrain Editor is an additional software package available for the MS-DOS, Macintosh, Amiga, and Atari systems. (The Commodore and color Mac versions of SimCity include Terrain Editor.) The Terrain Editor versions cost about half the price of the SimCity package and should be available where you purchased SimCity.

Your New Job Title

With the Terrain Editor software, you can "paint" a 10-mile-by-10-mile area with water, trees, and dirt. You can create the starting ground for the city before you begin working in SimCity. You then load the city file and begin building your city. Not only are you the mayor, tax board, and zoning commission, you are the Army Corps of Engineers.

Terrain Editor enables you to return to an existing city to rearrange some of the terrain if you like. Add a little dirt to the shoreline to squeeze in a few more (lucrative) residential zones. Grow forests at the click of a button. Or, build a new lake or river. If you want to do some serious urban renewal, jump into Terrain Editor and bulldoze the zone clean at no cost! You can even reset the game play level and year anytime you like. (Sorry, you can't mess with the funds with Terrain Editor. There *are* other ways to do that, though.)

Terrain Editor Installation

The Terrain Editor installation program and information in the manual are pretty straightforward. If you installed SimCity, you can handle Terrain Editor. Unlike SimCity, Terrain Editor does not have any sounds. The installation program asks about sound, anyway.

On our MS-DOS system, we put Terrain Editor in a subdirectory called TE under the SIMCITY directory. So when asked where on the hard drive to install the Terrain Editor, our response was `C:\SIMCITY\TE`. Putting Terrain Editor in its own subdirectory keeps our "raw" designs away from the other city files in the main directory.

Notice also that the installation program does not copy the additional city files to your system. You'll have to do that using standard operating system commands. (Those cities are worth taking a look at, too.) Review the sections on copy protection and registration in Chapter 2, if you have not already read those. Because Terrain Editor is not copy protected, we urge you to respect the rights of the software developer and not make additional copies for others to use.

We'll assume you know how to use your mouse, joystick, or keyboard to move the pointer around. Remember that even if you specify a joystick and have a mouse driver installed, the joystick will not work. When you start Terrain Editor, you'll see one of only two known pictures of a Sim, as shown in Figure 11.1. (The other Sim appears on the Park icon.) This Terrain Editor opening screen gives a revealing look at a Sim.

Figure 11.1 *A Sim 'dozer driver and a very strangely designed bulldozer.*

Windows

As in SimCity, you'll use windows in Terrain Editor: the Edit and City Map windows. Both windows remain open, but move from front to back when you click on one or the other. Flip windows back to front by pressing **<CTRL-M>** or **<CTRL-E>**. All the icon and menu selections are active in either window. Figure 11.2 shows the two windows of the Terrain Editor screen and the icons.

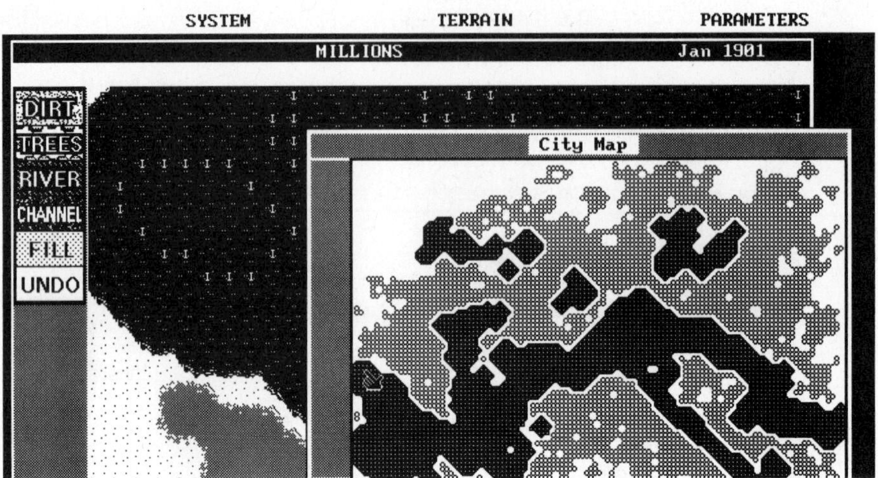

Figure 11.2 The City Map window shown in front of the Edit window.

Edit Window

The Edit window contains the detailed working area. Like the SimCity Edit window, it has a title bar, resize box, and icons. You can also scroll over the map in the Edit window.

Title Bar

The Title Bar across the top of the window contains the city name and date. Unlike SimCity, the city date does not progress as time passes. You can change the city name and date using the Parameters menu. Clicking on the title bar allows you to relocate the Edit Window if the window is not full screen size.

Resize Box

Located in the lower right corner of the window, the resize box is just a + (plus) sign. Resize the Edit window by moving the pointer to this corner and then clicking and dragging the corner. You can make the window wider or narrower but not shorter. We use this feature to place the Edit and Map windows side by side on the screen.

Scrolling

One of the most confusing aspects of navigating in SimCity or Terrain Editor is scrolling around. In the Edit window, scroll around the area by moving the pointer to the edge of the screen. The **<CTRL>** and Arrow keys also move the landscape in this window.

The pointer disappears as the landscape scrolls across the window. The landscape continues to scroll until you move the pointer away from the edge of the screen. Once you reach an edge or corner of the landscape, the movement stops but the cursor remains hidden.

An effective method to use the mouse or joystick to scroll is to "bump" the pointer against the window edge to move the landscape. If you just touch and back away from the window edge, the screen adjusts and you see the cursor again. To move more, just bump again. As you get familiar with this method, you'll learn to judge the length of time to bump for the distance you want to move.

***Tip:** To turn off mouse and joystick scrolling, press the **<SCROLL LOCK>** key. Your work area won't go scooting away from you, but you'll have to use the **<CTRL>** and Arrow keys to move the Edit window around or use the City Form map to move quickly.*

Icons

Icons appear on the side or bottom of the window, depending on the system you are using. The currently selected terrain icon—Dirt, Trees, River, or Channel—is highlighted and appear at the bottom of the window. The Fill and Undo icons trigger events. Icons are covered in more detail later in this chapter.

City Map Window

The Map window provides a view of the entire landscape including all features, natural and man-made. You can't display crime or population like you can in SimCity. Also, you can't resize the Map window.

There are only two ways you can change the City Map window. You can move it by pointing to the Title bar and dragging. And you can put it behind the Edit window by **<CLICK>**ing on the Edit window or by pressing **<CTRL-E>**.

This window is the most convenient way to create your landscape. The painting icons are in effect with this map, as well. The trick is to paint slowly in this window. The broad strokes you use can be 10 miles long. It takes the system time to record these brush strokes.

Mousers and stickers can just **<CLICK>** and drag slowly to paint the terrain. Unfortunately, there is no convenient way to do this with the keyboard. Keyboard users may want to use the Create choice on the Terrain menu, and then make changes in the Edit window.

Menus

Menu names, you'll remember, appear across the top of the screen. Terrain Editor has System, Terrain, and Parameters menus. We review each in turn.

System Menu

Similar to the SimCity System menu, this menu displays choices for loading and saving your work, printing the city (terrain), and exiting the game. Remember to save your terrain often!

The following descriptions of the menu choices include both point (joystick or mouse) and keyboard instructions to select each choice. Remember, to **<SELECT>** you move the pointer to the specified word or icon and press the left button on the mouse or joystick or press the **<SPACE BAR>**.

About Terrain

 **<SELECT>** `SYSTEM`, **<SELECT>** `About TERRAIN`

 **<ALT-S><SELECT>** `About TERRAIN`

Because great software programs don't have opening credits (we don't know why not, they are works of art), the authors and artists include another way to let users know who they are. When you select this command in the MS-DOS 1.07 version of Terrain Editor, the screen displays six names, the copyright notice and year, and the address and phone number of the company, including the fax number. A version number could have been helpful.

Print

 **<SELECT>** `SYSTEM` **<SELECT>** `Print`

 **<ALT S><SELECT>** `Print`

Terrain Editor, like SimCity, prints your city to a compatible printer. You can print a one-page map or eight-page poster. The default selection is the one-page map. Change your mind, and you can cancel.

Starting Over

 **<SELECT>** `SYSTEM` **<SELECT>** `Start New City`

 **<ALT-S><SELECT>** `Start New City`

Choosing this menu selection creates a new, random city just like SimCity. If you want to start with a blank (dirt) area, use the Clear Map command.

When you choose Start New City, Terrain Editor ignores any Terrain Creation Parameters you may have set. The random generator uses 50% trees, 50% lakes, and 50% river curviness parameters. You may want to choose Start New City and then make changes to suit yourself.

Before letting you start over, the system does as if you want a new game. When you choose yes, you lose whatever you were working on. If you have something you want to save, use the Save City As... or Save City command before choosing Start New City.

Load a City

 **<SELECT>** `SYSTEM` **<SELECT>** `Load City`

<CTRL-L>

This command lets you load an existing city to rework the terrain. A pop-up box appears and works just like the one in the SimCity program. Review that material if you need help.

You can only work with the dirt, trees, and water. Of course, if you put trees on top of man-made structures, the structures disappear. After completing a bit of urban renewal, your first action in SimCity will be to reconnect zones if you knocked out a few in between. If you have a terrain you like, but forgot to save it before building, Terrain Editor allows you to Clear Unnatural Objects.

Save City (New Name)

 **<SELECT>** `SYSTEM` **<SELECT>** `Save City As...`

 **<SELECT>** `SYSTEM` **<SELECT>** `Save City As...`

If you are compulsive, you probably won't want to save one version of your city over the old version. Use the Save City As... command instead of the Save City command. Every time you save the city with this command, you can rename it. Each version of the city might be numbered, as in DAN01, DAN02, and so on. Then you can go back to the good old days by loading a previous version. Not that anyone would do this, mind you. Oh all right, some of us do.

Save Your City

 **<SELECT>** `SYSTEM` **<SELECT>** `Save City`

<CTRL-S>

Remember to save your efforts early and often. Even mousers and stickers should remember the keyboard command to save the current version of their city. As you have no doubt discovered by now, if you lose power to your computer system, you'll also lose any work you've completed since you last saved. Get into the habit of using the **<CTRL-S>** keys often. We try to save at least every 15 minutes.

Quitting

 **<SELECT>** `SYSTEM` **<SELECT>** `Exit`

<CTRL-X>

When you select this command, Terrain Editor asks if you're sure you want to exit. If you did not save your file before this step, you'll lose some work. Are you sure?

Terrain Menu

While the icons on the edge of the Edit window provide for the detail work, the Terrain menu choices affect the entire city. When you choose some of the Terrain menu commands, you can specify additional choices as well. You'll be able to clear the map, clear buildings and roads, and smooth the edges of the trees and water. You can also specify the amount of trees and lakes, and how curvy the river should be. Want to create your own island? You can do it with these menu commands.

Clean Off the Map

 **<SELECT>** `TERRAIN` **<SELECT>** `Clear Map`

<CTRL-C>

Be very careful with this command! There is no warning that you will lose anything that you have created. Press **<CTRL-C>**, and everything vanishes: trees, water, buildings, and roads. Use this only when you want to crumple up your "sheet of paper", throw it in the trash, and start over.

Clean Off the Buildings

<SELECT> `TERRAIN` **<SELECT>** `Clear Unnatural Objects`

 **<SELECT>** `TERRAIN` **<SELECT>** `Clear Unnatural Objects`

If you have a city terrain you really like but the Sims didn't, you can start over with the same land. Load the city file into Terrain Editor and select Clear Unnatural Objects to scrape everything down to the ground, Sims and all. We've noticed that shouting, "Take that, you twits!" enhances the pleasure of this command.

As with the Clear Map command, there is no warning that you will lose your work when you use this command. If you issue this command by mistake, just reload the old version of the city.

How Many Trees and Rivers?

 **<SELECT>** `TERRAIN` **<SELECT>** `Terrain Creation Parameters`

<CTRL-T>

This command is the most interesting of the Terrain Editor commands. With it, you can specify the number of trees, number of lakes, and the curviness of the river. (Actually, you specify percentages.) For example, by increasing the percentage of lakes, you have more lakeside property to zone as Residential, resulting in higher land value. The same applies to trees.

When you select this command, a pop-up box appears and displays the three variables, as shown in Figure 11.3. Below each variable are arrows pointing left and right. You can change the values by **<POINT>**ing to the arrow and pressing the **<SPACE BAR>** or left mouse or joystick button. The number changes as you hold down the key. (Remember, you can use the + key to hop from point to point in this or any menu box.) When you're ready to see the terrain changes a percentage provides, **<SELECT>** `GO`, press **<G>**, or press **<ENTER>**. The system will terraform your new landscape.

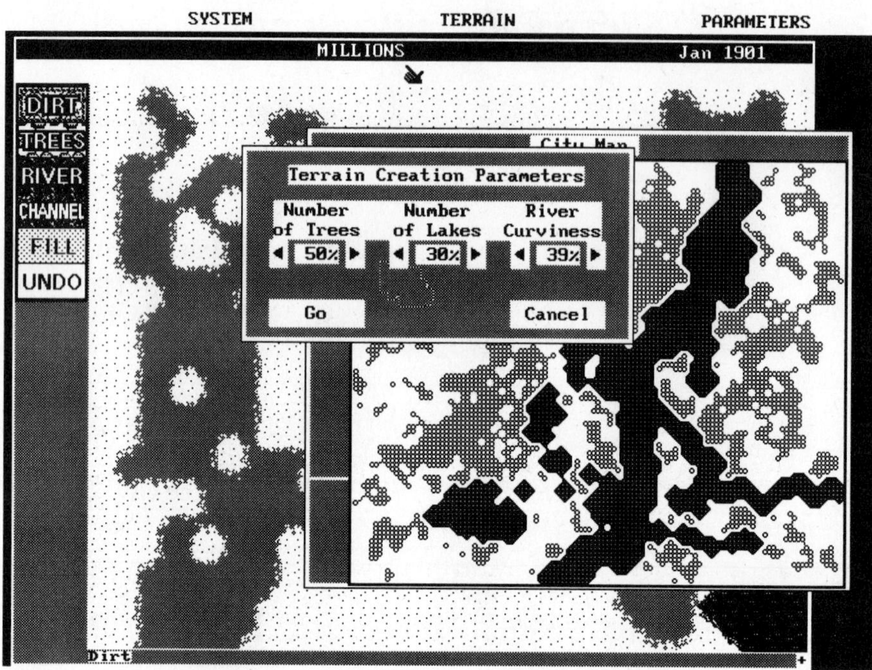

Figure 11.3 *The variables you can change when creating random terrain. These settings created the island shown in Figure 11.6.*

Notice again, the system does not warn you that you may be wiping out your previous efforts.

If you like curves, you can try 100% for the river setting. If you don't want a river at all, set this value to 0%. If you don't want trees, set the number of trees to 0%. And if you don't want lakes . . . well, you get the idea. Set them all to zero and you have a good start on boredom. Try getting the Sims to move into that!

Because we like trees, we tend to set this value at 80%. Lakes are nice but not necessary, so we use 30% here. A curvy river is harder to build on so we use 20% here.

Round the Edges

<SELECT> `TERRAIN` **<SELECT>** `Smooth Trees/Rivers/Everything`

<SELECT> `TERRAIN` **<SELECT>** `Smooth Trees/Rivers/Everything`
<CTRL-A> Smooths everything
<CTRL-R> Smooths rivers only

If you've designed your terrain by hand, you'll notice that the trees and lakes and rivers are pretty squarish. This might have something to do with the square "paintbrush." You can solve that problem with the Smooth commands. Figures 11.4 and 11.5 display the results of using the Smooth commands.

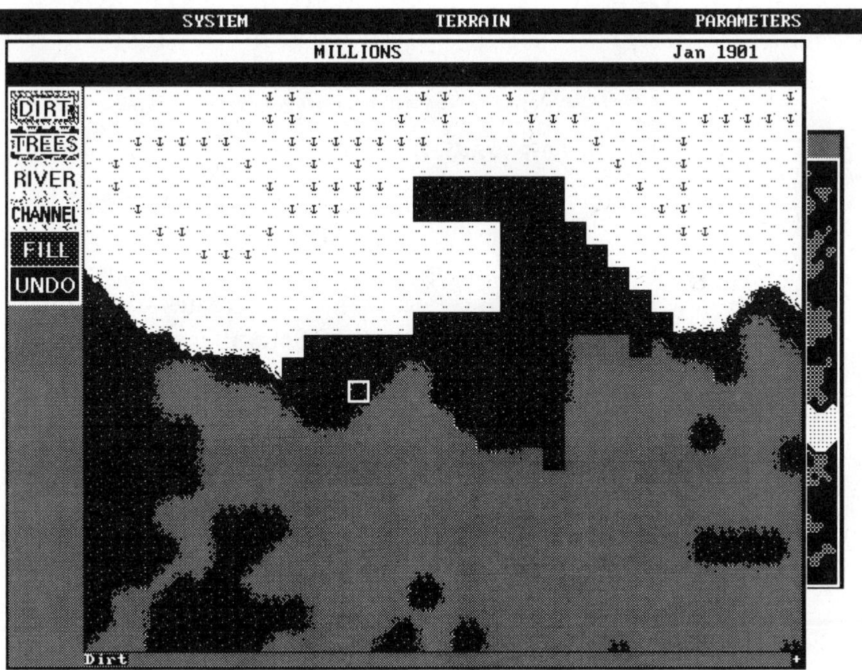

Figure 11.4 *Using Dirt to change the shoreline. Notice how the treeline is also squared off.*

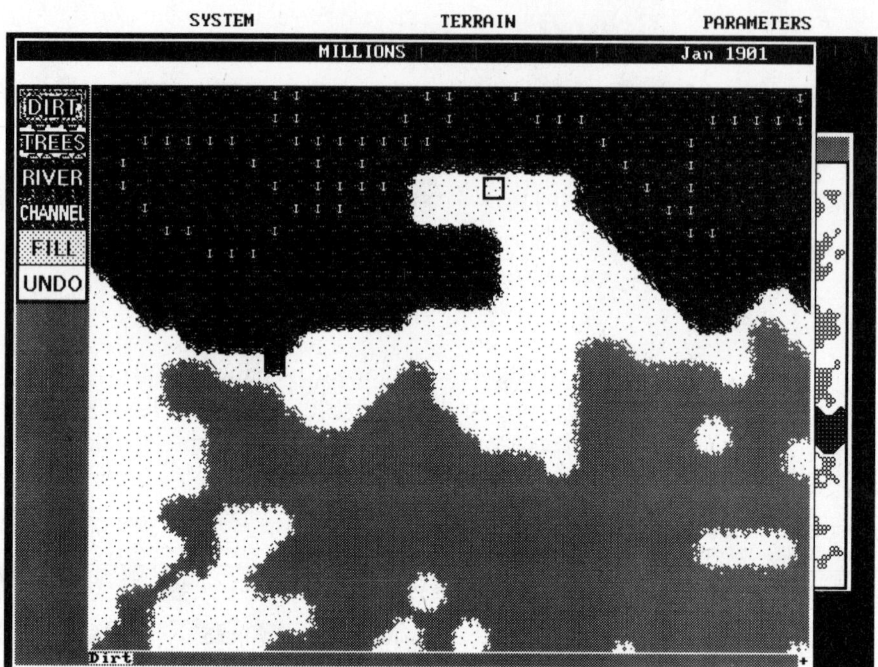

Figure 11.5 *The results of using the Smooth Everything menu choice.*

The menu choices include Smooth Trees, Smooth Rivers and Smooth Everything. Pointing to the Trees or Rivers (water) results in rounded edges for that item (those items?). It also creates shoreline (dirt) next to most of the water areas. Repeating the Smooth Everything command shifts the trees slightly but doesn't affect the water. Because we can't imagine a world with squarish trees *or* water, we always use Smooth Everything.

Simple Islands

 **<SELECT>** `TERRAIN` **<SELECT>** `Create Island`

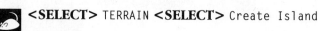

<CTRL-I>

Ever want to create an island paradise? This is your chance. The Create Island menu choice is a toggle. Choose it the first time, and a marker appears at the left edge of the word. This indicates that the next time you use Create Random Terrain, Terrain Editor produces an island similar to the one shown in Figure 11.6. This toggle stays on until you make that choice again to turn it off.

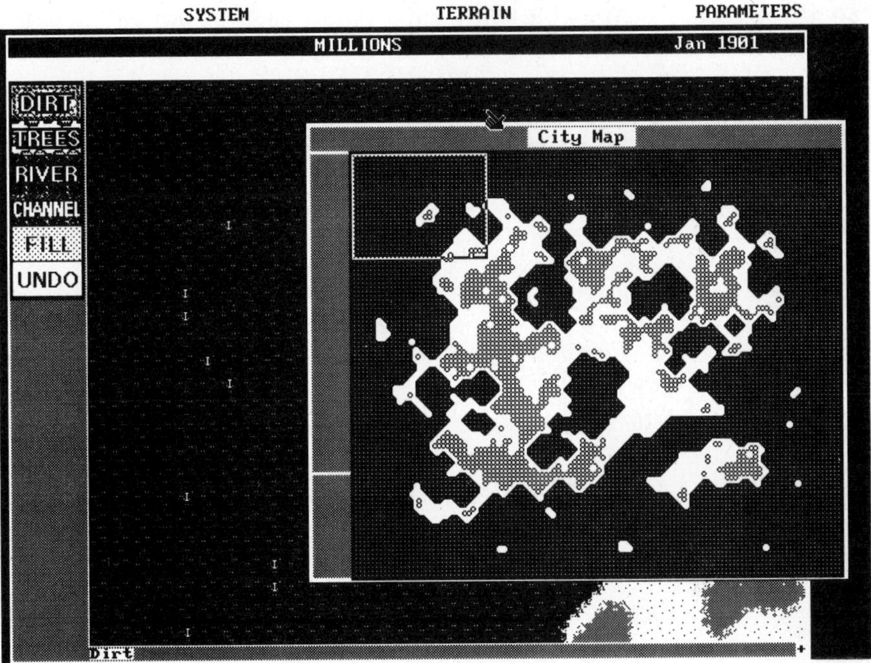

Figure 11.6 *The island that results from using the settings in Figure 11.3, and selecting Create Island. The Number of Lakes could have been set lower and the River Curviness set to 0% for more land in the island.*

Be careful here with the number of lakes and river curviness. If you set over 20% lakes, you will lose an awful lot of your island. Because you will have plenty of beachfront property to sell, you may not even need a river. Set the river curviness to 0%. If you do want a river, try something around 50%, and the river will cut through your island. More or less than 50%, and the river winds in and back out, on one edge of the island.

Parameters Menu

The Parameters menu can take years off your city, allow you to change the name and game play level of the city, and turn the sound off. You can make these changes to a city at any point with Terrain Editor. (The MS-DOS version has problems with the commands on this menu. Read the next few sections carefully if you have that version.)

Rename and Change the Game Play Level

 **<SELECT>** `PARAMETERS` **<SELECT>** `Name & Level`

 **<ALT-P><SELECT>** `Name & Level`

Making this choice brings up a familiar screen with which you can rename the current file. Notice that, as when you create a city, you may type more than eight characters, but MS-DOS only recognizes the first eight. (Some systems allow more characters.) Terrain Editor also allows spaces in the city name. While you can call up that city file by pointing to it, a space in the first eight characters of a city name might cause problems for the DOS operating system.

When you start a new city, the most noticeable difference between the Game Play Levels is the funding. The Easy level provides $20,000. The Medium level provides $10,000, while the Hard level provides only $5,000. Once you have established your city, you can use this command to increase the difficulty level. The scaling constant (a factor used in the simulation formulas) changes when you use Terrain Editor to adjust the Game Play Level. The Sims become more difficult to manage, but you can get a higher score by changing to a tougher level.

We found a bug in the MS-DOS version of Terrain Editor. When you use the Name & Level command to change the Game Play Level, the funding *returns* to the beginning amount for the level you select. (Hey, this might be good if your city's about to go broke!) And when you reload the city in SimCity, the Evaluation window still shows the previous level. Maxis Software is aware of this "bug," but has not had a chance revise this version of Terrain Editor. You'll encounter a similar problem if you try to change the game year using Terrain Editor's MS-DOS version.

Game Year

 **<SELECT>** `PARAMETERS` **<SELECT>** `Game Year`

 **<ALT-P><SELECT>** `Game Year`

You may have a very successful city. Part of that success may be due to your willingness to let your computer run overnight to generate lots of tax revenue. This technique ages your city, perhaps prematurely in your view. You can rejuvenate a city by resetting the game year with the Game Year command on the Parameters menu.

Another bug in the MS-DOS version of Terrain Editor makes resetting the year produce unpredictable results. We've reset the year to 1900 and ended up in -1000. (Is that B.C.?) Making another change resulted in a positive year. We had no idea how old the city really was. Before you try to issue the Game Year command, save any changes using the Save City As... command so you don't end up with a messed up city year (or funds).

Sound

 **<SELECT>** `PARAMETERS` **<SELECT>** `Sound on/off`

 **<ALT-P><SELECT>** `Sound on/off`

When you create a city in SimCity, you may turn the sound on or off. This menu choice in Terrain Editor toggles that setting on and off. When the menu choice indicates Sound is off, selecting the command turns the sound on and returns you to the main screen. Select the command again, and the sound will be off. Use **<ESC>** if you don't want to make any changes.

While this feature seems to be a minor one, it may prove useful if you bring a city file to work and want to make sure you don't have monster or tornado noises immediately upon starting a city. (You wouldn't think of letting a city grow on your computer at lunch time, would you?)

Icons

The icons appear on the edge of the Edit window. While the SimCity icons are just icons (little pictures), Terrain Editor uses words as well. This may be because it is difficult to create a Dirt icon which looks decidedly different from a Tree icon on a monochrome screen.

Activate all Terrain Editor icons by **<CLICK>** ing on the icon or typing the first letter of that icon name. Notice that the border around the active (selected) icon changes to dashed lines.

Dirt

What can you say about dirt? In Terrain Editor, all you get is Dirt. The groundwork begins on Dirt. If you were too enthusiastic with the Tree or Water icon, use the Dirt icon to "erase" trees or water.

You can place tiles with the Dirt icon, as well as the Tree and River icons, over any other terrain or man-made object. Regardless of which icon you've selected, the right mouse button places a dirt tile on-screen.

Trees

Ah, you can have shady, cool trees—lots of them, if you like. You *will* like them because the Sims like them. Leave plenty of trees into which you can drop Residential zones. We like to select Trees, and then use the Fill command (noted later), to create a completely tree-covered terrain. It does cost to bulldoze trees, while you can zone directly on dirt. Plan ahead, and you can save the cost of clearing off trees you discover you didn't really need.

River

This icon might more accurately be labeled "Water." (The word WATER appears at the bottom of the screen when this icon is active.) With this icon active, **<CLICK>**ing or pressing **<SPACE BAR>** places a square of water. You may create a river by drawing a waterway from end to end, or just create lakes. The Sims love water. The more you create, the more waterfront (high value) property you'll have.

Channel

Any water that reaches the edge of the map can carry a ship. The ship can only travel in a channel you designate with the Channel icon. When you create a terrain with rivers, they contain channels, indicated by small ship anchors. (Anchors also appear randomly in lakes.) You can only see anchors in Terrain Editor.

If you create your own river and expect to have a seaport, you'll have to create a channel which attaches to one or both river ends at the edge of the map. This is where the ship will travel, bringing commerce and prosperity to SimCity.

Place the channel markers in a continuous line near the center of the waterway. Locate the channel too close to land, and you might have a shipwreck. (He, he!) Erase channel markers by placing water tiles over them.

Fill

The Fill icon works with the Dirt, Tree, and River icons. When you select Fill, it covers an area with the selected terrain type. Fill saves a lot of time, especially if you use it as follows:

1. Select the icon for the type of terrain you want to create.
2. Draw an outline of the area you want to fill using the Map or Edit window. Make sure the outline is completely closed.

3. Select the Fill icon.
4. **<CLICK>** in the middle of the area you have outlined, or move the pointer there and press **<SPACE BAR>**.
5. Watch carefully as the Fill takes place, noting where on the outline the Fill spilled out. (It usually takes one or two tries to create a leak-proof outline.)
6. If the Fill goes out-of-bounds, select the Undo icon.
7. Move to the area which leaked, and repair the outline.
8. Return to Step 3.

Undo

Selecting the Undo icon reverses the last operation. You'll use Undo most after unsuccessful Fill attempts. If you select the Undo icon after laying tiles of Dirt, Trees, or Water, it just removes the last tile. Undo also returns terrain to the "square look" after a smoothing operation.

Graphic Sets

SimCity can be divided into three areas for consideration. The first, and most critical, is the set of rules used for the simulation. These rules determine how the program runs and how each change made affects all the other changes.

The second area to consider is the *user interface*. (This is a computerese way of saying "how the user tells the program what to do.") The user interface is how you save the city file, select icons, and create zones. In many programs, the structure is rigid, allowing only responses to specific questions. SimCity asks an open-ended question: How will you design your city? The keyboard, joystick, or mouse actions you make answer that question. The simulation tests your answer against its rules. Growth or atrophy are the programmed responses.

The final and most colorful area to consider is the *graphic images* used to represent the elements of a city. SimCity's designers could have used a big PP in the middle of a square to represent a power plant. Or roads could have been strings of RRRRRs. (What would railroads have been?) The pictures that represent the game elements are *graphics sets*. You can change the pictures without changing the simulation rules or user interface.

We've explained all this to provide a perspective on the use of the graphics sets. They provide a pleasant diversion, allowing a true change of scenery in the middle of an intense building session. While they are interesting to look at, and listen to, the graphics sets do not affect the SimCity rules.

The "noisy" part of each graphics set may or may not interest you. The graphics files do contain new sounds to go with the new images. The sounds in the Classic (original SimCity) graphics set are not particularly impressive in the MS-DOS version, and are not that much better in these MS-DOS graphics sets. In the following information, we do not give details about the sounds with the various graphics sets, because we pay attention to the sounds only long enough to turn them off.

We had an opportunity to preview the two graphics sets available for the MS-DOS version of SimCity. While we take you on a tour of these new views of SimCity, keep in mind that Maxis might throw some changes into the final release versions.

Installation

To install the graphics sets we saw, you use an installation program that's new, and much slicker than the one provided with SimCity. Also included with the graphics sets is a SETTINGS program which allows you to change the SimCity configuration (joystick, mouse, etc.) without using the original installation disks.

When we used the graphics set installation program, it made changes to SimCity which allow the simulation to use the alternate images. It also copied specific files from the disks for each of the graphics sets to the hard disk. When we changed the display type, it loaded more files to the hard disk. With the multiple graphics sets, the SimCity program may take several megabytes of hard disk space.

When our SimCity starts now, it notes on the screen that it is loading the graphics image. Once loaded, the last-used graphics is active for a new city, saved city, or scenario. A new choice on the System menu allows changes to the graphics anytime during the session.

Figure 11.7 shows a city with the normal (*Classic*) SimCity graphics set. The city includes an airport in the upper left corner, a stadium next to the airport, and a coal power plant at the lower right. Water is dark in this figure. Trees are gray. The next several figures will show the same city displayed with different graphics sets. Not all the elements will be the same in each picture. For example, Figure 11.7 includes a plane over the water and other figures may not.

Graphics Set #1

This set of replacement city graphics sets looks to the past with *Wild West*, *Ancient Asia*, and *Medieval Times*. In addition to the changes in the city graphics, these graphics files change some of the Edit window icons to reflect "new" functions. For example, power lines become waterways (canals). Table 11.1 lists the icons in the Classic graphics set, and the changes made by each of the other graphics sets in this group.

Table 11.1 Graphics Set #1 icon variations.

Classic	*Asia*	*Wild West*	*Medieval*
Bulldozer	Plow	Plow	Plow
Road	Road	Road	Path
Power Line	Waterway	Waterway	Waterway
Rail	Rickshaw Path	Stage Coach	Road
Park	Park	Park	Park
Residential	Residential	Residential	Residential
Commericial	Commercial	Commercial	Commercial
Industrial	Industrial	Industrial	Industrial

Continues

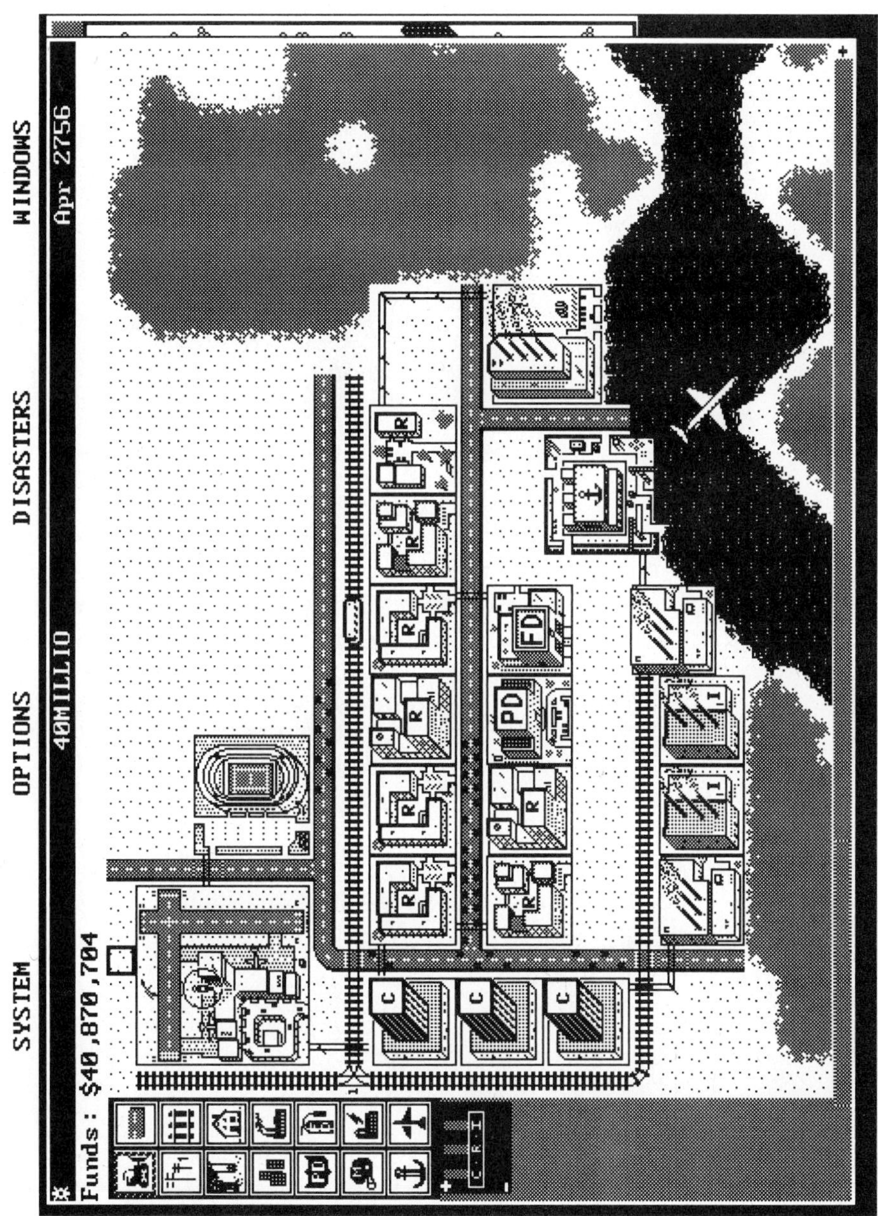

Figure 11.7 *The basic Classic graphics set city for comparison with the new graphics set pictures in this chapter's remaining figures.*

Table 11.1 *Continued*

Classic	*Asia*	*Wild West*	*Medieval*
Police	Police	Sheriff	Castle Guard
Fire	Fire	Fire	Fire
Stadium	Sumo Arena	Rodeo	Jousting
Power-Coal	Well	Water Wheel	Well
Power-Nuclear	Waterwheel	Steam Pump	Waterwheel
Seaport	Harbor	Harbor	Harbor
Airport	Palace	Gold Mine	Castle

Not only do you get new buildings to look at, the Disasters are more appropriate for the new eras, as noted in Table 11.2. Each character set has its own types of disasters with appropriate changes in the graphics. Note that the disasters all behave the same way, regardless of their appearance. Note also the timeless quality of a good earthquake.

Table 11.2 Graphics Set #1 disaster variations.

Classic	*Asia*	*Wild West*	*Medieval*
Fire	Fire	Fire	Fire
Flood	Tsunami	Flood	Flood
Plane Crash	Dragon Blast	Balloon Crash	Dragon Blast
Tornado	Typhoon	Twister	Tornado
Earthquake	Earthquake	Earthquake	Earthquake
Monster	Monster	Tumbleweed	Monster

Ancient Asia

Combining elements of Japanese and Chinese culture, this graphics set bases its transportation on water ways and rickshaw paths. The Sims are humble in this set, addressing you as "Master". The airport becomes a palace, and the traffic helicopter, a kite. The kite does still circle over all the peasants congregating on the paths. In Figure 11.8, a monster has begun to wreak havoc on the locals, and appears headed for the palace—must be a source of heavy pollution.

Wild West

A Gold Mine is the motherlode of the Wild West graphics set. Just like an airport, it costs $10,000. Take a stage coach to travel to the rodeo. You just might ask the sheriff if the giant tumbleweed did much damage the other day. Too bad the power source couldn't have been buffalo chips.

Medieval Times

A witch and a griffin keep watch over the Medieval city, shown in Figure 11.9. The witch circles the heavy traffic on the paths, while the griffin launches itself from the castle. The fire department better have access to the roads when it has to put out the dragon blast disaster, otherwise the Medieval fire fighters have to walk to the fire on the paths. Even though the citizens call you "Sire," they still let you know what they need to make them happy.

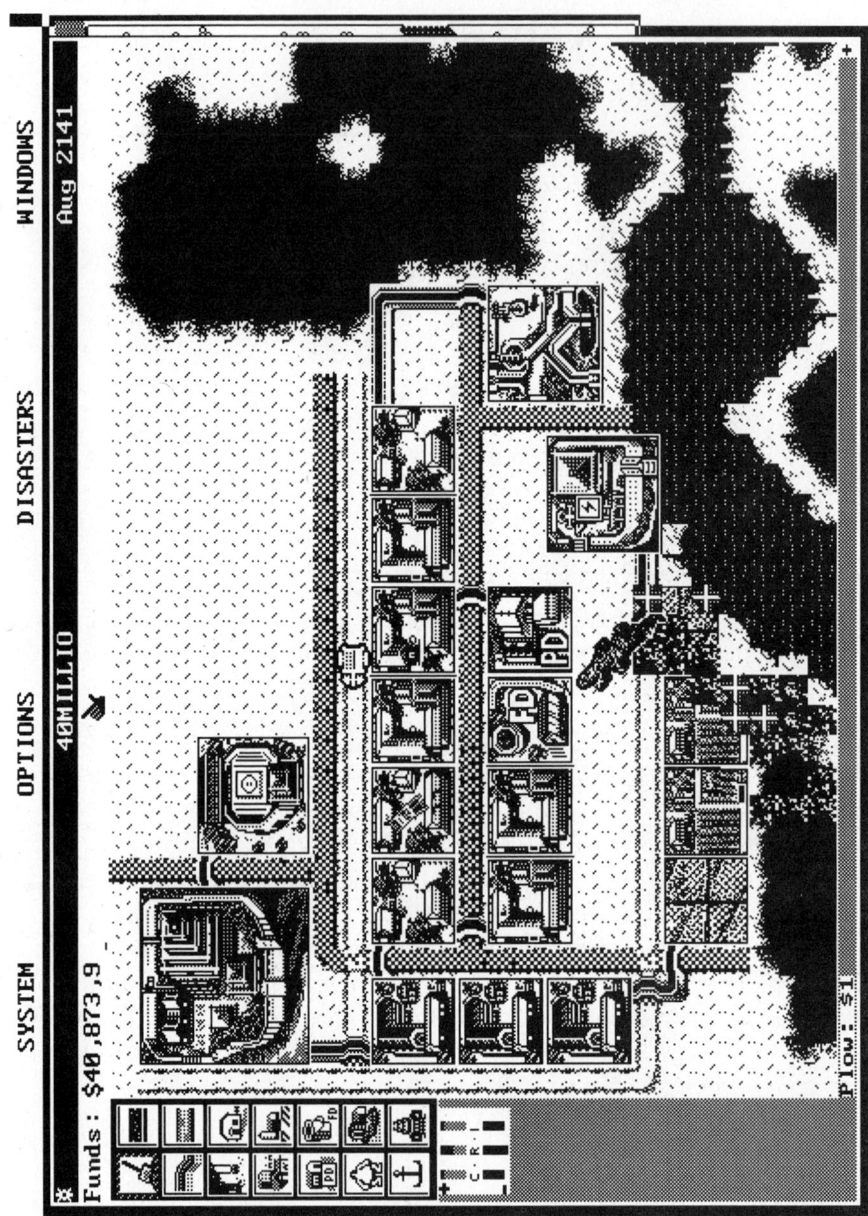

Figure 11.8 *An Asian SimCity. At least the Sumo Arena is close to the Palace.*

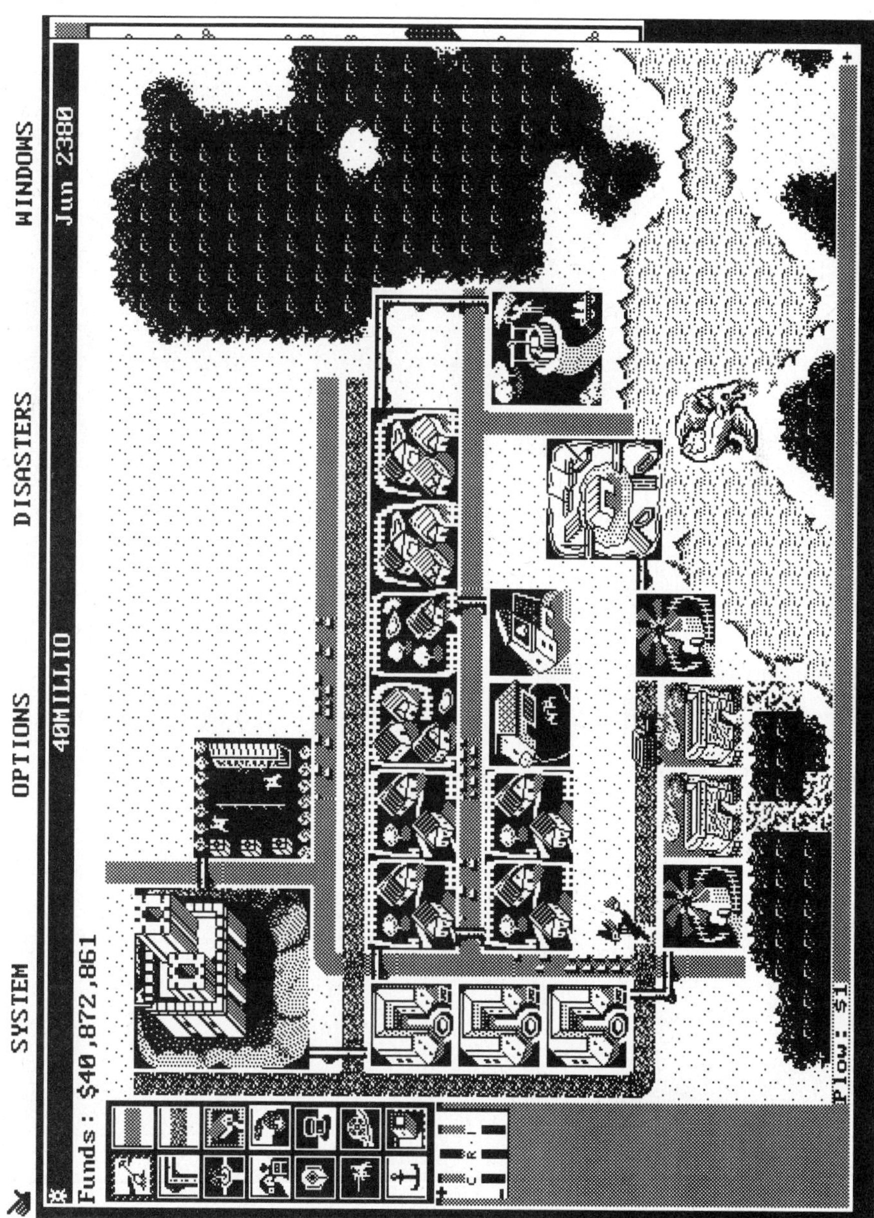

Figure 11.9 *A Medieval view of our little city worth over 40 million dollars. Notice the jousting stadium next to the castle and the witch watching weary workers walk the path.*

Graphics Set #2

This set of replacement city graphics focuses on the future, with *Future USA*, *Future Europe*, and *Moon Colony*. These sets change the icons, too. Table 11.3 shows the changes included with these graphic sets.

Table 11.3 Graphics Set #2 icon variations.

Classic	*Future USA*	*Future Europe*	*Moon Colony*
Bulldozer	Disintegrator	Disintegrator	'Dozer
Road	Transport Tube	Road	Road
Power Line	Power Line	Power Line	Power Line
Rail	Mag-Rail	Monorail	Rails
Park	Park	Park	Park
Residential	Residential	Residential	Residential
Commericial	Commericial	Commercial	Commercial
Industrial	Industrial	Industrial	Industrial
Police	Police	Metropol Station	Moon Patrol
Fire	Fire	Fire	Fire
Stadium	Laser-Bot	3-D Soccer	Low-G Rec Center
Power-Coal	Fission	Fission	Nuclear
Power-Nuclear	Fusion	Fusion	Gravity Wave
Seaport	Hovercraft	Hovercraft	Rover Port
Airport	Space Port	Space Port	Shuttle Port

Disasters are not as different with this set. The only changes are in the Moon Colony. Table 11.4 shows the different disasters which can occur on the Moon.

Table 11.4 Graphics Set #2 disaster variations.

Classic	*Moon Colony*
Fire	Fire
Flood	Acidic Mold
Plane Crash	Shuttle Crash
Tornado	Meteor Shower
Earthquake	MOONquake
Monster	Monster

Future USA

The basic power source of the Future USA set is fission. The high-level power source is fusion. Still, at the $3,000 and $5,000 prices, these power sources are a bargain. Citizens of the future use transport tubes and mag-rails for transportation, as shown in Figure 11.10. They clear their land and zones with a disintegrator instead of a bulldozer.

Recreation time calls for a rousing game of Laser-Bot, score Phzzts 7.036 to Clicks 2.2e3. (Put 100 credits on the Clicks. They always come from behind.) And if you thought there was nothing as fast as Fastest, the Future USA Sims have other ideas. Their speeds start at Yawn and move through So So to Zooming to Ultra, the fastest.

Future Europe

Definitely international in flavor, Future Europe Sims make their needs know politely in several languages, with "s'il vous plait" and "bitte" at the end of their requests. (For some strange reason, Future USA Sims still make "demands" instead of requests.) Future Europe must not be as far in the future as Future USA. While the Future EuroSims still use roads (see Figure 11.11), at least they do use a monorail for volume transportation.

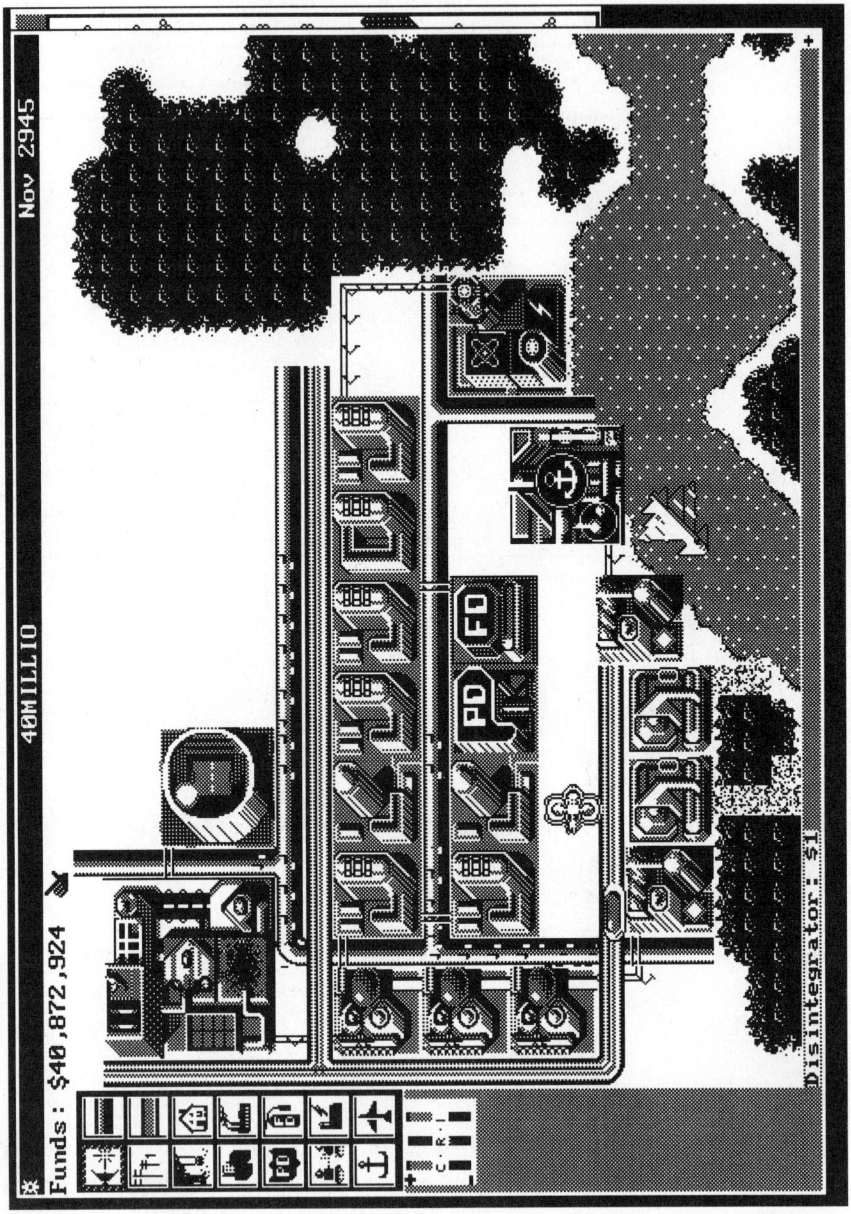

Figure 11.10 Future USA action graphics. Notice the traffic Hovercraft flying away from the transport tube.

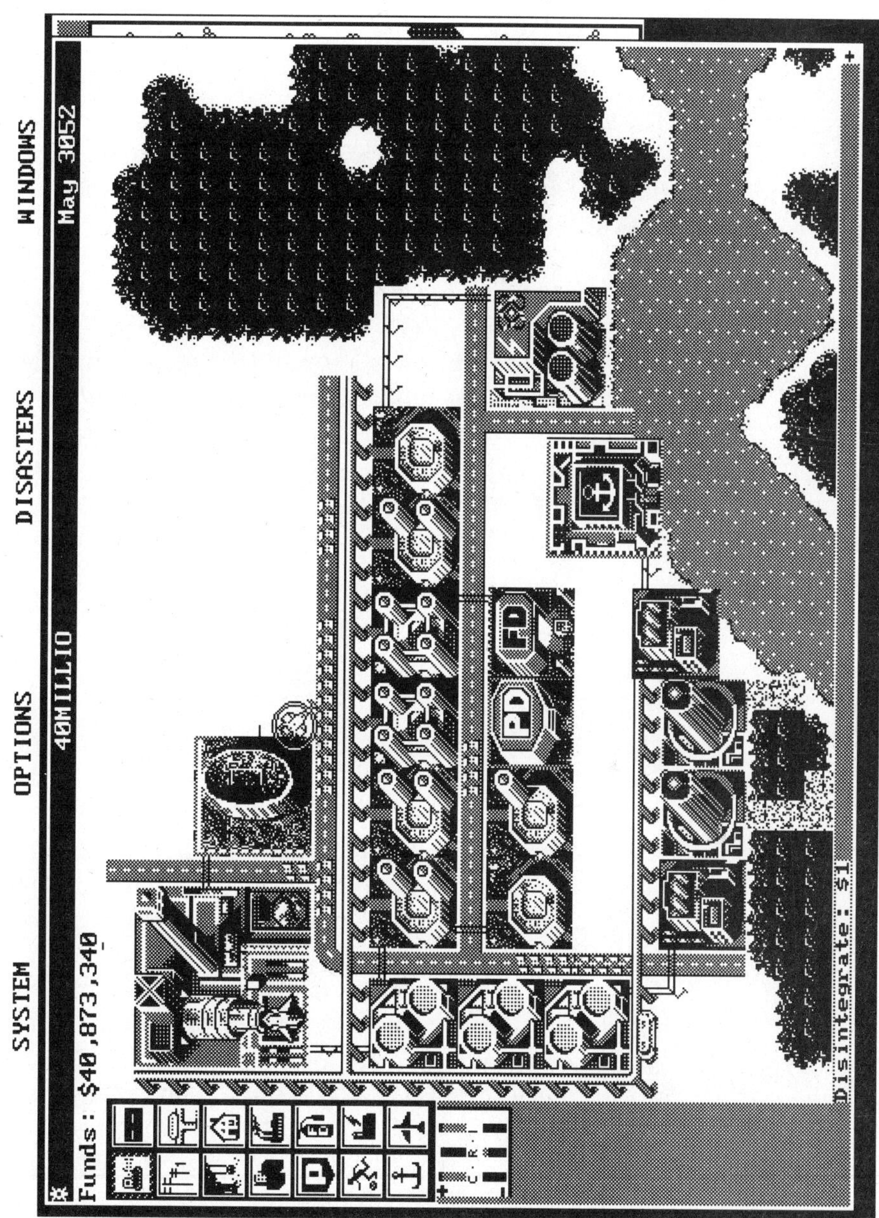

Figure 11.11 *Future Europe, including the monorail mass-transport system. Watch closely for the ball to come your way in their 3-D Soccer stadium.*

Moon Colony

The lack of atmosphere in this set sort of sucks the wind out of how SimCity operates. On the Moon, water becomes pools of dust, which look rather dark in Figure 11.12. Sims live in domes rather than buildings and have to deal with craters instead of trees. They enjoy recreation in a Low-G Center. The MoonSims must like looking out over the craters and dust pools. Residential zones are worth more in these locations.

The MoonSim disasters present some delightful differences. They must contend with new acidic molds, shuttle crashes, and meteor showers. The monster has a rather alien look, too. The ever-popular and timeless earthquake becomes a MOONquake. Imagine that. We can't quite figure out how the fires spread in the vacuum of space, but what do you want, good graphics or good sense?

To Buy, or Not to Buy

These SimCity extras are just that, extra. Except for Commodore and color Mac users, Terrain Editor costs extra. For the serious SimCity user, we can't imagine creating cities without the ability to rework the terrain. We look forward to trying even more variations in our cities once the Game Play Level and Game Year command bugs are fixed in the MS-DOS version.

The Graphics Sets are not quite as compelling as Terrain Editor. Because you learn to "read" a city with the Classic graphics set, you must relearn all the images in the different sets to understand what is happening in your city. They are interesting to look at, but we returned to the originals very quickly. There are new sounds with each set. If hearing a different type of monster scream is of interest, there may be something here for you.

The most significant element we saw in the pre-release set of graphics was the new SETTINGS program. This software greatly simplifies making changes to the SimCity program. Because we were constantly changing settings while we wrote this book, using the SETTINGS program saved us a lot of time. We hope Maxis includes the new version of the installation program and the SETTINGS programs with the new releases of SimCity.

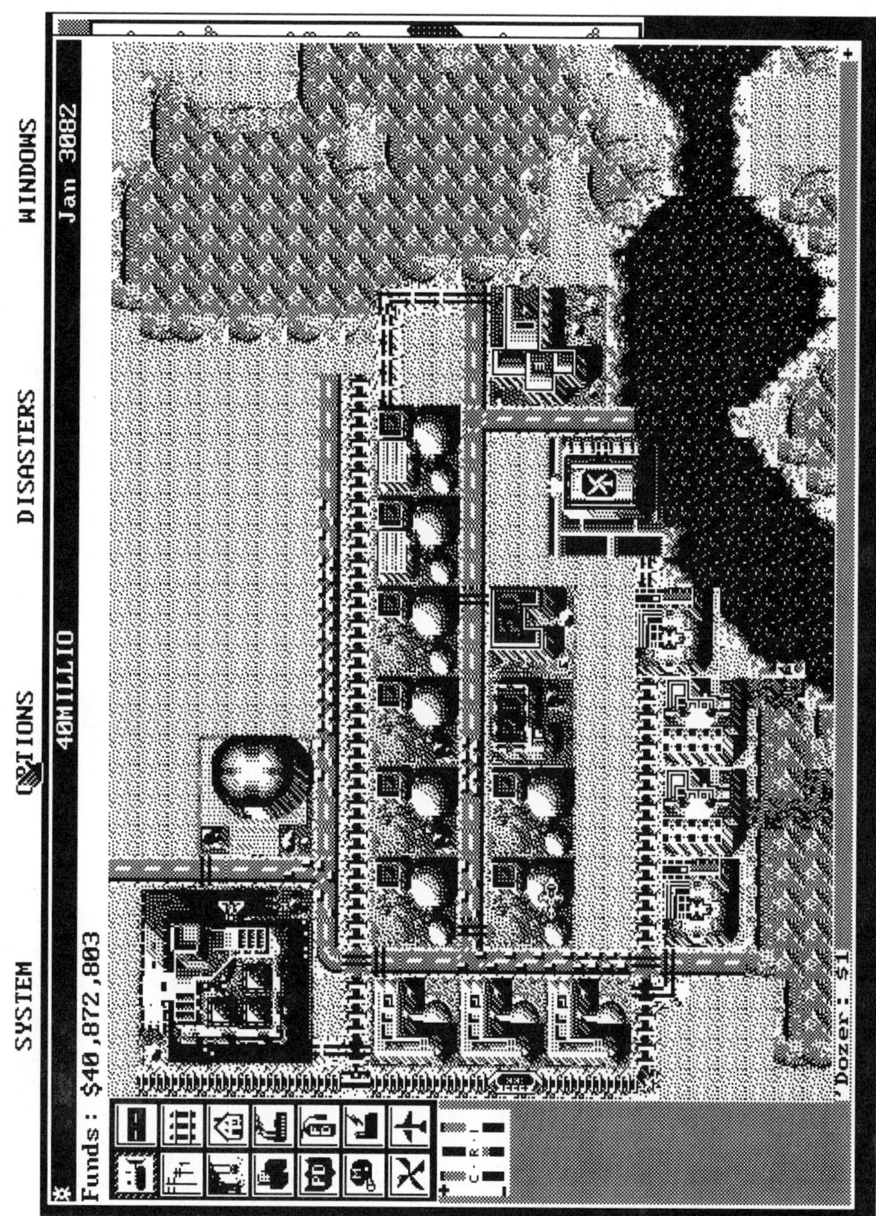

Figure 11.12 *Dark dust pools and medium gray craters. Many of the Residentials are domed as well.*

12 SimCity Quick Reference

Air Quality	See: *Pollution*
Air Crash	Typically happens near airport Causes fires Build Fire Department adjacent to contain crash fires
Airport	$10,000 to build an airport Build only when city growth levels off Build near water and/or city edge Airplanes can crash if Disasters are enabled Helicopter reports heavy traffic constantly High pollution area
Animate All	Toggle switch in Options menu Mark next to it indicates that it is on Leaving it off speeds up the simulation Not saved with city file See also: *Speed*, *Time Lag*

Assessed Value
: Value of the city-owned property, (not owned by the Sims)
: Displayed in the Maps Evaluation window

Auto-Budget
: Choice on the Options menu
: Mark next to it indicates it is on
: Automatically collects taxes and funds
: Manually make adjustments to budget if needed
: Use only with a positive "cash flow"
: See also: *Budget*, *Cash Flow*

Auto-Bulldoze
: Choice on the Options menu
: Mark next to it indicates that it is enabled
: Allows building without bulldozing every tile
: Clears all natural objects
: Still costs $1 per tile when used
: See also: *Bulldoze*

Auto-Goto
: Choice in the Options menu
: Mark next to it indicates that it is enabled
: Automatically moves Edit window to event
: Use **<TAB>** to move to event and return instead
: See also: *Goto*

Bern
: The scenario with a traffic problem

Boston
: The scenario with a nuclear meltdown

Bridges
: $50 per tile over water
: Straight line only
: See also: *Roads*

Budget
: Taxes collected yearly and the bills paid
: Watch your cash flow carefully
: City Services grace period until Jan., when city loaded
: Unlike real world—deficits not allowed
: 5% to 7% best tax rate
: Population over 200,000 lower for better growth
: See also: *Auto-Budget*, *Taxes*, *Cash Flow*

Bulldoze
: $1 to bulldoze each tile
: All terrain must be bulldozed except open land

	Turn on the Auto-Bulldoze for speed Use the right mouse or joystick button Can't undo a bulldoze action, so be careful Use to create a fire break around a fire Bulldoze burned zone tiles to regenerate Bulldoze center tile of zone to clear entire zone See also: *Auto-Bulldoze*, *Fire Break*
Cash Flow	Taxes remaining after all funds paid Cut the funding levels for better cash flow (Other problems will result from this, though) City cannot survive without a positive cash flow See also: *Budget*
Categories	Based on population Automatically reported with growth Village — 0 to 999 Town — 2,000 to 9,999 City — 10,000 to 49,999 Capital — 50,000 to 99,999 Metropolis — 100,000 to 499,999 Megalopolis — 500,000 and up Ghost town — Simless
CGA	PC-compatible monitor SimCity shows up in chunky black and white only
Church	A public building in Residential zones Appears automatically Bulldozing causes the wrath of God (tornado)
City Center	Center of your SimEarth city High land values and easy access to surrounding areas Mainly contains Commercial zones as the city grows Avoid Industrial zones nearby, or land values will plummet
City Dynamics Chart	Supplied in software box Shows plus and minus areas of influence

Reference Card	Supplied in software box Shows built-up zone values
City Form Map Window	Displays the entire city Use to plan the initial layout of your city Letters on the map: A = Airplane H = Helicopter M = Monster R = Railroad S = Ship T = Tornado
City Services	The police and fire departments You set the funding in the Budget window See also: *Budget*, *Police Stations*, *Fire Stations*
Clear Land	Open areas on city map (dirt) Need not be bulldozed
Coal Power Plant	$3000 to build Supplies power to about 50 zones Causes major pollution No yearly funding See also: *Nuclear Power Plant*
Commercial Zones	Cost $100 each Place near Residential zones and city center for highest land value Placing near Industrial zones lowers value Slowest to develop
Copy Protection	Encourages honesty: one owner, one player Red copy protection sheet with city name or population Question asked at the start of a SimCity session Three improper responses bring nonstop disasters
Covox Sound Master Board	Optional sound board for MS-DOS computers Reproduces the sounds better than the internal speaker Cute at first, but gets old quick See also: *Sound*

Crime Alert	Warning: Reduce the crime level
Crime Rate Map	Shows the intensity of crime in the city Use this map after a Crime Alert Use before building a police station Industrial zones have the most problems with crime See also: *Crime Alert*, *Police Stations*
Demand Indicator	Located in the Edit window Bar graph indicates zones in demand The time it takes for Sims to fill empty zones is a better demand gauge
Density Key	Used in some of the maps to show what varying display intensity means Hard to see without a color monitor
Detroit	The scenario with a high crime rate
Disasters	Enabled/disabled in the Disaster menu Save your city before you start a disaster Simulation starts with Disasters enabled Turn Disasters off immediately after loading a city See also: *Earthquake*, *Tornado*, *Flood*, *Monster*, *Air Crash*, *Fire*
Dullsville	The scenario with no (yawn) excitement
Earthquake	Very powerful, very destructive, 8.0 Richter scale Fires after 'quake cause the most destruction Use fire breaks to minimize the damage Can build fire stations immediately to help Try not to be on 10th floor when it hits
Edit window	Main window for zoning, building and observation
EGA	PC-compatible monitor SimCity shows up in 16 colors
Embezzling	Just what it says: more funding by cheating Type `FUND` in all capital letters to get $10,000 After three "collections," a *major* earthquake occurs Allows a maximum of $80,000

ESC key	Key to press when in doubt about menu or icon action
Evaluation Window	Located under Maps menu Shows city ratings, Overall City Score and Sims' complaints See also: *Public Opinion*, *Statistics*, *Overall City Score*
External Market	Economic conditions outside the city Completely determined by the simulation Does vary during city growth
Factors	Used by the simulation to determine the city score *Major:* city growth rate, crime, fire protection, housing costs, pollution, taxes, traffic, unemployment, unpowered zones *Minor*: bad attitude, burning fires, city service funding, not building airport, not building seaport, not building stadium
Fire	Caused by explosions and disasters Have good fire coverage to quickly extinguishes fires Can do serious damage Spreads quickly through forest and buildings See also: *Fire Stations*
Fire Break	Bulldozed area around fire Necessary if insufficient fire coverage Helpful after earthquakes and bombings
Fire Protection Map	Click on the City Form icon after selecting Maps from the Window menu, then select `Fire` Shows the fire protection area from each station Use to determine where to build more stations Overlapping areas cost more without benefits Amount of funding affects the coverage of each station
Fire Stations	Cost $500 to build $100 per year to maintain at the full funding level

	Good coverage increases land values Essential for disaster recovery See also: *City Services*
Flood	Slow spread of water in the areas on the shoreline Bulldoze shorelines to reduce heavy flooding
Forest	Green or dark area on map represents trees Must be bulldozed prior to zoning See also: *Auto-Bulldoze*
Fountains	Randomly appear as you build parks About every fifth park is a fountain Can build and destroy a park until fountain appears Use right then left mouse or joystick buttons until fountain appears
Frequent Animation	Toggle switch in the Options menu Mark next to it indicates it's on Controls movement on the screen Turning it off increases speed of simulation Setting not saved with city file See also: *Speed*, *Time Lag*
Funds	Displayed on the message bar Keep a positive cash flow so funds don't run out Run out of funds, and the Sims leave (fair-weather friends) See also: *Budget*, *Cash Flow*, *Embezzling*
Game Play Level	Selected at the start of a new city Changed only with Terrain Editor Three levels of difficulty and funding Easy $20,000 Medium $10,000 Hard $5,000 Hard is really difficult
Ghost Town	Sims' way of expressing dissatisfaction with the mayor

Goto	Located on the message bar Assist in locating problems and disasters **<CLICK>** on the Goto button to jump to the problem area **<TAB>** key also jumps **<TAB>** again to return to original location Can waste time following every traffic problem Useful when you *want* to locate roaming disasters See also: *Auto-Goto*
Graphics Sets	Extra disks with alternative settings for SimCity See also: Chapter 11
Graphs	Located in Maps window Show the changes in 10- or 120-year statistics View the populations for each of the types of zones View crime rate, pollution level, and cash flow Difficult to use unless seen on a color monitor With monochrome, view each item separately
Hamburg	The scenario bombed by the allies in WWII
Heavy Traffic	Turn off the sound when you're tired of the traffic reports See also: *Traffic*, *Helicopter*, *Airport*
Hospitals	Buildings created by the Sims in Residential zones Bulldozing may affect land values and is definitely rude
Housing Costs	Complaint in the evaluation window If all housing is expensive, Sims will complain Place Residential zones in low value areas near Industrial zones, away from city center, and complaints will subside
Icons	Tools used in various windows Enables building or zoning according to the selected tool If dimmed, there are not enough funds to use the icon

Industrial Zones	Cost $100 Zone on the edge of the city to spread pollution over edge Will always have a high crime rate Will lower the surrounding land values
Internal Market	Internal production for goods consumed by the Sims Food stores, gas stations, retail stores, etc. Grows slowly at first, becomes larger as city grows See also: *Commercial Zones*
Island	Created using Terrain Editor Randomly produced by SimCity when terraforming a new city See also: *Terrain Editor*, *Terraforming*
Island, Small	Avoid building on one unless the tax base justifies a bridge Forget rail access (tunnels are expensive)
Joystick	Steers small airplanes and jets Computer pointing device
Key to the City	What you win when you successfully complete a scenario
Keyboard	Necessary for typing in city names Also necessary for answering the copy protection question You can play SimCity with just the keyboard The Keyboard Reference Chart is essential in this case
Land Value Map	Select the City Form icon on the Maps window Shows the land values in your city Use to find profitable areas to zone Values based on terrain, accessibility, pollution, and distance to downtown
Landfill	Bulldozed areas along the shoreline One tile out into the water

Mass Transit	This is the railroad system Best transportation system in SimCity Only one SimEarth train visible at a time
Marina	See *Seaport*
MCGA	IBM PS/2 Model 25 and 30 screens Displays in black and white Special edition for color available from Maxis software
Megalopolis	500,000 or more Sims Usually ugly See also: *Categories*
Message Bar	Underneath city name in the Edit window Messages from the Sims and the simulation program Some messages can be ignored such as `More roads required`
Metropolis	100,000 to 499,999 Sims See also: *Categories*
Monster	Large creature crushes buildings, causes fires Heads for highly polluted areas Entertaining for the kids May be a red lizard or green dinosaur May stay for a while
Mouse	Small furry animal Computer pointing device
Net Migration	Statistic in the Evaluation window Sims leaving: Not Good Sims moving in: Good
Nuclear Meltdown	Rare occurrence from nuclear power plants Makes area uninhabitable for many years Cheat: Go into Terrain Editor and bulldoze the affected area
Nuclear Power Plant	$5000 to build Powers about 150 zones

	No pollution unless melts down Supplies more power for the money See also: *Coal Power Plant*
Open Spaces	Open areas on city map (dirt) Need not be bulldozed See also: *Open Land*
Overall City Score	Composite score based on several factors Over 800 very good See also: *Factors*
Parks	Costs $10 each Build around zones to increase value See also: *Fountains*
Plane Crash	Catches the area on fire Good fire protection helps extinguish the blaze quickly See also: *Airport*
Police Protection Map	Select `Maps` from the Windows menu, select the City Form icon, choose the `Police` option Shows the areas covered by the stations Use when building new stations Don't overlap the areas too much Amount of funding affects coverage of each station
Police Stations	Cost $500 to build $100 per year to maintain at full funding level Avoid overlapping coverage (wastes funds) Don't place near the city edge Don't build more than necessary Build only when demanded by Sims See also: *City Services*
Pollution	Spread out the Industrial zones to reduce pollution Heavy traffic causes it Avoid placing Residential zones next to heavy pollution

Pollution Alert	A warning to reduce the pollution levels
Pollution Index Map	Can view by selecting `Maps` from the Window menu and choosing the City Form icon Shows intensity of the pollution in the city Use to locate the worst pollution after a pollution alert
Population Growth Map	Can view by selecting `Maps` from the Window menu and choosing the City Form icon Shows the increase and decrease in SimEarth population Use to find areas with rapid growth See also: *Density Key*
Population Density Map	Can view by selecting `Maps` from the Window menu and choosing the City Form icon Shows the population density More problems with crime in high density area Build police stations nearby
Power Grid Map	Can view by selecting `Maps` from the Window menu and choosing the City Form icon Shows power coverage of city Use after a disaster to locate areas without power (dark)
Power Lines	Electrical lines connect the zones to the power stations Zones without power never develop Zones which lose power deteriorate, eventually become empty Power travels through connecting zones without power lines Long lines lose some power due to transmission inefficiencies
Printing	Print a copy of your city using the System menu Prints a one-page map or eight-page poster Only works with specific printers
Public Opinion	Can view by selecting `Maps` from the Window menu and choosing the City Form icon

	Displays the results of a yearly poll of Sims Gives you rating as mayor Displays the worst problems If complaints are higher than 10%, do something to reduce them
Query Function	Place the pointer on a tile, press **<Q>** and **<CLICK>** or **<SPACE BAR>** Pop-up window gives you information on Crime Pollution levels Land value Population density What the tile represents Use to determine problems bringing down the property values Use to determine high crime area
Quick Reference	See: *Reference, Quick*
Railroad	See: *Mass Transit*
Random Terrain Generator	Invoked when you start a new city Also a function in Terrain Editor Allows you to (sort of) control Terraforming See also: *Terrain Editor*
Reference Card	Card with Simcity: Zone evolution chart (value of buildings) City dynamics chart (interrelated factors) Keyboard reference (movement and menu keys)
Reference, Quick	See: *Quick Reference*
Registration	Register with Maxis when you purchase SimCity Maxis Software can update you on improvements Registered customers receive help with technical problems
Residential Zones	Cost $100 per zone Zone near water and forests Stay away from high pollution areas Zones on the edge of the city have low land value

Rio De Janeiro	The scenario flooded by rising sea levels
Roads	Costs $10 per section Costs $1 per section to maintain Use rails for in high density areas Avoid surrounding single zones (not cost effective) Bracket with zones to assure maximum value for each section Avoid long, open stretches (which don't pay for themselves) See also: *Bridge*, *Mass Transit*, *Trip Generation*, *Traffic*
Rules	Heart of the simulation Determine SimCity behavior
San Francisco	The scenario with the *major* earthquake
Scenarios	Provided with SimCity Each has a problem to solve Choose from the Scenarios menu The only way to "win" with SimCity
Score	See: *Overall City Score*
Seaport	Costs $5,000 to build a seaport Helpful if built on shoreline Build only when industrial growth has leveled off Occasional shipwrecks Lowers surrounding land values
Shipwreck	Only when you have a seaport Ship hits a bridge or is caught by a monster
Shoreline	Edge between water and land See also: *Landfill*, *Water*
Smoothing	Function in Terrain Editor Use to get the effect of natural boundaries
Terrain Editor	Allows manual terraforming
Trip Generation	The method the simulation uses to determine traffic flow

	Traffic conditions fluctuate quickly See also: *Traffic, Roads*
Traffic	Heavy traffic causes pollution Pollution causes complaints Provide several routes for traffic Double roads (boulevards) cause too much pollution Avoid road and rails next to each other See also: *Roads, Mass Transit*
Sound	A toggle choice on the Options menu Turning it off helps the simulation run faster See also: *Covox Sound Master Board*
Speed	Simulation action time Run fastest to collect more taxes Can build in pause mode, but collect no taxes See also: *Sound Animate All, Frequent Animation*
Stadium	Costs $3,000 to build Build only when Sims "demand" a stadium Query function tells the score during a game
Statistics	Select `Eval` from the Windows menu Review frequently
Taxes	Collected once a year Displayed in the Budget window Low taxes mean less income High taxes mean no Sims, no income Taxes between 6-9% work the best See also: *Budget*
Terraforming	Automatic with a new city Process of randomly generating terrain Use START NEW CITY over and over until you like the result See also: *Terrain Editor*
Terrain Editor	Additional program allows custom-built terrain Can be used to alter existing cities

	Provided with Commodore and Color Mac versions Extra with all other versions Worth the money
Tiles	Smallest unit of land in SimCity Each section of road or rail is one tile Zones have nine tiles Query function shows values for each tile See also: *Query*
Time Lag	Screens update delay Varies, depending on computer and city size Turning off animation and sound decreases the time lag See also: *Frequent Animation*, *Animate All*, *Sound*
Toggle	**<CLICK>** or **<SPACE BAR>** once on a menu item to change its status A triangle indicates an option is toggled on
Tokyo	The scenario with a monster attack
Tools	See: *Icons*
Tornado	Powerful funnel cloud wanders aimlessly around May stick around Quick stop: save and load the city again
Town	Population from 2,000 to 4,999 See also: *Categories*
Traffic	Indicated by the moving cars on the roads Replace heavy traffic areas with mass transit High population density always has traffic problems See also: *Roads*, *Mass Transit*
Traffic Alert	Warning to reduce the heavy traffic problems
Train wreck	Happens when train is caught by monster or tornado
Trains	See: *Mass Transit*, *Transit Lines*

Transit lines	Cost $20 per section of track Costs $4 per year at full funding See also: *Tunnels*
Tunnels	Mass transit under water Cost $100 per section Plan to span small areas of water Can only lay in a straight line See also: *Transportation, Mass Transit*
Unemployment	Public opinion problem in the Evaluation window Above 10% level, zone more Commercial and Industrial areas
VGA	Nice screen, but no advantage with SimCity
Village	Population from 0 to 999 Sims See also: *Categories*
Water	Areas of blue or medium gray represent rivers, lakes, and oceans
Zone Evolution Chart	See: *Reference Card*
Zoning	Designating an area for SimEarth buildings Sims determine what will be built in each zone Each zone costs $100 Remove a zone quickly by bulldozing the center tile Bulldozing a zone costs $9, $1 for each of the nine tiles

PART

3

SimEarth: The Gaia Theory

13 Creating a Planet

The ultimate goal of SimEarth is for all civilization to leave for the stars. When you achieve that goal, planet Gaia gives you a last message: `Good Riddance`. The lesson comes through. Some people believe we're messing up the planet and better figure out what to do. SimEarth is an interesting way to discover how we may be able to save ourselves.

Long-term planning aside, SimEarth offers a way to learn a great deal about our Earth. As much as the continents in SimEarth may be different from the real thing (with a few exceptions), the life forms in the simulation are all based on the only life forms we know of in the universe—those on this planet. The evolution of these life forms is also consistent with what scientists believe about the evolution of life on Earth. The challenge of the game also provides learning experience.

SimEarth Philosophy

Behind any game program there is a philosophical base, a meaning and intent to the program. The program creator designs and develops the program as a way of communicating to a lot of people, the players and users of the program. The pictures, control, and goals of the program communicate the creator's message. If enough people agree with the game's viewpoint, the program sells and the creator is happy.

In many cases, the basic intent of a game or simulation program is just to have fun. Many people need to be entertained and challenged to have fun. Good graphics, nice music, and quick response, then, continue to be the surface features of a program leading to success. The deeper issues of how well the program depicts reality and if the goals are constructive or destructive are not quite as obvious as the heroes' theme song.

This section contains our perspective on where SimEarth fits in the continuum of fun to serious and frivolous to meaningful. Our opinion results from our experience with this and other programs and does not necessarily represent how the creators of SimEarth feel about the program.

What We Need

Humans need to stick labels on everything. It is a prerequisite of communication. We must agree on the word to be used for this object shaped like a . . . whatever it is. As long as we consistently use the word "telephone" for an object which gives us the ability to talk with others at a distance, we can communicate reasonably well. The name for that device, "telephone," is valid because we say it is and use it consistently.

In addition to applying names to objects (using the word very broadly), we like to categorize these objects. We put telephones in the same class as cameras: *man-made devices*. We can put apples and peaches in the same class: *fruit*. But recognize that these classes are also artificial. We make them up! Those items could also be grouped together in the class: *things that weigh less than five pounds*. Or the class may be: *things that can be thrown across the room*. While the thought of throwing the camera across the room may be horrifying to some, putting the camera in that class is still valid. It is valid because we say it is!

In addition, how we name and group these things comes from our perspective, not to mention our language. An individual who had never seen a telephone would have no idea what to name it or how to use it. They would have no perspective of a telephone at all. So—the way we name and classify comes from our viewpoint, or perspective, of what we chose to name and classify.

Looking at the Earth

Look down. You probably see two feet, carpet, a few wires, maybe a software manual or two. This is your most intimate perspective of the Earth. Golly gee! You are perched right on top of the Earth. What is your perspective of the Earth from where you sit?

Run around the building. What is your perspective of the Earth now? It still looks pretty flat. As you see it, you have no idea how big it is. You have no idea what is more than six feet under the Earth. You look up and have no appreciation for the sea of air above you.

Now travel straight up about 6,000 miles. What does the Earth look like now? Different perspective, eh? What category does this Earth thing fall into? What name do we give it now that we can see the whole object? Does our name for this object affect how we perceive it?

The Gaia Theory

The Gaia theory says we have not been looking at this thing called Earth from the proper perspective. James Lovelock has been discussing his perspective for 25 years. He sees the Earth as one living thing. All parts interact with the other parts. His perspective encompasses the whole Earth, not just the parts we can see.

The word *Gaia* comes from Greek mythology. Gaia is the Earth personified as a goddess. Alternately pronounced "gay-ä" or "geye-ä," this name used by Lovelock represents a new way of viewing our world. Use of the new term *Gaia* provided a new way of looking at this thing we call Earth.

Look through a microscope and examine a single-celled life form. It has all the necessary parts and functions to be "alive," as we define the term. Taken apart and examined, the one-cell organism has things like genes made of DNA which allow the cell to reproduce. (Well, these things would allow it to reproduce if we hadn't taken it apart.)

If we take that microscope and make it into a "macroscope," we can examine the Earth as we examined that one-cell life form. According to the Gaia Theory, if we would take away some parts of the Earth, other parts will die. The theory says we need to look at the Earth as one large organism. While the Earth is no more conscious than a tree, its forces still work to ensure the survival of all its parts so the planet as a whole can survive.

The SimEarth Perspective

And then there is SimEarth. SimEarth takes the Gaia Theory of the Earth and provides an interesting—and yes, entertaining—perspective of this world view. This game's creator wanted to make the program more than just easy to use and interesting to look at. The creator wanted users to see a new way of looking at the Earth when they work with the program.

On the continuum of fun to serious, the program definitely leans toward the serious end. From frivolous to meaningful, SimEarth is well into the meaningful end. This does not suggest that you'll have to "work" at having fun or that you should try SimEarth because it is good for you. You will hardly notice the program's inherent message as you try things out. But over time, you'll begin to appreciate what SimEarth has to say to us all.

Planet Management

In the SimEarth scheme of things, you can be an observer. Many of the basic planet choices will allow you to sit and watch. After all, the entire concept of Gaia is that the planet should be self-regulating and need no help to thrive. In this game, you sit above the planet like an alien from outer space and watch the action below.

As an observer, you will discover that the planet is self-regulating during the first two time scales, before intelligent life appears. Once the natives begin to build fires and fight, you as the observer must get involved to keep the planet growing. The assumption here is that intelligent life does need external guidance to succeed on the planet. You become a *planet manager*. But again, you may choose your level of involvement.

As a planet manager, you adjust the planet in dozens of ways. You make changes in response to messages and watch the results. Do the plants and animals continue to grow? Do the civilizations advance to the next level? Is technology on its way to the stars?

A planet manager interested in maintenance only just watches the messages. This manager makes moderate adjustments when messages appear to restore the planet's equilibrium. This manager's actions are just reactions, a quiet and passive approach to planet management.

A bolder, more controlling planet manager anticipates the needs of the planet and makes adjustments. Or, the manager may make adjustments to observe the results. Of course, radical adjustments create other problems which, in turn, must also be solved. The planet's balance is delicate and easily upset by radical actions. Controlling managers can take on more difficult assignments, problems which already exist, and solve the problems without the help of the planet's natural regulatory mechanism.

Whether *you* choose to act as an observer, maintenance manager, or controlling manager, for the simulation to continue the planet must still progress from each time scale to the next. The final goal of the simulation is to have the life forms leave the planet for the stars.

Choose a Starting Point

SimEarth presents a number of ways to start a planet. Chapter 15 provides more detail about these choices, but we'll provide an overview here. Once you select `New Planet` from the File menu, you must make two decisions: What level of energy and which of the eight "canvases" do you want to start with?

Energy

You'll determine the amount of energy available when you select the game play level. All levels but Experimental Mode provide a limited amount of energy. You start with this amount, use energy units as you make changes to the plant, and the energy slowly returns over time. *BUT* the amount of energy that accumulates will not exceed the initial amount of energy provided. Letting the simulation run for long periods of time *will not* accumulate extra energy.

Having said that, we highly recommend that you use the Experimental Mode, at least at first. This game play level provides unlimited energy. Once you limit the energy available by selecting any other mode, you do not have the luxury of making large-scale changes to see if they work. If you make a drastic change, the planet runs out of energy, and you can make corrections or changes only after energy builds up after time passes. After you have learned what works in SimEarth, starting with limited energy presents a challenge. Until then, limiting your resources just results in frustration.

Planet Canvas

SimEarth lets you choose from eight different starting planets. Four present immediate problems. Three offer interesting starting points. The last planet lets you form a random world, depending on the time frame you choose.

Problem Planets

These planets have problems to solve, some quite severe but not impossible to overcome. Chapter 17 provides tips and ideas for conquering these challenges. We just provide starting information here.

- **Stag Nation**—The sentient species evolved but had the misfortune to start on a small continent. They can't just hop a plane and fly out. They are stuck in the stone age. Help them spread to the rest of the world and advance to the Nanotech Age. Not a bad place to start to learn how to nurture intelligent life.
- **Earth**—Modern day Earth presents problems of its own: pollution, war, limited food, and a high birth rate, to name a few. This is not a starting point for a timid planet manager, but provides insight into the balancing act required when "intelligent life" begins messing with Gaia.
- **Mars**—After being teleported to Mars, you face a lifeless, cold ball of rock. The simulation provides special tools and unlimited energy to help you bring the planet to life. Oh yes, you have to do it within 500 years. This task is very difficult to accomplish.
- **Venus**—This ball of rock is hot enough to melt your shoes, teeth, and hair. Cool it off with special tools. In 500 years, maybe someone will come to visit—or then again, maybe not. This one is also very difficult.

Starting Points

Each of these established planets offers a unique situation. They lend themselves to experimentation and discovery. Prior experience using SimEarth is not as important with these planets, described as follows:

- ❑ **Daisyworld**—Daisies cover the planet. Daisyworld demonstrates the planet's ability to self-regulate, as proposed in the Gaia Theory. Don't eat the daisies.
- ❑ **Aquarium**—You can develop designer continents on this ball of water. Create life from single-celled animals and up. Just remember to use your designer genes.
- ❑ **Earth**—The Cambrian Era Earth starts out 550 million years ago. This starting point gives a striking spectacle of continental drift.

Random

Random planets provide additional choices depending on the time scale. You may choose to begin in any time scale or advance from one to another. Once you've chosen the starting time scale, the simulation randomly places continents and life forms. Following are the time scales:

- ❑ **Geologic**—This time scale, which runs itself, begins just after the planet cools enough to hold water and ends when single-celled life begins.
- ❑ **Evolution**—Life continues to evolve in this time scale, moving from single-celled organisms to sentient life forms. Our bias in favor of mammals does not hold here. A variety of life forms may become intelligent, including dinosaurs. This time scale also runs without assistance.
- ❑ **Civilized**—This time scale starts with the sentient life form in the Stone Age. Without your guidance, life quickly reverts to pre-civilization conditions. Your goal is to help the life forms to the Industrial Revolution. Unless you have just moved up from the Evolution time scale, the simulation will randomly pick the intelligent life form.

- **Technology**—The last step is to head for the stars. Energy and pollution become big issues in this last time scale. Succeed here, and the entire population leaves the planet for outer space. After the pesky intelligent life forms leave, the planet returns to the Evolution time scale.

Approaching SimEarth

The SimEarth manual advises us to "go slowly" when we play with a planet. Because so many interactions occur, it may take time before results of a change you make become obvious. Make an adjustment, and then wait to see the results. This is not a program to rush through. Take time to enjoy it. In addition to the "go slowly" advice, we suggest that you make one change at a time and watch carefully for the results.

SimEarth provides many variables to adjust. Each variable can affect dozens of others, which may affect dozens more. For example, raising the planet's core heat may increase the sea temperature. This will, in turn, affect some of the life forms. Some may die, while others can adapt. Those who adapt may have a better chance of evolving onto land. Had the core heat remained the same, a completely different life form may have crawled out of the sea. Changing the core temperature may affect the continental drift rate, the number of volcanoes, and so on.

If you make more than one adjustment, say also increasing the air-sea thermal transfer, you would not know if the core heat is what changes the course of life or if the change to the air-sea thermal transfer is having impact. Of course, the combination of the two changes could result in a new course of life and create even more interesting possibilities.

When you make one change at a time, you must carefully observe the results. Making the change without knowing the outcome is of little use to you. Because you are watching for patterns, you have to observe the changes over time to find the patterns which work. Even if the change does not work, you have still learned what you can do with no affect. Taking note of your results enables you to test the next change.

This process of making controlled changes and watching the results is certainly not unique to SimEarth. Scientists have been using this method for a long time. Similarly, this process works well with any computer program you learn. First learn what changes create what results, then use the program to accomplish the desired task.

The alternative to a diligent, controlled approach is to stumble around in SimEarth, making changes at random. If you eventually do accomplish your goal, you will have little idea how you got there and may not be able to repeat your success.

On the other hand, the "random learn" approach takes less conscious thought and provides more action. Enough random sessions also will eventually provide the pattern for success. In fact, children learn randomly most of the time. SimEarth provides the chance to experience the value of trial and error when learning complicated topics.

Measures of Success

Success in SimEarth is well defined. In a random planet simulation, success means to advance to later time frames—from geologic to evolution to civilization to technology. Once your planet reaches the technology period, help its inhabitants leave for the stars. Each scenario comes with specific problems to solve. These are clear-cut goals, easily measured while playing the simulation. Completing these goals is one measure of success.

Another measure of success would be in learning to use the method of controlled change and observation noted in the "Approaching SimEarth" section. Learning to learn by trial and error is a significant accomplishment. We have taught thousands of adults and quite a few children how to use many different computer programs. The successful students knew or learned how to use this process of making simple changes and observing the results. SimEarth provides a nonthreatening way to learn this vital skill.

You could consider coming to appreciate the message inherent in SimEarth as another measure of success. Whether or not you believe in the Gaia Theory, it is difficult to play the simulation for any time and not appreciate how all life interrelates.

Some of you may need a more concrete measure of success. OK. Take comfort when you don't boil the oceans away within the first 15 minutes of your planet's life.

14 Getting Started with SimEarth

Just opening the SimEarth box provides a hint about the complexity of this simulation software. The manual is thick and includes references to "biomes" and "energy units" and "hydrosphere." It contains lots of information about SimEarth that you'll want to read someday. For now, this chapter will provide you with a quick start to planet building.

SimCity Users

For those of you moving from city building to planet building, or considering the move, Table 14.1 provides a quick comparison of SimCity and SimEarth.

Table 14.1 How SimCity and SimEarth differ.

Aspect	*In SimCity*	*In SimEarth*
User's title	Mayor	Supreme being
User's powers	Spend money	Create life
Domain	100 square miles	Entire planet
Number of variables	Dozens	Hundreds
Timeframe	Centuries	Eons
Typical problem	Need more roads	Oceans boiling away
Funding	Money	Energy
Orientation	Man made	Natural
Win condition	Stable city	Head for the stars

It's only fair to warn veteran SimCity players that you have just had a taste of the challenge of a simulation. Each of these programs has its own feel. The SimCity city did not grow unless you zoned and built to suit the Sims. In SimEarth, the planet Gaia takes care of itself. Life evolves without much intervention. Whereas growth is the goal in SimCity, it is inevitable in SimEarth. In SimEarth, you make changes which can affect that growth and watch the results. Testing your planet-sized theories can result in intelligent dinosaurs or a lifeless, planet-sized cinder.

SimCity provided one dimension to control (two if you want to count the tax rate), funding; SimEarth has dozens of variables you change. Each variable provides for hundreds of possible combinations to encourage or inhibit growth.

SimCity player or not, we'll get you started quickly in this chapter with a quick note about the installation, basics about the enhanced windows in SimEarth, and a quick start to building PLANETQ.

Installation

The large SimEarth manual provides information about all computer versions of SimEarth. This makes it a generic manual. Each software version, such as MS-DOS or Macintosh, also contains installation instructions in a separate document. We'll note the minimum system requirements to install and use SimEarth and review the basics of installation for MS-DOS users. To use SimEarth you must have

- ❑ A hard disk with at least 1.5M available storage space.
- ❑ 640K of memory.
- ❑ An AT or faster system.
- ❑ A graphics screen.

If you do not have even one of these items, you will not be able to use SimEarth. The MS-DOS version can use any graphic monitor available, including Hercules and MCGA. We highly recommend an EGA or VGA screen. The sound boards supported include AdLib, Sound Blaster, Game Blaster, Game Master, and the Tandy sound chip, as well as the system's internal speaker. We recommend a mouse for MS-DOS SimEarth users. There are just too many controls to try to move the pointer around with the keyboard. A joystick will NOT work in SimEarth. Chapter 20 provides more details about all these devices.

From Floppy to Hard Disk

The *Disk #1* in the SimEarth package contains the installation program. You must use this program to copy the files to the hard disk and configure the program for your system. Once you've completed that procedure, you can run SimEarth. Because SimEarth will only run on a hard disk, the following are the only installation instructions for MS-DOS users:

1. Start your system as you normally do. This usually involves turning on all the switches and waiting for the opening screen to appear.

2. To be exceptionally safe, you should make copies of your program disks using DOS's DISKCOPY command before you install SimEarth. We've never seen the INSTALL program write anything on the disk, but it would not hurt to make the backups for later use as well. At least put write-protect tape over the notch.

3. If you have a menu system, drop out so that you see the DOS prompt, which should look something like `C:\>` or `C>`.
4. Insert the first SimEarth diskette in drive A:, usually the top or only floppy drive on the computer.
5. Type `A:` and press **<ENTER>**. The prompt should change to `A>`.
6. Type `INSTALL` and press **<ENTER>**.

At this point, the INSTALL program will take over the installation process. INSTALL will present a series of choices. The default (what the program is guessing) answer will contain an asterisk in brackets, as in `[*] A: [ ] B:` Use the → and ← to move the asterisk if necessary. In our experience, you'll rarely need to make any changes. The program is very good at guessing the proper answers. If you need to make changes, you may do so later by re-running the INSTALL program.

For most hard disk users, you will install the program from drive A: to drive C: The INSTALL program will create a subdirectory called \SIMEARTH and will copy all the necessary files to the hard disk. If you have trouble installing the software, the notes in the SimCity section or in Appendix A may provide some solutions.

Start Up

Once the installation is complete, you'll need to use the following procedure to start SimEarth:

1. Remove the diskette currently in the disk drive. Don't put the program diskettes too far away. You'll need them if you find you need to change the answers you gave when you ran the INSTALL program.
2. Type `C:` and press **<ENTER>** to return to the root directory of the hard drive.
3. Type `CD\SIMEARTH` and press **<ENTER>** to move to the subdirectory with the SimCity program. The prompt may look like `C:\SIMEARTH>` or it may still look like `C>`.

4. Type `SIMEARTH` to start the program.
5. In a few moments, the SimEarth opening screen should appear. Each time you want to use SimEarth, you'll have to repeat steps 3 and 4. The steps move you from the root directory into the SIMEARTH directory and start the program named SIMEARTH.

Quick Screen Tour

SimEarth uses the standard screen and menu window controls appearing in most programs which use windows. While the ability to have more than three windows on the screen at one time may sound overwhelming, you'll soon want even more screen real-estate as you make changes and study the results of your planet.

Windows

Each window contains common elements. Some windows have all of the common elements we'll describe, while others have just two: a close function and move function. Just looking at the window will provide clues. Figure 14.1 has little arrows pointing to the various parts of the windows. By the way, once you master the basics of these windows, you'll find they are consistent with windows in many types of programs.

SimEarth allows many windows to be open at one time. No one window must be open to use another window. And you can move all the windows around on the screen. Windows can be lined up neatly side by side, or more likely, stacked like pieces of paper on a desk. Each window provides information about or control over some variable in SimEarth. By selecting windows and moving them to different areas on the screen, you can create your own monitoring station for your planet. Like a TV control room, you can watch many views of the same event and select which controls to use as you direct the show, er, planet.

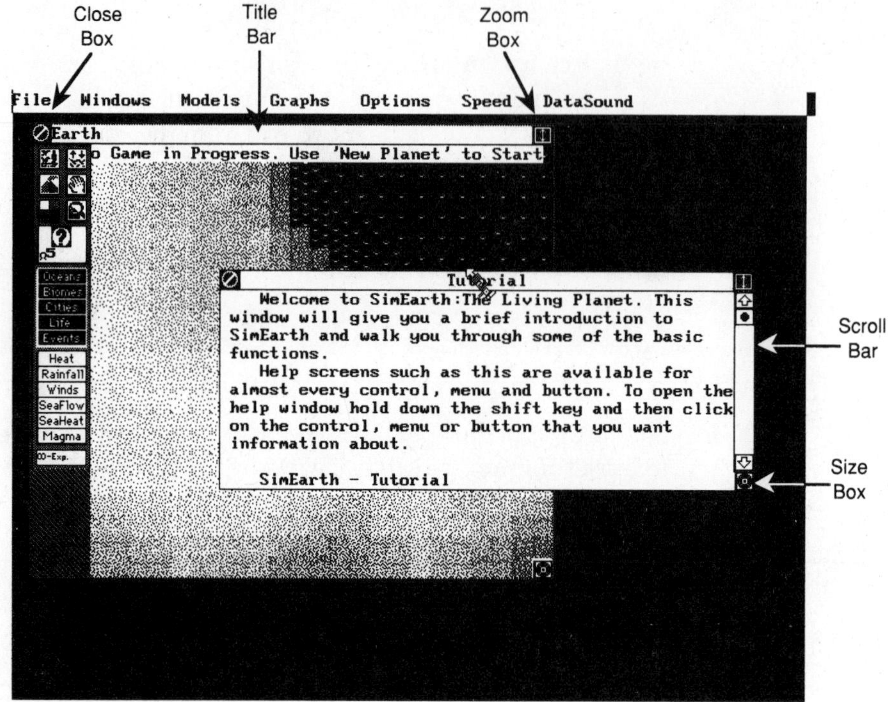

Figure 14.1 *Common parts of windows.*

Close Box

In the upper left corner of each window will be a small symbol, the *close box*. On some systems it is just a small square. On the MS-DOS version of SimEarth, it's a slashed circle, the universal NO symbol. Even though different systems use different symbols for the close box, **<POINT>**ing to that corner and **<CLICK>**ing closes the window. Reopening the window requires a menu or icon selection. Keyboard users can just press **<CTRL–>** to close the top window. Use the **<CTRL>** key then press the minus key on the numeric keypad.

Title Bar

The area across the top of each window, called the *title bar*, serves several functions. It contains the *window title* (name), the *close box*, and the *zoom box*, and it enables you to reposition the window. By using **<CLICK-DRAG>** anywhere on the title bar, (put the pointer on the title bar, **<CLICK>**, and hold the mouse button while moving the mouse) you can position the window anywhere on the screen. While you're moving a window, only the window's outline will move on the screen. When you release the mouse button, the actual window moves to the new location. Keyboard users can press **<CTRL-P>** and then use the Arrow keys to move the window. Press **<ENTER>** when finished with the move.

Because windows may overlap, a repositioned window appears on the top of the stack. **<CLICK>**ing on any part of another window brings it to the top. Stacking several windows on the screen allows quick access to many views or actions. Depending on other settings in the program, SimEarth constantly updates just the top window or all the windows.

Scroll Bar

Not all windows contain *scroll bars*. This part of the window enables you to move the material or image within the window up, down, right, or left within the window. Located on the right side and/or bottom of the window, the scroll bar has an arrow box at each end and a slider square somewhere in the middle.

<CLICK>ing on the arrows at the end of the bars moves the window materials in the specified direction a little bit at a time. Using **<CLICK-DRAG>** on the slider square moves the image more quickly. After you **<POINT>** to the slider square, **<CLICK>** and hold the mouse button. As you move the mouse up or down, (or right and left using the bottom slider), the image in the window moves in the specified direction. At all times, the position of the slider represents the relative part of the entire image displayed in the window. For example, pulling the slider to the top or bottom of the bar shows either the very top or very bottom portion of the full image.

Confused? Don't think about it too much. Just do it. You'll see the results and get the hang of it.

Size Box

A few of the windows contain a *size box* in the lower right corner. Using **<CLICK-DRAG>** on this symbol provides an outline of the window as you move the corner up, down, right, and left. Once you release the button, SimEarth resizes the actual window. You can then use the title bar to move the window, if you like. Keyboarders can use **<CTRL-A>** to adjust the window. Arrow keys then change the size. Press **<ENTER>** when you've sized the window to your specifications.

Zoom Box

Similar to the size box, the *zoom box* on the right side of the title bar changes the size of the window. **<CLICK>** on the zoom box to "zoom" the window to full-screen size. **<CLICK>**ing the zoom box again returns the window to the former size. **<CTRL-Z>** will perform the same action for keyboarders.

This zoom process can become confusing if you forgot the zoom box and used the resize box to expand the window to the full size of the screen. In that case, when you **<CLICK>** on the zoom box, nothing happens. Because the resized window is the same size as the zoomed window, you see no change. The only help is to look for the resize box in the lower right corner of the window. If there's a resize box, you can resize this window.

Other Window Items

Windows also contain *message bars*, *message boxes*, and *icons*. Message bars may appear at the top or bottom of the window, depending on the type of window. The message remains on the window until you resolve the problem or something more urgent happens. These messages provide such subtle clues as `Mass Extinctions Occurring` or `Oceans Boiling Away`. You do need to deal with the problem. A planet is a terrible thing to waste.

While message bars usually alert you of problems, message boxes pop up to announce positive events. Because you can't do anything until the message box is gone, **<CLICK>** anywhere outside the window to remove it. It will disappear in 30 seconds, even if you don't remove it.

Icons typically appear on the left and/or bottom of the window. There is so much to tell about icons, we discuss them briefly below and at length in Chapter 16.

Menu Selections

Menu names appear across the top of the screen. **<CLICK>**ing on any menu name makes a pull-down menu appear. You can then **<CLICK>** on the menu choices provided. You also may **<POINT>** to a menu name and **<CLICK-DRAG>** to the specific menu choice; when you release the mouse button, SimEarth activates that menu choice.

Keyboard users can use the Arrow keys to move through the menu choices and **<CLICK>** with the **<SPACE BAR>**. But there are a number of shortcut keys for menu choices and program functions. Because this is a quick tour, we won't review all the keys here. **<CLICK>**ing with the **<SPACE BAR>** will get you going. Later, when you want to become more efficient, you can review other sections of the book to discover the shortcut keys.

Moving Around

Three windows enable you to move over the planet surface: the Map, Edit, and Globe windows. While the Map and Globe windows provide the satellite view, the Edit window provides a close-up look at the planet surface.

A box on the display area of the Map and Globe windows represents the area currently displayed in the Edit window. (Actually, the box is a trapezoid in the Globe window.) Moving the box changes the view in the Edit window. The Map and Globe windows each offer a different way for you to reposition the Edit view box.

We provide many more details about these windows in Chapter 16. For now, we just provide the basics of moving around.

Map Window

To examine a portion of your planet more closely, position the pointer anywhere inside the rectangle in the Map window. If the Map window is not open, **<SELECT>** `WINDOWS` from the top of the screen, then **<SELECT>** the `Map` choice; or just use **<CTRL-M>**. The Map window, shown in Figure 14.2, appears. Use **<CLICK-DRAG>** to move the Edit box to the area you want to examine. Once you release the mouse button, the Edit window will show the selected portion of the planet surface. As you move the Edit box in the Map window, the contents of the Edit window change. **<CLICK>** in the Edit window or **<SELECT>** `WINDOWS Edit` to bring the Edit window to the top of the window stack. The Map window also contains icons at the bottom of the screen and several special window buttons. These icons provide views of different conditions on the planet, including temperature, the location of life, and continental drift. We cover these icons in more detail in Chapter 16.

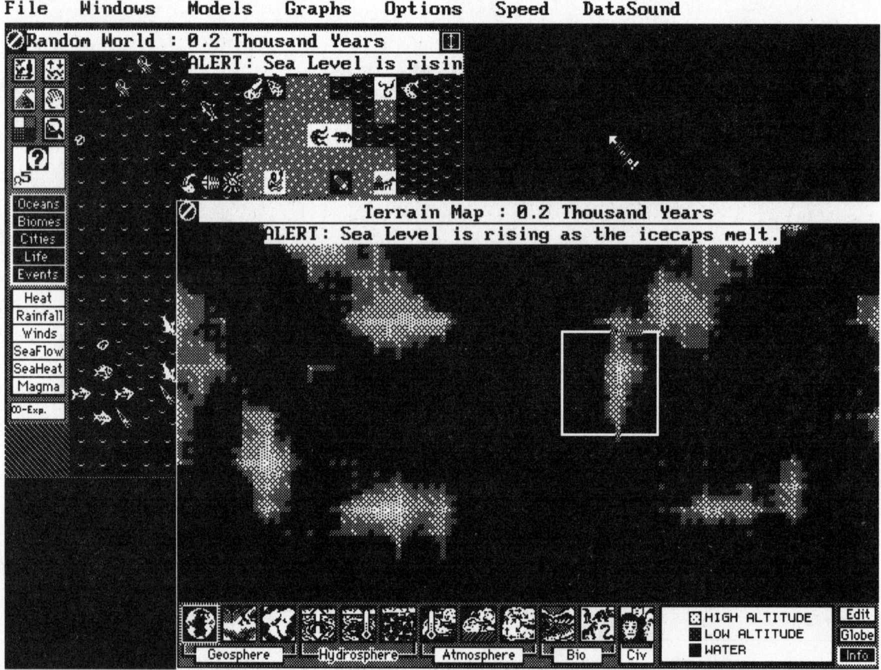

Figure 14.2 *The Map window always contains a square representing the Edit window view.*

Edit Window

The Edit window enables you to make changes to the planet surface. While working in this window, you can move to other parts of your planet by moving the pointer to any edge of the screen. This begins to move the Edit window view in that direction. Moving the pointer back away from the edge stops the movement. (Mac users have scroll bars on the edge of this window.)

Be careful when approaching the edge of the screen if you have the Edit window open. If you accidentally bump the edge of the screen, you'll move the Edit window view. This is no great disaster, but you'll have to move the view back when you bring the Edit window back to the top of the stack.

Globe Window

As shown in Figure 14.3, the Globe window provides a "rounded" world view. The area in the trapezoid represents the view in the Edit window. **<CLICK>**ing inside the trapezoid (let's just call it a box) will stop the rotation of the planet. **<CLICK>**ing to the right or left of the box will move the planet in that direction. **<CLICK>**ing above or below the box will move the box in that direction.

(Authors: Stopping the planet rotation sounds dangerous to the life forms on the planet. Is it? Your Editor) (Dear Editor: After considerable research, we discovered that all life forms on these planets wear Velcro boots. Stopping planet rotation is dangerous only to creatures who wander off the Velcro paths. DWD/DRD)

Using Icons

Icon hardly begin to tell all about icons. (Sorry about that.) Chapter 16 provides all the details about what each icon in SimEarth does, where each is located, and the best ways to use each one. We'll just look at the two different kinds of icons. Mouse users can just point to the icon and **<CLICK>** the left button. Keyboard users will move the pointer to the icon and press the **<SPACE BAR>**. Both of these methods are indicated below as **<SELECT>**ing.

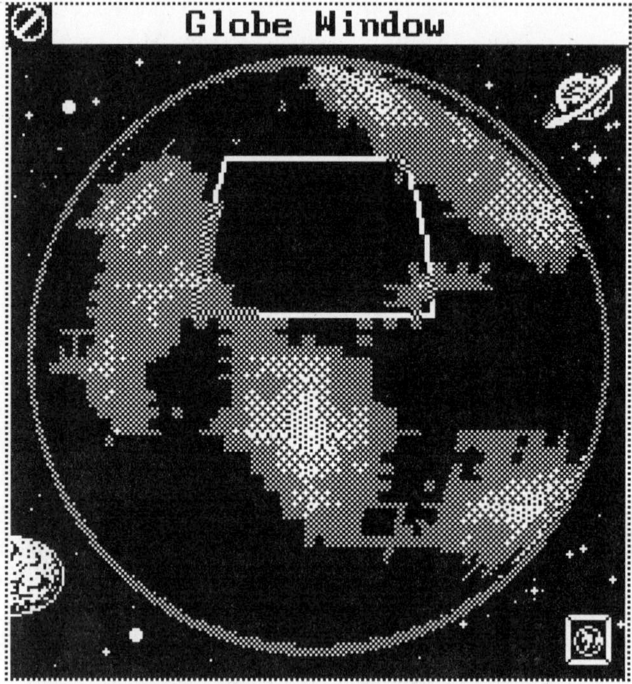

Figure 14.3 *The Globe window, with the trapezoid Edit view in the middle.*

View Icons

<SELECT>ing one of the View icons provides a view of different conditions in the window's contents. For example, the View icons at the bottom of the Map window provide indications of weather currents, civilization, continental drift, or several other conditions. In most cases, choosing a View icon turns off the currently selected View icon.

In some cases, more than one View icon can be active at once. When such a View icon is selected, the icon changes color or intensity to indicate it is active. **<SELECT>**ing it again turns it off. The appearance of the window contents also changes depending on the View icons selected. For example, the Edit window contains these multiple View icons. You can **<SELECT>** one or more of these to show oceans, events, and other features of the planet. In some cases, because a tile area contains more than one symbol, turning these icons on and off shows the layers of information more clearly.

Tool Icons

Tool icons enable you to directly shape the planet by placing items, by changing the surface of the planet, or by viewing a small portion of the surface. In some cases, selecting the icon displays additional selections in a pull-down box. The trick here is to keep the mouse button down while moving the pointer to the proper choice. When you release the mouse button, it selects the icon the pointer was located on.

In all cases, the icon box displays the currently selected icon. With over 40 possible selections, you'll need to watch that icon box closely before **<POINTING>**ing and **<CLICK>**ing anywhere in the Edit window. Accidently planting a volcano instead of a city upsets the locals quite a bit—blows them away, actually.

Build PLANETQ

SimEarth can be overwhelming. There are so many windows, menu choices, and tools, you can spend hours just poking around to see what happens. For those of you who want a quick shot at managing a planet, we've provided the steps to create PLANETQ. After completing this section, you'll have started a planet and be on your way to the stars.

Step by Step

In this PLANETQ tour, we'll just provide the keystrokes or mouse movements to get you started. You'll find much more detailed information for planet building in later chapters. Our instructions appear in two columns. The left column will have the specific action to take. The right column briefly explains what we are telling you to do and what the results will be. You may want to read the right column first.

Because the mouse allows the screen pointer movement at any angle, we'll give directions such as **<SELECT>** EASY. This instruction means to move the screen pointer to the EASY on-screen and press the left mouse button once. If you are not familiar with using a mouse, you may want to review the end of Chapter 2.

Keyboard users will use the Arrow keys to move the pointer and the **<SPACE BAR>** to **<SELECT>**. In some cases, the instructions will include the keyboard shortcut keys. And, in a few places, everyone will have to use the keyboard to type some information. Notice that specific keys are contained in the < and > symbols. For example, **<ENTER>** means press the Enter (sometimes called Return) key on the keyboard.

Let's Go

Do what it takes to get to the opening screen of SimEarth. Review the start-up section of this chapter if you are not sure how to get the program started. Read through the following instructions and look at all the pictures before you begin.

Instructions	**Notes**
Start the game	You should see several windows with the SimEarth logo window on the top. You may also hear the Gaia theme music. The screen will look like Figure 14.4.
Use the mouse or Arrow keys and move the pointer around	This action helps you find the pointer on the screen.

Figure 14.4 *The opening screen of SimEarth.*

<SELECT> the SimEarth logo window

<SELECT> means to put the cursor on the icon or word and press the mouse button or **<SPACE BAR>**. If you don't **<SELECT>** the logo window within a few seconds, it will go away by itself. If you get in stuck later, return to this point to start over.

Look at the screen

Notice that there are three windows, each overlapping the other. The top window is the Help window, the next window is the Map window. On the bottom is the Edit window. Nothing will happen to the simulation while you look at this screen. Nothing has started yet.

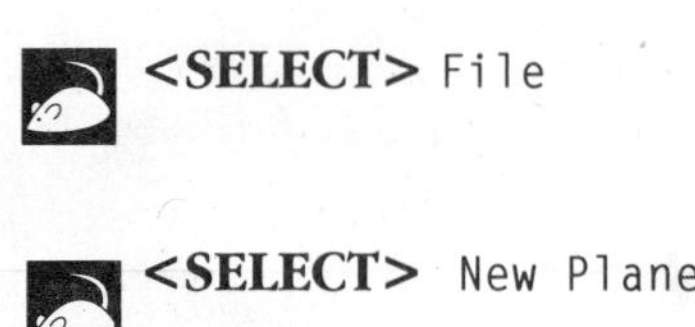

<SELECT> `File`

You need to tell the program that you want to start a new planet.

<SELECT> `New Planet`

<CTRL-N>

Once you begin to do something specific with the program, the copy protection method kicks in with a question similar to the one shown in Figure 14.5.

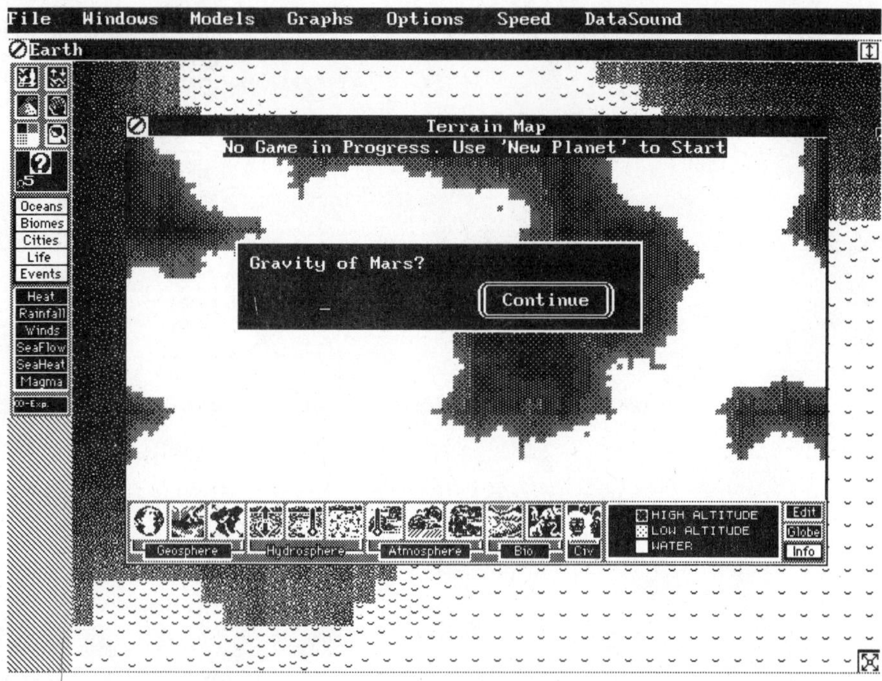

Figure 14.5 A SimEarth copy protection question.

Type the answer, then press **<ENTER>**

The answer to the question is in the back of the SimEarth manual. Make sure you include any minus sign or decimal point with any answer. If you don't provide the proper answer, the program just returns you to the opening screen.

Look at the screen

This is the jumping off point for any world you start. The screen will look similar to Figure 14.6.

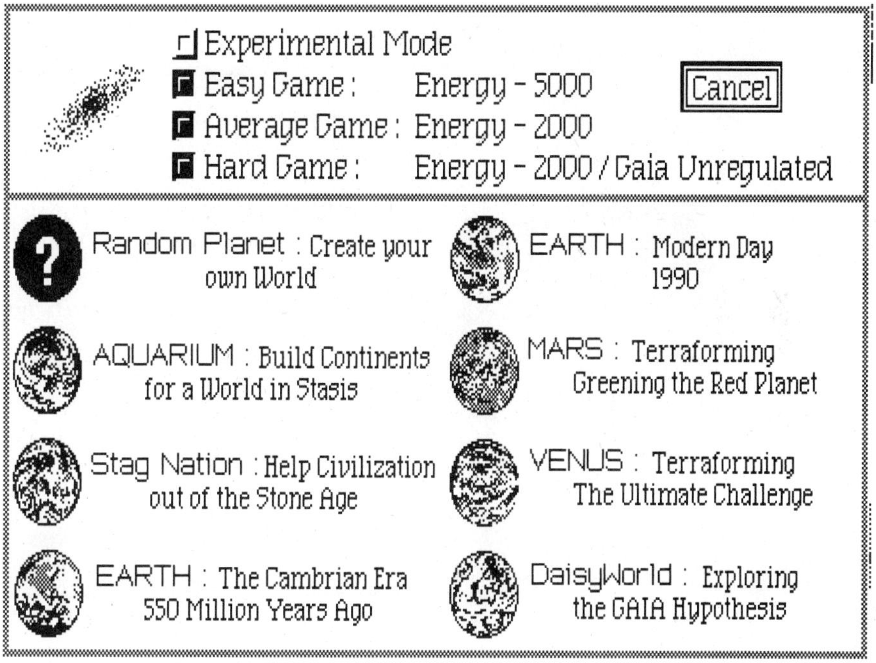

Experimental Mode
Easy Game : Energy - 5000
Average Game : Energy - 2000
Hard Game : Energy - 2000 / Gaia Unregulated
Cancel

Random Planet : Create your own World
EARTH : Modern Day 1990
AQUARIUM : Build Continents for a World in Stasis
MARS : Terraforming Greening the Red Planet
Stag Nation : Help Civilization out of the Stone Age
VENUS : Terraforming The Ultimate Challenge
EARTH : The Cambrian Era 550 Million Years Ago
DaisyWorld : Exploring the GAIA Hypothesis

Figure 14.6 *The starting point for many planets.*

<SELECT> `Experimental Mode`

This top button of the four Game Play level choices may already be selected. Experimental mode provides you with unlimited energy for your planet building. At this point, you'll need all the energy you can get.

<SELECT> `Random Planet`

This choice allows you to pick the exact time scale of the planet and start from scratch. (The other planet choices already have their own problems.)

Examine the screen

The pop-up box that appears (see Figure 14.7) allows you to choose the time scale of your new planet.

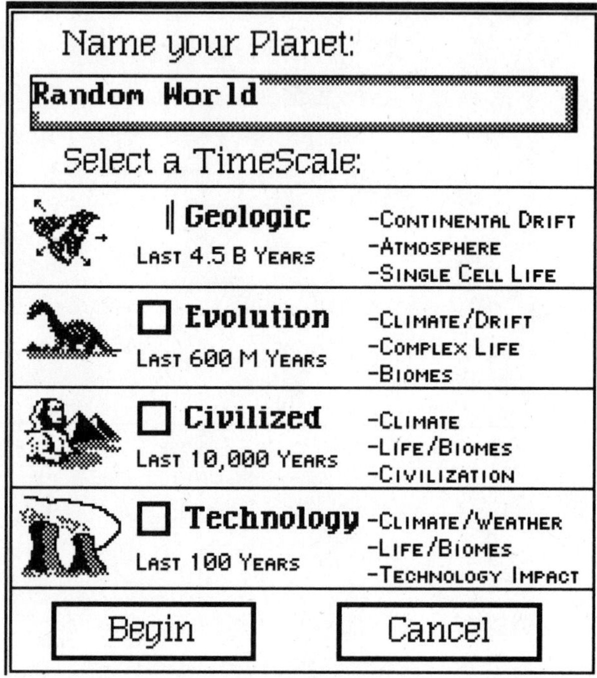

Figure 14.7 *The time frame choices for a Random planet.*

<SELECT> `Geologic`

This time scale begins as the beginning. What better place to start?

<SELECT> `Begin`

This is a box at the bottom of the screen. **<SELECT>** `Cancel` to return to the opening screen (if you do this, you're on your own from here).

Notice the screen

You didn't want us to keep saying, "Look at the screen," did you? Figure 14.8 shows the introduction window for `THE DAWN OF GAIA`. Each of the time scales provides preliminary information, including the goal to reach to advance to the next level.

THE DAWN OF GAIA

Out of the interstellar dust a planet begins to form. It cools and a solid crust forms on the surface. Your first task will be to promote the formation and survival of life. If you can survive the shift to an oxygenated atmosphere and evolve multicellular life you will reach the Evolution time scale.

Figure 14.8 *The beginning of a planet.*

Action	Result
<CLICK> Outside the window **<CTRL ->**	**<CLICK>**ing outside any information window closes the window. Keyboard users press the Ctrl key and the – (minus) key.
<SELECT> `Speed` (See next step)	Things happen quickly in this world. Depending on the speed of your computer, you probably want to slow everything down.
<SELECT> `Slow` **<1>**	In Figure 14.9, we set the simulation on its slowest rate. Even at that speed, .1 billion Sim years passed in the several seconds it took us to make the choice. You can always adjust the speed Pause to Fast by pressing the `0`, `1`, `2`, or `3` keys.
Sit back and watch	Within a few million years, (several seconds to you) oceans will begin to form as shown in Figure 14.10.

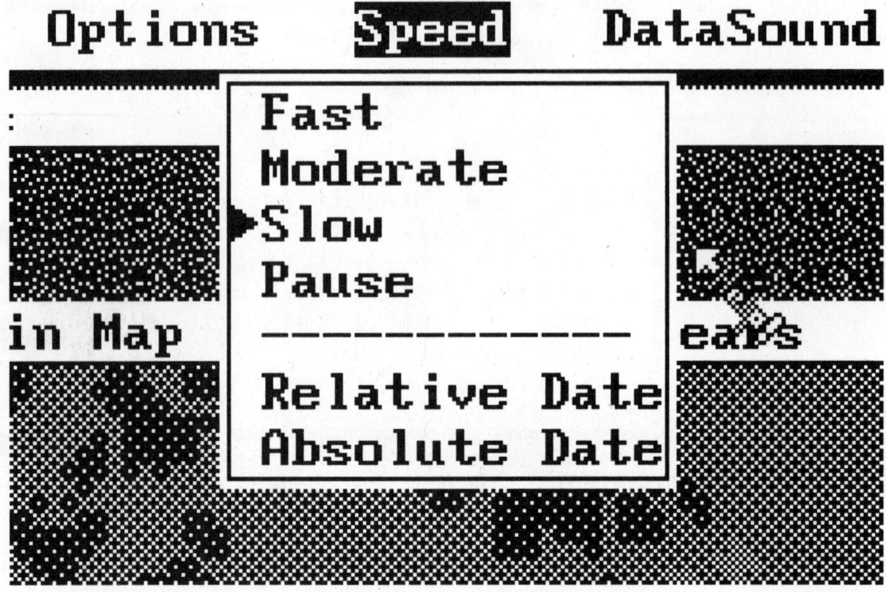

Figure 14.9 Slow things down with the Speed menu.

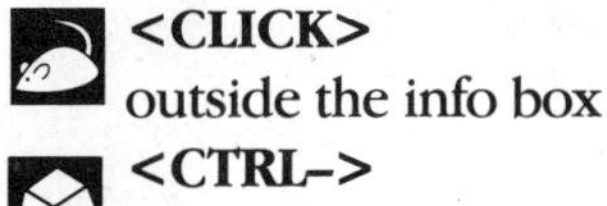

<CLICK> outside the info box
<CTRL->

Whenever a message box appears, just **<CLICK>** outside the box so it will disappear. They will also clear on their own after a few seconds.

Still watching

After another few million years, you'll get a message that life has formed, as shown in Figure 14.11. Press **<3>** if you are getting impatient.

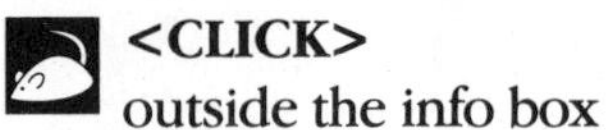

<CLICK> outside the info box

This closes this window.

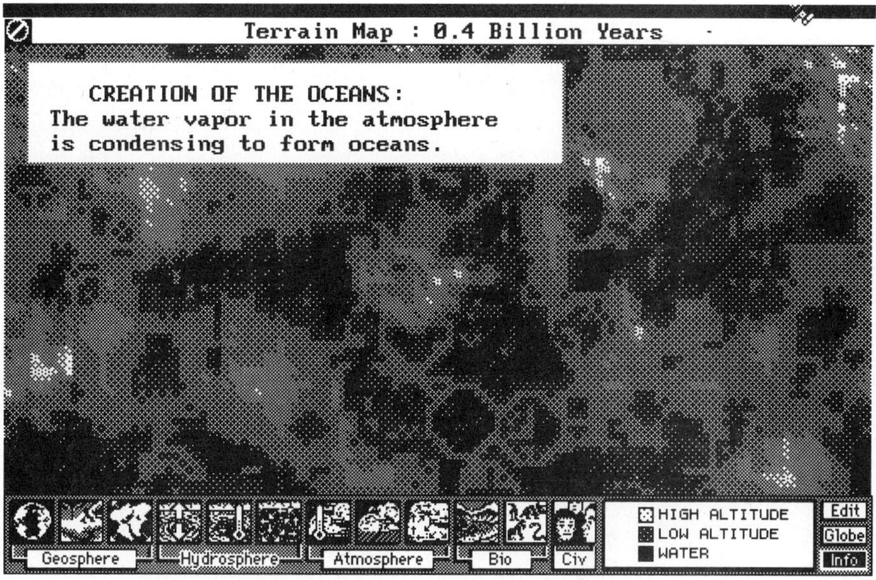

Figure 14.10 *The creation of the oceans.*

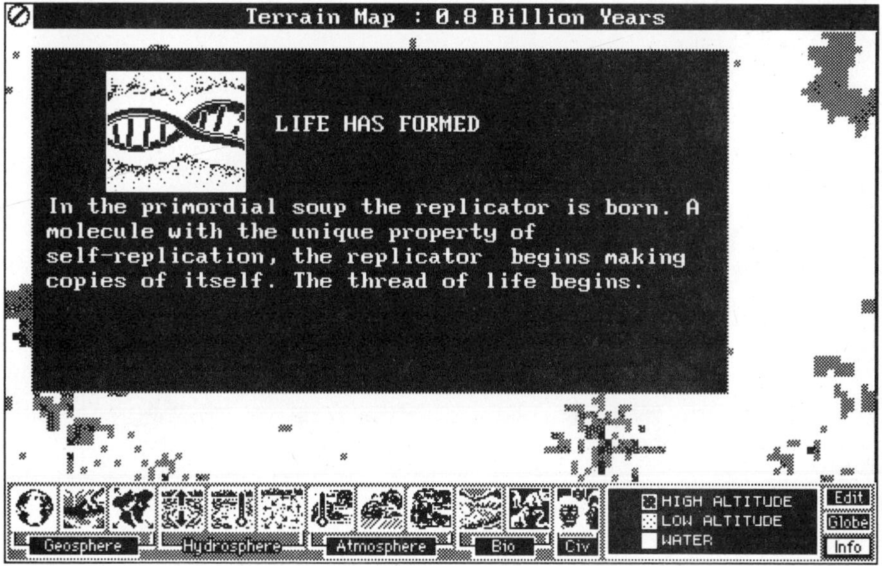

Figure 14.11 *Announcing the creation of life on the planet.*

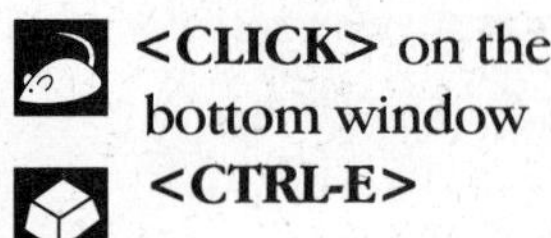 **<CLICK>** on the bottom window **<CTRL-E>**	**<CLICK>**ing on any window brings it to the top of the stack of windows. This is the Edit window. The Map window provides the entire planet picture. This Edit window shows the details as shown in Figure 14.12. Mousers—If you can't see the Edit window on the screen, use **<CTRL-E>**.
<SELECT> `Oceans`	All five of this cluster of buttons in the Edit window control panel start off active. By **<SELECT>**ing, you turn them on or off. You just turned off the Ocean option, and the water is "invisible" now.
<SELECT> `Oceans`	Yes, do it again. Now the water is visible. Sorry keyboarders, there is no quick way to do this. You'll have to move the pointer with the Arrow keys and press the **<SPACE BAR>**.
Try the other buttons now	See how the view changes. Some choices won't make any difference because you don't have cities or smart animals, yet.
Time passes quickly	After about 10 million years, radiates, a life form, will evolve. The simulation will announce their presence with a message box like the one in Figure 14.13.

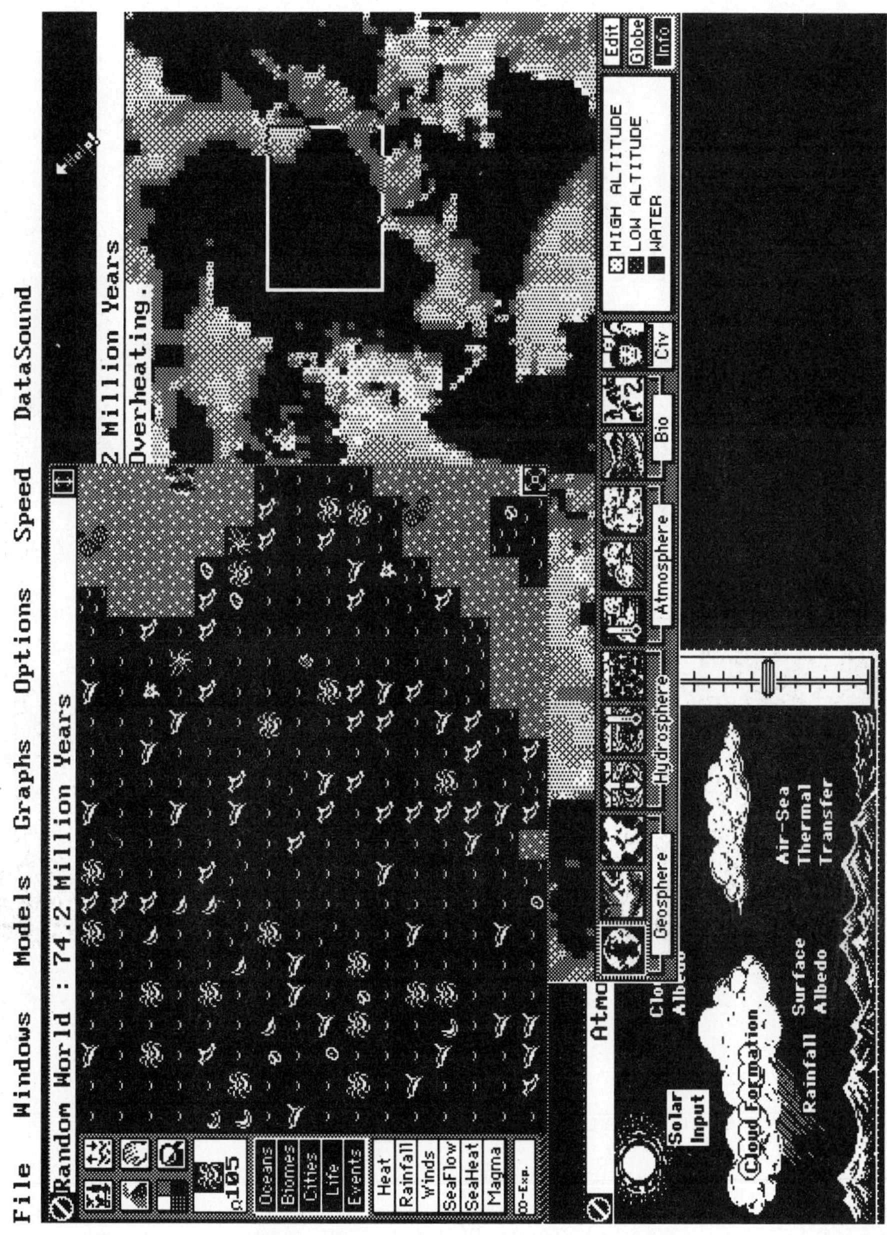

Figure 14.12 *Stacked windows—Edit window, then the Map window, and in the lower left corner, the Atmosphere Model control panel window.*

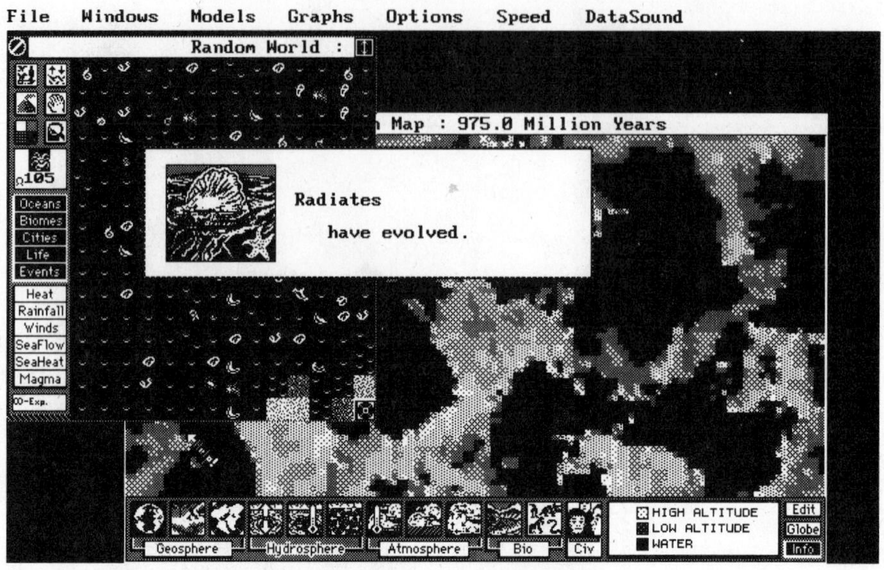

Figure 14.13 *Radiates have evolved. (Contrary to popular belief, radiates do not glow in the dark. These jellyfish are just one step of the evolutionarily ladder.)*

<SELECT> `Models`
<SELECT> `Atmosphere`

Now, we'll use the Models menu choice at the top of the screen. The Atmosphere Mode control panel appears on-screen.

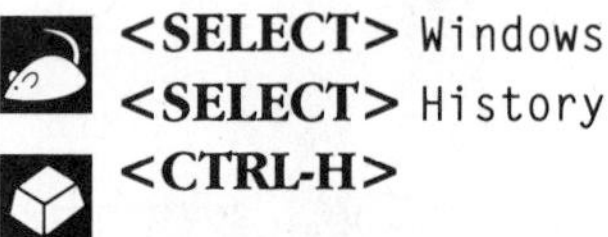

<SELECT> `Windows`
<SELECT> `History`
<CTRL-H>

We'll go back to the Windows menu and select `History`. After this new window pops up, there are four windows on the screen.

<SELECT> `Air Temp`
<SELECT> `Biomass`

The History graph can show up to four different aspects of the planet's readings at once. We'll just select the two which concern us: air temperature and the total amount of living matter on the plant, the biomass. Like pieces of paper stacked up on the desk, our windows are beginning to get messy.

<CLICK-DRAG> `History` to lower right corner

<CTRL-P>

You may move around and stack all windows. **<POINT>** to the top bar of the window, press the left mouse button, and hold it down. As you move the mouse, an outline of the window moves. When you let go, the window shifts to that location. Keyboarders can "loosen" the active window with **<CTRL-P>**, then use the Arrow keys to reposition the window. Press **<ENTER>** when the window is where you want it. Mousers should also remember this **<CTRL-P>** trick.

<CLICK-DRAG> `Atmosphere Model`

<CTRL-P>

Positions this window in the lower left corner of the screen, as shown in Figure 14.14.

<CLICK> on the Map window

<CTRL-M>

With the windows positioned similar to those in Figure 14.14, you can **<CLICK>** on any window to bring it to the top of the stack. **<CTRL-M>** just brings the Map window to the top. If SimEarth is not updating the windows at the same time, use the following sequence.

<SELECT> `Options`
<SELECT> `Update Background`

<CTRL-U>

If the background windows are not being updated, this will toggle them on. This is indicated with an arrow to the left of the word `Update Background`. If this choice is on and you do this step, you will have turned it off.

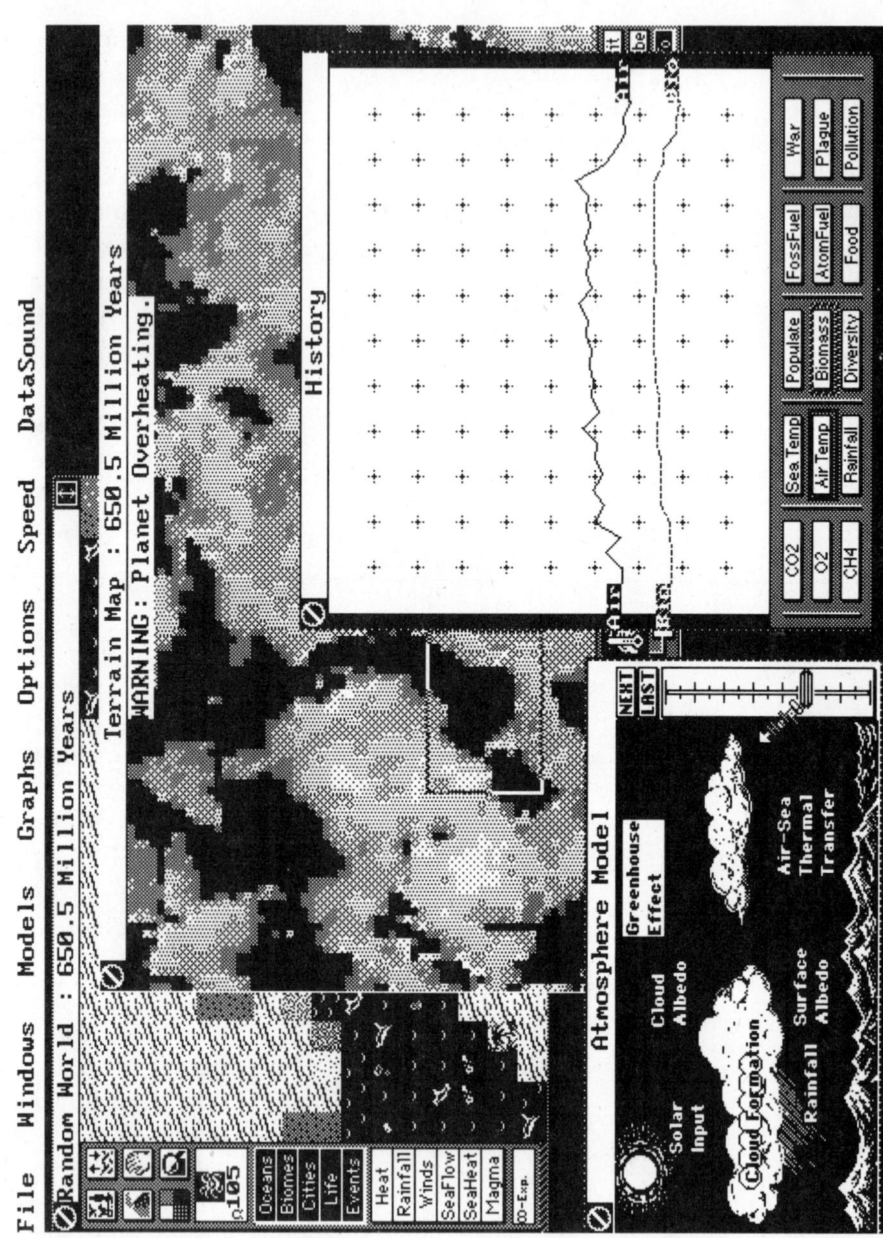

Figure 14.14 *The windows neatly arranged on the screen.*

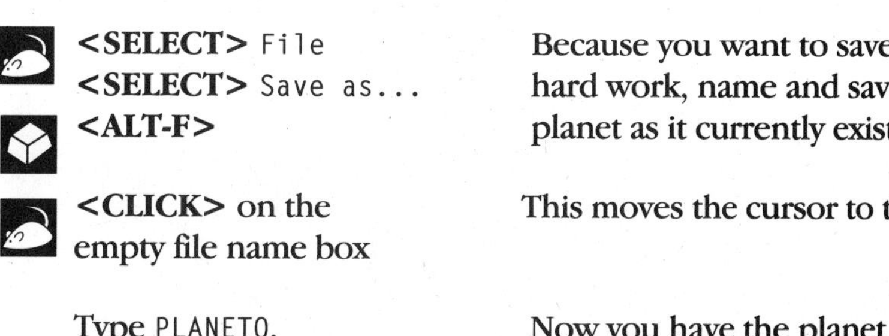

<SELECT> `File` **<SELECT>** `Save as...` **<ALT-F>**	Because you want to save all your hard work, name and save this planet as it currently exists.
<CLICK> on the empty file name box	This moves the cursor to that box.
Type `PLANETQ`, press **<ENTER>**	Now you have the planet saved on your default disk in the SIMEARTH subdirectory.

What's Next?

These first few steps are just the beginning of your journey. There are so many worlds to create and explore. Here are a few quick tips as you continue your trip:

- ❏ Most worlds will evolve without much intervention. In the beginning, make adjustments only as needed and observe the natural process of things.
- ❏ When making adjustments, make small changes in just one or two areas. Observe the results of these changes before making more changes.
- ❏ You can affect the whole planet level or the surface. Working on the surface will not do any good if the whole planet is not yet stable.
- ❏ Use Experimental mode to try out your ideas. The limited energy available in the other modes runs out very quickly when doing things by trial and error.
- ❏ Remember the Gaia Theory states that everything is connected. Changes to one area can and do affect many other areas.
- ❏ Forget using the Gaia window. (You'll know what it is when you discover it.) It's like having your mother watch while you have a good time.

15 Windows and Menus

In this chapter, we describe most of the windows you use to examine and work on your planet. The Edit and Map windows are so complex, we devote Chapter 16 to them. We start by describing the opening windows that greet you when you start the simulation. Then we move on to the menus and describe what to watch for in the more important areas of the SimEarth simulation.

Opening Windows

When you load SimEarth, the logo window shown in Figure 15.1 greets you. You can see the Edit and Map windows in the background, but they're not functional at this point. **<SELECT>** `File` from the top of the screen to display the File Menu.

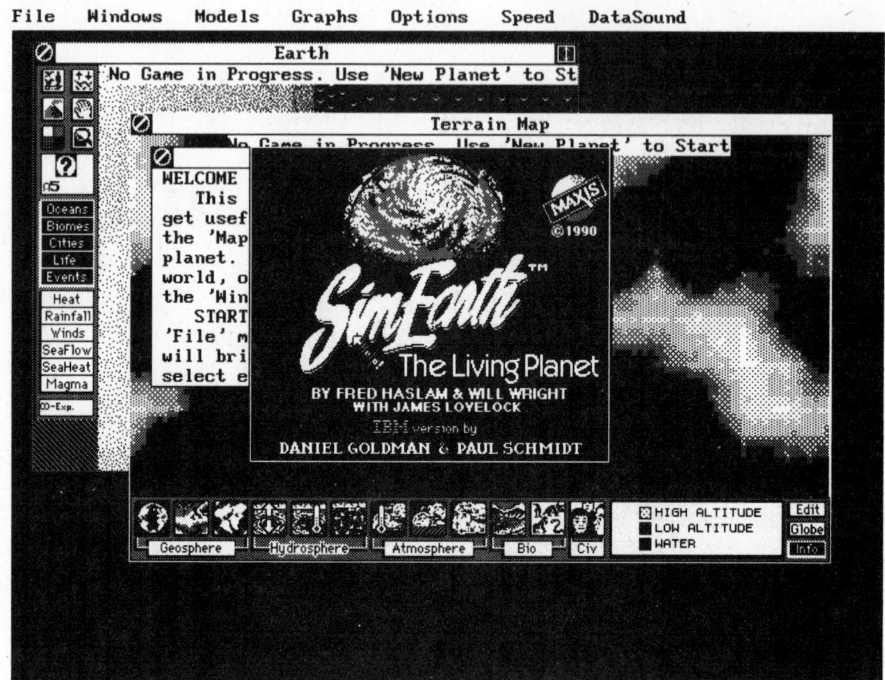

Figure 15.1 *A nice title window with a little song.*

When you start a new planet, you have to make some choices. First you have to answer the question from the copyright pop-up box, shown in Figure 15.2. Look up the answer to the pop-up box question in the Planet Specification Sheets in the back of the SimEarth manual and type it in. Now **<SELECT>** `New Planet` to start the simulation.

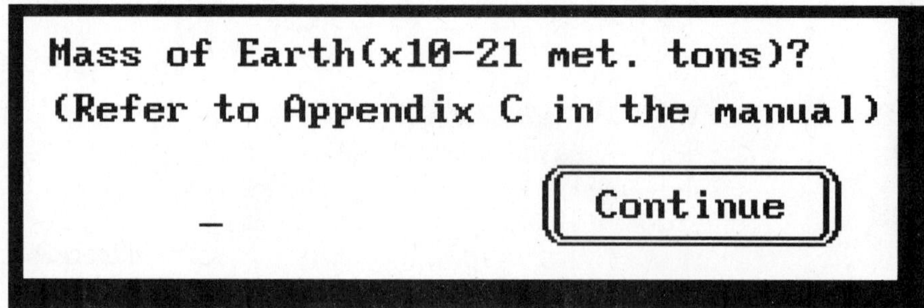

Figure 15.2 *If you don't remember the answer to this question from your science classes, you can look it up in the back of the manual.*

Choose a Game Play Level

The first choice you must make is to select the level of difficulty for the simulation from the screen shown in Figure 15.3. Your choice affects the *rules* the simulation follows and the amount of *energy* you have to help your planet evolve. The energy level determines what changes you can make to your planet. You might say this is your money. You are restricted to a "budget" according to the level of difficulty you choose. Every time you make a change to your planet, you use some of your energy supply.

Figure 15.3 *The four modes (levels) of play and the planet choices.*

The simulation replenishes your energy supply at a pace determined by the simulation rules. Replacement energy comes from the stores of the planet in the form of geothermal, wind, and solar energies. Once a life form becomes intelligent, the simulation adds some of the energy produced from this sentient life form to your supply. Don't get any ideas, though. You have limited control of the amount of energy you will receive. If your technology level is high, the energy output of the life form is higher, so you will receive more energy.

When you choose a game play level, you start with the specified amount of energy, and no matter how much you receive from the simulation, your energy supply "bank account" will not exceed the original amount. In other words, you have to use your energy to make room for more to use later.

Once you choose your level of play, the planet will continue at this level whenever you load it. If you choose `Hard Game`, the planet will always be a tough cookie. **<SELECT>** the button next to the game play level you want. This will darken the button so you can see the level that is set.

Experimental Mode

In this mode, recommended for beginners, your "bank account" of energy will always be unlimited. Until you learn how to fine tune a planet to use little energy, start in this mode. Even advanced users can use this mode to experiment on some new or bizarre ideas. Try radical settings in this mode to see what will happen before trying those settings on a more difficult planet. Selecting this mode randomly sets the *model control panels* in average positions so the planet will survive with little work, to make using SimEarth easier for beginners.

Easy Game

Once you know a little about what you need to do to keep a planet in good shape, this level will challenge you to do so with a "budget." This mode starts your planet with an energy level of 5,000 E.U.(*Energy Units*). Remember, you will never have more than 5,000 E.U., as this is the cap on your "bank account." This level sets the model control panel as in Experimental mode. You'll have to make few changes to enable the planet to survive, and you must budget the changes you want to make. Once you understand what it takes to produce needed results, you will be ready for the next level.

Average Game

With a little less energy to spend, you now must watch what you do much more closely. If you have paid attention to results of your actions in the easier modes, you can use your energy wisely. Your planet starts with only 2,000 E.U.s. The simulation randomly sets the model levels for more extreme conditions which will require you to make changes. These changes will cost you some of the E.U.s in your more limited supply.

Hard Game

This level is for only the Simmers who have mastered many of the aspects of the simulation. The Gaia (which normally regulates the original settings) is unregulated, so you will be responsible for regulation of the climate, atmosphere, and life.

This level also provides only 2,000 E.U.s. The model levels will be even more extreme and will require a lot of fine-tuning. Bring up the Gaia window and watch the little guy make faces as you really mess things up. If Gaia is smiling at you, then you know that you've mastered the simulation and have a complete understanding of the Gaia theory. Go ahead, pat yourself on the back. If you fail miserably, join the majority of the population and try and learn from your mistakes. At least you can start with a new planet.

Planets

You also must choose the type of planet you want to start with. Some of the choices are scenarios that give you specific challenges. Just **<SELECT>** the planet you want. For more on the scenarios, see Chapter 17. Following are the available planet selections:

- **Random Planet**—This choice directs the simulation to generate a random planet in the given time scale, which you also can choose. **<SELECT>** this icon, and SimEarth displays a dialogue box that enables you to name your planet and choose one of the four time scales.
- **Aquarium**—What makes you think this is all water. Does the word "fishbowl" come to mind? This planet is like a huge fishbowl. No continents will appear on the planet unless you say so. This choice is for people who want to make "designer" planets. Create your own shapes for the continents. This planet starts in the Evolution time scale.
- **Stag Nation**—The poor souls that live on this planet are stuck on one small island. The scenario starts in the early part of the Civilization time scale. You can help the sentient life to spread, or bring another life form up to take over the world. Anything will be an improvement from the stagnant world you start with.
- **Earth: The Cambrian Era**—This is a simulation based on Earth in the Evolution time scale (555 million years ago). This scenario reproduces the continental drift that occurred on Earth.
- **Earth: Modern Day**—Find out what it takes to keep the present world from nukin' itself. This scenario actually reproduces the oil tankers running aground. Win this scenario and feel relieved that we might survive, after all.
- **Mars**—Return to *War of the Worlds*? No, just invade Mars and try to make it habitable for the Sims. You will find no hostile aliens here, just a dead planet that needs a little work.
- **Venus**—This planet is much the same as Mars. It just has a little more hostile environment you must try and control.
- **DaisyWorld**—The simulation offers a simplified version of the SimEarth simulation. James Lovelock used DaisyWorld to test the Gaia Theory.

Name and Time Period

If you choose Random Planet, another window appears, as shown in Figure 15.4. Use this dialog box to name your new planet and choose the starting time period.

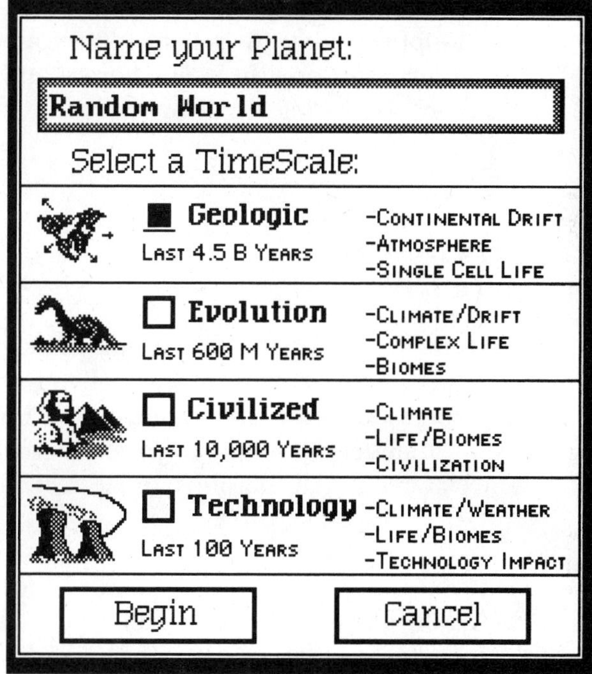

Figure 15.4 *Name your planet and select your time scale.*

To name your planet, move the pointer to the box under `Planet Name`. **<CLICK>** or press **<SPACE BAR>**, and a cursor appears in the box. Type the name you want and press Enter.

Next choose the time scale to start your planet in. If you start at Geologic, your planet will evolve through all four time scales. Each time scale uses a different set of factors in running the simulation. The simulation uses the factors to determine the results after your inputs. In both the Civilization and Technology time scales, for example, you can increase the advancement of the sentient beings using the Monolith, which appears with the Terraformers in the Place Life menu. The Monolith sometimes speeds up the Sims' evolution. For more information on terraformers and the monolith, see "Tools" in Chapter 16. If the Sims become too technological, you may find that they use up the fossil fuels quickly. Make sure that you allow enough time in the Geologic and Evolution time scales to form an ample supply of fossil fuels. Remember your geology? The things that died a long time ago now heat our homes and power our cars (and make pollution). Following are descriptions of the time scales.

Geologic

This time scale starts at the beginning of the planet's existence. The planet is cooling and the oceans are forming, as shown in Figure 15.5. (On Earth, this process started four-and-one-half billion years ago.) The simulation demonstrates such conditions as continental drift, atmospheric composition, extraterrestrial collisions, single-celled life, and climate.

The main thing you can do is adjust factors important to the formation of multi-celled life. Making the atmosphere favorable for life and the development of temperate climates will lead to the formation of multi-celled life forms. Once the multi-celled life forms appear, the planet advances to the next time scale. The time scale moves more quickly than the others, as the processes in this era normally would require more time in comparison to the rest of the simulation.

The Time/Simulation cycle is the amount of the planet's time passing between each time the computer updates the simulation. This cycle changes in each of the different time scales.

Each Time/Simulation cycle in this time scale covers 10 million years. Your planet will last about 10 billion years, so you must try and complete this Time Scale in about three to four billion years. Each Time/Simulation cycle will add one E.U. onto your energy budget—that doesn't sound like much, but then, not much is happening on the planet in this time scale.

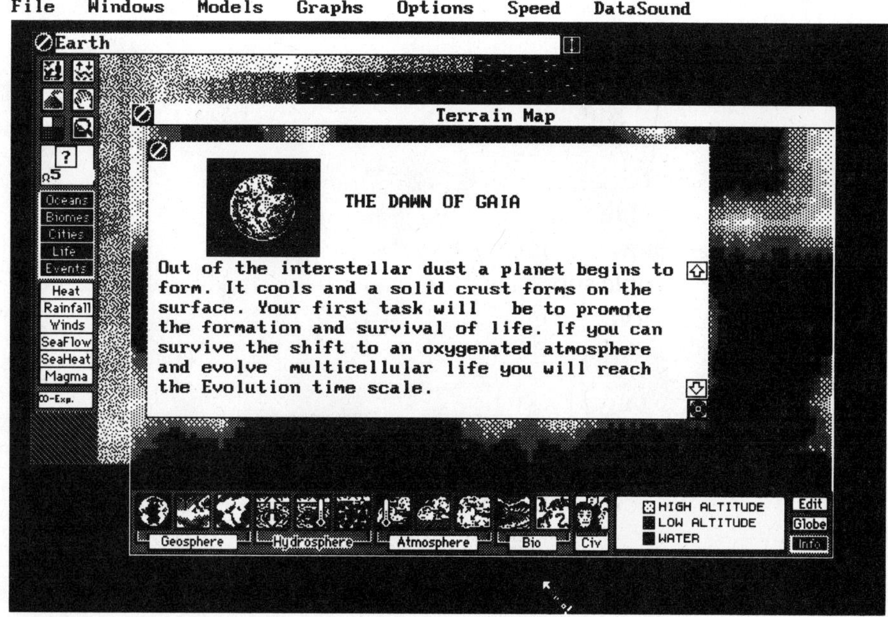

Figure 15.5 *When the ball of rock cools....*

Evolution

With the appearance of multi-celled life, your planet enters the Evolution time scale. The Time/Simulation cycle slows down in this time scale to 500,000 years. Things mutate and grow all over, and eventually crawl out of the ocean, as shown in Figure 15.6. The factors simulated in this time scale are life, biomes, climate, atmospheric composition, and continental drift. You can experiment with such factors as climate and atmospheric composition to see what makes the life forms thrive or die. You should complete this time scale in two or three billion years. Again, you earn one E.U. for each Time/Simulation cycle. When intelligent life forms, the planet enters the next time scale.

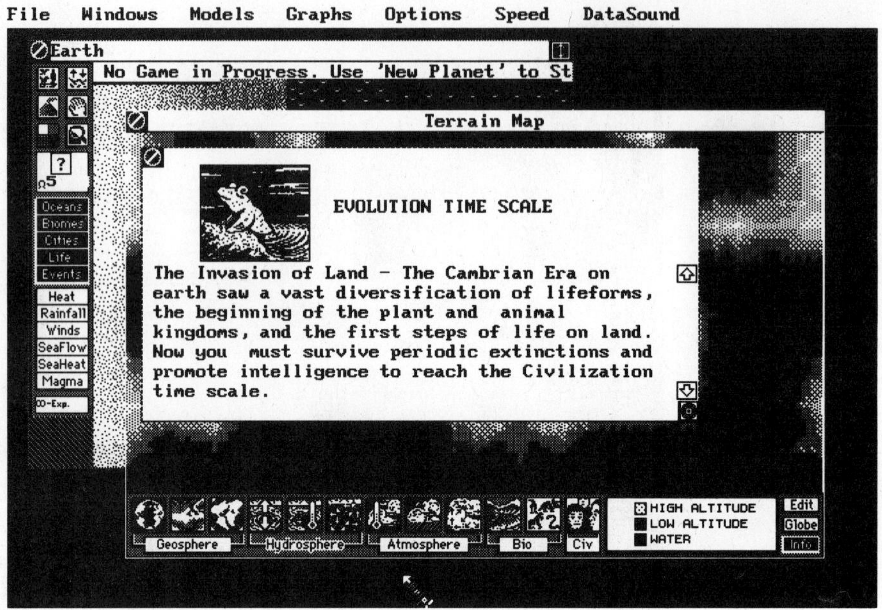

Figure 15.6 *Kermit crawls from the sea.*

Civilization

Life forms must be intelligent to be considered *civilized* life forms. Whatever the life form, intelligence is the key here, as shown in Figure 15.7. You can influence many factors in this time scale. The simulation mimics civilization, life, biomes, climate, and atmospheric composition. You must manipulate these factors to promote the rise of technological, sentient beings to advance to the next time scale. Setbacks such as wars and poor energy supplies make your task difficult. The Time/Simulation cycle slows down to a 10-year period. The energy gained depends on the highest technology level: Stone Age Time/Simulation cycles earn two E.U.s, while the Bronze and Iron Age cycles earn three and four E.U.s. With only 10 billion years for the life of the planet, you should complete this time scale when the planet is nine to nine-and-one-half billion years old. When technology arrives at the Industrial Revolution, the planet advances to the next time scale.

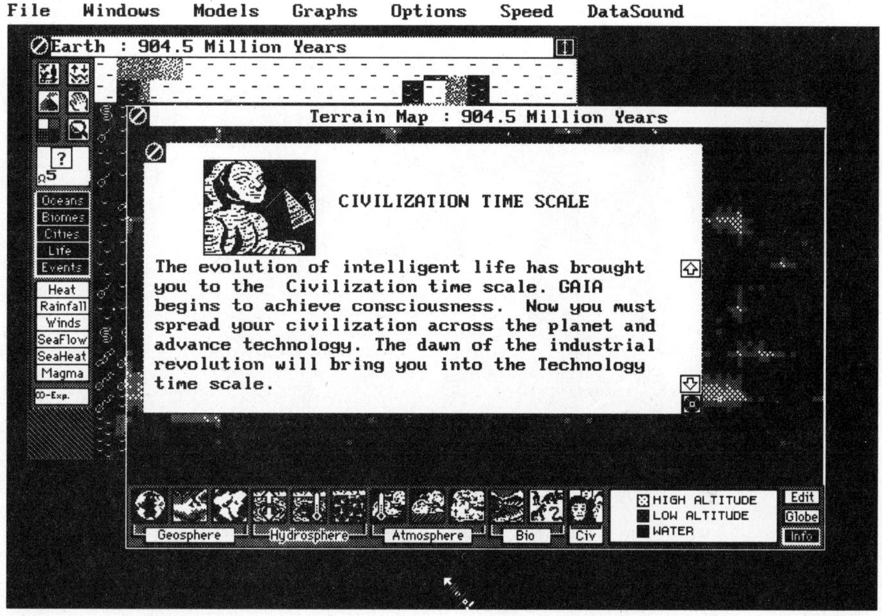

Figure 15.7 Now you have to deal with intelligence. What a headache.

Technology

The object of the last time scale is to help your planet bloom and spread its seeds. Your sentient beings should become capable of interplanetary travel and leave your planet to colonize other worlds. The Time/Simulation cycle slows even further to one year per cycle. You earn five E.U.s for each cycle in the Industrial Level, six E.U.s in the Atomic Age, seven E.U.s in the Information Age, and eight E.U.s for the Nanotech Age.

In this time scale, the simulation works on civilization, life, biomes, sentient expansion, climate, and atmospheric composition. You must keep the Sim beings from destroying the planet, as warned in Figure 15.8. Fine-tuning the energy forms used will help stop pollution and the depletion of fuel supplies. If your Sims pack up and blast into space to colonize other worlds before the planet "dies," you've won. The planet then returns to the Evolution time scale.

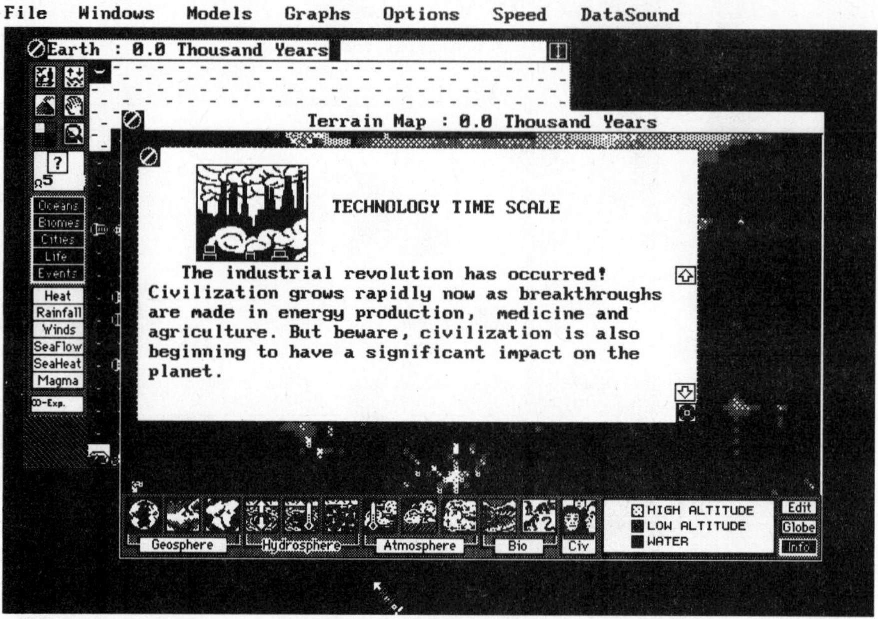

Figure 15.8 *Now you must protect the planet from the Sims.*

Pull-Down Menus

After you have chosen the planet and time scale, you'll begin to work with the pull-down menus listed across the top of the SimEarth screen. To **<SELECT>** a pull-down menu, move the pointer to the title in the bar across the top and **<CLICK>**. The menu drops down to display your options. Point and **<DOUBLE-CLICK>** on your selection, or use the ↑ and ↓ then **<ENTER>**, to execute the command or bring up another menu. In this simulation, many graphs and menus are available from more than one source. When you first play the simulation, pull-down menus offer the easiest way to find everything. Later, you can learn many shortcuts.

Each menu or choice will include mouse and keyboard instructions. If there are no keyboard instructions, there are no short-cut keys. Just follow the mouse instructions to get to that command.

File Menu

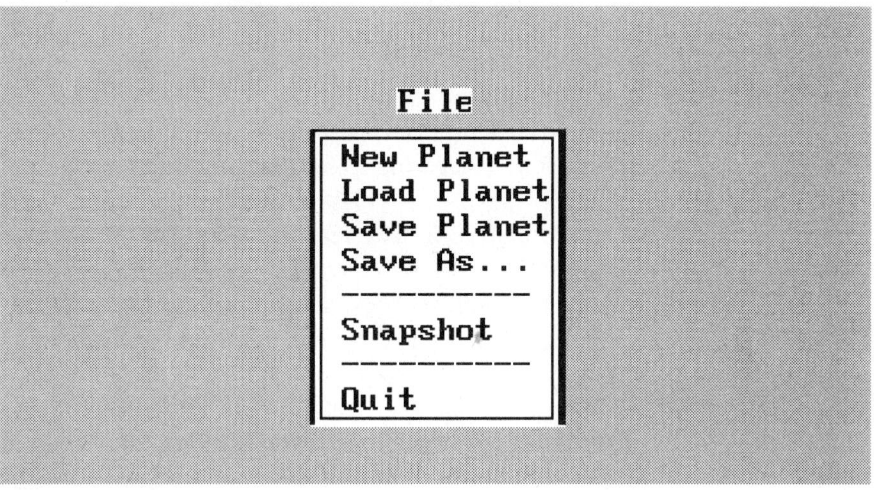

<SELECT> `File`

<Alt-F>

The file menu is the first menu you'll use. Use this menu to start and quit the game, as well as save what you have done.

New Planet

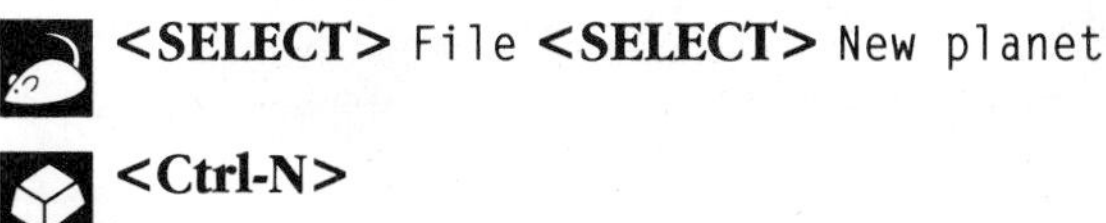
<SELECT> `File` **<SELECT>** `New planet`

<Ctrl-N>

Make this selection to start a new game. You will have many choices to make, as described earlier. At any point while playing, if you find the planet a hopeless mess, select this menu choice to start over and try again. If you choose `New Planet` while working on another planet, SimEarth will give you the option of saving the current planet first.

Load Planet

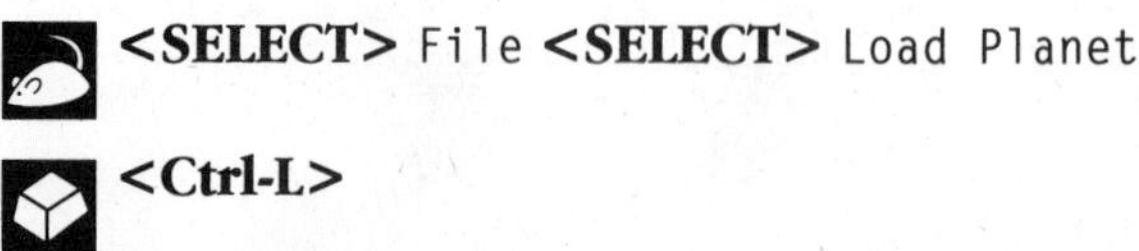

<SELECT> `File` **<SELECT>** `Load Planet`

<Ctrl-L>

You can load planets you have worked on (and saved) before with this choice. **<SELECT>**ing `Load Planet` brings up the Load World Window, shown in Figure 15.9. This window displays a series of boxes across the top which contain disk drive letters. **<SELECT>**ing one of these displays the directories or files with the .PLA extension in the selected drive in the file window below the `Path:` display. For example, **<SELECT>** the `A:` box, and any directories or world files on the floppy disk in your A: drive appear on-screen.

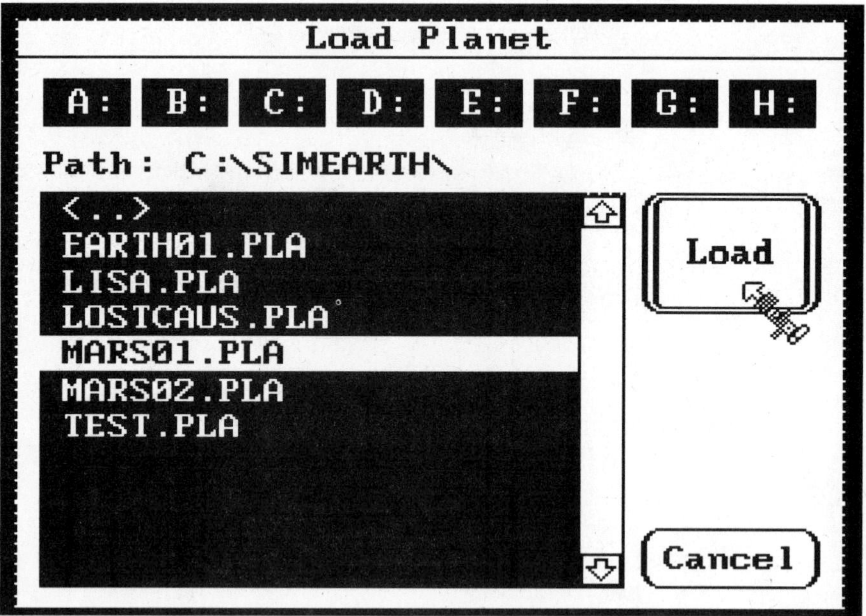

Figure 15.9 *Gentlemen, load your world!*

The `Path:` display shows the current path of the files displayed in the scrolling file window beneath it. The scroll bar, on the side of the file window, enables you to **<CLICK>** on the ↑ or ↓ to scroll through the files in the current directory. To load a planet, **<SELECT>** the box for the drive containing your files and **<SELECT>** the appropriate directory to display your world files. Highlight the world file you wish to load, then **<SELECT>** the `Load` button. If you decide not to load a file, just **<SELECT>** the `Cancel` button in the lower right corner of the window to return to the previous display.

Save Planet

 **<SELECT>** `File` **<SELECT>** `Save Planet`

<Ctrl-S>

<SELECT>ing this menu option brings up a window similar to the Load World window. The Save World window displays `Select world to save` **at** the top, with a box. The box contains the name of the planet you have been working on. If you wish to rename the planet, just **<SELECT>** this box and delete the current name. Type a new name, and **<SELECT>** the `Save` button at the right side of the File: window. If you wish to store the planet in a different directory, **<SELECT>** the box with the letter of the drive you wish to use. SimEarth displays the directories of the drive you select in the File: window. **<SELECT>** the directory you want, or just save the planet in the root directory.

After you have saved your planet once, **<SELECT>**ing `Save Planet` will only prompt you to make sure you want to overwrite the older version of the file. **<SELECT>**ing `Yes` returns you to the simulation after quickly saving the world. If only it was so easy to save the real world.

Save As...

<SELECT> `File` **<SELECT>** `Save As...`

This choice on the File menu brings up the Save World window to enable you to rename your planet if you choose to do so. After you have saved your planet once, the Save Planet choice alerts you to the fact you are overwriting the old version of the planet. Save As... enables you to rename your planet if you are keeping separate versions of the planet, which is handy if you are trying new planet-altering techniques. If your plan fails, you can call up the last "good" version of the planet. Who wants to throw away five billion years' worth of work?

Snapshot (Print)

The procedure for printing a planet varies greatly between the MS-DOS and Macintosh versions of SimEarth. The Mac version calls this menu choice `Print` while the MS-DOS version menu option is called `Snapshot`.

The black and white Mac version of SimEarth prints the whole planet in a compressed view, including the Report window, the Biome Ratio graph, the Atmospheric graph, the Life Class Ratio graph, and the planet scenario and level of play. SimEarth for the Mac includes two versions of the program in the package, but only the black and white version enables you to print. Color Mac users must use the black and white version to print a planet.

Nothing at all prints when MS-DOS users choose `Snapshot`. It just saves one or four screen files to disk. A program which supports the PCX graphic file format can print these files. PC Paintbrush is one of the more common MS-DOS graphic software packages that can print SimEarth planets.

Once you select `Snapshot`, a second selection provides a choice for one image of 1024 x 512 pixels or four images of 512 x 256. If the screen is set at a lower resolution, these numbers will also be smaller. Color screens are captured in colors, black and white in, well, black and white. Any Map selections active at the time are included in the image.

Because so much is compressed into the large image (1024 x 512 in high resolution), the resulting PCX file is not very useful. We created snapshots of both black and white and color images, and printed the results. The printed image was as useful as those photographs of a house with someone on the porch. You know that someone's there, but you just don't exactly know who they are unless someone tells you.

The smaller image file, (it takes four small files to capture the entire planet) is only marginally better. The biomes and cities are visible in the image. You have to print all four and tape them together to get the complete picture.

Snapshot is careful to check the disk prior to writing the files. If you previously named and numbered a screen capture as SNAP01.PCX, the program will save the next file as SNAP02.PCX. The quadrant images are named SNAP01A.PCX, SNAP01B.PCX, SNAP01C.PCX and SNAP01D.PCX.

Quit

 **<SELECT>** `File` **<SELECT>** `Quit`

<Ctrl-X>

<SELECT>ing this command makes all the Sims quit smoking. Just kidding. It's really for ending a session of SimEarth. The Quit command brings up a prompt asking if you are sure you want to quit. **<SELECT>** `Yes` and go back to working on that report for your boss.

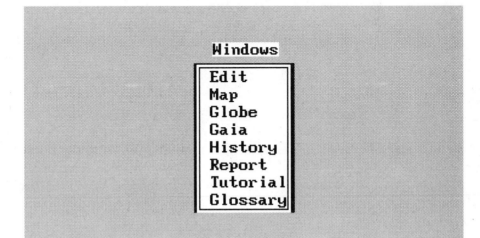

Windows Menu

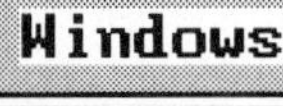

Edit
Map
Globe
Gaia
History
Report
Tutorial
Glossary

<SELECT> `Windows`

<Alt-W>

The Windows menu enables you to access various windows in SimEarth. You can open most of the windows in other ways, but using the menu is the easiest way to start to use the windows. You can bring any open window to the front of the display by **<CLICK>**ing on any exposed part of the window. If none of a window is visible, **<SELECT>** it from the menu to bring it to the front.

Edit

<SELECT> `Windows` **<SELECT>** `Edit`

<Ctrl-E>

This menu selection opens the Edit window or brings it to the front if it is already open. You can find out more about the Edit window in Chapter 16.

World

<SELECT> `Windows` **<SELECT>** `World`

<Ctrl-M>

This menu choice opens a window which displays the entire world as a flat map. If the window is already open, this menu choice brings it to the front. A blinking rectangle highlights the area of the world currently displayed in the Edit window.

Globe

 **<SELECT>** `Windows` **<SELECT>** `Globe`

<Ctrl-O>

The Globe window choice opens a window which displays the planet in its true round form. The displays in the Globe window show the same attributes displayed in the World window. The Globe window shows whatever the World window displays. **<DOUBLE-CLICK>**ing on any area but the blinking trapezoid, (which indicates the Edit window area), displays the interior of the planet, as shown in Figure 15.10.

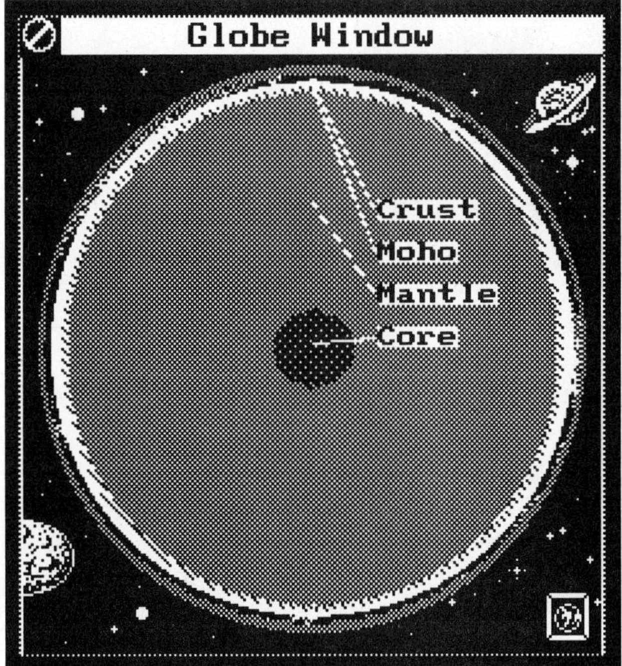

Figure 15.10 *The planet interior revealed.*

Gaia

<SELECT> `Windows` **<SELECT>** `Gaia`

<Ctrl-G>

This is the little caricature which represents the Gaia that is maintaining your planet. Open this window and watch how Gaia reacts to your meddlings with the planet. Gaia is cute for a while, but eventually seeing him may get old for you. Besides, with Gaia in the way, you won't have enough room to display everything you want to see on your screen.

Tutorial

<SELECT> `Windows` **<SELECT>** `Tutorial`

<Ctrl-T>

The Tutorial selection brings up a scrolling dialog box which gives you some information about the simulation. After you've played the simulation a few times, this window will have little value to offer you.

History

<SELECT> `Windows` **<SELECT>** `History`

<Ctrl-H>

The History window provides a graphed record of various conditions. By tracking changes in chemical composition, life, humidity, and other variables, the graphs enable you to follow the development of your planet. The bottom of the window displays several buttons you turn on and off by <CLICK>ing. You can select as many as four variables at once for graph display. Following are the 15 variables tracked in the History Window:

- ❑ **CO_2** displays the carbon dioxide levels.
- ❑ **O_2** displays the oxygen levels.
- ❑ **CH_4** displays the methane levels.
- ❑ **Sea temperature** displays an average of the overall water temperature in the oceans.
- ❑ **Air temperature** displays an average of the planet's air temperature.
- ❑ **Rainfall** displays an average of the planet's rainfall.
- ❑ **Population** displays the planet's population of Sims.
- ❑ **Biomass** displays the total weight of plant and animal life on the planet. (Plant life forms contribute 99% of the total weight.)
- ❑ **Diversity** displays the number of different species on the planet. Periods with major extinctions will be obvious here.
- ❑ **Fossil Fuels** displays the fossil reserves within the planet. The fossil fuel supply grows during the Evolution time scale and is depleted by civilization.
- ❑ **Atomic Fuel** displays the reserves of atomic fuel within the planet.
- ❑ **Food** displays food production on the planet.
- ❑ **War** displays the amount of armed conflict for the entire planet.
- ❑ **Plague** displays the number of plagues that occur.
- ❑ **Pollution** displays the total amounts of pollutants released by the Sims.

The amount of time displayed on the graph changes according to the time scale that your planet is in. A line divides each of the time scales. The total number of years the History window can display at one time for each time scale is as follows:

Geologic	1,000,000,000
Evolution	70,000,000
Civilization	2500
Technology	50

The window, shown in Figure 15.11, scrolls right to left as time advances. There is no way to back up and evaluate conditions earlier in the planet's evolution.

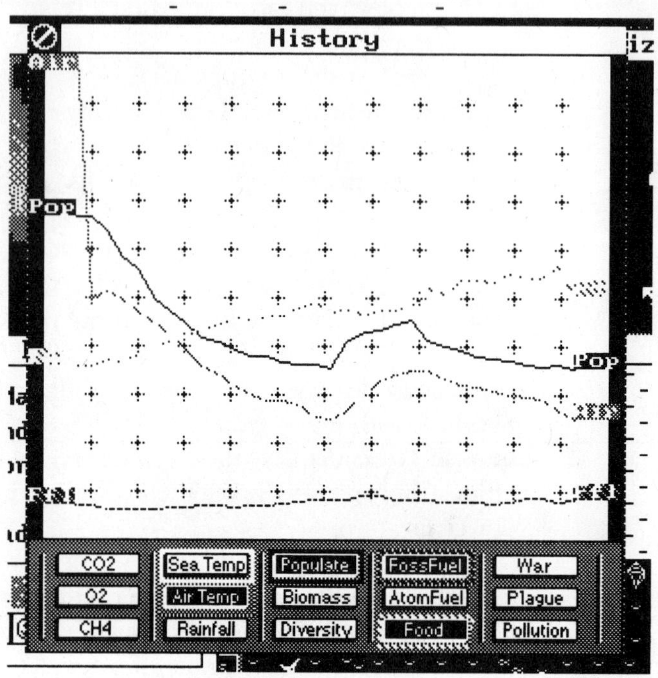

Figure 15.11 *This History window shows the population, air temperature, fossil fuel supply, and the food supply.*

Report

 **<SELECT>** `Windows` **<SELECT>** `Report`

 **`<Ctrl-R>`**

The Report window gives you feedback about how well your planet is doing. Watch this window to see just how well you're manipulating your resources. There are two different report windows, depending on which time scale the planet's in. A simple report gives information about the first two time scales. The second report, for the last two time scales, shows more detailed statistics.

The Report window for the Geologic and Evolution time scales (in Figure 15.12) shows the three most intelligent life forms, including an intelligence rating, or rough IQ estimate, for each. This window's IQ scale is not comparable to human IQ ratings; the window's IQ scale just provides a basis for comparing the intelligence of the various simulated species. When a specie's IQ rating reaches 100, the life form becomes *sentient*, or has perception. The report lists life forms according to development. The top of the list shows the sentient species, if there is one. Then the list gives the highest class after the sentient and the median class. Next the report indicates the *zoomass* and the *biomass*. The zoomass is the combined mass of all the animal forms; biomass is the total mass of plant life.

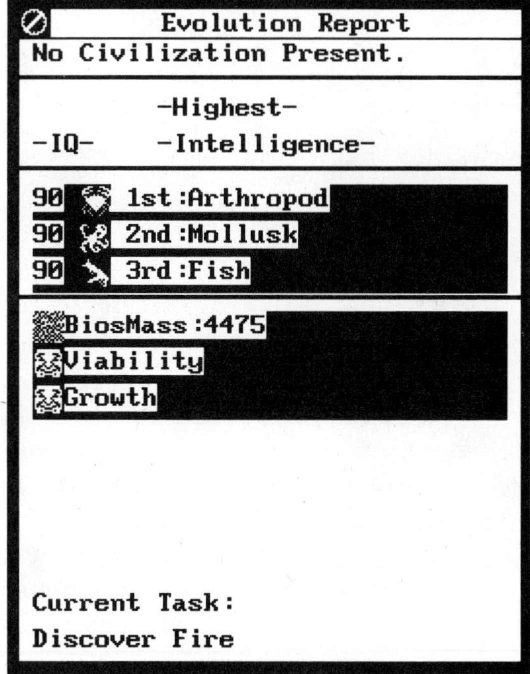

***Figure 15.12** The Evolution Report window.*

The Report window for the Civilization and Technology time scales displays much more information because the planet it describes has become more complex. Figure 15.13 shows an example Technology Report window. The `Sentient Type:` field tells you which life form has become the dominant, most intelligent species. The `Highest Tech:` field tells you how far the sentient species has evolved in some area of the planet. Next, the `Median Tech:` field tells you the average advancement for the entire planet. The report shows the `Population:` of Sims on the planet.

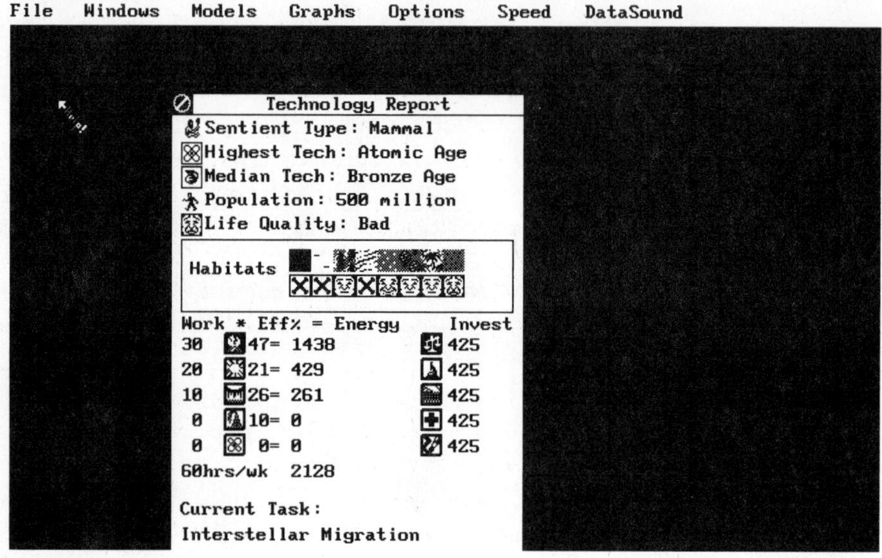

Figure 15.13 *The Technology Report window.*

The last item on the list gives the `Life Quality:` for the Sims, the sentient species. The Life Quality is for the common "Sim on the street." In other words, the Life Quality rating reflects the average living conditions. The two factors which the simulation uses to judge Life Quality are the number of work hours per week and the allocation of resources to the `Art/Media` category. (Look at the Civilization Model control panel shown in Figure 15.13 to see the Energy Allocation categories.) If you are the dictator type, you will use more energy for the `Science` category than for `Art/Media`. As a result, the Sims will live like slaves only working to produce the goods for the upper classes. If you try reducing the work hours to 0 (we'll explain how to do this later), the living conditions will reach the best immediately. Unfortunately, when we let the Sims get out of working, our civilization soon collapsed. The different `Life Quality` levels are Heavenly, Marvelous,

Good, Pleasant, Tolerable, Unpleasant, Bad, Miserable, and Hellish. The better the living conditions, the faster the technology levels will advance.

In the middle of the Civilization and Technology Report windows is a box which displays the Habitats (biomes) on the planet and how the Sims like each one. The `Habitats` box gives you an idea of where the Sims thrive. The Sims' rating for each biome indicates how well they have adapted to living in the biome. Four different symbols depict the ratings for biomes. An "X" indicates that the Sims can't live in the biome. A "sad face" means Sims can live in the biome but hate it. When Sims can live in a biome and like it, the box shows a "straight face." A "smiling face" indicates a biome that is what we all want—a paradise.

The bottom of the Civilization and Technology Report windows gives information on Energy. The Energy information in the Report windows is the most valuable because you can use it in conjunction with the Civilization Model control panel. Open both the control panel and this window and place them side by side. As you adjust the energy levels using the control panel, you can see the results in the Report window. The left column lists the amount of hours committed to each energy type and shows the Energy icons. To the right of the icons is the efficiency rating, followed by the energy calculated from the formula. The bottom of the column gives the total of the hours worked for the energy sources, and the total energy produced.

You control the hours allocated for each energy source using the Civilization Model control panel. Watch the Report window carefully, and use the most efficient form of energy (which depends on whether your planet is in the Civilization or Technology time scale). Using the most efficient energy form means the planet gets the most energy for the hours worked, and the Sims will be happy. Use the left column of the control panel to change the number of hours invested in each energy type. As you make changes in the left column of the control panel, you will see the hours allocated to the different energy types change accordingly. The energy types are

- ❑ **BioEnergy**—This is the natural power produced by animals and the Sims which do the work. This energy source also includes plant power (farming) and burning wood for cooking and heating. BioEnergy is always one of the most efficient energy types.
- ❑ **Solar/Wind**—This energy type includes things like sun-drying clothes and food, as well as modern uses like solar heating. Wind energy powers windmills, wind-powered generators, and sailing ships. The Solar/Wind efficiency will increase as your species advance technologically.

- **Hydro/Geo**—This energy type is the use of water to power waterwheels and hydroelectric power generators. Geothermal energy includes natural sources that heat homes or caves, or power steam generators. Hydro/Geo also becomes a more efficient energy type with time.
- **Fossil Fuel**—This energy type, otherwise known as coal and oil, comes from earlier species that died off. Fossil Fuels become important in the Industrial Age, with a high efficiency rating. If you use them too heavily, you will run out, and they'll have no efficiency rating at all. This energy type also increases the "Greenhouse Effect."
- **Nuclear**—The use of atomic energy to produce electric power becomes important in the later stages of civilization as the efficiency improves with the technology. Again, overuse will deplete the fuel supplies and kill the advantages of technological advances.

As shown in the right column of the Civilization Model control panel, you allocate the energy to five different categories. How you divide the energy can affect the Sims' happiness, as well as the advancement of civilization. The categories include

- **Philosophy**—The Philosophy category controls how much time the species will think about things before they do them. Allocating energy to Philosophy will deter war. The Sims will have fewer conflicts if you give the right amount of energy to Philosophy.
- **Science**—You must allocate energy to Science to advance to a higher technology. Giving too much energy to Science will produce a quick peak, followed by a lot of wars and plagues. A slow, even rise in technology will occur if you use the right amount of energy for Science.
- **Agriculture**—Energy for Agriculture affects the output of the food for the sentient species. Increasing the amount of energy for Agriculture will help to increase the population.
- **Medicine**—Without any energy for the Medicine category, the planet's population will die off from plagues.

- **Art/Media**—Giving energy to this category will increase the quality of life by increasing the entertainment available. This assumes that you allow the sentient beings time to do something besides work.

The bottom of the Report window displays the Current task. You must complete the current task so your planet can move on to the next time scale.

Glossary

<SELECT> `Windows` **<SELECT>** `Glossary`

The Glossary window is simply an on-line help window with definitions of words commonly used in SimEarth. **<CLICK>** on the up and down arrows on the scroll bar to move through the text. Keyboarders can press the ↑ and ↓ keys to scroll. Once you're familiar with the simulation, you won't use this window often.

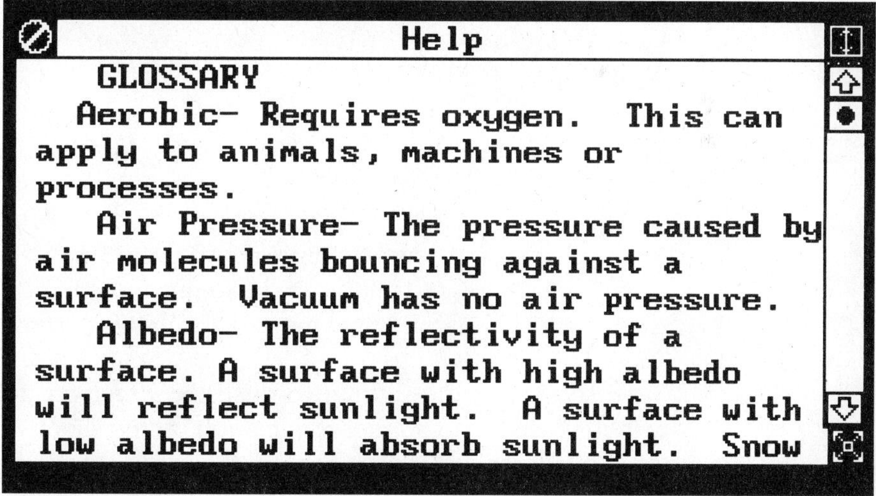

Figure 15.14 The Glossary window.

Models Menu

 **<SELECT>** `Models`

<Alt-M>

The model control panels enable you to fine-tune the many different settings that affect your planet. The control panels are the only screen areas used for input only. You will not see how the changes you make to the settings in the panels affect the planet. The control panels only display settings; other windows display results. To **<SELECT>** an item in a control panel, you must **<CLICK>** on the item to highlight it. An indicator bar appears next to each item to indicate the item's current setting. Each item has 16 possible settings.

To change the setting, you use the *slider* on the right side of the window. Move the pointer to the knob on the slider, and **<CLICK>** and hold down the left mouse button. Move the slider up or down, and the indicator bar increases or decreases accordingly. This method of changing a setting will cost you 150 E.U., no matter how much you move the slider. You can *bump* the slider by positioning the pointer under or over the knob and **<CLICK>**ing once. This technique moves the slider one position down or up and costs only 30 E.U. The main thing to remember is that if you want to move the slider a little, bump it. Moving the slider all the way up or down will cost 450 E.U. if you bump it one level at a time. For any major adjustments, slide it. In the upper right corner are the `NEXT` and `LAST` buttons. These will cycle you through all four control panels when you <SELECT> them. There is some time lag between when you make adjustments and when an adjustment affects your planet. The length of the time lag depends on the speed of the system and your selected speed setting.

Geosphere

<SELECT> `Models` **<SELECT>** `Geosphere`

The Geosphere Model control panel, shown in Figure 15.15, enables you to control the composition of the Geosphere, the core and crust of the planet. You also can control the impact of meteors from space and the tilt of the planet in relationship to the sun. Following are descriptions of the items in this panel:

- ❑ **Volcanic Activity** controls the amount of activity from volcanos.
- ❑ **Erosion** controls the rate of erosion, which affects the amount of CO_2 in the air.
- ❑ **Continental Drift Rate** controls the rate at which the continents drift.
- ❑ **Core Heat** controls the heat of the center of the planet, which affects the direction of the magma flow and the severity of the volcanic activity.
- ❑ **Core Formation** controls the rate at which the core forms. As the core forms, the planet size increases. This affects the magma flow, which impacts the volcanos and continental drift. (Just like reality—everything affects everything, or something like that.)
- ❑ **Meteor Impact** controls the amount of times the planet gets slammed by some object from space.
- ❑ **Axial Tilt** controls the tilt of the axis the planet rotates around. This tilt gives us seasons. More tilt than Earth's 22 degrees would result in more severe seasons. Go figure.

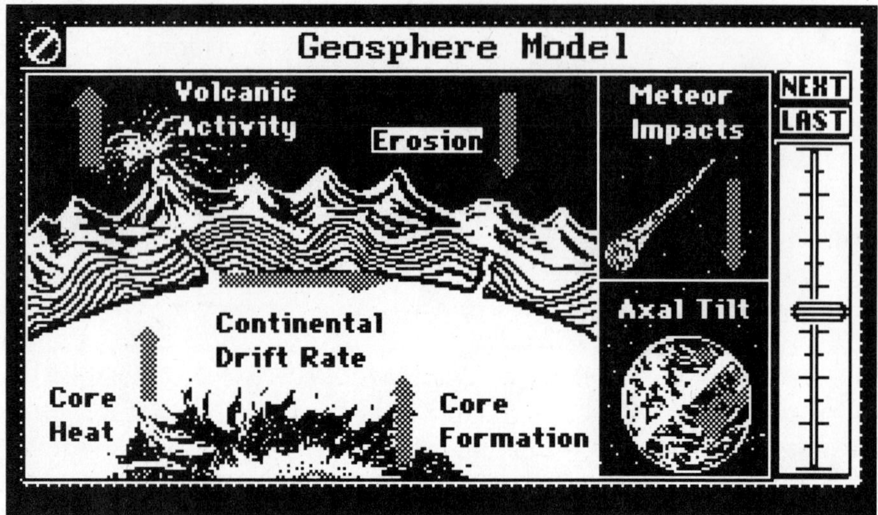

Figure 15.15 The Geosphere Model control panel.

Atmosphere

<SELECT> `Models` **<SELECT>** `Atmosphere`

The Atmosphere Model control panel, shown in Figure 15.16, enables you to regulate conditions that affect air temperature and weather. We found ourselves using this panel quite often. If you're not paying attention to the temperature, the oceans have a nasty habit of boiling away when it gets REAL hot. You can monitor the air temperature in the World window by selecting the temperature icon under the Atmosphere group. You can adjust the following conditions:

- ❏ **Solar Input** adjusts the incoming sun beams that produce heat. To make it night permanently, turn the slider all the way down. Fun, eh?
- ❏ **Cloud Albedo** affects the clouds' ability to reflect sun rays. The greater the reflection of the rays, the less heat reaches the surface of the planet, reducing the planet surface temperature.

- **Greenhouse Effect** controls the intensity of planet warming from the Greenhouse Effect. Gases blocking outgoing radiation increase the heat trapped in the atmosphere and the overall temperature. The Greenhouse Effect causes ice caps to melt, covering all small islands on the planet. Then your Sims will never get to see all the reruns of Gilligan's Island. Turn this setting way down when your Sims use a lot of fossil fuels and fill the air with those nasty gases.
- **Rainfall** controls the average yearly rainfall of the entire planet surface. Use this setting to determine whether the planet is a dust bowl or a wet tropical planet (with warm temperatures).
- **Surface Albedo** is the planet surface's ability to reflect solar radiation back into space. This setting also will affect the surface temperature of the planet.
- **Air-Sea Thermal Transfer** controls the rate at which the air and sea transfer heat. A higher setting stabilizes the planet's temperature, because sea temperatures do not change as fast as air temperatures.

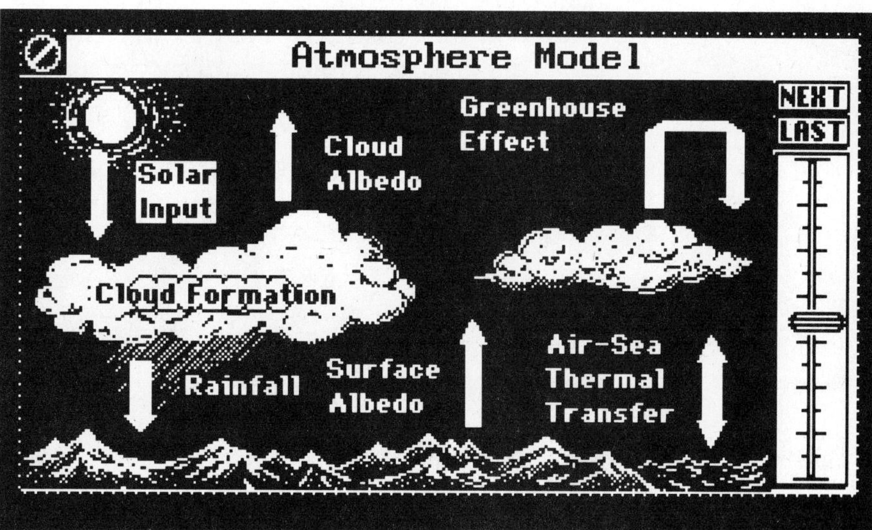

Figure 15.16 *The Atmosphere Model control panel.*

Biosphere

<SELECT> `Models` **<SELECT>** `Biosphere`

Shown in Figure 15.17, the Biosphere Model control panel enables you to regulate the biosphere, or living matter, on your planet. This control panel is very useful during the Evolution time scale. It gives you some control over what evolves to become the sentient species. In this panel you adjust the following factors:

- ❑ **Thermal Tolerance** controls the range of temperatures which the life forms can tolerate. The higher the setting, the larger the acceptable temperature range.
- ❑ **Reproduction Rate** controls the amount of fun allowed, which affects the number of young life forms which affects . . . well, you know.
- ❑ **CO_2 Absorption** controls the ability of plant forms to cleanse the air of carbon dioxide.
- ❑ **Mutation Rate** controls the rate at which life forms mutate. Mutations can make the evolution of a species jump ahead of normal. Some people we know are proof that this actually takes place.

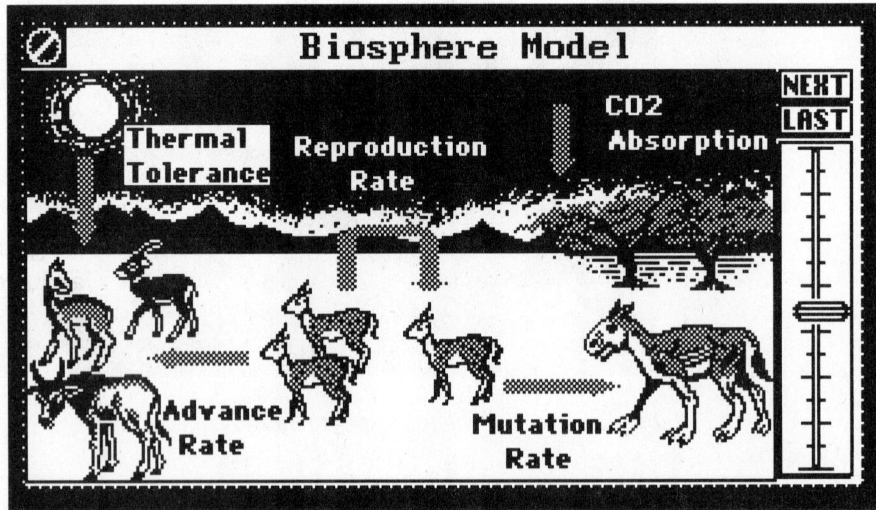

Figure 15.17 *The Biosphere Model control panel.*

Civilization

<SELECT> `Models` **<SELECT>** `Civilization`

Using the Civilization Model control panel, you can fine-tune whatever has become the sentient species of your planet. This is where the real challenge in SimEarth lies. You must make decisions and set priorities for the energy sources and uses. This control panel's results are best shown in the Report window. Open that window when you make adjustments in this panel, as shown in Figure 15.13.

The Civilization Mode control panel has two sections. Use the left side to make investments of the workers' labor. Your choices produce the energy that sustains the Sims. By watching the efficiency of each power source, you can increase the energy output with the least amount of work. The efficiency levels change with technological advances, so watch these indicators closely. The length of each indicator bar represents the working hours dedicated to its corresponding energy source. If you want none of a particular energy source, slide the control to nothing. The five energy sources are BioEnergy, Solar/Wind, Hydro/Geo, Fossil Fuel, and Nuclear. For more on this, refer to the section earlier in this chapter on the Report window.

The right side shows the energy allocations for each of the five categories of energy usage. All the energy produced is used. The indicators in this part of the panel are a comparison. The difference between indicator lengths is the important part. Having all the bars at the halfway point is the same as having all of them at full length. You don't want to turn one all the way down, as this can severely affect the efficiencies of the energy sources. If your efficiency levels decline, this can reduce your technology and cause your planet to slip back to the previous level. The categories of energy usage are Philosophy, Science, Agriculture, Medicine, and Art/Media. For more details on these, refer to the earlier section about the Report window.

Graphs Menu

 **<SELECT>** `Graphs`

<Alt-G>

There are four graph windows which you can access from the Graphs menu or icons in the Map Window. See Chapter 16 for more on the Map window icons. You can display only one graph at a time.

Atmospheric Composition

<SELECT> `Graphs` **<SELECT>** `Air Sample`

The Atmospheric Composition Graph window, shown in Figure 15.18, gives the current contents of the air on your planet. The graph displays four gases, the dust particles, and the water vapor in percentages of the total atmosphere. The Air Pressure is last on the list. The four gases are Nitrogen, Oxygen, Carbon Dioxide, and Methane (natural). The bars beside each percentage can be confusing if you don't pay attention to the shading. The graph compares only bars that are the same shades, as some of them represent less than 1% of the atmosphere, while others indicate percentages above 10%, and so on. Looking at the numbers in conjunction with the bars will tell you which is which. A plus (+) or minus (–) indicates that an item is increasing or decreasing. Things to watch for are lack of life-sustaining oxygen, and the lack of carbon dioxide for plant life.

This graph is handy in the Mars and Venus scenarios. You can use the terraformers to adjust the atmospheric levels to support the Sims.

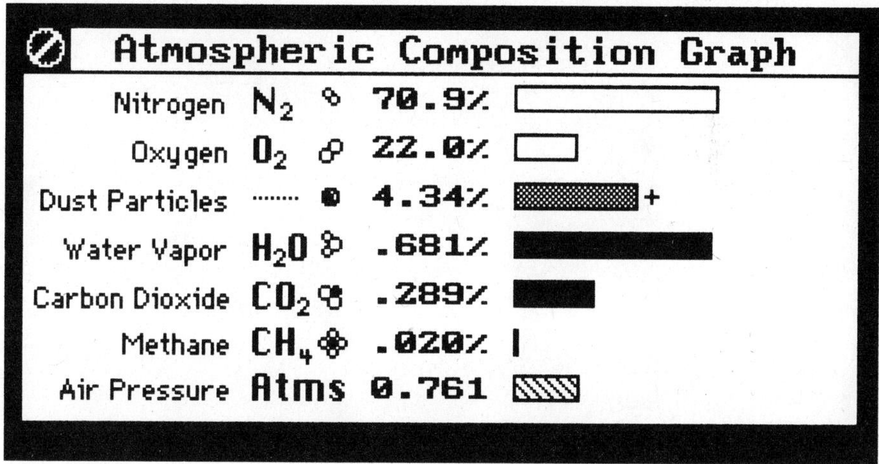

Figure 15.18 *The Atmospheric Composition Graph window.*

Biome Ratio

<SELECT> `Graphs` **<SELECT>** `Biomes`

The Biome Ratio Graph window, in Figure 15.19, displays the relative amounts of the seven different biomes in a three-dimensional form. This shows the history of which biomes have thrived and which have died. The bar in front is the most recent period, the bars stacked behind it give the variation back to when the biome appeared on the planet.

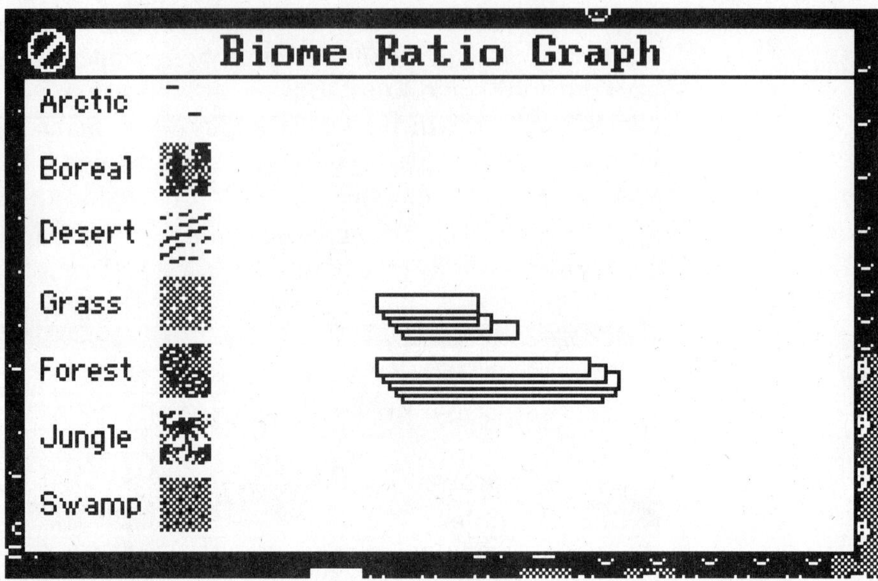

Figure 15.19 *The Biome Ratio Graph window.*

Life Class Ratio

<SELECT> `Graphs` **<SELECT>** `Life Forms`

This Graph window displays the 14 different life forms available with the Place Life tool, and that wild and crazy mutation, the Carnifern. This is what happens when programmers stay up all night. They create a life form that can only appear on your planet by mutation. Not only that, it can become the sentient species. It is a mobile carnivorous plant that prefers to hang out in all night bars (otherwise known as meat markets). This graph (in Figure 15.20) is like the Biome Ratio Graph, because it shows a history with the three-dimensional display of the indicator bars.

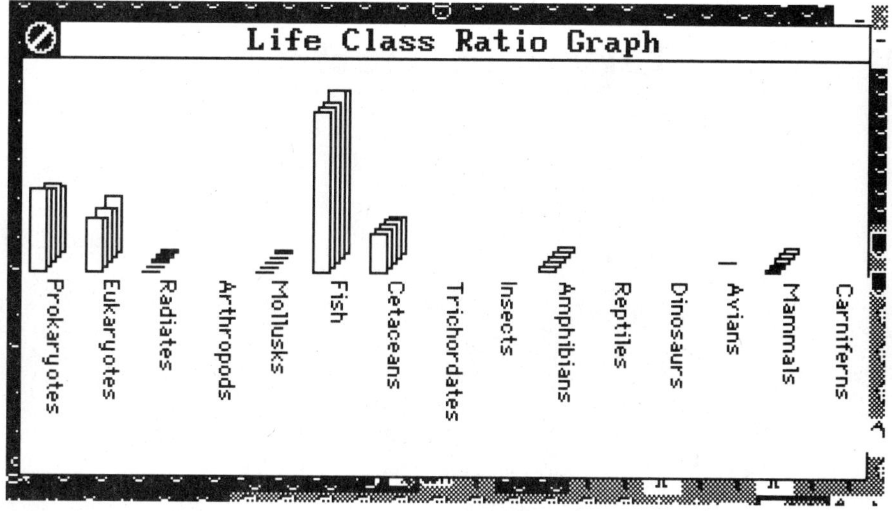

Figure 15.20 The Life Class Ratio Graph window.

Technology Ratio

<SELECT> `Graphs` **<SELECT>** `Technology`

As shown in Figure 15.21, the Technology Ratio Graph window displays the different technologies and portion of the population living in areas with each type of technology.

Technology Ratio Graph
Stone Age
Bronze Age
Iron Age
Industrial Age
Atomic Age
Information Age
Nanotech Age

Figure 15.21 The Technology Ratio Graph window.

Options Menu

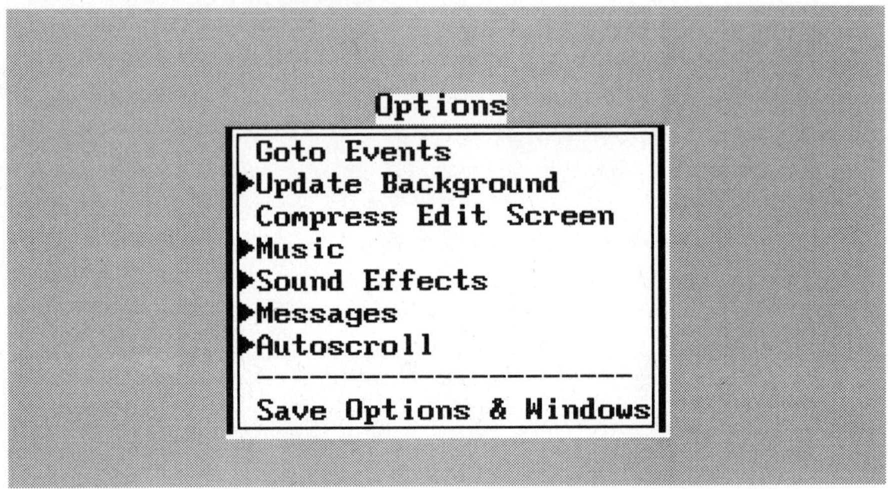

 **<SELECT>** `Options`

<Alt-O>

Windows available through the Options menu allow you to set up the simulation to suit your personal preferences. Some things you might use for a while but later find annoying, so this menu enables you to turn features off and on. When an option is in the active mode, an arrow appears next to it.

Goto Events

<SELECT> `Options` **<SELECT>** `Goto Events`

This feature works when you are in the Edit window only. When you choose this Options menu item, it "zooms" you to the spot when some sort of event occurs. This is not a really useful feature, as there is nothing you can do but watch the event. This is one option that we always leave in the default setting, off.

Update Background

 **<SELECT>** `Options` **<SELECT>** `Update Background`

<Ctrl-U>

This option is important to those who have a slower computer. It allows you to run only one window at a time, even when you have other windows open. With the Update Background option off, the simulation updates only the window in which you're working. This means the system has to perform less work, so the simulation runs faster. If you have a fast machine like we do, it is best to leave this option on, because you need to see the results of what you do in one window in another window. The simulation decides if you have a fast system and sets the default setting for this option accordingly.

Compress Edit Screen

<SELECT> `Options` **<SELECT>** `Compress Edit Screen`

This setting determines the area displayed in the Edit window. The normal view shows more detail in a smaller area. The compressed view shows only every other tile, including a larger area. This choice is useful for systems with small displays, like the Macintosh. The default setting for the Compress Edit Screen option is off. Because we used the Edit window so little, we paid little attention to this option.

Music

<SELECT> `Options` **<SELECT>** `Music`

The Music option simply enables or disables the music played during the simulation. This is one of those things that is cute at first but gets old after a while. We are glad that Maxis Software has given the player the option to turn this music off. You will be too. This option's default setting is on.

Sound Effects

<SELECT> `Options` **<SELECT>** `Sound Effects`

This option turns off the sound effects that happen in the game. As with the music, it is nice to be able to turn the sounds off. Especially when you might be playing at work. Oh, excuse us! We should know that no one plays games at work. The default setting for this option is off.

Messages

<SELECT> `Options` **<SELECT>** `Messages`

The Sims will contact you through the message displays from time to time during the simulation. If you tire of being interrupted by the complaints from your planet's citizens, turn the Messages option off. The default setting is on.

Autoscroll

<SELECT> `Options` **<SELECT>** `Autoscroll`

This option enables you to scroll the Edit window while you are using a tool at the edge of the window. As you move out of the display area, the window will then continue to scroll in the direction you are moving. We are not really sure why you would want to turn this option off. The default setting is on.

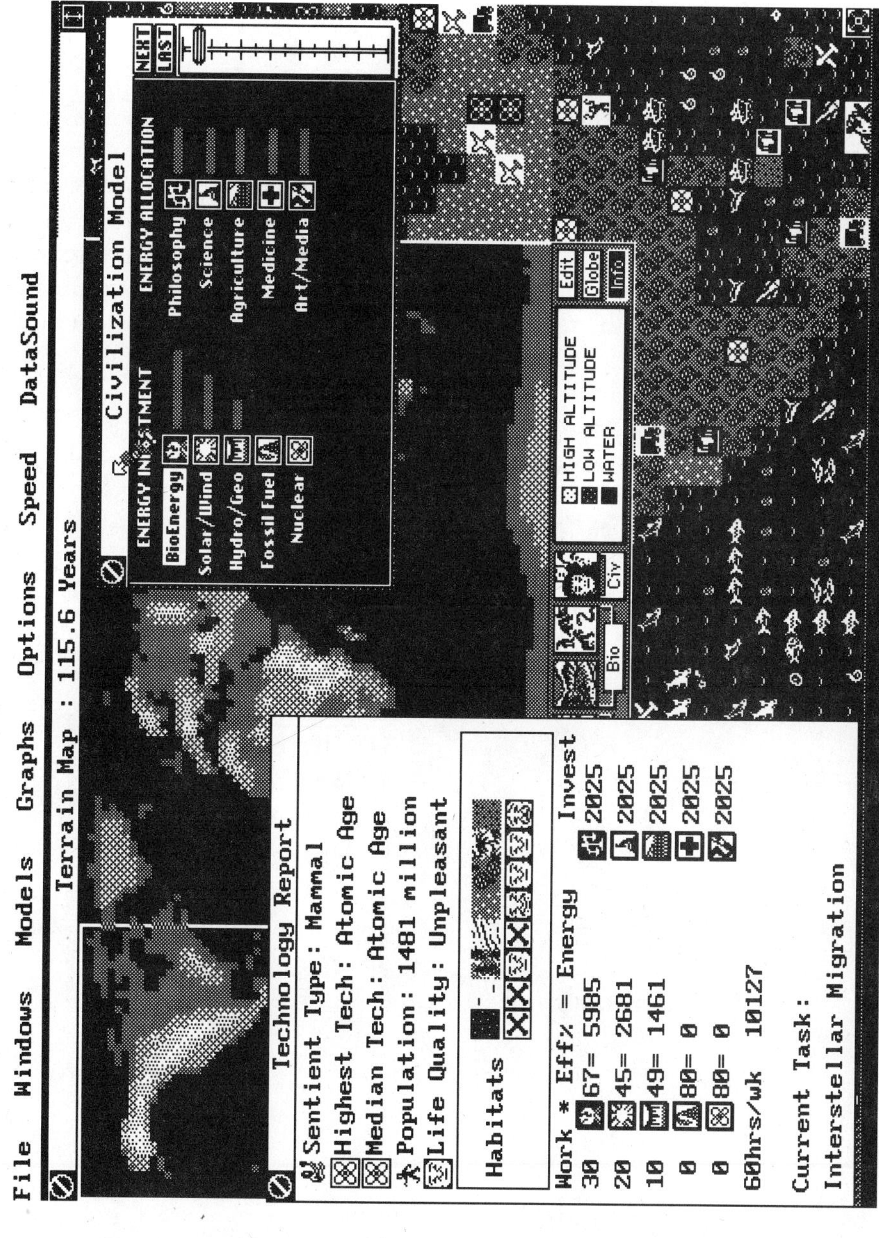

Figure 15.22 *The Civilization Model map, report, and control panel displayed with the Edit window.*

Save Options & Windows

<SELECT> `Options` **<SELECT>** `Save Options & Windows`

After you have set up all the options the way you want them and have the windows the way you want them to appear on your screen, **<CLICK>** once on this menu choice. This menu option saves the window configuration and options to disk for the active world file. The next time you load this world file, the screen windows will appear as you saved them, and the options you specified will be active. Figure 15.28 shows one of our favorite configurations.

Speed Menu

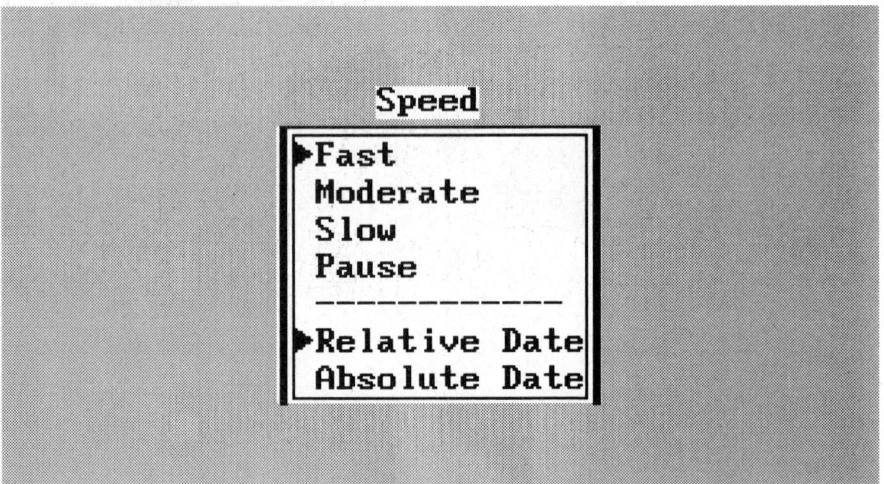

 **<SELECT>** `Speed`

<Alt-S>

The speed menu enables you to set the speed at which your system "crunches" the numbers that control the simulation. You also can control how the date appears on the message bar.

Fast

<SELECT> `Speed` **<SELECT>** `Fast`

<3>

Choosing this menu option runs the simulation at the fastest setting your machine can handle. We were running the simulation on 386s and found that the planet would die of old age in a couple of hours when we chose the Fast setting.

Moderate

<SELECT> `Speed` **<SELECT>** `Moderate`

<2>

This setting runs the simulation at approximately 75% of the fastest speed. This is the default setting when you start a planet.

Slow

<SELECT> `Speed` **<SELECT>** `Slow`

<1>

This menu choice sets the simulation to run at approximately 25% of the fastest setting. We finally learned that this was the best setting to use on our systems. At the fastest setting, the oceans could boil off in two minutes if the temperatures got too hot and we weren't watching closely.

Pause

 **<SELECT>** `Speed` **<SELECT>** `Pause`

<0>

Choose `Pause` to stop the time cycle but still allow you to use the planet manipulation tools.

Absolute Date

<SELECT> `Speed` **<SELECT>** `Absolute Date`

Choose this menu item to show the date as the time since the planet cooled. If you started your planet in a later time scale, the absolute date will be an estimate made by the simulation. Who's going to argue with that?

Relative Date

<SELECT> `Speed` **<SELECT>** `Relative Date`

This is the default setting when you start a new world. Relative Date shows the date as the time elapsed since whenever you started the simulation. It will not really be the age of the planet.

DataSound Menu

DataSound

Tone Monitor
Play Data Song

▸Altitude
Air Temperature
Rainfall
Sea Temperature
Biomes
Life
Civilization

 **<SELECT>** `DataSound`

 **`<Alt-D>`**

The DataSound menu enables you to use audible tones (sounds) to monitor some of the factors which affect your planet. The first two menu items determine the ways in which you can use the sound taken from data readings. The last seven options enable you to choose which data to use.

Tone Monitor

<SELECT> `DataSound` **<SELECT>** `Tone Monitor`

This plays an intermittent tone at a pitch determined by a reading from the selected data. The higher the reading, the higher the tone. For example, if you **<SELECT>** `Air Temperature` at the bottom of the DataSound menu then **<SELECT>** `Tone Monitor`, a high tone would mean that the average temperature of the planet is high. If the next tone was lower, then you would know that the temperature is dropping. When the Tone Monitor is selected, you can monitor various planet factors without having to refer to the appropriate display all the time.

Play Data Song

 **<SELECT>** `Datasound` **<SELECT>** `Play Data Song`

<Ctrl-D>

Data Songs are another of the cute features in this simulation. They're not very useful except for entertainment. The simulation divides the data selected from the planet into 32 evenly spaced readings. Then Data Song converts these readings into 32 notes and plays them in a song. Lawrence Welk, eat your heart out. The Sims are startin' a band.

Factors to Monitor

The bottom part of the menu contains the different elements on which the simulation bases the tones or songs. You can select only one of the following seven items at a time.

Altitude
Air Temperature
Rainfall
Sea Temperature
Biomass
Life
Civilization

Using these displays and menus are key to your success in developing a thriving planet. Make sure and check out all the choices on the menus just so you will know where to look for information when you need it. You will find that some things are next to useless or are just entertaining. Others will be necessary for specific tasks. Explore them all. The next chapter will tell you more about the "tools" with which you make the changes to the planet surface.

16 The Edit and Map Windows

The Edit and Map windows enable you to observe and modify the planet surface. We usually had both these windows open when playing the simulation. With these two views, you see the planet events as they happen.

Edit Window Title Bar

The Edit window, shown in Figure 16.1, presents a close-up view of the planet surface. Used for making changes to the planet, the Edit window is also known as Local Input in the SimEarth manual. You can move the Edit window around on the planet surface to investigate events. This is basically the only input and output window in the simulation. The main parts of the Edit window are the title bar, display area, and the control panel. On some systems, you will have scroll bars on the right side of and across the bottom of the window.

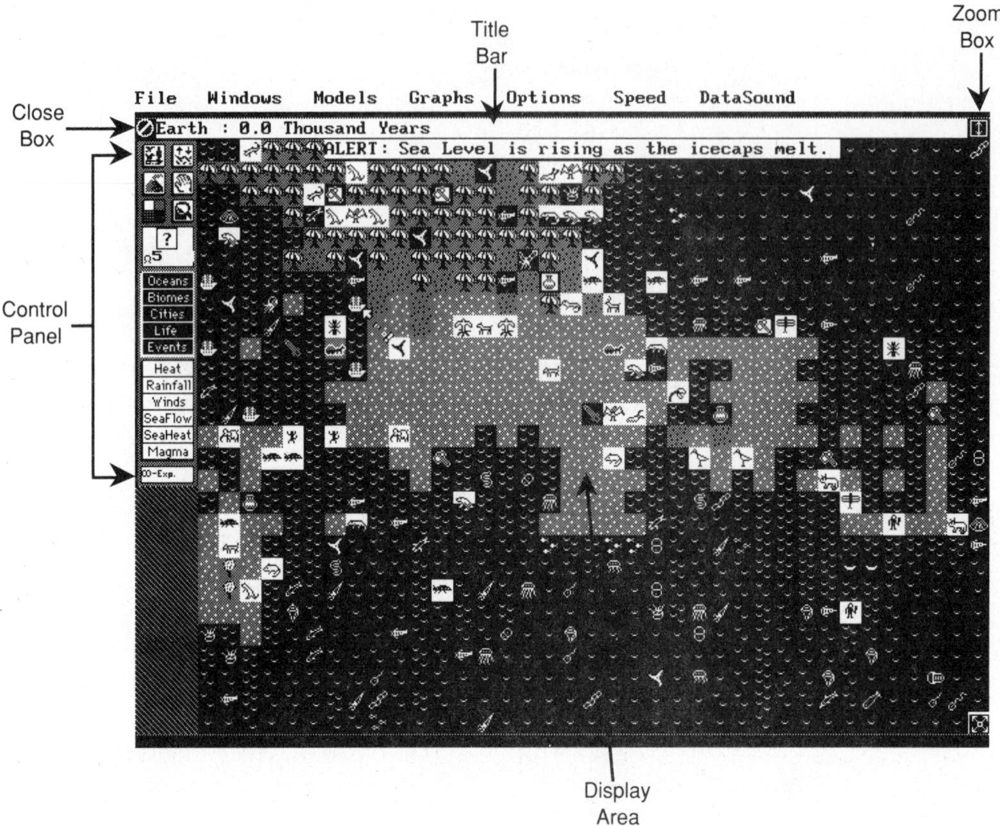

Figure 16.1 *The Edit window displaying the planet surface.*

Located across the top of the Edit window, the title bar displays the planet name and the date. The date displayed depends on the active date selection in the Speed menu, Absolute or Relative. The close box is located on the left end of the window, and the zoom box is on the right end. If you close the window, you can reopen it using the Windows menu. **<CLICK>**ing on the zoom box will make the window fill the entire screen. **<CLICK>**ing on the zoom box again will shrink the window back to the former size. Keyboarders can adjust the size of the window with **<CTRL-A>**. Use the Arrow keys to change the window size and press **<ENTER>** to finish the adjustment. **<CTRL-Z>** toggles window zooming.

You can reposition the Edit window like the rest of the windows. With the pointer on the title bar, **<CLICK>** and hold the left mouse button, and move the window to the position you want.

Edit Window Display Area

Using the planet manipulation tools, you can alter the planet surface shown in the display area. This is the only way you can work directly on the planet's surface and life forms. You can scroll around the entire planet a number of different ways. Some methods depend on what kind of computer system you're using. If you have scroll bars on the side and bottom of the Edit window (Macintosh), you can use them to move around. On MS-DOS systems, just move the pointer to the side of the display, and it will scroll in that direction. Vertical movement of the display is limited to the area between the top and bottom of the Map display. Moving horizontally, you can go around the world as long as you want. Near the top of the display area, SimEarth will display messages about the planet. Watch for the messages, as they can help you to eliminate problems that could wreck your planet.

Edit Window Control Panel

The Edit window control panel appears below the title bar, along the left side of the display area. Use the control panel to select the information displayed and to access tools for planet modification. Use the Help window to learn more about all the tools and icons. Hold the **<SHIFT>** key down and **<CLICK>** on the item you want more information about. SimEarth displays a small window about that tool or display item, as shown in Figure 16.2. Use the scroll bar to the right of the displayed text to access more information. The **<DEL>** (Delete) key on the keyboard will also bring up the Help window describing the item at the current pointer position. Hit **<DEL>** again to clear the Help window.

In the control panel, the tool icons enable you to make (or break) your planet. **<SELECT>** these items to perform an action or to bring up a menu with more choices.

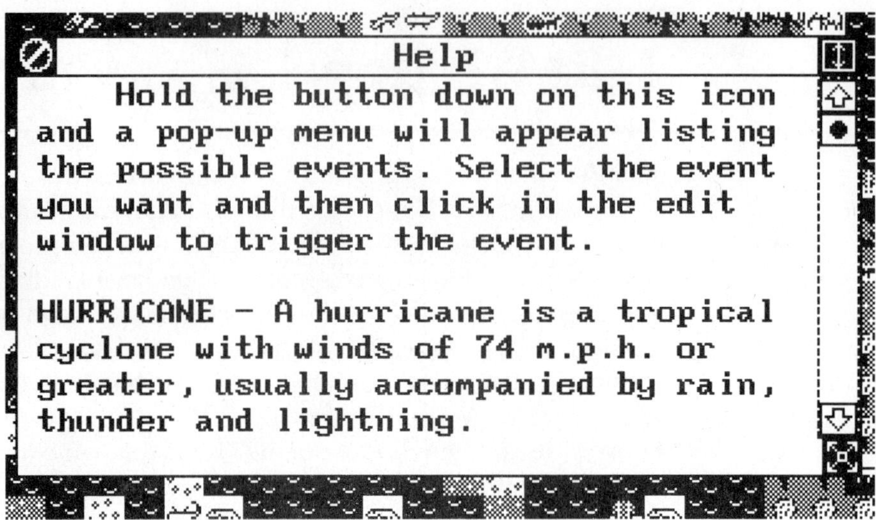

Figure 16.2 *The Help window, displaying information about the Event*

Place Life Tool

<SELECT>ing the Place Life tool icon from the upper left corner of the control panel displays the Place Life menu, shown in Figure 16.3. **<SELECT>** a life form, city, or terraformer from the menu to place it on the planet surface. There are 14 different life forms, seven types of cities, and seven terraformers to select from the menu. Of the life forms, seven are sea creatures and seven are land dwellers. Each time you place life, you will be charged E.U.s (Energy Units).

To place a life form, use the following procedure:

1. Move the pointer to the icon for the life form, city, or terraformer you wish to place.

2. **<CLICK>** on it with the left mouse button or press **<SPACE BAR>**. The selected item appears in the current tool display, with the E.U. costs underneath it.

3. Move to the area in the Edit window where you want to start the life form and **<CLICK>**.

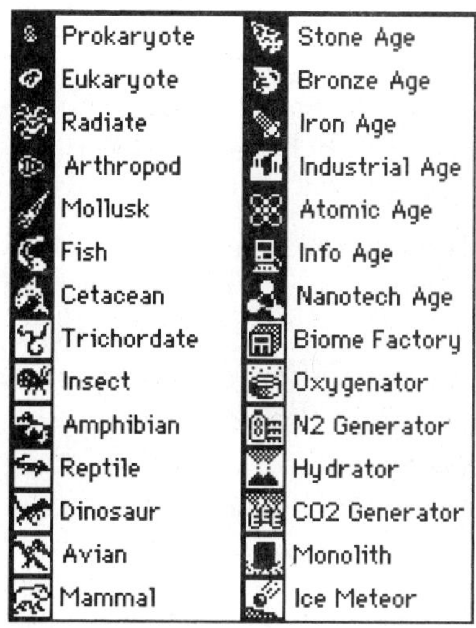

Figure 16.3 *The Place Life menu.*

The life form has life! If you have not placed it in an area where it can live, it will immediately die and your E.U.s will not be refunded! No guarantees in this world. A description of each life form, city, and terraformer, and the E.U.s charged for each, follows.

Sea Life

The sea is where life began. In SimEarth, Sea life forms range from simple single-celled bacteria to the rulers of the sea, Cetaceans. Following are the Sea life forms:

Prokaryote—Single-celled bacteria.	35 E.U.
Eukaryote—Single-celled amoebas.	70 E.U.
Radiate—Simple multi-celled starfish.	105 E.U.
Arthropod—Crabs, lobsters, crayfish.	140 E.U.
Mollusk—Snails, clams, octopi, squid.	175 E.U.
Fish—What else? Fish.	210 E.U.
Cetacean—Whales, dolphins, Flipper.	245 E.U.

Land Life

In the Evolution time scale, life crawls from the sea. After that happens, you can try your luck with the following Land life forms:

Trichordate—Simple animal with spines.	280 E.U.
Insect—Creepy, crawly, yech!	315 E.U.
Amphibian—Frogs, newts, toads.	350 E.U.
Reptile—Slithery sneakies and turtles.	385 E.U.
Dinosaur—Big lizards.	420 E.U.
Avian—Birds.	455 E.U.
Mammal—Humans, apes, rodents, lawyers, etc.	490 E.U.

Cities

You can place seven types of cities, each from a different time period. You cannot place a city until your planet is in the Civilization time scale. Cities are expensive and really designed to be used in the Experimental mode. The seven cities with the E.U.s charged are

Stone Age—Oldest culture, uses stone tools.	500 E.U.
Bronze Age—Uses bronze tools.	1000 E.U.
Iron Age—Uses iron tools.	1500 E.U.
Industrial Age—Uses machinery.	2000 E.U.
Atomic Age—Uses atomic power.	2500 E.U.
Information Age—Uses information as a tool.	3000 E.U.
Nanotech Age—Don't need tools.	3500 E.U.

Terraformers

You'll use the terraformers in the scenarios, which Chapter 17 covers. Once placed, a terraformer will keep working. The only way to stop a terraformer is to slam it with a meteor, burn it with fire, or try something equally destructive. There are five terraformers, the Monolith tool, and the Ice Meteor in this section of the Place Life menu, as follows:.

Biome Factory—Once placed, these factories look at the surrounding terrain and produce a biome which can exist there. The Biome Factory monitors the climate and will create different biomes if necessary. These cost 500 E.U.s.

Oxygenator—Oxygenators take carbon dioxide out of the atmosphere and replace it with oxygen. For life to survive, the atmosphere must be between 15 and 25 percent oxygen. Too much oxygen causes fires to burn a long time and destroy much of the planet. Because it eliminates carbon dioxide, a gas that contributes to the greenhouse effect, an oxygenator will help to cool a hot planet. These cost 500 E.U.s.

N_2 Generator—These are used to build up the nitrogen (N_2) level, increasing atmospheric pressure. Atmospheric pressure affects the temperature by controlling heat loss. The more dense the atmosphere, the more heat it retains. Making the atmosphere more dense also stabilizes the other gases. N_2 Generators will set you back 500 E.U.s.

Vaporator—These add moisture to the air, causing more humidity and thus more rainfall. Vaporators cost 500 E.U.s.

CO_2 Generator—These produce carbon dioxide (CO_2), which is necessary for plant life. If you have an Oxygenator, eliminate it first. Otherwise it would simply cancel the effects of the CO_2 Generator. These also cost 500 E.U.s.

Monolith—This is not a terraformer, but it's in the Place Life menu for convenience. The Monolith tool speeds up evolution. Maxis credits Arthur C. Clark's story *2001: A Space Odyssey* for this concept. To use the Monolith, **<SELECT>** it, then immediately **<SELECT>** a life form. There is a one in three chance that you will successfully force mutation to a higher life form and automatically move your planet to the next time scale. If you use the Monolith in the Technology time scale, you might trigger the Exodus. (Exodus is the win situation for the simulation.) The Monolith does not work on all life forms. We managed to use it to start the Exodus on a planet, then advanced Carniferns to the sentient species. Using it some more, the Carniferns eventually started the Exodus themselves, all in a 10-minute period. Using the Monolith costs 2,500 E.U.s, whether it works or not.

Ice Meteor—<SELECT> the Ice Meteor to make a large chunk of ice fall from space. This is handy when your planet has little or no water. A couple of these will start the oceans on Mars. Ice Meteors cost 500 E.U.s.

The Extinct Function—This is an added function that enables you to wipe out a life form. Hold down **<CTRL>** (the **<OPTION>** key on some systems), and **<CLICK>** on the life form in the Place Life submenu. Gone!

The Event Trigger Tool

The icon below the Place Life tool icon activates the Event Trigger tool. **<SELECT>**ing the Event Trigger tool icon displays another menu, shown in Figure 16.4. The choices on this menu start specific events wherever you specify. By triggering these events, you can better understand events that occur naturally in the simulation. There are 11 different events that occur in the simulation. You can trigger all but three of them—war, pollution, and the Exodus. To choose one of the events, use the following steps:

1. Move the pointer to the icon for the event you wish to trigger.
2. **<CLICK>** on it with the left mouse button or press **<SPACE BAR>**. The current tool display shows the event you selected, along with the cost of 50 E.U.s for each use.
3. Move the pointer to the location in the Edit window where you wish to trigger the event and **<CLICK>** or press **<SPACE BAR>**.

Following are the events you can trigger using the Event Trigger menu:

- ❑ **Hurricane**—High winds and rain. Hurricanes add moisture to the atmosphere.
- ❑ **Tidal Wave**—A large wave gets everything wet. These are also triggered when you crash an Ice Meteor into the sea.
- ❑ **Meteor**—A large piece of space debris slams into the planet and destroys everything in the immediate area. Meteors kick up a lot of dust if they hit on land. The Air Sample graph can show the dust level.

Figure 16.4 *The Event Trigger menu.*

- ❑ **Volcano**—The planet springs a leak, and the inner molten lava pours out. Volcanos can build islands in the sea or create mountains on land. They also destroy everything around. Small problem.
- ❑ **Atomic Test**—Whoops! Somebody leaned on the button. The area will remain radioactive for quite awhile.
- ❑ **Fire**—And smoke. Fires will burn a lot if there is a high oxygen content in the atmosphere.
- ❑ **Earthquake**—This choice displays a submenu that enables you to point to the direction that you want the quake to move the crust. This way you can use it to direct the crust together to form mountain ranges. Are we having fun or what?
- ❑ **Plague**—Some deadly disease will spread and kill off many life forms on a random basis. In the Edit window, a skull and crossbones chewing gum represents a plague.

Plant Biome Tool

The Plant Biome tool icon appears below the Event Trigger tool icon. **<SELECT>** the Plant Biome tool to bring up the menu shown in Figure 16.5. *Biomes* are areas filled with plant life forms that thrive in a specific type of environment. For example, the Arctic biome thrives in the cold areas but vanishes in the tropic areas. There are seven different biomes, each thriving according to certain altitudes, temperatures, and rainfall. Like the life forms, the simulation will automatically place biomes on the planet in a natural order. You can experiment by placing your own. Of course, nothing says that what you place is going to survive.

Figure 16.5 *The Plant Biome menu.*

To place a biome, use the following steps:

1. Move the pointer to the biome which you wish to place.

2. **<CLICK>** with the left mouse button or press **<SPACE BAR>**. The current tool display shows the selected biome along with the cost of 50 E.U.s for each biome placed.

3. Move to the area in the Edit window where you wish to place the biome and **<CLICK>** or press **<SPACE BAR>**.

Following are the different biomes and the environment in which each thrives.

- ❑ **Rock**—This is really no biome.
- ❑ **Arctic**—Place in areas that are cold and dry.
- ❑ **Boreal Forest**—Grows well in cold areas with moderate rainfall.
- ❑ **Desert**—Place in very hot areas with little rainfall.
- ❑ **Temperate Grasslands**—Place in areas with moderate temperatures and rainfall.
- ❑ **Forest**—Best in areas with moderate temperatures and high rainfall.
- ❑ **Jungle**—Thrives in areas with high temperatures and rainfall.
- ❑ **Swamp**—Place in areas with high temperatures and moderate rainfall.

Set Altitude Tool

Next to the top tool in the second column is the Set Altitude tool icon, which looks like up and down arrows. Use the Set Altitude tool to raise and lower sections of land. You can make islands in the sea or lakes on land. Creating islands or lakes destroys any life in the area and changes the climate in the surrounding space. So, it's best to use the Set Altitude tool before life forms are on your planet. There are 32 different levels of terrain possible in SimEarth; using this tool, you can adjust areas to your liking. Use it to create your own continents, or spell your name.

To use the Set Altitude tool, follow these steps.

1. Move to the Set Altitude tool icon and **<CLICK>** or press **<SPACE BAR>**. This sets you up to raise the level of the land. In the current tool display, you will see an up arrow. **<SELECT>** the icon again, and it turns to a down arrow, which means it will lower the land altitude.
2. Move the pointer to the area on the Edit window that you want to change.
3. **<CLICK>** and hold the left mouse button or **<SPACE BAR>**. You can move the pointer around to change large areas or just give a short **<CLICK>** to change a small area. You are charged 50 E.U.s for each **<CLICK>**, so **don't release the button until you've finished**. We were able to eliminate the oceans on a planet for 50 E.U.s. Needless to say, the civilization collapsed and the planet died. Just had to find out if we could do it.

Moving Tool

The Moving tool icon, below the Set Altitude tool icon, has a hand on it. This tool enables you to pick up any biome, niche, or civilization and move it. If you need to move a population to another continent or separate warring tribes, the Moving tool can be very handy. Simply **<SELECT>** the icon and move the pointer to the item you wish to relocate. Using the mouse, **<CLICK-DRAG>** the item to a new location. Release the button, and the moved item settles into the closest location. Using the Moving tool costs 30 E.U.s.

Examine Tool

The Examine tool icon, is the last icon, and is represented by a "?" in the current tool display. Use this handy tool to look at individual spots in the Edit window. To use the Examine tool, **<SELECT>** the icon, then move the pointer to the Edit window location you want to investigate. **<CLICK>** and hold the left mouse button (keyboarders press and hold the **<DEL>** key), and the Examine window appears with information about the selected area, as shown in Figure 16.6. Move the pointer without releasing the button or key, and the information for each new area you move into appears. Each time you **<CLICK>** the mouse, SimEarth charges you 5 E.U.s.

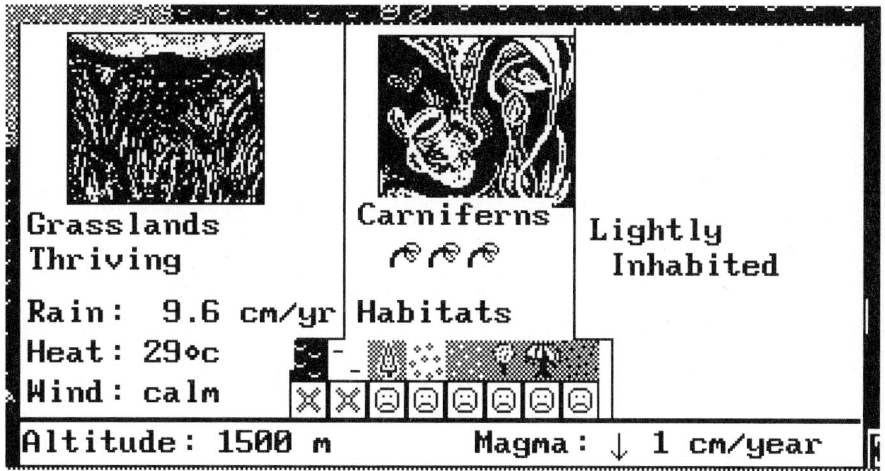

Figure 16.6 *The Examine window showing where those wild and wacky Carniferns live.*

There are four parts to the Examine window, as follows:

Biome Section—This section at the left side of the window shows a picture of the biome, if there is one. It indicates the biome's current condition, either `Thriving` or `Dying`. Next, it displays the rainfall amounts, the average temperature, and wind direction.

Life Section—If there is a non-sentient life form that dominates this area, a picture will be displayed here, to the right of the biome section. Three species of the life form class appear below the picture: the original species, the present species, and the species that will evolve if all goes well. Finally, this section gives a chart showing how that life form survives in the different habitats. If there are no life forms in the selected area, the life section will say `No Animals`.

City Section—The right side of the window gives information about the sentient species if there is one. If there is a city, this section displays a picture of the type of city. Underneath appears the species the city belongs to with the time period of the city. This section also lists the city's population or identifies traveling populations. If there are no sentient life forms in the area, the city section displays `No Sapients.`

Altitude/Magma Section—The bottom of the window displays the altitude of the area and information about the magma. If the selected area is in the sea, this section displays the depth instead of the altitude. This section gives the direction of magma movement and the amount of movement per year.

Current Tool Display

The *current tool display* appears below the six tool icons. This box just displays the tool icon last chosen along with the E.U.s charged per use of that tool.

Data Layer Buttons

Eleven Data Layer buttons used to control what is displayed in the Edit window appear next in the control panel. By selecting different buttons, you show the layers of information that suit your personal needs. Using these buttons does not affect the planet in any way. The Data Layer buttons only control what you see. There are no charges for using these buttons, because they change nothing in the simulation. **<SELECT>** a Data Layer button to toggle it off or on accordingly. Mouse users can simply **<CLICK>** on the button. The first five buttons show the planet's life forms and living areas; these can be all on at the same time. The last six buttons display the climate. You can only use the climate display buttons one at a time. Following are the control panel Data Layer buttons.

- ❑ **Oceans**—This button removes the oceans when turned off, so you can see the ocean floor.

- **Biomes**—This button removes the biomes so you can see the elevation and cities more clearly.
- **Cities**—When you use this button to turn city display off, you can't see the cities anymore.
- **Life**—This button displays all the species on the planet, 240 different species. Turning the Life button off enables you to see the cities more clearly.
- **Events**—This button controls the display of the events as they happen in the area displayed by the Edit window.
- **Heat**—Turning this button on displays the air temperatures. Darker shades indicate higher temperatures.
- **Rainfall**—Turn on to see darker shades that indicate more clouds and higher rainfall.
- **Winds**—Turning this button on displays the wind currents.
- **Sea Flow**—This choice displays the sea currents.
- **Sea Heat**—Choose this button to see the sea temperatures.
- **Magma**—The Magma button displays the magma currents under the crust.

Available Energy Display

The energy display, below the Data buttons, is the "bank account" of your available E.U.s (Energy Units). This reading decreases as you perform functions using E.U.s. As the simulation produces energy, the display adds in the additional E.U.s..

Map Window Title Bar

The Map window displays the entire planet surface area. Figure 16.7 shows an example Map window displaying the planet's air currents. The Map window opens when you start the simulation. If the window is hidden so that you can't bring it to the front by **<CLICK>**ing on it, you can **<SELECT>** `Map` in the Windows menu to do so. Use this window only to observe the planet.

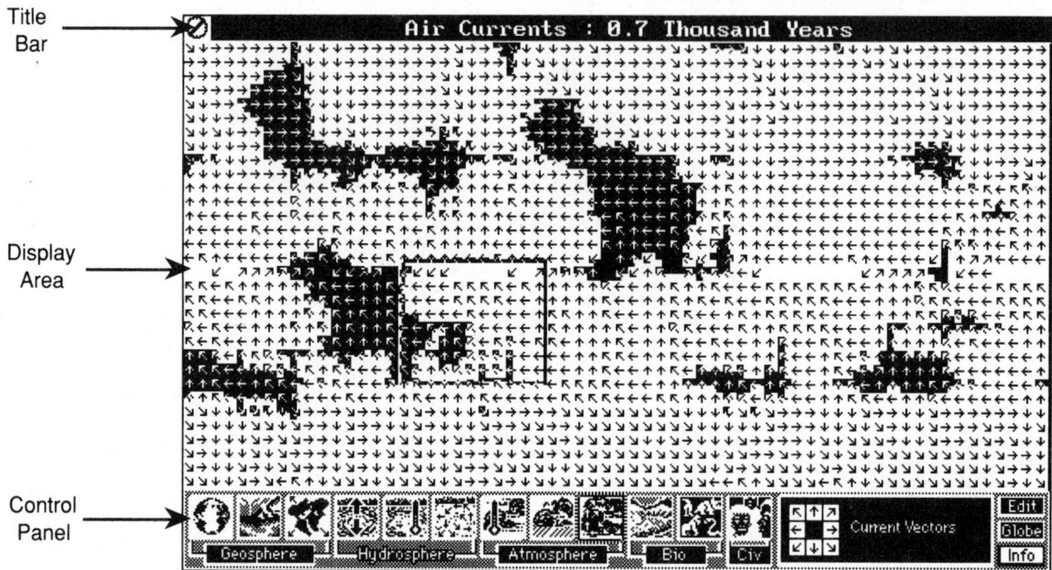

Figure 16.7 *The Map window displaying the air currents.*

The title bar at the top of the Map window shows what the map is currently displaying and the date. To the far left side of the title bar is the close box. **<CLICK>**ing on the close box will close the window. **<CLICK>**ing on the title bar itself enables you to position the window on the screen.

Map Window Display Area

The main part of the Map window is the *map display area*. Use the Map window control panel below the display area to select the type of display. A blinking rectangle appears in the display area, indicating the area currently displayed in the Edit window. If you **<DOUBLE-CLICK>** on the rectangle, the Edit window comes to the front. If you **<CLICK>** and hold on the rectangle, you can drag it around to choose a new area for display in the Edit window.

Map Window Control Panel

The Map window control panel below the display area enables you to select the information to be shown in the display area. You also can access all the Model control panels, the History window, the Edit window, and all the graphs using the control panel. Chapter 15 contains more information about these panels and windows.

Starting at the left, the control panel displays icons you select to control the Map window display. There are 12 icons divided into five groups: Geosphere (three choices), Hydrosphere (with three icons but four choices), Atmosphere (three choices), Biosphere (two icons), and the Civilization icon. Following is more information about these icons.

Geosphere Group

The Geosphere choices will give you information about the Geosphere of the planet. The Geosphere consists of the terrain, events, and the magma flow. **<CLICK>**ing on the word `Geosphere` will bring up the Geosphere Model control panel—explained more completely in Chapter 15.

Terrain Map—The first icon is the terrain map, shown as a world. When selected, this map displays the oceans and the altitude of the planet. Water is blue or black, depending on your system. The land altitude will be displayed with the higher elevations being the lightest color. The information box to the right of the icons displays a legend of the different altitudes. **<DOUBLE-CLICK>**ing on this icon will bring up the Gaia window.

Global Event Map—This icon choice will display the events that take place all over the planet. Events are represented by small symbols as they take place. The key to the symbols appears in the information box.

Continental Drift Map—The continents drift according to the magma flow underneath the planet's crust. This icon will show the direction of the magma flow, determining the continental drift.

Hydrosphere Group

The following icons give you information about the Hydrosphere, more commonly known as oceans. There is no model control panel to select for this group.

Hide/Show Oceans—**<SELECT>**ing this icon toggles an on/off switch. "On" shows the oceans. "Off" makes them disappear. The oceans don't go away; you just can't see them. This option will work in conjunction with other displays.

Ocean Temperatures—This icon displays the average temperatures for the oceans. The information box to the right shows the legend. By **<CLICK>**ing on the `Info` button in the lower right hand corner of the control panel, you can display a graph in place of the legend. This graph shows the average temperatures over a period of time.

Ocean Currents—The Ocean Currents icon shows the direction of the oceans' surface currents.

Atmosphere Group

This group of icons gives you information about the atmosphere and the climate. **<CLICK>**ing on the word `Atmosphere` will bring up the Atmosphere Model control panel. **<DOUBLE-CLICK>**ing on any of the icons in this group will bring up the Atmospheric Composition graph.

Air Temp—This choice shows the average air temperatures on the planet over a period of one year. **<CLICK>** on the `Info` button to display a graph in the information box, showing the average temperature for a period of time.

Rainfall—Choose this icon to display the average yearly rainfall for the planet. This icon, too, has a graph in the information box.

Air Currents—Choose the Air Currents icon to see the average air currents that flow over the planet's surface. The currents result from the disequilibrium and Coriolis effect (clockwise movement of fluids in the Northern Hemisphere and counter-clockwise on the moon or in the Southern Hemisphere). **<CLICK>** on the `Info` button to see a graph.

Biosphere Group

Use these icons to find out about the life on the planet. **<CLICK>**ing on `Bio` displays the Biosphere Model control panel.

Biomes—This icon displays the distribution of the various biomes on the planet. The graph display, in the information box, will show the average of the Biomass over a period of time. **<DOUBLE-CLICK>**ing on this icon brings up the Biome Ratio graph.

Life—This choice displays the life forms on the planet. As with the other displays, the legend gives an idea of what life forms are where and in what quantity. The graph display, in the information box, will show the genetic diversity over a period of time. **<DOUBLE-CLICK>**ing on the icon will produce the Life Class Ratio graph.

Civilization Icon

This is the last icon and is a group of one. Choose the Civilization icon to display the civilizations of the world. The more advanced the civilization, the darker the dot. Terraformers appear as black dots. **<DOUBLE-CLICK>**ing on the icon brings up the Technology Ratio graph. **<CLICK>**ing on the `Info` button brings up another graph showing the population of the sentient species over a period of time in the information box. **<CLICK>**ing on `Civ` brings up the Civilization Model control panel.

Information Box

The information box appears to the right of the last icon. This box displays legends corresponding to the information in the Map window display area and the graphs. The graphs displayed are taken from the History window. You can bring up the History window by **<DOUBLE-CLICK>**ing in the information box. (This is a shortcut for **<SELECT>**ing `Windows` then **<SELECT>**ing `History`.

Buttons

There are three buttons to the right of the information box. The Edit button brings the Edit window to the front. The Globe button brings up or opens the Globe window. The Info button changes the display in the Information box from a legend to a graph.

Gaia Window

<DOUBLE-CLICK> on the Terrain Map icon to access the Gaia window. The Gaia displays a caricature of the Earth as a living organism. Gaia's face planet tells you what he thinks of what you are doing to him. He makes faces and fusses at you when he thinks you are messing up the planet. He keeps his eyes on the pointer as it moves around the screen.

We found that the best thing to do was to poke him in the eye and hear him moan. Until life forms, he sleeps. When the planet's life is about to end, the little sun in the corner of this window will grow and burn up the Gaia. That means it is time to start another planet. This feature of the simulation may get old after a while.

Figure 16.8 *The Gaia window, with us poking Gaia in the eye. Oh my!*

17

Scenarios

The scenarios provided with SimEarth give you the ability to see and learn aspects of planet building. With the scenario files, you can prepare to build your own planet. Just think. You probably can't add a room on to your house, but you will be able to build your own planet. A window, shown in Figure 17.1, lists the scenarios with a brief description of each.

<CLICK> ing on the planet form next to the title and simulation loads the scenario, or use the + key on the numeric keypad (**<GRAY+>**) to move to each choice and hit **<SPACE BAR>** to select one. The Help window opens, giving you a description of what you have to work on. By **<CLICK>** ing on the sizing button in the top right corner of the window with the mouse or Arrow keys, you can expand this window to full-screen size and see all the text. The text tells you the time period and gives you general information like the problem with the planet, some methods for solving the problem, and a few other hints. The text explains the mission you need to accomplish to "win" the scenario.

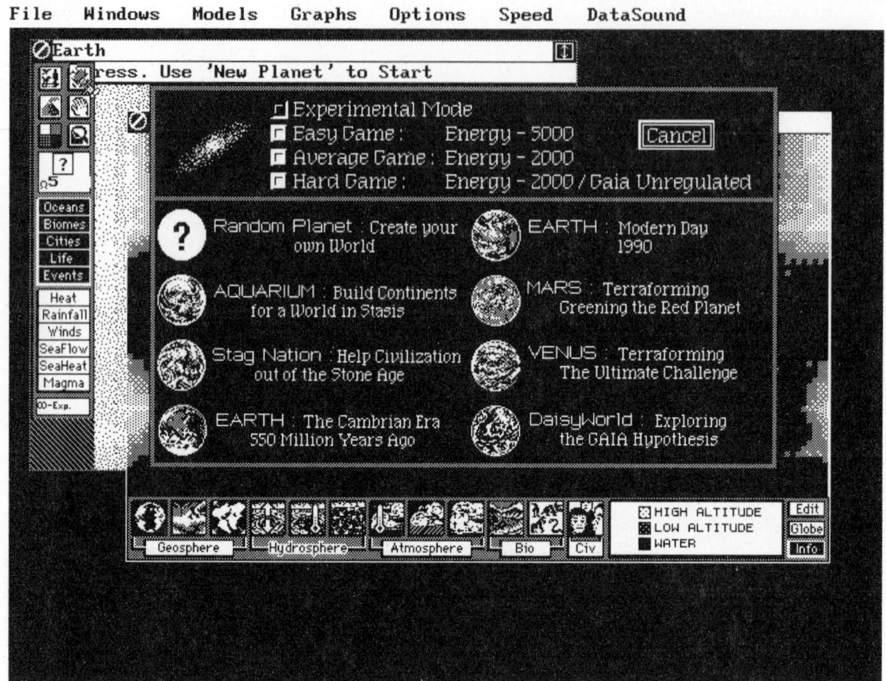

Figure 17.1 *A window presents the game play levels and scenarios.*

You can play each of the scenarios in any of the four modes. We figured that a person who can win the Mars or Venus Scenarios in Hard Game mode should see if NASA would like hire them. For the most part, you need to play in Experimental mode. With an unlimited number of Energy Units, you have one less thing to worry about. How can you concentrate on E.U.s when you're trying to set the planet's O_2 (oxygen) level? We had a limited amount of time to master these scenarios and found that there probably are several different ways to approach the problems and win. In the following descriptions, we'll give general information about each scenario and share some of our skilled (or lucky?) approaches for winning the scenario.

Aquarium

Water, water everywhere, and no place to dry off. As you figured, this planet has no land on its entire surface. Life flourishes in the large area of sea, but no life form can become sentient without fire. Without something dry to burn and some dry land to burn it on, fire just can't happen. Guess what you need to do?!

- ❑ **The Setup**—The Aquarium planet starts in the Evolution time period. Lots of sea life has already evolved on this mostly stable planet. Because of the planet's waterlogged state, no life form can develop into an intelligent species.
- ❑ **The Goals**—You need to build some continents to make possible the development of fire, food cultivation, shopping malls, and other things necessary for intelligent life forms.
- ❑ **Tips**—Aquarium is the simplest of the scenarios. All you have to do is build some continents. The simulation will take over and continue the evolution of land life forms. If you want to speed up the evolution in this or any other planet you build, use the Biosphere Model control panel. Turn the Reproduction Rate, the Advance Rate, and the Mutation Rate all the way up. This will give the life forms the "urge" to reproduce. They will happily oblige. Your planet will soon overflow with life forms. To build your continents, use the Set Altitude tool to raise the land where you choose. If you're careful, you can shape the continents to form your name. We made a big "X" and called it Landerhere, as shown in Figure 17.2. We designed Landerhere to attract space travelers and tourist aliens.
- ❑ **Our Luck**—As we said earlier, Aquarium is an easy scenario for players who understand how to build continents. The life forms grew on Landerhere like wildfire after we set the Biosphere Model controls to the maximum levels. Waiting for a life form to become sentient is sometimes a boring process. We used the Monolith quite often to speed up the process. Using the Monolith is expensive, so it made even more sense to start in Experimental mode where we could have unlimited E.U.s. We made the Dinosaurs the sentient life form. Another couple of **<CLICK>**s with the Monolith tool, and the Exodus (the win condition) began. We won, at least technically. You may think we cheated. We call it blindingly(?) fast research.

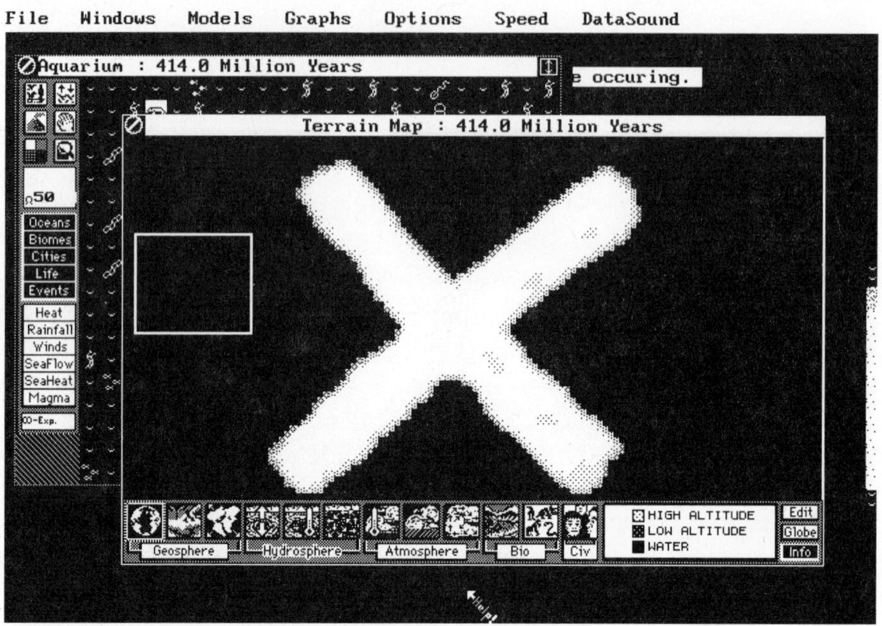

Figure 17.2 *Our plant "Landerhere."*

Stag Nation

Stagnation. We've all had days where we don't have the spunk to get up off the couch. The Sims on planet Stag Nation have a similar problem. They hate water, and can't seem to figure out how to get off the island where they evolved. All the sea cruise ships are booked until the Nanotech Age. Anyway, these Sims are into walking. Evolution on Stag Nation has stopped.

- ❑ **The Setup**—You start out in the Civilization time scale. The Mammals are sentient. The planet is fairly stable, but has only Stone Age technology. The life forms are stuck on one small continent. The sentient beings discovered that using stone to build ships causes mass drownings.
- ❑ **The Goals**—To help these Stone Age Sims increase their technology, they need to travel and explore the rest of the planet. You need to help them travel, without the massive drownings.

- **Tips**—Your best bet is to build a land bridge. Use the Set Altitude tool, which will be least destructive. You can create land with volcanos, but volcanos destroy everything around them and fill the air with dust. The Set Altitude tool only destroys the immediate area and doesn't fill the air with dust. The most clean method is to use the Helping Hand (moving tool). Pick up the city and move it to another continent. Or place a city on another continent using the Place Life tool. Any of these methods will spread the Sims all over the planet. For information on volcanos or using the tools, see Chapter 16 under "Edit Window."
- **Our Luck**—We tried all the methods we gave for moving the Sims to another continent and found each technique worked just fine. The land bridge idea takes a while. It was like opening a bird cage door, and having the bird just sit there. The Sims take a while to move across the bridge. The fastest way to move the Sims was to use the Place Life tool. Choose the Stone Age City (the simulation will not allow you to place anything more modern), and place several all over. A couple of **<CLICK>**s with the Monolith, and the Exodus took place. We were done.

Earth Cambrian Era

Figure 17.3 shows Earth as it was 500 million years ago. The life forms were moving onto land. This scenario is more of an educational experience than the others. It is a reproduction of the continental drift of the real Earth. In this one, you can just sit back and watch the continents drift if you like.

- **The Setup**—You start with the old Earth, in the Evolution time scale, and try to nurture the evolution of life in a fashion similar to the real Earth's. As shown in Figure 17.3, the planet starts with the large continent of Pangaea, which broke down into all Earth's continents. You will recognize the continents when the simulation reaches the current time period. Beyond 200 million years, the simulation just guesses where the continents will head. You can watch a replay of the continental drift by **<CLICK>**ing and holding on the Info box in the Map window. Slowly drag the pointer back and forth along the bar displayed, and you will see the continents move as they have throughout the simulation.

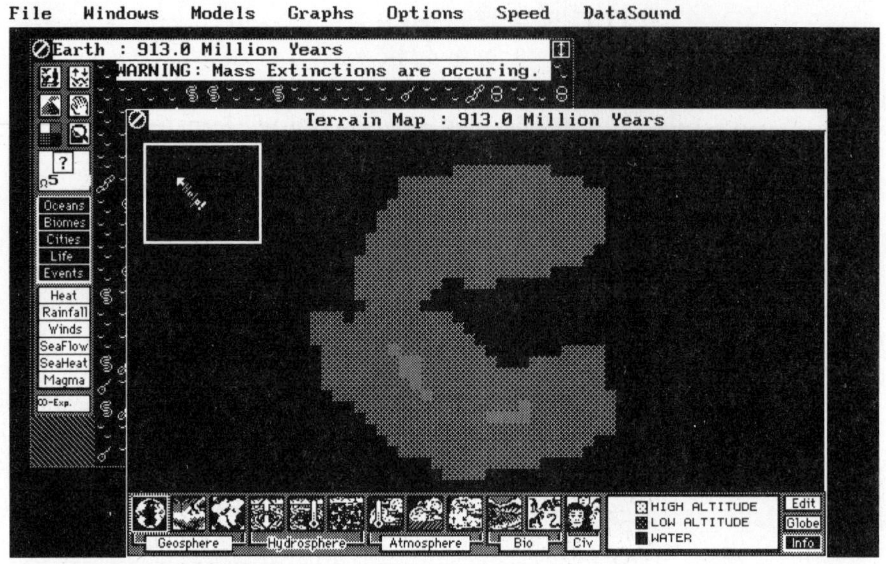

Figure 17.3 *The Earth, 500 million years ago.*

- **The Goals**—Simply, you want to bring about the evolution of life forms. The idea, as we said, is to simulate Earth's history. Or, you can try to develop Earth as you'd like to see it. Maybe you'd have Avians (birds) as the sentient life form instead of Mammals. Big Bird would like that.
- **Tips**—There's not much we can tell you to increase your luck. The best tip we have is to get something to drink and some munchies and watch the continents do their thing. Watch for the heat levels to rise. If the planet becomes hot enough to boil away the oceans, there's not much continental drift to see. Turning the Greenhouse Effect down in the Atmosphere Model control panel will help cool the air temperature.
- **Our Luck**—By the time we could finish two Mountain Dews and a bag of Doritos, we had nothing left but a planet full of Carniferns. We play in the fastest mode, in which things have a way of happening before you can stop them. The trip to the refrigerator to get the second Dew cost us the oceans.

Earth Modern Day

What a mess. The sentient species has been treating the Earth terribly. Open the Gaia window, and Gaia complains about the pollution levels. You have to try and deal with all the environmental challenges that modern humans face and not let the species destroy the planet.

- ❑ **The Setup**—Just as the scenario name says, welcome to modern day Earth. The problems the planet faces include pollution, wars, famine, energy supplies, and choosing which city gets to host the Super Bowl every year.
- ❑ **The Goals**—Keep the Sims from destroying the planet. Eventually inspire the Sims to leave in the Exodus. Enable your hometown to host the Super Bowl.
- ❑ **Tips**—Try to control the wars and plagues. Increasing the allocations of energy for the Arts/Media and Philosophy categories in the Civilization Model control panel will keep the wars under control. More energy for the Medicine category will help reduce the severity of plagues.
- ❑ **Our Luck**—If we were to say we won this scenario honestly, we'd be lying. After struggling to settle down the restless humans who always want to go to war, we gave in to the old standby solution. We used the Monolith to start the Exodus and make our little Gaia say, "Good riddance," as shown in Figure 17.4. The planet was clean again. Are they (the authors of the program), trying to tell us something?

Mars

In this scenario, you are the first of the colonizers from the home planet. The Exodus is about to begin at home, and you must prepare this planet for habitation. The last person who attempted to prepare Mars for the Sims failed. There are some fat Carniferns somewhere because of the prior failure to prepare the planet. You must use the technological tools you have

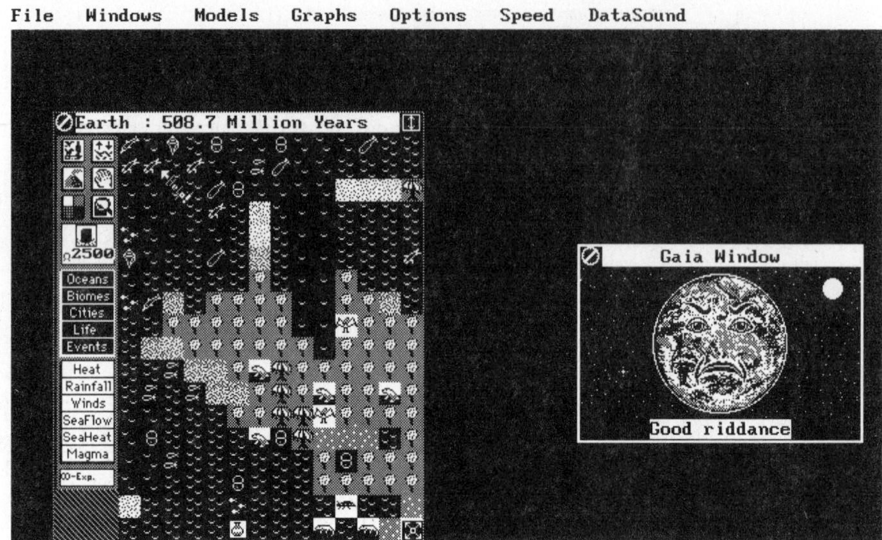

Figure 17.4 Gaia likes it when the pesky Sims leave.

at your disposal. Use the Terraformers. You have a mere 500 years to do your job.

- **The Setup**—Mars has no water, no atmosphere, no plants, and no animals—just plenty of rock. The average temperature is –53 degrees Celsius (–63 degrees Fahrenheit). Mars starts in the Technology time scale. Maxis didn't seem to think the basic challenge was hard enough, so they also disabled three of the control panels. The Civilization Model control panel works, but you have to be lucky enough to get a civilization started first. Gaian regulation is disabled, so no life forms develop spontaneously.
- **The Goals**—To make the planet habitable, the atmosphere must be able to support life. The temperature must be livable. There must be water. Once you have fixed these basic problems on Mars, you must start up life forms of all species. Once the life forms thrive, you must populate the planet with cities. If all goes well, then you've won!
- **Tips**—This is a tough job. If you get a chance to slip off of Mars before you fail, you may save yourself from the Carniferns. Use the Terraformers to make the planet habitable. For more information about the Terraformers and Biome Factories, see Chapter 16's

section about the Place Life tool. Use the Biome Factories to start a foothold for your life forms. A few Ice Meteors will water down the planet, and the oceans will form. Sprinkle with life and stir vigorously. You will end up with either a nice planet, or a mess.

- **Our Luck**—We realized the Mars scenario is missing one of the real planet's familiar features—the canals. Using the Set Altitude tool, we dug a series of canals and then filled them with several Ice Meteors. Figure 17.5 shows this work in progress. We built up the atmosphere with a few Oxygenators and a few N_2 Generators. Then we sprinkled the planet with Biome Factories. The planet kept trying to take off, but something was missing. Finally, after a liberal sprinkling of Vaporators, the Biomes started growing like crazy. We placed a few Nanotech cities, and everything was smooth sailing. We were saved from the Carniferns.

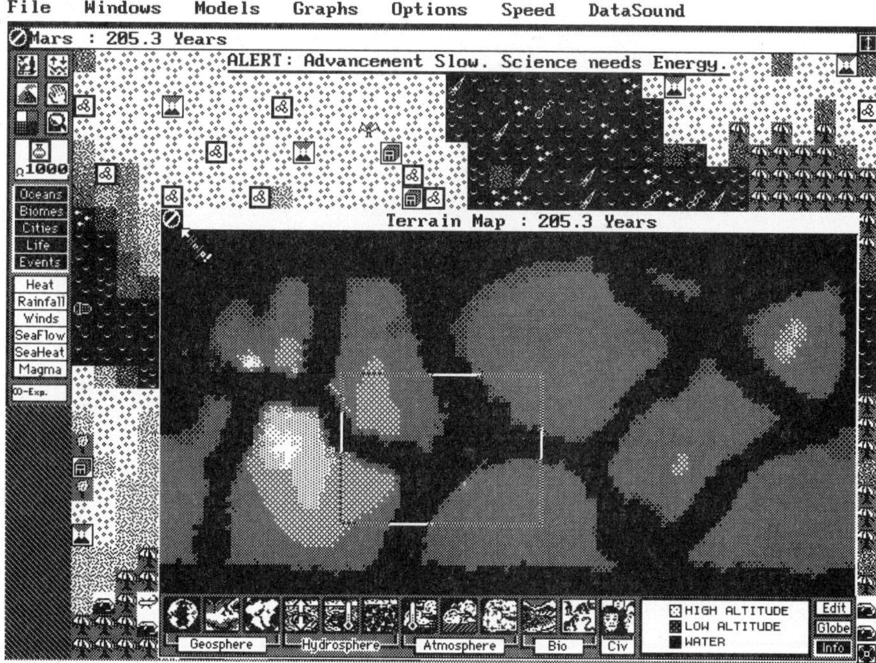

Figure 17.5 *The Mars planet, with canals added.*

Venus

We thought Mars was a challenge, then we tried Venus. Mars is cool, Venus is hot. In this scenario, too, all the control panels but the Civilization Model control panel are disabled.

- ❑ **The Setup**—Venus starts as a hot, dry planet. The average surface temperature is 477 degrees Celsius (890 degrees Fahrenheit). Everything on this planet is cooked, as in "well done." At least Venus is already in the Technological time scale, so you can use the Terraformers.
- ❑ **The Goals**—As in the Mars scenario, you must make Venus habitable for the Sims on your home planet. If not, you will be fired and forced to live on this planet. In that case, your goose is cooked.
- ❑ **Tips**—The first and most important step is to cool the planet. Oxygenators will cool things off while producing needed oxygen. Once the temperature's cool enough, a few Ice Meteors can form the ocean. Then, many of the same techniques that work in the Mars scenario will work for Venus.
- ❑ **Our Luck**—We started by using a few Oxygenators. With the World window displaying the temperatures, we added a few more. Nothing seemed to be working. Finally, after we placed about 100 Oxygenators, the temperature finally dropped to a livable range. Watch the elevation when placing all these Terraformers. When you make your oceans, the lower altitudes will be flooded. If you place your terraformers in the low areas, they will be flooded and will no longer produce anything. After a large number of Ice Meteors, Venus became a cool, wet planet with two large continents. We sprinkled these with Biome Factories, and life forms took off. We placed a few life forms and our Nanotech cities, and everything was just fine and dandy, as shown in Figure 17.6.

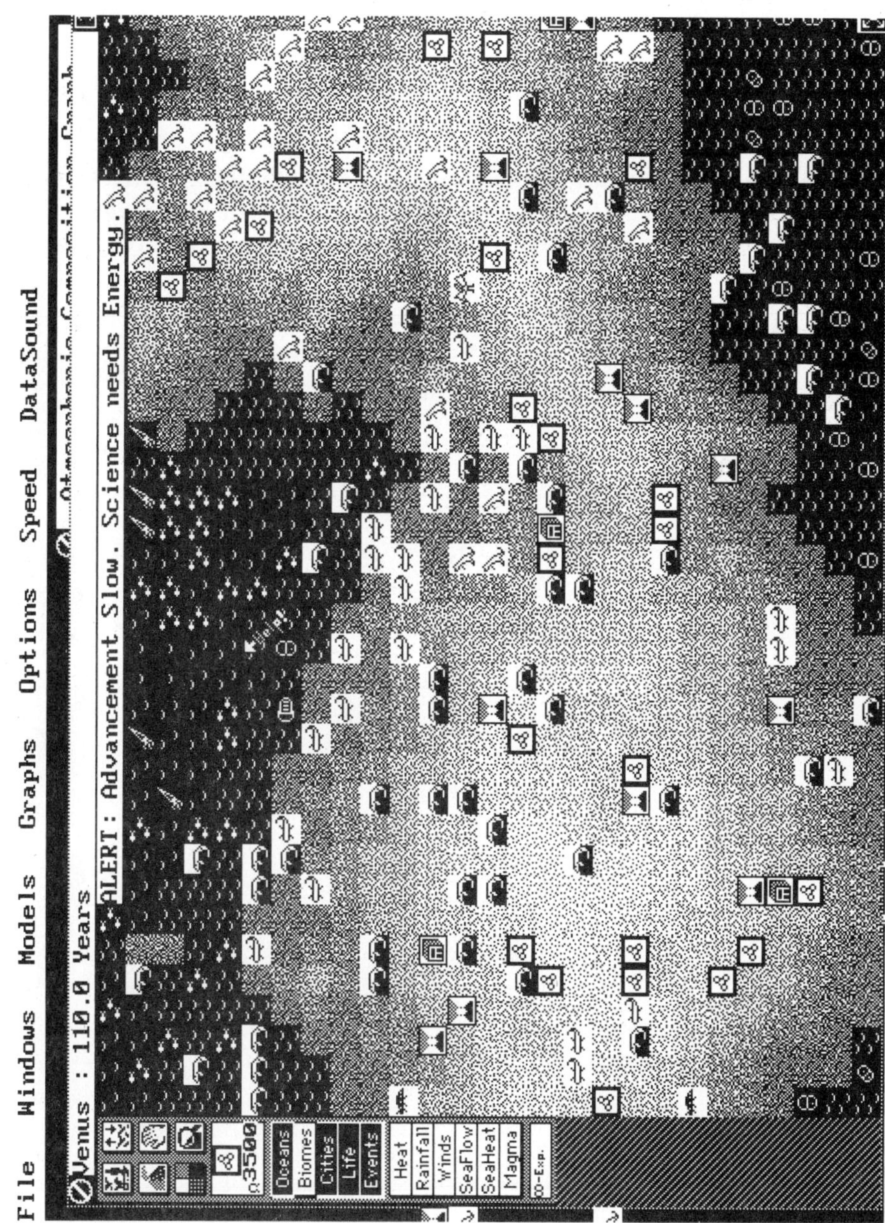

Figure 17.6 *The thriving Venus colony.*

DaisyWorld

This scenario is nothing like the other ones. It loads differently each time. It will come up as a random planet, but with Daisies instead of biomes. The DaisyWorld scenario is based on the original Daisyworld program that James Lovelock developed to test the Gaia Theory. According to the theory, the Earth's average temperature will remain constant, despite increases in the Sun's heat. The Daisyworld scenario tests whether the planet itself can keep the temperature at a level that will support life forms, as postulated in the Gaia Theory.

The planet's self-regulation is really tested as the simulation slowly increases the solar output of the Sun. DaisyWorld has daisies in eight colors instead of the Biomes. The different shades, ranging from white to black, each reflect solar radiation differently. White is most reflective and black the least reflective. There is not much for you to do except experiment. You can destroy some of the daisies and watch the resulting temperature changes by displaying the air temperature in the World window. The Gaia system will replace the daisies as needed and will keep everything under control. Whoops! We just told you all you would see if you play this scenario. If DaisyWorld makes you want to learn more about the Gaia Theory, see the reference section in Appendix B for names of books on the topic.

18 Cooperative Learning with SimEarth

If we hadn't known better, we would have thought SimEarth was designed for the classroom. Students can explore many educational topics using SimEarth: geology, biology, zoology, meteorology, ecology, and many more "ologies." Just watching the interplay of forces in SimEarth will produce a torrent of questions from student and teacher alike.

Learning Perspectives

The introduction to Chapter 10 includes some perspectives on computer learning in the classroom. If you're an instructor, the "Tip For Teachers" section in Chapter 10 explains how to make this book easier to use. This chapter provides some additional comments about SimEarth and then jumps right into the SimEarth lesson plans.

Audience

SimEarth is a sophisticated, and at times overwhelming, program. It contains dozens of controls and operates according to hundreds of concepts, many of which will take most adults some time to master. For this reason, we would imagine students in 5th and 6th grades would require a lot of guidance to use the program effectively. While 5th and 6th graders could use the mouse to point and click their way around, their random actions would give them little understanding of cause and effect. Students ages 10 to 14 will need firm guidance, and most other students will need at least some help.

Windows

Effective planet management requires the ability to view many areas and conditions at one time. Multiple windows give those views. Anyone using SimEarth will need to be familiar with opening, closing, positioning, and resizing windows. In addition, anyone who wants to plan and manage a planet over more than one computer work session will need to know how to save and load files.

Teacher's Experience

These lesson plans assume that you, the teacher, have a reasonable amount of experience with the computer. We do not recommend SimEarth as a first program for teachers, much less students. We'll assume you know how to

- ❑ Turn on (boot) the computer system.
- ❑ Start different programs.
- ❑ Use the mouse (required in SimEarth).
- ❑ Open, close, move, and resize windows.
- ❑ Load the printer with paper and ribbons.

- ❑ Copy disks (make backups).
- ❑ Save files to disk (specific to each program).
- ❑ Turn off the computer properly.
- ❑ Take care of floppy diskettes.

As always, if you get stuck, remember to look in the computer manual for possible solutions to computer problems. Refer to Appendix A for information about some problems you might encounter in SimEarth.

Lesson Plans

Each lesson plan will follow a typical outline for the educational setting: objectives, materials, preparation, activities, teamwork, discussion questions, and notes. Have your students complete the first three lesson plans in order. In sequence, the first three lessons provide the basic steps for using and learning more about SimEarth. The remaining lessons build on the skills taught in earlier lessons, and students need not necessarily complete them in order. Students do need to master the material presented in the first three lesson plans before moving on to later lesson plans.

It's not easy to set the structure of a SimEarth cooperative learning team. Because all the elements within SimEarth are interrelated, specific jobs and tasks are hard to define. The best approach may be to let the students determine and assign individual tasks as the jobs become more apparent. In some cases, SimEarth may be better used as a demonstration tool. As always, flexibility will be the key to getting the most out of a computer in the classroom.

Overview

Each lesson begins on a new page. If a lesson plan references a handout, it appears at the end of the lesson. References to the SimEarth manual and other parts of this book provide a source of background information.

We suggest using the Experimental mode for all lesson plans, regardless of the planet or scenario chosen. In this mode, there is no restriction on looking at or changing the parameters in SimEarth. Even the 5,000 E.U.s provided in the Easy Game level run out quickly, because changes made in a model and placement of biomes and life forms cost energy.

Some of the lesson plans encourage exploration, while others lead to a specific goal. In any case, allow enough time for the students to investigate the variables in the program. Some of the lesson plans could easily last for four hours or more. Some of the lesson plans will take a lifetime to complete. Table 18.1 provides an overview of the lesson plans.

Table 18.1 This chapter's lesson plans.

This Lesson Plan	*Teaches How to*
1. SimEarth Tour	Handle a planet.
2. Windows Orientation	Do windows.
3. PLANETQ	Build a planet step-by-step.
4. Ball of Rock	Form land masses.
5. Sun, Wind, and Rain	Do something about the weather.
6. Get a Life	Raise plants and animals.

1

SimEarth Tour

Learning a new program on the computer is very exciting. SimEarth provides a wide variety of choices and options from the very first step. This lesson covers the basic skills needed to use SimEarth effectively. We assume the students know and understand the basics of computer care and use.

Objectives

- ❑ To start and exit the program.
- ❑ To make menu and icon selections.
- ❑ To learn the basics of using a mouse with the program.
- ❑ To use the Help system.
- ❑ To reverse menu and icon selections.

Materials

Computer system and SimEarth software.

SimEarth Help Study Guide (lesson handout) for each team.

Preparation

The teacher or guide should be familiar with the SimEarth program. Make sure the system works, including the mouse, before the class demonstration. Reviewing Chapters 14, 15, and 16 might be useful.

Activities

- ❑ Review the process of starting the computer and software.
- ❑ Demonstrate how to use the copy protection information at the back of the SimEarth manual.
- ❑ Show how to move the mouse, **<CLICK>**, **<CLICK-DRAG>**, and **<DOUBLE-CLICK>**.
- ❑ Show the menu system and how to make choices.
- ❑ Show how to cancel (get out of) the menu choices.
- ❑ Demonstrate the windows available and how to move from one to another.
- ❑ Show how to choose an icon and place that object in the Edit window.
- ❑ Briefly explain the symbols on the Map window.
- ❑ Show how to use the Help function.
- ❑ Explain the areas to fill in on the SimEarth Help Study Guide.
- ❑ Show how to exit the program properly.

Teamwork

- ❑ Each team will need to select the "driver" for the first round.
- ❑ Once a team has started the program, each member should practice making menu choices, moving between windows, and selecting icons.
- ❑ Each team should complete the SimEarth Help Study Guide.

Discussion Questions

1. Can anyone manage a planet? How close can a software program come to showing what a planet really is?
2. What might the closest job title be for someone who plans a planet in real life?
3. Why shouldn't people just make copies of the SimEarth program diskettes to give to friends?

Notes

Practice on your part is important here. You need not have a complete understanding of how to build a planet, but knowing how to use the software is critical for the demonstration. If you don't have the time to become familiar with the program, you may consider letting a student with computer experience spend some time with the program. Let that student demonstrate the program while you explain. Completing the SimEarth Help Study Guide will provide notes for later reference and reinforce the material

SimEarth Help Study Guide

By exploring the menu system, you can learn how to use the *SimEarth* program. The answers to this handout's questions are all available by looking around *SimEarth*.

1. What are the main menu choices?
2. How do you get the Help function cursor?
3. How do you get to the Globe window?
4. How do you pause the program?
5. What do the icons at the bottom of the World window represent?

   Geosphere ______________________________

   Hydrosphere ______________________________

   Atmosphere ______________________________

   Bio ______________________________

   Civ ______________________________
6. How do you save a planet?
7. How are a **<CLICK>** and **<DOUBLE-CLICK>** with the mouse different?
8. Why shouldn't you make copies of this program to give to friends?

2

Windows Orientation

Many computer programs display information in *windows*. These windows are small boxes which may be arranged on the screen in a number of ways. This lesson focuses on using windows to provide the easiest control and multiple views of SimEarth. We also cover SimEarth's readily available tutorial system.

Objectives

- ❑ To review starting and ending the program.
- ❑ To learn to open, close, move, and resize windows.
- ❑ To experiment with multiple open windows.

Materials

Computer system and SimEarth software.

Blackboard or drawing pad.

SimEarth Windows Study Guide for each team.

Preparation

Review the window functions, including opening a window with a menu choice, closing the window by **<CLICK>**ing on the upper left corner, resizing a window with **<CLICK-DRAG>** on the lower right corner, using zoom on the upper right corner, and moving a window with **<CLICK-DRAG>** on the title bar.

Activities

- ❑ Start by drawing a square on the blackboard. As you demonstrate each function in class, add that feature to the window.
- ❑ Open a window from the menu.
- ❑ Close the window.
- ❑ Open the window again, then zoom it. Unzoom it.
- ❑ Resize the window to one quarter the screen size.
- ❑ Move the window to one quadrant of the screen.
- ❑ Open another window and move it to another section of the screen.
- ❑ Open another window and make sure it overlaps with the open windows.
- ❑ **<SELECT>** each window to activate it.
- ❑ Close all the windows, one at a time.
- ❑ Open the Tutorial window and demonstrate how to use the scroll bars to read the text.

Teamwork

Each team should complete the SimEarth Windows Study Guide.

Discussion Questions

1. What do windows contain on the computer?
2. How many windows can you have at one time?
3. How will these different views of the planet building process be helpful?

Notes

These skills for using windows will serve everyone well. The skills have become standard and work with most character and graphic window programs.

SimEarth Windows Study Guide

Like multiple TV cameras focused on the same sports event, windows show different views and perspectives of the planet in process. Techniques for using SimEarth windows follow software standards and will work with most character and graphic window programs.

1. Draw a large square below. Include, label, and explain the following parts:

   Close Box ______________________________

   Title Bar ______________________________

   Scroll Bar ______________________________

   Resize Box ______________________________

   Zoom Box ______________________________

2. How do you move a window?
3. Which windows have resize boxes?
4. Which windows have scroll bars?
5. Why don't all windows have a Zoom box?
6. Why are windows so important in SimEarth?

3

PLANETQ

The first two lessons covered the basics of using the tools and windows available in SimEarth. This lesson covers the basic steps to create a planet. Once the SimEarth teams have completed this lesson, they will have the basic skills to work with the program.

Objectives

- ❑ To build a planet.
- ❑ To save the resulting work to disk.

Materials

Computer system and SimEarth software.

PLANETQ Study Guide for each team.

A Formatted diskette for each team.

Preparation

Distribute the PLANETQ Study Guide, which the teams will use to build a planet.

Activities

- ❑ Outline the steps to building a planet.
- ❑ Review the process of saving and loading a planet.
- ❑ Wish the teams luck.

Teamwork

Each team will use the PLANETQ Study Guide to create a planet.

Discussion Questions

1. Where does SimEarth save the planet files?
2. What is the advantage to saving the planet in process under different names (such as PLAN01, PLAN02, etc.)?

Notes

Depending on your system, saving planets to a floppy diskette will involve slight variations to the instructions in the PLANETQ Study Guide. Letting the students keep their own diskettes helps provide a sense of control over the computer and this game. This is also a good opportunity for students to learn how to care for diskettes. Losing the contents of the diskette by doing something like laying it on top of a speaker at home will cause less trauma if the diskette was full of SimEarth files instead of files for a term paper.

PLANETQ Study Guide

Do what it takes to get to the opening screen of SimEarth. Read through these instructions and look at all the pictures before you begin. Chapter 14 provides more detailed instructions.

Instructions	Notes
Start the program	If you get stuck later, return to this point to start over.
<SELECT> `File`	You need to tell the program that you want to start a new planet.
<SELECT> `New Planet`	Once you begin to do something specific with the program, the copy protection question appears.
Type the answer to the question, then **<ENTER>**	The back of the SimEarth manual has the answer.
<SELECT> `Experimental Mode`	This top button of the four may already be highlighted.
<SELECT> `Random Planet`	This choice enables you to pick the exact time scale of the planet and start from scratch.
<SELECT> `Geologic`	This time scale starts at the planet's birth.
<SELECT> `Begin`	This is a box at the bottom of the window.
<CLICK> on the upper left corner	This action closes the window.
<SELECT> `Speed` **<SELECT>** `Slow`	Sit back and watch. Within a few million years (several seconds to you), oceans will begin to form.
<CLICK> on the info box	Whenever a message box appears, just **<CLICK>** in it, and it will disappear.

<CLICK> on the upper left corner	This closes this window.
<CLICK> bottom window	**<CLICK>**ing on any window brings it to the top of the stack of windows. In this case, the bottom window was the Edit window. The World window provides the entire picture of the planet.
<SELECT> `Speed` **<SELECT>** `Fast`	You might want to speed things up here because you might be heading for your first planetary crisis. Sometimes the planet will overheat. If so, there are ways to deal with the crisis. Next are the steps you might need to take. Even if your planet is not overheating, follow the next steps to see the results.
<SELECT> `Models` **<SELECT>** `Atmosphere`	Now you are ready to deal with the overheating crisis. Increasing the Rainfall isn't a solution to this problem, unless you want your planet to be a huge steam bath.
<SELECT> `Solar Input`	Decrease the amount of sunshine.
Put the pointer at the bottom the slider	The slider is located on the left of the window and looks like a thermometer.
<CLICK> three times	Notice how the handle on the slider moves down a notch with each **<CLICK>**.
<SELECT> `Greenhouse Effect`	Another way to reduce the heat on the planet's surface is to let more heat out by reducing the greenhouse effect.

<CLICK-DRAG> the slider handle down three notches	Another way to move a slider is to slide it. Use the History graphs to find out how the world is doing.
<SELECT> `Windows` **<SELECT>** `History`	Use the Window menu choice at the top of the screen. (There are now four windows on the screen.)
<SELECT> `Air Temp` **<SELECT>** `Bio Mass`	Look at air temperature and the total amount of living matter on the plant, the biomass.
<CLICK-DRAG> the History window to the lower right corner **<CLICK-DRAG>** the Atmosphere Model control panel to the lower left corner **<CLICK>** on the Globe window	Rearranges the windows to provide a better view.
<SELECT> `Options` **<SELECT>** `Update Background`	If the background windows are not being updated, this will toggle them ON. If they are already on, this step turns them OFF.
<SELECT> `File` **<SELECT>** `Save As...`	To save all you hard work, name and save this planet as it currently exists.
<CLICK> on the empty file name box	This moves the cursor to that box.
Type `PLANETQ`, press **<ENTER>**	Now you have the planet saved on disk.

4

Ball of Rock

The Geosphere represents the molten rock and crust which makes up most of the plant. The Geologic time scale in SimEarth begins just after the planet has cooled enough to allow water to remain on the surface. Continents drift as the planet cools. With the proper conditions, single-celled life begins on this newly formed planet.

Objectives

- ❑ To study continent formation.
- ❑ To use the Geosphere Model control panel.
- ❑ To use the History graph.
- ❑ To understand the need to manipulate only a single variable.

Materials

SimEarth software and computer.

Additional materials from the library or a science text.

A Ball of Rock Study Guide for each team.

Preparation

Review the questions in the Ball of Rock Study Guide. Gather additional material on planet formation and continental drift which might be of interest.

Activities

For this and the remaining lesson plans, briefly review the study guide as the demonstration. You can introduce additional material or references from your science text or library.

Teamwork

Complete the Ball of Rock Study Guide.

Discussion Questions

1. What factors affected the planet most quickly?
2. Can humans control any of the factors in real life?
3. Does life continue to evolve even as you make modifications?
4. What's wrong with making several changes to a model and then watching the results?

Notes

This lesson introduces the need to make adjustments to just one variable at a time and observe the results. If the students understand and use this principle of exploration, they will have gained a great deal from this lesson. Continue to emphasize this technique as students explore this program, other programs, and life in general.

Ball of Rock Study Guide

Thousands of years will soon pass before your eyes. Use the following steps to set up your experiment. Read through the instructions first before starting the steps.

1. Start a Random planet in Experimental mode and choose the Geologic time scale.
2. Close the World window.
3. Close the Edit window.
4. Under the Model menu choice, **<SELECT>** `Geosphere` to bring up the Geosphere Model control panel.
5. Move this window to the upper left side of the screen.
6. Under the Windows menu, **<SELECT>** `History`.
7. Move this window to the right side of the screen.
8. Under the Speed menu, **<SELECT>** `Fast`.
9. Under the Graph menu, **<SELECT>** `Air Sample`.
10. Move that window to the lower right corner of the screen, below the History window.
11. At various times, information windows will pop up, announcing the arrival of various life forms. Just **<CLICK>** on the window and proceed.
12. In the History window, **<SELECT>** `Sea Temp`, `Air Temp`, `Biomass`, and `Diversity`.
13. The Geosphere Model window will allow you to make changes to seven different aspects of the geosphere. You'll make adjustments to one area at a time and then observe the results for a minute or so. The key is to make adjustments to just one area and then watch. If you make changes to more than one area, you cannot be sure which adjustment affected the planet.
14. Increase Volcanic Activity setting by **<CLICK>**ing on the those words in the Geosphere Model control panel. Once the words

are highlighted, move the pointer above the slider bar on the right of the window. **<CLICK>** three times to move the slider up three notches. You'll notice the arrow next to `Volcanic Activity` became fatter. What has happened to the O_2 ratio of the planet? The Dust Particles? What about the Air Temperature?

15. Bring the Volcanic Activity setting down to the middle again by **<CLICK>**ing below the slider. Now highlight `Meteor Impacts` and increase that factor by five notches. What happened to the Air Temperature? What happened to the Biomass (living matter)?

16. Before you continue, return the Meteor Impacts setting to the normal level. If you don't, you just might kill everything on the planet.

17. Using these same steps, discover what you can about changes to your planet's Core Heat, Continental Drift, and Axial Tilt.

5

Sun, Wind and Rain

To sustain life, a planet must have a useable atmosphere. The interaction of the sun and the planet surface creates the weather. This lesson focuses on changing the factors which affect the sea of air surrounding the planet.

Objectives

- ❏ To observe changes to the Biomes Ratio Graph.
- ❏ To make changes in the Atmosphere Model control panel.
- ❏ To explore the greenhouse effect.

Materials

SimEarth software and computer.

Additional materials from the library or a science text.

A Sun, Wind and Rain Study Guide for each team.

Preparation

Review the questions on the Sun, Wind and Rain Study Guide. Gather additional material on weather conditions which might be of interest.

Activities

Review the study guide. If you wish, introduce additional materials or references from your science text or library.

Teamwork

Each team should complete the Sun, Wind and Rain Study Guide.

Discussion Questions

1. How many of the atmospheric factors can we really control?
2. What causes the greenhouse effect?

Notes

Remember that the simulation will proceed without intervention. Making changes to the Atmosphere Model and other control panels upsets the balance but does allow for observation.

Sun, Wind and Rain Study Guide

As much as we complain about the weather, we can't do much about it. We can't do much unless we control our own planet. In this session, you'll control the rain, the clouds, and even the sun. Explore the greenhouse effect and see how life changes in response.

1. Start a new planet using the Experimental Mode and Random Planet, Evolution time scale choices.
2. Open the Atmosphere Model control panel, the History window, and the Biome Ratio Graph. Arrange all these windows on the screen so that you can see them all at the same time. Parts of the windows will overlap.
3. **<CLICK>** on CO_2, O_2, `Air Temp`, and `Biomass` in the History window.
4. Just sit back and watch the Biome Ratio Graph and History window as life progresses on the planet. You may want to set the Speed to Fast while you watch. Does the Biomass increase as the Biomes increase? How is the CO_2 level affected? Do the Arctic Biomes increase with lower Air Temperature?
5. Adjust the Rainfall setting in the Atmosphere Model up five notches. What is the affect to the Biomass? Return this setting to normal.
6. Adjust the Solar Input setting up four notches. What is the affect on the Biomass and Air Temperature? Which Biomes increase? Which decrease? Return Solar Input to normal.
7. Adjust the Greenhouse Effect setting up four notches. What happens to the Biome ratios? Adjust the Greenhouse Effect to the top of the scale. What happens then? Now increase the Solar Input. What happens?
8. What changes to the Atmosphere Model control panel will kill all life on the planet?

6

Get a Life

Nurturing the plant and animal life on the planet is essential in SimEarth (and other places we know and love). This lesson plan looks at some of the 240 species of animal life as well as the seven types of sea life, and 16 types of land dwellers on SimEarth planets. Not only does the lesson cover the many life forms, it explores the biomes where life forms can thrive, just survive, or die.

Objectives

- ❑ To determine the number of biomes in SimEarth.
- ❑ To observe life tolerance in various biomes.

Materials

SimEarth software and computer.

Additional materials from the library or a science text.

A Get a Life Study Guide for each team.

Preparation

Review the questions on the Get a Life Study Guide. Gather additional material on species and habitats which might be of interest.

Activities

Review the study guide as the demonstration. Introduce additional material or references from your science text or library.

Teamwork

Each team should complete the Get a Life Study Guide.

Discussion Questions

1. Can you think of any additional real biomes on Earth?
2. Does a real biome just support one life form, as in SimEarth?
3. How many life forms are there on Earth?
4. How do humans change Earth's biomes?

Notes

This is the last of the six lesson plans. By now, the students know how to use SimEarth and explore the possibilities of this simulation. Guidance may consist of specific questions to answer, or providing the resources to answer the questions that arise as the students play and use SimEarth.

Get a Life Study Guide

Without plants, animals cannot survive. SimEarth provides six different types of plant "environments." Two consist of just rock or ice which do not support any life in SimEarth. Use the Place Life icon to discover which life forms can live in which biomes.

1. Under the File menu, select `New Planet`.
2. Select `Experimental Mode` and `Earth: The Cambrian Era`.
3. Under the Speed menu, select `Slow`.
4. Move the edit square to an area of land.
5. Bring the Edit window to the top of the window stack.
6. **<CLICK>** on the magnifying glass. The pointer now looks like a magnifying glass.
7. Move the pointer to any area and **<CLICK>**.
8. What information appears in this information window?
9. Under the Speed menu, select `Pause`. Using the magnifying glass, determine the types of biomes within the current Edit window.
10. **<CLICK>** on the Place Life icon in the upper left corner of the Edit window. The first seven icons relate to life in the sea. How many are land dwellers? (Count amphibians even though they can live in the sea and on land.)
11. **<CLICK>** on dinosaurs. Place a dinosaur in a biome. Now switch to the magnifying glass and examine the dinosaur where you have placed it. What is the biome?
12. Notice the faces under the life form section of the window.
    _____ Will the dinosaur barely exist here (frowning face)?
    _____ Exist fairly well (neutral face)?
    _____ Or thrive here (smiling face)?
13. Select several other life forms and complete the same questions.

Life form	Biome	Survival
________	________	________
________	________	________
________	________	________
________	________	________

13. Because the simulation is still on Pause, the life forms will not progress. Under the Speed menu, select `Slow`. What happens to the all the life forms?
14. What happens to land life forms placed in the sea?
15. What happens if you place a lot of the same life forms in the same area?
16. What happens if you place a lot of different life forms in the same area?

19 SimEarth Quick Reference

Absolute Date	Set in Speed menu Date as number of years since original cooling of planet If planet began at later time scale, will estimate See also: *Speed Menu, Relative Date*
Albedo	The reflectivity of a surface
Altitude	Level of planets surface 32 different levels of terrain Adjusted with the Set Altitude tool See also: *Set Altitude Tool*
Amphibian	One of the Land life forms Frogs, newts, and toads and puppydog tails Costs 350 E.U.s Available in the Place Life menu

Aquarium	One of the scenarios Planet with no continents Good for those who want to build their own continents In Evolution time scale See also: *Scenarios*
Arthropod	Crabs, lobsters, and crayfish Uses 140 E.U.s One of the Sea life forms
Arctic	Snow-covered area with low temperatures
Atomic Age	Begins in the 1950s Use of atomic power Costs 2,500 E.U.s City in the Place Life menu
Avian	One of the Land life forms Birds, Tweety and friends Costs 455 E.U.s Available in the Place Life menu
Axis	The planetary center of rotation
Bioenergy	One of the energy sources Use of animal labor and the cultivation of crops See also: *Energy*
Biomass	The combined weight of the living matter on a planet 99% of all life is plant
Biome	An ecosystem such as a desert or grassland Can be placed with the Place Biome tool

Biome Factory	One of the Terraformers Looks at terrain and produces appropriate biome Costs 500 E.U.s See also: *Terraformers*
Bronze Age	Begins 3500 B.C. Use of bronze tools Costs 1,000 E.U.s City in the Place Life menu
Carniferns	Mobile carnivorous plants The result of a bad dream
Cetacean	Whales and dolphins Uses 245 E.U.s One of the Sea life class
CO_2 Generator	Available in the Place Life menu Produces CO_2 (Carbon Dioxide) One of the Terraformers Costs 500 E.U.s See also: *Terraformers*
Compress Edit Screen	Useful for computers with small screens, (Mac) When active, displays every other tile in edit window Default setting is off
Continental Drift	Movement of Earth's continents
DaisyWorld	One of the scenarios Simplified version in SimEarth Used to test Gaia theory Designed by James Lovelock See also: *Scenario*

Data Song	Option in DataSound menu Plays 32 evenly spaced samples of data from top to bottom More fun that useful See also: *Datasound Menu*
DataSound Menu	Controls sound functions First two items control ways of using sound Last seven choose data from which to generate sound See also: *Tone Monitor, Play Data Song*
Desert	Hot and dry ecosystem
Dinosaur	One of the Land life forms Big, big lizards Costs 420 E.U.s Available in the Place Life menu
Earth Cambrian Era	One of the Scenarios Earth in Evolution time scale Continental drift re-creates real Earth See also: *Scenario*
Earth Modern Day	One of the scenarios Deals with today's problems See also: *Scenario*
Ecosystem	Group of plants/animals which live in an area together
Edit Window	Is close-up view of planet Used for local input (making changes to planet) Used for output (investigating planet)

Energy	The uses of planet resources to maintain the planet Player given a budget set by the level chosen Used up as the player makes changes to the planet
Eukaryote	Complex single-cell life form Uses 70 E.U.s Otherwise know as amoebas One of the Sea life forms Source of bad puns in manual
Event	An occurrence which affects the planet surface or the life forms 11 events, eight can be triggered with the Trigger Events tool
Evolution	The process through which life forms change over time
Extinction	The dying off of a species One of the Sea life forms Fishes, all kinds of 'em Uses 210 E.U.s
Fossil Fuel	One of the energy sources Contributes to greenhouse effect Limited supply See also: *Energy*
Gaia	A theory about the evolution of the Earth The basis for SimEarth Proposed by James Lovelock
Goto Events	Automatically transports you to an event when it occurs Default setting is Off See also: *Event*

Greenhouse Effect	The warming of the air temperature due to trapped heat Caused by greenhouse gases See also: *Greenhouse Gases*
Greenhouse Gases	Cause the greenhouse effect Contain carbon dioxide, methane, and water vapor
Hydro/Geo Waterwheels	One of the energy sources Use of water to drive mills and generators See also: *Energy*
Hydrosphere	The water portions of the planet
Ice Meteor	A choice from the Place Life menu Used to create oceans on a dry planet Costs 500 E.U.s
Industrial Age	Begins in late 18th century Use of powered machinery Costs 2,000 E.U.s City in the Place Life menu
Information Age	Begins 2000 A.D. Costs 3,000 E.U.s City in the Place Life menu
Insect	One of the Land life forms Creeping, crawling, buzzing little—well, you know Uses 315 E.U.s
Iron Age	Begins 1000 B.C. Use of iron tools Costs 1500 E.U.s City in the Place Life menu
Jungle	Thrives in hot wet climate

Mammal	One of the Land life forms Humans, apes, and other warm blooded animals Costs 490 E.U.s Available in the Place Life menu
Mars	One of the scenarios Dead planet that you have to bring to life See also: *Scenario*
Methane	Produced by microorganisms in the intestines of animals Otherwise know as flatuence
Microbe	Single-celled life form
Mollusk	Snails, clams, oysters, scallops, octopuses, and squid Uses 175 E.U.s One of the Sea life forms
Monolith	Is an evolution speed up device Costs 2,500 E.U.s Available in the Place Life menu
Nanotech Age	Sometime in the future Costs 3,500 E.U.s City from Place Life menu
Nitrogen	Heavy stable gas comprising 80% of Earth's atmosphere
NO_2 Generator	One of the Terraformers Produces $N0_2$ (Nitrogen) Increases the atmospheric pressure Costs 500 E.U.s See also: *Terraformers*

Nuclear	One of the energy sources Only useable after Atomic Age Also used as weapons in battles See also: *Energy*
Options Menu	To adjust many features of SimEarth When options are active, checkmark appears left of item
Oxygen	Gas used by life forms to respirate (breathe)
Oxygenator	One of the Terraformers Produces oxygen while removing carbon dioxide Costs 500 E.U.s See also: *Terraformers*
Place Life Menu	One of the Planet Manipulation tools in the Edit window
Prokaryote	One of the Sea life forms Simple single-celled life form Uses 35 E.U.s Otherwise known as bacteria Source of bad pun in manual
Radiate	Simple multicelled life Uses 105 E.U.s Otherwise known as a starfish One of the Sea life forms
Relative Date	Set in Speed menu Date as number of years since present time scale Default setting See also: *Speed Menu, Absolute Date*

Reptile	One of the Land life forms Lizards, snakes, and turtles Costs 385 E.U.s Available in the Place Life menu
Sapient	Adjective: Full of knowledge, wise
Scenarios	Planets with various problems Played in Easy, Medium, Hard, or Experimental mode Selected in the Choose Planet window
Sentient	Adjective: Conscious
Solar Wind	One of the energy sources Use of sun to dry and to power solar cells See also: *Energy*
Speed Menu	Enables you to set speed and date Fast = Maximum for the computer Moderate = Approximately 75% of fast Slow = Approximately 25% of fast Pause = Stops simulation, tools still active See also: *Relative Date, Absolute Date*
Stag Nation	One of the scenarios Sim life forms stuck on one small continent In early Civilization time scale See also: *Scenarios*
Stone Age	Oldest human culture Use stone tools Costs 500 E.U.s City in the Place Life menu
Swamp	Extremely wet grasslands

Terraformers	Available from the Place Life menu Used to make the environment habitable Used mainly in the scenarios
Tone Monitor	Plays intermittent tone based on settings Higher tone means increase in item being monitored Lower tone means decrease in item being monitored Enables you to monitor without checking maps Option in DataSound menu See also: *DataSound Menu*
Tool Icons	**<CLICK>** to access tools for modifying planet Six icons, three have submenus Box below displays active icon and budget information Every use will deplete E.U.s
Trichordate	One of the Land life forms Simple three-chord-spine animals Uses 280 E.U.s
Update Background	Enables you to choose to update all windows When option is off, only front window is updated When option is on, speed of simulation is slower Default setting depends on computer's speed of operation For slow computers, leave option off
Vaporator	One of the Terraformers Adds water to the atmosphere Costs 500 E.U.s See also: *Terraformers*

Venus	One of the scenarios The ultimate challenge to terraform a planet See also: *Scenario*
Zoomass	The weight of all animal forms on the planet See also: *Biomass*

PART

4

Hardware

20 SimCity/SimEarth Versions

To write this book, we worked on an MS-DOS system. Most of our experience with SimCity and SimEarth was with the MS-DOS version. While we have been assured by the designers of SimCity that the versions are very similar, we knew that we had to make some allowances for the differences between machines. We did this by pouring over the documentation and testing out the various versions on different machines. We didn't have the luxury of spending the hours on each machine which we've spent on the MS-DOS systems. So our comparisons are more technical (from the manuals) than subjective (based on play time).

This chapter deals most with the MS-DOS versions of both programs, because those are the versions we lived with for Sim centuries. There are a number of hardware differences for MS-DOS systems, such as screen type and added sound boards. We'll cover all these differences for both SimCity and SimEarth. Additional comments about other system versions appear at the end of this chapter.

Note that SimCity and SimEarth will run on systems with any display EXCEPT a monochrome (text-only) monitor. You can use SimCity with a number of input devices, including keyboard, mouse, and joystick. You can use the keyboard and mouse with SimEarth. SimCity works with the system's internal speaker or the COVOX Sound Master. SimEarth works with the internal speaker, as well as a number of popular sound boards mentioned in the next section.

MS-DOS Computer Systems

This chapter contains our opinions about the hardware necessary or nice to have for SimCity and SimEarth. Table 20.1 lists the hardware we recommend for each program. Review the table to help you decide what sections you need to read in the first part of this chapter.

Table 20.1 Recommended hardware for SimCity and SimEarth.

Option	*SimCity*	*SimEarth*
Microprocessor	8088 (XT)	80286 (AT)
Sound Board	Internal	Sound/Game Blaster
Display	CGA	EGA
Input	Mouse/Joystick	Mouse recommended

MS-DOS System Speed

MS-DOS-based computers are run by increasingly more powerful *microprocessors*, starting with the *8088 (XT)* and moving through the *80286 (AT)* and *80386 (386)*. The newer the microprocessor chip, the faster a program runs—this proved true with our informal tests on SimCity.

While it is highly unlikely that a dedicated Sim player would get a faster computer just to have quicker sessions, if you've been considering a new system, Table 20.2 may bolster your argument. We tested SimCity on three machines and tried to get all variables as equal as possible. We measured the real time for one Sim year. As you can see in Table 20.2, we measured a Sim year for both an empty city and the Rio de Janeiro scenario. We turned off the Animate All, Frequent Animation, and Sound options for these time trials. We set the program at the fastest speed.

Table 20.2 System speed (minutes:seconds) for one Sim year.

System	*Speed for Empty City*	*Speed for Rio*
8088	01:40	10:00+
80286	01:30	02:22
80386	00:04	00:17

While running these trials, we also noticed the speed difference between each speed setting (slow through fastest) was approximately a factor of seven. A year passed about seven times faster each time we chose a faster speed level. On a 386 machine, if one year took 2:30 in Rio on slow, it only took about .43 seconds on the fastest setting. A century in Rio takes only 43 seconds on that machine.

Speed is even more essential in SimEarth. Even set on the fastest setting, the effects of our efforts on an 8088 (XT) occurred so slowly they were almost imperceptible. We don't recommend even trying SimEarth on an XT system, even if it has a turbo speed.

MS-DOS Sound

While the display is important for any computer program, the sound in a simulation or game adds to the fun. Sound also provides another channel of output. For example, SimEarth has a Data Tone feature which may be set for one of several variables. The regular tones provide information about another variable not necessarily represented on the screen. For example, if you set the Data Tone feature to monitor rainfall, a higher tone tells you that there is plenty of rain. A lower tone suggests you should adjust the RAINFALL setting upward.

When it comes to sound on MS-DOS machines, there isn't much to say. The small speaker provided is fine for beeping but not much more. These systems were never intended to provide sophisticated sounds. Fortunately, a number of companies have stepped in to offer *sound boards* which add a great deal to the system.

Tandy systems are unusual among the mainstream MS-DOS systems. Tandy systems include special sound chips built in to provide enhanced sounds. The catch is that a program must be written to take advantage of that special sound chip. We tried SimCity on a Tandy machine and did not notice much difference between the typical internal speaker sounds and those emitted by the Tandy.

Special sound boards for MS-DOS systems cost from $85 to over $200, depending mostly on the board quality and features. There is not just one board or type of sound driver (way to make the sounds). Programmers must include specific instructions in the software so a program can use a particular sound board.

You must install sound boards inside the computer. In some cases, you'll have to set *jumpers* for the *DMA* and *Interrupt channel*. While this work is not dangerous, it can be very frustrating. If you're considering purchasing a sound board or other hardware by mail order, make sure technical help is available BEFORE you make the purchase. If you're purchasing a sound board from a local dealer, you may want to ask how much extra it costs to have it installed for you.

The following sections describe some of the available sound boards and how well they work with SimCity and SimEarth.

Sound Master

The MS-DOS version of SimCity includes an ad for the *COVOX Sound Master*. In addition to providing stereo sound on its own speakers, the board enables you to use two contact-type joysticks. The COVOX board can also replace your system's internal speaker.

The board includes two black plastic "Hi Fi Mini Speakers" for stereo sound. They have their own non-removable cords and do not need external power. The speaker in each mini speaker box is about two inches in diameter. To use these speakers in place of the internal speaker, connect a wire from this sound board to the system in place of the system internal speaker. Any game or other program which uses the internal speaker can use these speakers instead.

The joystick ports for the COVOX board are not for standard MS-DOS joysticks. MS-DOS or Apple joysticks use variable (analog) movement for input, but on/off contact controls the COVOX ports. The COVOX joysticks just report the position of the stick as it makes contact, just like the types of joysticks used with Atari and Commodore systems. This contact type of joystick is reportedly quicker to use.

The Sound Master comes with software to enable you to edit and play back recorded sounds. We recognized the software from another COVOX board, the Voice Master, which enables speech input and playback. The software with the Sound Master is interesting, but the limited sounds provided with the board might be frustrating. The included software also enables you to calibrate the joysticks.

While the Sound Master is a reasonable investment, it is not worth purchasing just to hear "better" sounds while playing SimCity. If COVOX included a music program of some type, this board might be a better buy. On the other hand, SimEarth does support this board and produces much better sounds with it than with the internal speaker.

If you are interested in better sounds from your system, you may want to consider another one of the boards profiled. As always, purchase of hardware should be based on your software needs. If you do have several programs which use the COVOX Sound Master, it may be an appropriate purchase.

Sound Blaster

The *Sound Blaster* from Creative Labs appears to be the front runner in the add-on board race. Not only does it handle AdLib compatible sounds (profiled later), it has its own C/MS stereo music synthesizer, digitized voice input and output, MS-DOS (analog)-type joystick port, and a MIDI (Musical Instrument Digital Interface) port.

First things first. SimCity does not use this board. SimCity won't make additional sounds after you install this board. We can only attribute purchase of this board by SimCity players to confusing the Sound Blaster with the COVOX Sound Master. We can make this statement with authority, because that's exactly what we did. We bought a $200 Sound Blaster thinking it was the same as a Sound Master. But our mistake worked out for the best because . . .

SimEarth uses the Sound Blaster board to add a whole new dimension of sound and music. Volcanos roar. Meteors crash. And theme songs for dozens of life forms announces their appearance on the planet. There is enough variety to make you look forward to hearing the next sound. We only turned the sound off during late night play.

In addition to outputting the Creative Music System (C/MS) sounds with 12 voices, this board also handles the 11-voice AdLib FM music system. Most game and simulation programs only cover one or the other of these music systems. The software provided with the Sound Blaster includes a music playing and recording program, called Intelligent Organ, which turns the computer keyboard into a musical keyboard.

Attaching any microphone and running the VOXKIT software enables you to record, edit, save, and play back sounds. You can add sounds together and even use sounds from other digitized sources. Play back sounds from the DOS prompt using the VOUT program.

The Sound Master, at $190, is worth a look. You'll have to contend with some jumpers as part of the installation process and supply your own speakers. The built-in amplifier will power the speakers.

Game Blaster

The *Game Blaster* is the little cousin to the Sound Blaster. It produces C/MS music and provides the joystick port. As for the Sound Blaster, with this board you'll have to provide your own speakers and may have to set a few jumpers. If you are just interested in the nice sound of music and want to use an analog joystick, this board selling for less than $80 is also worth considering.

Creative Music Systems offers additional software for playing and composing music. This library includes pop-up music, sing-alongs, and classics; a graphics presentation program, and a music composer.

AdLib

The *AdLib* board was one of the first add-on boards for the MS-DOS market. While it only plays music for one channel, the software is easy to use with a mouse. You'll need to amplify the speaker or use headphones. Because this board had been around the longest, there may be more programs written to use this board. There are a lot of files available from amateur musicians composing music for the AdLib. Even with its good price of $150 and the software music editor, this board is showing its age. If you can get a used one with the software for under $60, it would be a good buy.

MS-DOS Displays

An enjoyable part of a successful game is the screen appearance. Even with the best interaction, a single-color screen containing just characters fails to hold a user's attention. Both SimCity and SimEarth are much more enjoyable with color, high resolution screens. The following comments about display formats apply to both programs.

When comparing screens, the standard reference for image sharpness is based on the number of dots displayed across the screen by the number of dots from top to bottom. The higher the numbers, the better the image is. More dots provide more detail in an image. The old CGA screen with 320 dots across by 200 dots down looks pretty clunky compared to the more common 640 x 480 available on VGA screens.

Hercules

Hercules display has become a standard format for systems using monochrome monitors. These monitors, according to the original IBM specifications, could only display the ASCII character set. These screens displayed their images clearly because they used a lot of dots for each character. They worked very well for users spending a lot of time staring at the screen.

Most systems, especially clones, now use the Hercules display format, which enables character-based monitors to display graphics in a 720 by 348 dot pattern. This graphic resolution is quite good, but the graphics program must have the drivers to use this screen type. Both SimCity and SimEarth present decent images using Hercules display.

If you have a monochrome monitor (say, at work?) but are not sure if the display card supports the Hercules standard, try to install SimCity or SimEarth. The programs can detect the Hercules card and will use it. If the display will not work, the installation program will let you know, and no harm will have been done.

CGA

The *CGA* (color graphics adaptor) was the first formal standard set by IBM for color displays. The characters are poorly formed because the resolution is so low. In SimCity and SimEarth, the image appears in black and white because the system must use the 620 by 200 mode.

MCGA

This special display mode, *MCGA*, exists only on the IBM PS/2 Model 25 and Model 30 computers. In some cases, these systems can display EGA and VGA resolution graphics. In many cases, they can't. SimCity has a special version of the program which will display the image in color on an MCGA system, but at the lowest resolution of 320 by 200. This display is "clunky"-looking but has lots of color. If you want sharper images in black and white, choose the VGA/MCGA b/w display format for SimCity or SimEarth.

EGA

Both SimCity and SimEarth have been optimized for the *EGA* (enhanced graphics adaptor) screen. With the 640 by 350 resolution and 16 colors offered by this display, the screen images appear much more distinct and identifiable. Once you see this screen, it is difficult to go back to anything less. If you have been considering purchasing a color screen and display card, don't stop with an EGA, though. Consider a VGA display.

VGA

The *VGA* (variable graphics array) represents the most readily available color graphics standard. While SimCity and SimEarth do not take advantage of the VGA standard, many programs do.

The difference in price between EGA and VGA is small compared to the potential. The EGA is limited to 640 by 350 resolution with 16 colors. The VGA is capable of much more. How much more will depend on your computer system. If you can afford it, get at least 512K of display board memory and a monitor capable of 640 by 480 resolution with 256 colors.

MS-DOS Input Devices

User control of any program is important. The easier it is to control the program, the more you can concentrate on placing the road or jungle tile. The following information may help you choose how you would like to control the SimCity and SimEarth programs.

Mouse

A computer *mouse* is a small device about the size of a bar of soap. When attached to the computer with properly installed software, it enables better control of the cursor or pointer on the screen. As the user moves the mouse across the table, the pointer moves in the same direction.

The buttons located on the mouse's top make selections on the screen through **<CLICK>** and **<CLICK-DRAG>** actions. The mouse contains a ball that sticks through the bottom of the case. The rolling action of the ball on the table provides the mouse software with the signals to move the pointer on the screen.

Mouse prices range from $25 to $100. Variations include serial or bus; mechanical or optical; one, two, or more buttons; and sensitivity of movement (DPI). All "mice" include at least the basic mouse software. More expensive versions include additional software, typically graphic drawing programs.

One of the keys to selecting a mouse is to look for MicroSoft compatibility. Most programs that use a mouse use the MicroSoft standard. Be careful when comparing prices. A $25 mouse might be all you need if you already have a graphics program. If you want to go for the best, buy the MicroSoft serial mouse with 400 DPI, which includes the PC Paintbrush drawing program.

A *trackball* is a variation of the mouse. This box rests on the table with the movement ball on the top. The user moves the ball in all directions to move the pointer. Trackballs also have two, three, or more buttons that function just like mouse buttons.

We've used the trackball as well as a mouse. The trackball has a definite advantage when there is little desk space to move a mouse over. Our Logitech trackball is designed so you can use your thumb to move the ball while your first and second fingers rest comfortably on the buttons. Because trackball prices are similar to mouse prices, and any mouse-aware program doesn't know the difference between the two pieces of hardware, choose whichever you're most comfortable using.

Joystick

Joysticks are more popular for the "game" machines, such as Commodore and Atari. Since most games can also use the keyboard for input, joysticks are not essential for MS-DOS machines.

Joysticks require a special port available on a joystick board or as part of another board (such as the sound boards discussed earlier). There are two main types of joysticks, *analog* and *contact*. Analog joysticks are used by the MS-DOS and Apple systems. These joysticks provide a continuous signal to the system. More movement provides more action.

Commodore 128 and Atari systems use the contact-type joystick. This joystick just reports contact when the stick is moved to one of eight positions. Contact joysticks are reported to be quicker to use with action programs. The COVOX Sound Master accepts two contact joysticks.

We have used both types of joystick and found no difference in SimCity. For action games, there may be some advantage to the contact type of stick. By the way, SimEarth does not use a joystick at all.

Keyboard

SimCity users with only a keyboard can employ a number of shortcuts. Making your own keyboard chart of these shortcuts will give you the format you want as well as help you learn those keys as you write them down. Potential SimEarth users should note that you need a mouse to run that program.

The Ultimate MS-DOS System

Way back in 1981, IBM introduced the IBM PC. It was not the fastest nor by any measure, the prettiest computer. It was designed for business and legitimized desktop computers in the office. IBM originally made few concessions to game players by offering an optional joystick port and a CGA color monitor. The joystick port did not work reliably, and the color screen offered very few colors on a low-resolution screen.

Things have changed a bit in the past few years. Some of the other current systems come with more built-in game-playing capabilities than MS-DOS systems. But if the issue is adding or upgrading to the current MS-DOS system to make it a better "game" machine, there are lots of options, as we've discussed in this chapter.

Our ultimate game and simulation MS-DOS computer system would consist of the following:

- ❑ **Speed**—We would buy an 80386-based system running at 33 mHz with a math co-processor. We'd get at least 4M of RAM to enable us to copy program overlay files to a RAM disk for speed.
- ❑ **Sound**—We'd attach Creative Labs Sound Blaster to a stereo system with enough power to rattle your teeth.
- ❑ **Display**—While a 14" VGA monitor like the NEC/MultiSync 4D would be nice, we'd include a wall projection system to allow for images at least 2 feet by 3 feet in size.
- ❑ **Input**—We'd include both a mouse and joystick to provide the flexibility to choose the proper device depending on the program being used.

- **Comfort**—A large recliner for the user would be an essential part of this system.

While we had our tongues a bit in cheek while we came up with this ultimate system, the system components we recommend do provide some ideas about how to maximize the fun and challenge of games and simulations on an MS-DOS system.

SimCity Versions

SimCity was originally written for the Commodore 64. It has also been written for MS-DOS, Macintosh, Color Macintosh, and Atari systems. With the exception of the Commodore version, all the city file formats are supposed to compatible. We were able to use city files from Atari and Amiga but were not able to use versions from the Macintosh systems. Following is summary information about all the non-DOS versions of SimCity.

Atari

While the Atari version of SimCity is very similar to the MS-DOS version, not as many copies of the Atari version have been sold. On the Atari, SimCity displays in color, in the low-resolution mode.

System You Need: 520 or 1040ST.

Latest Version: 1.0.

Drives You Need: 1 floppy (second floppy or hard disk optional).

Disk Format: 3.5-inch.

Screen: Atari Color, displays in low-resolution mode.

Memory Required: 512K minimum.

Input: Mouse required.

Copy Protection: Red Sheet.

Registration Card: Pink.

Software Included: None.

Notes: Images in the manual are slightly different than those displayed on the screen. You'll require at least one extra disk to save city files.

Monochrome Macintosh

The monochrome Mac of SimCity has gone through several versions and is now at version 1.2. The latest version removed the disk-based copy protection method.

System You Need: 512e, Plus, SE, SE/30, IIx, IIcx (will not work on IIci).

Latest Version: 1.2.

Drives You Need: 1 floppy.

Disk Format: 3.5-inch, 800K, double-sided.

Screen: Standard.

Memory Required: 512K minimum, 1M preferred.

Input: Mouse.

Copy Protection: Versions 1.0 and 1.1, disk-based; 1.2, red sheet.

Registration Card: Yellow.

Software Included: None.

Notes: Older Macs with 64K ROM many not run dependably. Systems with 512K memory will not include all sounds. Disasters include Air Crash.

Color Macintosh II

Maxis calls this version of SimCity "SimCity Supreme." Even though it's billed as the "ultimate version," most of the documentation for this version is the same as that for the Monochrome Mac 1.0 and 1.1 versions.

System You Need: Color QuickDraw in ROM (for the Macintosh II, IIx, IIci) or the Macintosh SE/30.

Latest Version: Color Mac II.

Drives You Need: 1 floppy, 1 hard drive.

Disk Format: 3.5-inch, 800K, double-sided.

Screen: Monitor capable of 16 colors or 16 gray scales.

Memory Required: 2M.

Input: Mouse.

Copy Protection: Red sheet.

Registration Card: Gold.

Software Included: Terrain Editor, extra cities.

Notes: The program requires an external monitor if you're using a Mac SE/30. Multifinder compatibility. This version includes documentation on Terrain Editor. Disasters include Air Crash.

Amiga

This version of SimCity contains two disks, one each for 512K and 1M machines. The smaller version provides only 16 colors, but runs faster and may be multi-tasked.

System You Need: 500, 1000, 2000, or 2500.

Latest Version: 1.2.

Drives You Need: 1 floppy, second floppy or hard drive optional.

Disk Format: 3.5-inch.

Screen: Color monitor.

Memory Required: 512K or 1M.

Input: Mouse optional.

Copy Protection: Red sheet.

Registration Card: Green.

Software Included: Two versions of SimCity.

Notes: Running SimCity requires Workbench 1.3; you can run with Workbench 1.2, but print options won't be available. Screens differ slightly from other SimCity versions, including having maps and graphs on a single screen and icons on the right side of the Edit window.

Commodore

The Commodore version of SimCity does vary quite a bit from the other versions of the simulation. The screens are different, as well as some of the basic functions. For example, the zones all require water instead of power. Terrain Editor is included as part of the software.

System You Need: 64 or 128.

Lastest Version: 1.1.

Drives You Need: 1 floppy.

Disk Format: 5.25-inch.

Screen: Color monitor.

Memory: N/A.

Input: Joystick required.

Copy Protection: Disk-based (unable to copy disk).

Registration Card: Yellow.

Software Included: Terrain Editor built into program.

Notes: Cities created on the Commodore are not compatible with other systems' cities.

MS-DOS

System You Need: XT, AT, 80386sx, 80386.

Latest Version: 1.07.

Drives: 1 floppy, second floppy or hard drive helpful.

Disk Format: 5.25-inch, 360K and 3.5-inch 720K.

Screen: Hercules, CGA, EGA, VGA.

Memory: 512K.

Input: Mouse or joystick optional.

Copy Protection: Red sheet.

Registration Card: White.

Software Included: None.

Notes: Both Terrain Editor and Additional Graphics sets are available. Supports COVOX Sound Master sound and joystick card. You must install this version before you can run it.

SimEarth Versions

SimEarth was originally released for the Mac and Color Macintosh systems. Shortly thereafter, the MS-DOS version hit the shelves. From extensive time spent on both these systems, there does not appear to be much difference between the Mac and MS-DOS versions. Maxis is planning an Amiga version.

City File Formats

For those Simmers who like to take things apart, this section describes the city data file format for SimCity. This description is valid for the IBM, Macintosh and Amiga versions of SimCity. Table 20.3 lists the data structures for the file parts.

Table 20.3 Data structures SimCity data files.

Data Structures	*Size (Bytes)*
Name	128
FinderInfo	480
ResHis	480
ComHis	480
IndHis	480
CrimeHis	480
PolluteHis	480
CashFlowHis	240
MiscVar	24,000
Map	27,248

FinderInfo—Only the Macintosh uses this part of the file. But the IBM and Amiga city files also create this in every file so you can move cities to the Mac easily.

ResHis—This is the data seen in the Residential population line graph. The first 120 integers represent the 10-year data (most recent first), and the second 120 integers represent the 120-year data. The next five structures in this list also follow this format.

ComHis—This part contains the commercial population data.

IndHis—This part contains the industrial population data.

CrimeHis—This part contains the average crime level data (scaled 0..255).

PolluteHis—This part contains the average pollution level data (scaled 0..255).

CashFlowHis—This part contains the CashFlow data (scaled 0..255, 128 is 0, <128 is negative CF, >128 is positive CF).

MiscVar—This array of integers stores various information, as follows:

MiscVar[1]	External Market Size
MiscVar[2]	Residential Population
MiscVar[3]	Commercial Population
MiscVar[4]	Industrial Population
MiscVar[5]	Residential Valve
MiscVar[6]	Commercial Valve
MiscVar[7]	Industrial Valve
MiscVar[8&9]	City Time (current year = City Time/ 48+1900)
MiscVar[10]	CrimeRamp (used to smooth graphs)
MiscVar[11]	PolluteRamp (used to smooth graphs)
MiscVar[12]	LandValue Average
MiscVar[13]	Crime Average
MiscVar[14]	Pollution Average
MiscVar[15]	Game Level
MiscVar[16]	City Class (village, town, city, etc.)
MiscVar[17]	City Score
MiscVar[50&51]	Total Funds (long value)
MiscVar[52]	Flag for Auto-bulldozer
MiscVar[53]	Flag for Auto-budget

MiscVar[54]	Flag for Auto-goto
MiscVar[55]	Flag for Sound On/Off
MiscVar[56]	City Tax Rate
MiscVar[57]	Simulation Speed
MiscVar[58&59]	Police Budget
MiscVar[60&61]	Fire Budget
MiscVar[62&63]	Road Budget

Map—This is the city map. The map is 120 horizontal by 100 vertical, with each tile represented by an integer. The lower 10 bits of the integer hold the index for the tile, and the upper six are "attributes" for that tile, as follows:.

Tile Attributes

Bits[0-9]	Tile index #. (0-1023)
Bit[10]	Is this a zone center tile?
Bit[11]	Is this tile animated?
Bit[12]	Can you bulldoze this tile?
Bit[13]	Can this tile burn?
Bit[14]	Can this tile conduct power?
Bit[15]	Is this tile currently powered?

Tile Index Numbers

0—Clear terrain

2—All water

4—River channel

5-20—River edges

21-36—Tree edges

37—All trees

40-43—Parks

44-47—Rubble

48-51—Flood

52—Radiation

56-63—Fire

64-78—Roads (no traffic)

80-142—Roads (light traffic)

144-206—Roads (heavy traffic)

208-222—Power lines

224-238—Transit lines

244—Low density and empty Residential zone center

249-260—Houses

265, 274, 283, 292—Residential zone centers (low value) from low to high density

301, 310, 319, 328—Residential zone centers (mid value)

337, 346, 355, 364—Residential zone centers (upper value)

373, 382, 391, 400—Residential zone centers (high value)

409—Hospital center tile

418—Church center tile

427—Commercial, empty zone center

436, 445, 454, 463, 472—Commercial zone centers (low value); 436-lowest density

481, 490, 499, 508, 517—Commercial zone centers (mid value)

526, 535, 544, 553, 562—Commercial zone centers (upper value)

571, 580, 589, 598, 607—Commercial zone centers (high value)

616—Industrial, empty zone center

625, 634, 643, 652—Industrial zone centers (low value)

661, 670, 679, 688—Industrial zone centers (high value)

698—Port center tile

716—Airport center tile

750—Coal powerplant center tile

765—Fire station center tile

774—Police station center tile

784—Stadium (empty) center tile

800—Stadium (full) center tile

816—Nuclear powerplant center tile

828-831—Open horizontal bridge

832-839—Radar dish

840-843—Park fountain

948-951—Open vertical bridge

Lots of Money

Psssst, want to have some money, lots of money, for your SimCity? Want to build anything you want? Not worry about taxes? Not even worry about having any Sims stay in your city? And have it all legally?

OK. It isn't illegal, but it's definitely cheating. We found a way to provide an existing city with around $2,000,000,000. That's right—two billion dollars. After we learned this trick, the city fund balance ranged from $1,979,665,929 to $2,147,420,889. We built a city with over 150 airports, and we didn't even dent the fund balance.

We've only tried this method on MS-DOS systems using DEBUG. You could make the same changes for any other systems by finding the right HEX string and making these same changes. You'll have to have the DEBUG program, which comes with most versions of DOS. DEBUG must be in the same directory as your city files or be available in your path statement. As always, make a copy of your city file before you attempt this maneuver.

Assume you have a city file called MINE.CTY and that you have the DEBUG program available. Start at the DOS prompt, and type the following lines exactly as they appear, pressing **<ENTER>** after each line:

```
COPY MINE.CTY MINEBACK.CTY
DEBUG MINE.CTY
E D24
7FE D25
FF
W
Q
```

When you've entered these lines and the DOS prompt reappears, jump into SimCity and load that city file. You should have more money than you can spend in a lifetime. The Fund balance is so large that messages overwrite the last few digits. Just look at the Budget window if you doubt the value of the city. (If this didn't work, you have a good copy of the city file called MINEBACK.CTY.)

If you want a quick way to update city files, you can build a data file to add the money in one step. First, build the data file in an ASCII editor or by using COPY CON:. We'll use the COPY CON method since it is the quickest way we know. Starting at the DOS prompt, type the following lines, pressing **<ENTER>** after each:

```
COPY CON: MONEY.DAT
E D24
7F
E D25
FF
W
Q
^Z
```

Press the F6 key for that last line, and you'll return to the DOS C:\> prompt. Type the following line (substitute the name of your city, including the .CTY extension, for MINE.CTY) at the DOS prompt to increase the value of any city file:

```
DEBUG MINE.CTY < MONEY.DAT
```

Now that you know this trick, you are less likely to be impressed with large cities with lots and lots of money.

Troubleshooting

We can divide the problems you might have into two types: problems you have *before* you get the program working and problems you have *after* you get the program working. This appendix covers both types of problems and offers suggestions on how to solve them. These potential problems apply to both SimCity and SimEarth. (Actually they apply to many software packages.)

Before It Works

The first type of problem is extremely frustrating. You just paid good money for software and expect a return on your investment. If you are like some people we know, you want that return as quickly as possible.

The opening scene might go like this: You rip the cellophane off the package, quickly examined the various items in the box, and then stick the first diskette into the computer. After a few seconds of hesitation, you paw through the remaining contents of the box for the installation instructions.

(The SimCity instructions are in the main book. The SimEarth instructions come on a separate manual for your specific computer.) You read through the instructions and see that you need to type INSTALL to put the proper program files on your hard or floppy disk. You type `INSTALL` and you get the response: `BAD COMMAND OR FILE NAME`. You're stuck.

Regardless of the type of computer system, there are a few basics to getting a program working properly. (If you are skimming this section and you already have SimCity or SimEarth installed, stick around. This advice applies to many programs.)

Getting a program working on a computer is not necessarily easy, especially if you use the procedure we just described. A little planning will help a great deal. Try the following simple steps. You'll soon be dancing like a pro.

1. Determine your system parameters.
2. Decide where the program will be installed.
3. Read and follow the instructions.
4. Test the results.

Determine Your System Parameters

What kind of computer system do you have, and what specific *parameters* control its operation? Knowing that the computer is an Atari or an IBM clone is not enough. You had to know that answer to know which version of the program to buy. Some of the smaller systems can only handle a limited number of parameters. Those programs you install just run as provided. MS-DOS systems have a number of possible combinations of parameters, so we'll discuss those systems as an example. The ideas for MS-DOS machines *STILL* apply to other computer systems and software installation.

There are many variables to consider when installing software, variables you'll have to know before the program will work properly. While SimCity and SimEarth are pretty good about "reading" your system for the answers, knowing the variables may help with the installation process for other programs or with problems you may encounter in installing SimCity or SimEarth. If you don't know the answer to the following questions, you'll have to look in your computer manual or ask someone to help you find the answers.

- ❑ **How much *memory* does the system have?** Few systems have less than 512K of memory. While it is possible to use some programs on machines with 256K of memory, you can't run SimCity or SimEarth with that amount. Most systems now have 640K of memory.
- ❑ **What kind of *monitor* (display) does the system have?** Possible choices might be monochrome, Hercules, CGA, EGA, VGA, and MCGA. This alphabet soup of choices represents a big difference in the image you'll see as you use the program. As mentioned, SimCity and SimEarth do a good job of finding out your system screen type.
- ❑ **How much space do you have on the hard disk? If you have floppy disk drives only, what size are they?** Most programs will let you know how much space they'll need for proper installation. If you don't have enough space, the program won't install properly or may not run after it has been installed.
- ❑ **What *devices* does your computer have?** Does your computer have a mouse or joystick attached? Does it have a special sound board? What kind of printer and what port does it use? Mouse connections are fairly generic and, in many cases, need not even be specified. The program can detect the mouse by itself. From that point, things get more complicated. There are two different types of joysticks, several types of sound boards, dozens of printer types, and five possible printer ports.
- ❑ **What version of the *microprocessor* (processing chip) does the system use?** While SimCity and SimEarth programs don't require one over the other, the chip level will affect the speed of the simulations. (SimEarth does work better on an 80286 or faster system.) Knowing the relative speed will help later when you decided if you want Frequent Animation and/or Animate All on or off.

With SimCity and SimEarth, go with the installation program if you are not sure what all this is about. If you don't know how to find the answers to these questions about your computer system, you'll have to learn a bit about MS-DOS. Perhaps a book about DOS would be a good purchase. Yeah, that's the ticket! Get a book about MS-DOS. We'll even recommend one by SAMS (our publisher). *The First Book of MS-DOS* by Jack Nimershiem comes highly recommended.

Following are some specific examples of MS-DOS systems that give you a good idea of how much variation is available. A system might have

- ❑ 640K memory.
- ❑ An EGA screen.
- ❑ A hard disk as drive C: with 2903392 bytes (almost 3M) of disk space.
- ❑ A mouse.
- ❑ An HP LaserJet II printer attached to port LPT1.
- ❑ An 80286 (AT) microprocessor.

Or, a system might have

- ❑ 512K memory.
- ❑ A CGA screen.
- ❑ Two 360K floppy drives (A: and B:).
- ❑ A joystick.
- ❑ An Epson printer attached to port LPT2.
- ❑ An 8088 (XT) microprocessor.

Know Where the Program Will Be Installed

When many INSTALL programs run, they copy program files and data files specific for your system to another disk. These programs cannot run off the original diskette.

If you have a hard disk, you can decide where the program files will be copied by specifying a subdirectory name. The INSTALL program will offer a suggestion. If you take this suggestion or provide a different subdirectory, write down this subdirectory name. You must know it later to use the program.

If you are using floppy diskettes, you have limitations on the number of files INSTALL can copy to each diskette. Whether or not you have one or two floppy drives will also affect how the program will work. Running the program from a floppy diskette will not necessarily limit your playing satisfaction, just the time required to load the program files and the occasional need to swap disks. (SimEarth requires a hard disk, though.)

Read and Follow the Installation Instructions

One of the difficulties of writing computer manuals (and computer books), is determining how experienced the readers are. If you assume that the reader has little or no knowledge about computers, you force experienced users to wade through too much material to find the small pieces they need. If you write for an experienced user, the novice may be lost on the first page and not even get started.

For example, we convinced a co-worker to purchase a copy of SimCity for her daughter's birthday. Our friend uses computers every day and is fairly proficient with DOS. She followed the instructions exactly, but the manual neglects to mention that you must be in drive A: before you type `INSTALL` to get the program going. Should an "average" user know that they need to move to drive A:?

As hard as this advice is to follow, do it anyway: Find the section of the manual or special installation card for your system and, before you do *ANYTHING*, read it completely. Then read each instruction and try it. If a step does not do what you expected, stop and try to decide what didn't work. Going further is likely to pull the knot of confusion even tighter.

Test the Results

Once you've completed the installation, it seems natural that you would "test the results." But in this case, just running the program does not constitute a good test. Unless you check over all the main elements of the program, you won't know if they will work when you need them.

Each step in a testing procedure should isolate a potential problem. Making the steps small makes it easy to identify the variable causing the problem.

Try the following procedure (which we used) to test SimCity and SimEarth. Start the program as instructed. Move the pointer around with the mouse, joystick or keyboard. Follow the instructions to get to the main window, including copy protection methods. Immediately exit the program. If the system returns to the expected prompt, you know you can load, use the pointer, and exit properly.

If the program doesn't load . . .

- ❑ Check the loading instructions and try again.
- ❑ Reinstall the program.

If you get an "out-of-memory" error . . .

- ❑ Check the system configuration for the memory available.
- ❑ If you're just plain out of memory, create a boot disk (see below).

If the screen is not readable . . .

- ❑ Reinstall the program.
- ❑ Allow the system to choose the screen type.

If the pointer may not move or the system locks up . . .

- ❑ If the keyboard moves the pointer, check the mouse or joystick cord connections.
- ❑ If you have a mouse, did you say NONE for the joystick setting?
- ❑ Did you install the proper Joystick?

After the program works, do some additional testing.

1. Test the menu selections by **<CLICK>**ing and viewing each pull-down menu. Just test the main selections first before trying selections under each choice.

2. Test any window or icon by **<CLICK>**ing on it and attempting to use it in some way. At this point, don't try to do anything in particular. You are just testing the tools for now.

3. Now go back and work on some of the menu pull-down boxes. You've already tried the most important procedure, exiting. Loading and saving files would be the next most important functions.

4. Begin to look for the important options such as the sound On/ Off option and Pause setting.

Throughout this process, you are initially testing the program to see that it behaves as you would expect. Another reason to take this "stroll" is to familiarize yourself with the location of the choices and icons. If the phone rings when you are in the shower or doing your best in a good program, do you remember where you found the Pause command? (That's in the program, not the shower.)

Notes from Maxis

The technical support people at Maxis Software did pass along some tips and comments about SimCity they've made to callers over the past few months. (SimEarth had not been released when we wrote this material.)

MS-DOS Tech Notes

According to Maxis, there are four factors which may cause your mouse to malfunction:

1. You chose a joystick option when installing SimCity.
2. You are running memory-resident software like AUTOMENU.
3. You haven't installed your mouse driver.
4. Your mouse is not compatible with SimCity.

What to do . . .

1. Reinstall SimCity, making sure to select the NONE option for joystick .
2. Make sure your mouse driver is properly installed.
3. If you are running memory-resident software and do not wish to alter your configuration, create a game boot diskette which will

   Start your system with all memory free.

   Load your mouse driver automatically.

   Change to drive C: and run SimCity for you.

Creating a Game Boot Diskette for SimCity

Creating a game boot diskette is very effective for solving mouse and other memory-related problems, according to Maxis. To create a game boot diskette, first find a blank diskette and place it in the drive A:, then type `Format a:/s`. This will copy the system files onto the new diskette and make it bootable. If you are using a mouse, be sure to copy mouse driver (probably the MOUSE.COM or MOUSE.SYS file) to the boot disk. Next create an AUTOEXEC.BAT file on the diskette in your A: drive by typing the following lines at the DOS prompt and pressing **<ENTER>** after each line:

```
COPY CON AUTOEXEC.BAT
PROMPT $P$G
MOUSE (type this line only if you are using a mouse with
the mouse.com file)
C:
CD\SIMCITY
SIMCITY
(Hit <F6> then <ENTER>)
```

If your mouse driver is the .SYS type (rather than .COM), you will need to create a CONFIG.SYS file on the diskette in drive A: by typing the following lines at the DOS prompt:

```
COPY CON CONFIG.SYS
DEVICE=MOUSE.SYS
FILES=20
BUFFERS=20
```

(Hit **<F6>** then **<ENTER>**)

Reset your machine with the new boot diskette in drive A: by pressing **<CTRL><ALT><DEL>**. When you are finished playing SimCity, simply remove this diskette from drive A: and reset your system.

Solutions to Common Problems in SimCity

Following are some of the most common problems users have called Maxis for help with, and steps you can take to resolve these situations.

1. If the computer locks up after you move past the first screen or shortly after . . .

   Make sure there are no programs running memory-resident on your system. To make sure your memory is free, create a boot diskette by following the instructions given earlier.

   When installing SimCity, use the graphics set that the asterisk lands on. The INSTALL program looks at your hardware and selects the correct option.

   To run in the EGA/VGA hi-res mode, you need at least 540K of memory. To check the amount of available memory, use the DOS CHKDSK command.

   When you run the INSTALL program, check to see which version of SimCity you are using. If you have version 1.03, please call Maxis for the latest version, 1.07.

If you are using DOS 4.01 make sure you are not running SHELL and FASTOPEN. We recommend creating a game boot diskette. (See the previous instructions.)

2. If you get an `access denied` or `cannot find EGA/VGA drivers` or `cannot load EGA/VGA blocks` message when running from a floppy diskette . . .

   Make sure you installed the simulation to a blank, formatted floppy diskette and not the original or a diskette that already has files on it.

3. If you would like the VGA upgrade . . .

   Please note that the 256-color version of the simulations mentioned in the README file on the program diskettes is an MCGA/VGA 320 by 200 low-resolution color version. This version was specifically created to allow MCGA users to run the simulations in color. The resolution is lower than your current display if you're using the EGA high-res option, so please keep this in mind when ordering.

   To order the MCGA color version, send Maxis a check or money order for $10.00 plus $3.00 shipping and handling to the address listed in the manual.

4. If you still can't get the simulation to run . . .

   Make sure you are in the proper subdirectory before starting the program. Including the SIMCITY subdirectory in the PATH statement will not work.

   Try running the MS-DOS GRAFTABL.

   Try turning the sound off.

   Try turning turbo mode off if your machine has it.

   Make sure you enter the NAME or POPULATION of the city when requested by the copy protection pop-up box.

   Try using SET NO87 = DISABLE in the AUTOEXEC.BAT file if you have a math co-processor.

   Remember that SimCity can only print on the IBM Proprinter and Epson or Epson compatibles.

Mac Tech Notes

If you experience Systems Bombs or other problems . . .

Try taking all inits (especially Suitcase II) out of your system folder. In addition, make sure your RAM cache is off. Be sure to restart your system after making any system changes.

For Mac color users . . .

If you have horizontal bars or lines across the screen, disable your Super Clock. If this doesn't work, try setting your monitor to four colors prior to running SimCity, then load SimCity and switch the setting to 16 colors.

Amiga Tech Notes

If you have printer problems . . .

The Amiga preferences that control printing have many different settings. If you are getting a solid, muddy picture, try changing the threshold setting and also the density to low values, such as one or two. You will have to boot your computer with WORKBENCH first, and then open up Preferences to make the changes. If you are not familiar with Preferences, please read your Amiga owner's manual.

If you have an expansion board . . .

Some people have encountered problems running SimCity on Amiga 1000's that have RAM expansion boards. Maxis doesn't have a good answer for this one, because it is not a problem for everyone. It is possible that there is a bad memory chip or that something is wrong with the memory board. If you cannot get SimCity to work, you can send Maxis your 1M version, and we will swap it with a 512K version that will enable you to run SimCity without your memory expansion board installed.

If the program won't boot . . .

If you have tried loading SimCity after running WORKBENCH or booting right from the SimCity disk and SimCity won't boot, check the version number of the game. If you have a version earlier than 1.2 that does not require the "red code sheet," then you may be having problems with the on-disk copy protection. This problem can be caused by several things, such as having a drive out of alignment or having a bad diskette. You can send us your SimCity diskette, and we will exchange it for a version 1.2 with the off-disk copy protection.

If you're having trouble saving cities . . .

If your SimCity game disks are completely full, there is no room on them for saving cities. To save your cities, you will need one or more floppy diskettes or a hard drive. Before saving to a floppy diskette, you must first initialize it, then name it anything you want except *SimCity*. We suggest naming the diskette *City Data*.

Final Thoughts

If you frantically raced through this chapter and found nothing to help you, sorry. Just be glad this isn't the new payroll program (imagine how you'd feel if 300 people weren't getting their paychecks tomorrow because you can't figure out what is wrong with the system).

Appendix B may provide some ideas about what to do next. If you're really frantic, you have our permission to call Maxis. There are a few tips about calling. Remember there may be a time difference between your part of the world and California. Calling at 2 a.m. will only work if you live in England.

B

Resources

During the first few hours they use a program, some users prefer to be left alone. They just want to explore and create on their own. But when a problem crops up or a particularly delightful city or planet takes shape, the solitary user may want to connect with other players. Here then, are a few ways to find help, swap tips, and share your best creations.

Getting Help

We all get stuck once in a while. Even if are not currently flipping frantically through this book looking for answers, knowing in advance where the answers are or who can supply them can save you several moments of panic.

Maxis Support

Most computer program publishers now realize that a lot of their success comes from providing help to users in trouble. Maxis has several people who provide this help by phone, letter, or FAX. They want you to enjoy the program and tell your friends how much you enjoy the program. They do want to help. But part of any problem using a program is knowing when a call to the software publisher is appropriate and what you need to have before you call.

The first step is to check the manual. This sounds obvious, but tech support people have a suggestion for people who ask questions plainly answered in the manual: *RTFM (Read The Flipping Manual)*.

If you don't find the answer in the manual, and you have tried everything you can think of, call the support people ONLY after you have made a note of the following:

- ❑ Your system type.
- ❑ Memory.
- ❑ Screen type.
- ❑ Program version.
- ❑ Steps leading up to the problem.
- ❑ Steps taken to resolve the problem.
- ❑ When you purchased the program.

Depending on the time of day and how recently the program was released, you may have to wait for some time to talk with someone. Remember that the tech support person just finished talking with someone and will be talking with someone after helping you. They'll spend a reasonable amount of time trying to solve your problem, but don't expect a long chat.

If the thought of spending more than three minutes listening to a radio station from Modesto, California bothers your budget, you can always write. Maxis will get back to you within a few days with some ideas about what you can do to solve the problem.

Possibly the best of all methods is the FAX machine. You wait in line at the FAX machine, but still pay lower long distance charges. FAXing a letter is still faster than the mail. Maxis receives about 10 FAXes a day which they dutifully respond to. Make sure you include all the information noted above and tell them where they can FAX their response.

In all cases, you can count on Maxis to verify that you are an owner of the program by checking their database of registered users. You did send in that card, didn't you?

Contact Maxis at

Maxis
1042 Country Club Drive
Suite C
Moraga, CA 94556
415/376-6434
FAX 415/376-1823

User Groups

Many cities now have computer user groups. Some groups are for users of specific systems types, while other groups cover all computers. A large computer store in your city should be able to provide the name of the local user group.

Membership fees are nominal and the meetings casual. These groups frequently have *SIGs (Special Interest Groups)*. The SIGs may focus on spreadsheet, database, or word processing programs. Some SIGs may include game and educational programs. Somewhere in the structure of the user group may be a cadre of SimCity or SimEarth players. Or, maybe not . . . .

Even if there is not a special group of Simmers, it is entirely possible that a show of hands may reveal some closet players. There is the start of your SIG. Everyone can share ideas and tips. Attend the next meeting and find the answer to that Sim-ple question.

Electronic Bulletin Board Systems

Another world awaits computer users with modems and communications software. Using a modem, users can call both local and worldwide electronic bulletin board services. Some local services are PC-based, while other commercial services use mainframes with gigabytes of data. Bulletin boards all represent a tremendous resource, not for just SimCity or SimEarth players, but for and about hundreds of topics.

Local BBS

Local *bulletin board systems (BBS)* are run on personal computer systems, usually as a labor of love. A user group may sponsor the BBS, or the *SYSOP (SYStem OPerator)* may just pay the expenses. In a few cases, you have to pay the SYSOP to call into the board.

Local boards have two main features: messages and files for downloading. Messages are left by callers for other callers. Like the messages on the community bulletin board at the local grocery, anyone can post a message on the BBS for everyone else to read. Messages may consist of questions, comments, announcements, or items for sale. Anyone can respond by leaving another message. Message strings can easily contain over a dozen responses to responses.

Depending on the number of callers to the BBS and the number of incoming phone lines, dozens of people may read the messages each day. Several dozen messages may be left every day. Someone might respond to a message like: *Anyone know how large a SimCity can get before police stations are required?*

Another BBS feature is the ability to upload (send) and download (receive) files to and from the host BBS computer. As a caller, you can have a file sent from their computer to yours. Because the files are compatible, you can download a SimCity city created on an Amiga and loaded on the BBS, and use the file on an MS-DOS system. This is an electronic version of "Show and Tell."

Commercial Systems

If your friendly local BBS system is like a house, the commercial versions represent a city—a large city. There are over a dozen commercial on-line information services easily available to computer users. These services run on large mainframes with gigabytes of data available for a service fee. Not only do commercial services include messages and files for downloading, they have stock quotes, buying services, libraries full of information, and dozens of other features.

Because there are thousands of messages, the service places the messages into special interest areas ranging from *Aviation* to *Zebras*. Simulations frequently have their own area, with dozens of messages from people around the world. We corresponded about SimCity via CompuServe with several people from all around the country. Commercial BBSs also have lots of space for files. We downloaded and reviewed several dozen SimCity files, also through CompuServe.

These services are not free. The companies make money because they have a service you want and are willing to pay for. Some services charge by the hour and others for just basic access. Prices and services vary but a two-hour session on-line can easily cost $10 in some places.

We provide the following numbers of services we have used and have been satisfied with. We can't guarantee there are SimCity or SimEarth users on-line, but it is hard to believe there aren't. Contact the toll-free numbers for more information.

CompuServe	800/848-8990
Prodigy	800/822-6922
Delphi	800/544-4005
	617/491-3393
Genie	800/638-9636

We spent the most time and had the most help from people in CompuServe in the GAMERS forum. To get there, type `GO GAMERS` at any ! prompt. There is a copy of a file named SIMDEMO.ZIP, which is an MS-DOS version of SimCity which has many of the program's features. The file does not enable you to load or save cities, limiting your efforts to one session.

Books

Both the SimCity and SimEarth manuals provide references for further reading. The following list includes those books, as well as a few others we discovered in the process of preparing this book. Titles without additional information were not readily available to us.

Titles are listed alphabetically. If the lines contain a "/", we found different versions or information about the book.

The Ages of Gaia, A Biography of Our Living Earth
Lovelock, James.
Norton, New York/Bantam, New York
1988/1990, 250 pages
ISBN: 0-553-34816-7
11th grade +
A 10-year follow-up to his original *Gaia: A New Look at Life on Earth*.

Architects Make Zigzags: Looking at Architecture from A to Z
Monroe, Roxie
National Trust for Historic Preservation, Washington, D.C.
1986, 60 pages
ISBN: 0-89133-121-2
4th grade +
Examples of architecture using the alphabet with line drawings.

Atmospheric Physics
Iribarne, J.V., and Cho, H.
Reidel Publishing Co., Holland
1980, 212 Pages
ISBN: 90-277-1033-3
12th grade +
Textbook.

The Challenge of Change (video)
American Institute of Certified Planners
15 minutes focus on how planning works and why planners find the profession both challenging and rewarding.
Contact American Planning Association, $19.95

The Citizen's Guide to Planning
Smith, Herbert H.
APA Planners Press, contact American Planning Association
1979, 208 pages
Introduction to planning for the layman and aspiring professional.

City: A Story of Roman Planning and Construction
Macaulay, David
Houghton Mifflin, Boston
1974, 50 pages
ISBN: 0-395-19492-X
5th grade +
Text and drawings show how Romans planned and built cities in 200 B.C. Fifth-grade son wanted to read immediately.

The City of Tomorrow and Its Planning
Le Corbusier
Dover Publications, New York
1971, 300 pages
10th grade +
Published in 1924, translated from French, interesting historical perspective, still relevant today.

Close-Up, How to Read the American City
Clay, Grady
Praeger Pub./U. of Chicago Press, Chicago
1973/1980, 190 pages
LC: 72-89482
8th grade +
Urban journalist photographs and discusses new ways to look at changing cities.

"The Day I Played God"
Elmer-Dewitt, Philip
Time Magazine, December 24, 1990
One-page article about SimEarth.

The Death and Life of Great American Cities
Jacobs, Jane
Random House
1961, 455 pages

8th grade +
First sentence: This book is an attack on current city planning and rebuilding.

The Dynamic Earth
Skinner, B.J. and Porter, S.C.
J. Wiley and Sons, New York
1989, 550 pages
ISBN: 0-471-60618-9
8th grade +
Geology text with color pictures.

Earth, 4th Edition
Press, Frank and Siever, Raymond
W.H. Freeman, New York
1986, 650 pages
ISBN: 0-7167-1743-3
12th grade +
College geology textbook.

Ecocity Berkeley
Register, Richard
North Atlantic Books, Berkeley
1987, 140 pages
ISBN: 1-55643-009-4
6th grade +
Ideas of how to improve Berkeley, CA.

Ecotopia
Callenbach, Ernest
North Atlantic Books, Berkeley
1975, 160 pages
LC: 74-84366
Eco (Greek oikos - home) topia (Greek - topos) place
Fictional account of travels to a utopian country.

From Settlement to City
Barker, Albert
Julian Messner
1978
Nonfiction for children.

Gaia: A New Look at Life on Earth
Lovelock, James
Oxford Press, Oxford
1979, 160 pages
ISBN: 0-19-286030-5
9th grade +
The original book about the Gaia Theory.

Gaia, an Atlas of Planet Management
Myers, Norman
Anchor Press/Doubleday, New York
1984, 350 pages
ISBN: 0-385-19072-7
6th grade +
Text and color drawings and photographs offer one possible approach to planet management using the Gaia Theory. Very colorful and interesting.

Gaia: The Growth of an Idea
Joseph, Lawrence E.
St. Martin's Press, New York
1990, 276 pages, $19.95

The History of Life
McAlester, A.L.
Prentice-Hall, New Jersey
1977

How to Read a City Map
Rhodes, Dorothy
Elk Grove Press
1967, 44 pages
LC: 67-21058
2nd to 6th grade
Basic text with photographs and what the corresponding area looks like on the map.

Introduction to Oceanography
Ross, D.
Prentice-Hall, New Jersey
1988

Introduction to the Atmosphere
Reihl, H.
McGraw-Hill, New York
1978

The Language of Cities
Hoskin, Frank P.
Schenkman Publishing Company, Cambridge
1972, 75 pages
LC: 70-183603
6th grade +
B/W photos showing how cities are, and are not, planned.

Life of the Past
Lane, Gary N.
Charles Merrill Publishing Co., London
1978/1986, 300 pages
LC: 85-62153 ISBN: 0-675-20508-5
12th grade +
College textbook.

The Little House
Burton, Virginia Lee
Houghton Mifflin, Boston
1942 (1969), 40 pages
LC: 42-24744 ISBN: 0-395-25938-X
2nd to 4th grade
Story of a little house showing changes as city grows up around it.

Local Government/The First Book of Local Government
Eichner, James A. and Shields, Linda M.
Franklin Watts, New York
1983/1976, 66 pages
ISBN: 0-531-04642-7
4th through 8th grade
Basics of city government.

Local Population and Employment Projection Techniques
Greenburg, M., D. Kruekeberg, and C. Michaelson
Center for Urban Policy Research, New Brunswick
1978, 273 pages

ISBN: 0-88285-049-0
12th +
Statistical methods handbook

The Lorax
Dr. Seuss
Random House, New York
1971, 70 pages
LC: 74-158378
2nd grade +
Dr. Seuss describes the results of the local pollution problem.

The Modern City: Planning in the 19th century
Choay, Francoise
George Braziller, New York
1969, 128 pages
LC: 77-90408
10th grade +
Historical look at 19th century city growth. Translated from Dutch or German. Very heavy reading.

Mrs. Torino's Return to the Sun
Murphy, Shirley and Pat
Shepard Books
1980, 18 pages
ISBN: 0-688-41921-6
Fiction for Children
2nd - 6th grade
Victorian house lost in the city finds a new location.

Nemesis, the Death Star
Muller, Richard
Weidenfeld and Nicolson, New York
1988, 190 pages
ISBN: 1-555-84173-2
9th grade +
Story of how a scientist explores the theory that every 26 million years the Earth undergoes a great catastrophe.

The New View of the Earth, Moving Continents and Moving Oceans
Uyeda, Seiya
W.H. Freeman, New York
1978, 216 pages
ISBN: 0-7167-0282-7
Translated from Japanese. Theory of continental drift and plate tectonics.

Places Rated Almanac: Your Guide to Finding the Best Places to Live in America
Boyer, Richard and David Savageau
Rand McNally & Co., Chicago
1986, 450 pages
LC: 84-43149
4th grade +
Covers climate, terrain, housing, health care, crime, recreation, education and more. Very interesting to browse through or use for research.

A Planners Review of PC Software and Technology
Klosterman, Richard, Editor
Planning Advisory Service, contact American Planning Association
1989, 102 pages, $36.00
Collection of nine reviews on microcomputers and planning.

Planning Magazine
American Planning Association
1313 East 60th Street
Chicago, IL 60637-2891
312/955-9100

The Practice of Local Government Planning
So, Frank S. and Getzels, Judith, Editors
International City Management Association, Washington D.C.
1988, 550 pages
ISBN: 0-87326-077-5
12th grade +
Text and reference book recommended by the American Planning Association.

Underground
Macaulay, David
Houghton Mifflin, Boston
1978, 80 pages
ISBN: 0-395-24739-X
5th grade +
Explains with drawings and text what the underground of the city looks like.

Understanding Our Atmospheric Environment 2E
Neiburger, Morris, Edigner, James G., and Bonner, William D.
W.H. Freeman, New York
1982, 450 pages
ISBN: 0-7167-1348-9
9th grade +
Textbook about weather.

Urban Geography, An Introductory Guide
Clark, David
The Johns Hopkins University Press, Baltimore
1982, 228 pages
ISBN: 0-8018-2965-8 hardcover
12th grade +
College textbook.

The Urban Pattern
Gallion, Arthur and Eiser, Simon
Van Nostrand Reinhold Co., New York
1950/1963/1986
10th grade +
Text and reference book for the student of city growth.

Urban Planning Analysis: Methods and Models
Kueckeberg, Donald
John Wiley & Sons, New York
1974

Voice of the Planet (video series)
Narrated by William Shatner
Five-series broadcast on TBS, October 1990.

Volcanoes
Peter Francis
Penguin Books, England
1976, 368 pages
6th grade +
No LC or ISBN number, printed in England. Black and white charts and photos. Lots of information about volcanoes.

Other Simulation Programs

There are quite a few programs which use the word "simulation" as part of their description. They include "Yeager's Advanced Flight Trainer" from Electronic Arts, "Street Rod" by California Dreams, and "Indianapolis 500: The Simulation" by Electronic Arts. While there is nothing wrong with these programs, they focus on driving fast machines. There are dozens more like them.

When we narrowed our search to include only constructive simulations, we found four we thought might be of interest to you. These are available in MS-DOS versions. They may be available for other machines as well.

Populous

Distributed by Electronic Arts and created by Bullfrog, this program does not simulate a world any of us know. But it does present an interesting premise. You are a deity and can control many aspects of the world, including the terrain. You can only "influence" the behavior of your "followers" with special icons.

Your energy fluctuates depending on how many followers you have and your latest actions. The only problem is that there is another deity in another part of the world. Deities being what they are, only one of you can rule the world. Your respective followers fight the battle for the planet.

The most interesting aspect of the program is the ability to link two computers with each player assuming the role of a deity. Lacking that connection, you play the computer deity.

The program will work on any MS-DOS system with a graphic screen. It will use a mouse or joystick if available. There is no music for specific sound cards. Copy protection is based on entering information from the manual.

Balance of the Planet

The writer of this program, Chris Crawford, distributes it. It uses limited graphics and includes 150 static screens describing problems currently being faced on our Earth. The program is described as "easy to play, (and) intellectually challenging." Crawford is reportedly more interested in the conceptual aspects of the problem than presentation. "Balance" makes that pretty obvious.

This program runs on any MS-DOS system with a graphic display and can use a mouse, if available. There is no special sound system. Copy protection consists of a picture of a couple asking that you not make copies to give to others.

Moonbase, Lunar Colony Simulator

Published by Wesson International and distributed by Merit Software, this program, at first glance, looks similar to SimCity. You build housing, create roads, and make connections with roadways—all on the Moon, of course. This program focuses more on the commercial aspects of civilization, with choices for what is to be produced as well as where it is to be sold.

You have a start-up budget from NASA. You build and explore for raw materials. You must deal with pressure loss, radiation leaks, and power outages. If your colony survives and becomes prosperous, you may declare independence. There is no on-screen animation except occasional spacecraft fly-overs. The manual is an interesting story, with instructions about the program included as part of the story. This is a very interesting approach to learning and using the program.

The MS-DOS version works with any system and graphics screen. A mouse can be used, if available. There is no special music or copy protection.

Railroad Tycoon

This program, created by Sid Meier and distributed by MicroProse, is the closest we've seen to SimCity. You design and build a financial empire based on the railroad industry of the 1800s. You pick from several locations as you begin this simulation of the railroad expansion of that era. Significant events are announced by newspaper headlines and stock market quotes. You decide what type of equipment to use and which cities to service with your rail lines. Making and keeping money is the bottom line in this program.

We first learned about this program from all the messages on CompuServe. With the program's imposed limit of 100 years, players want to know how to become more efficient in their planning and investing.

The program runs on any MS-DOS system with at least 512K memory and a graphics card. A mouse is optional but highly recommended. The box includes nicely laminated color reference cards showing economic relationships and map icons. Sound is enhanced with an AdLib card or on a Tandy system. Copy protection is based on answering a question from the manual.

Our Pick

Like any software program, you should choose a simulation program which meets your needs. After mastering SimCity and SimEarth, you have several directions you can go. SimCity enthusiasts may want to consider looking on **Moonbase** for their next challenge. **Railroad Tycoon** is a more complicated choice.

Those interested in exploring more about the Earth might consider **Balance of the Planet**. If a more direct confrontation appeals to you, **Populous** will let you assume the role of a supreme being. You can then maneuver your pawns on the planet into a battle for world domination.

Oh, you want to know which one we will buy? We have them all! Just as soon as we finish this book, we plan to dive into **Moonbase**. Or maybe we'll work on **Railroad Tycoon** next. But **Populous** does look like fun. And, then again . . . .

Index

Symbols

A

B

C

D

E

M

N

O

S

T

U

V

W

Z

Fold Here

From:

____

____

____

YOU BUY THE STAMP
PLACE
STAMP
HERE
WE'LL BUY THE DISK

Maxis
953 Mountain View Drive
Suite #113
Lafayette, CA 94549

Staple or tape here